T0176153

USAMA IBN MUNQIDH was born on 4 July 1095 at his family's castle at Shayzar, on the banks of the Orontes River in northern Syria. His clan, the Banu Munqidh, was an established aristocratic Muslim Arab family who had gained political prominence locally and elsewhere in the medieval Near East at a time when the Muslim world was adjusting to the Turkish invasions of the eleventh century, and still reeling from the Crusades of the twelfth. Exiled from Shayzar by an uncle who saw him as a rival, Usama took up service with many of the most prominent courts of the region, in Iraq, Syria and Egypt, giving him ample opportunity to hone his skills as a warrior, diplomat and man of letters, and to observe the strange customs of his new Frankish neighbours. Usama was a political schemer of the first order, and much of his wandering can be attributed to his involvement in numerous failed adventures. In 1157, most members of his family were killed in an earthquake that left Shayzar in ruins and Usama and his ambitions wrecked. In the last decades of his life, he retired from active service and concentrated on writing, collecting his scattered poems into a much-praised *Diwan*, but specializing in topical anthologies of poetry and prose like the *Book of the Staff* or *Kernels of Refinement*, both excerpted here. Usama's last patron was the mighty sultan Saladin, for whom he intended his most famous work, translated here in full, his charming and heavily autobiographical meditation on Fate, *The Book of Contemplation*. He died in Damascus in 1188.

PAUL MICHAEL COBB is a native of Amherst, Massachusetts. He is Professor of Islamic History in the Department of Near Eastern Languages and Civilizations at the University of Pennsylvania. He studied Anthropology at the University of Massachusetts at Amherst and then Near Eastern Languages at the University of Chicago, where he took a PhD in Islamic history in 1997. His publications include *White Banners: Contention in 'Abbasid Syria* (2001) and *Usama ibn Munqidh: Warrior-Poet of the Age of Crusades* (2005). His work has been supported by (among others) the National Endowment for the Humanities, the Fulbright Foundation and the John Simon Guggenheim Memorial Foundation.

USAMA IBN MUNQIDH

The Book of Contemplation
Islam and the Crusades

Translated with an Introduction and Notes by
PAUL M. COBB

PENGUIN BOOKS

FOR LMH
Concordiam in populo

PENGUIN CLASSICS

Published by the Penguin Group
Penguin Books Ltd, 80 Strand, London WC2R ORL, England
Penguin Group (USA) Inc., 375 Hudson Street, New York, New York 10014, USA
Penguin Group (Canada), 90 Eglinton Avenue East, Suite 700, Toronto, Ontario, Canada M4P 2Y3
(a division of Pearson Penguin Canada Inc.)
Penguin Ireland, 25 St Stephen's Green, Dublin 2, Ireland
(a division of Penguin Books Ltd)
Penguin Group (Australia), 250 Camberwell Road, Camberwell, Victoria 3124, Australia
(a division of Pearson Australia Group Pty Ltd)
Penguin Books India Pvt Ltd, 11 Community Centre, Panchsheel Park, New Delhi – 110 017, India
Penguin Group (NZ), 67 Apollo Drive, Rosedale, North Shore 0632, New Zealand
(a division of Pearson New Zealand Ltd)
Penguin Books (South Africa) (Pty) Ltd, 24 Sturdee Avenue, Rosebank, Johannesburg 2196, South Africa

Penguin Books Ltd, Registered Offices: 80 Strand, London WC2R ORL, England

www.penguin.com

First published in Penguin Classics 2008

026

Copyright © Paul M. Cobb, 2008
All rights reserved

The moral right of the translator and editor has been asserted

Set in 10.25/12.25 pt PostScript Adobe Sabon
Typeset by Rowland Phototypesetting Ltd, Bury St Edmunds, Suffolk
Printed and bound in Great Britain by Clays Ltd, Elcograf S.p.A.

ISBN: 978-0-140-45513-7

www.greenpenguin.co.uk

Contents

Acknowledgements

Much of this book was written with the support of an utterly undeserved Fellowship from the John Simon Guggenheim Memorial Foundation. The History department of the College of Arts and Letters at the University of Notre Dame rather too gleefully provided me with the semesters off to enjoy the honour, and Notre Dame's Institute for Scholarship in the Liberal Arts provided the administrative help in dealing with it all.

Many individuals had some role to play in the final form of this book, though I can name only a few of them here. Any faults that remain are of course entirely my own. Niall Christie, Don-John Dugas, Anne Lester and John Meloy were valued sounding-boards for some of my editorial decisions at an early stage. Andrew Dimock and Megan Reid read more mature and lengthy versions of the text, and their comments were correspondingly crucial. Drs Meloy and Reid in particular gave generously of their time to help me hunt down and bag super-fluities of prose. Many others provided key moments of clarity and assistance, including Remie Constable, Bruce Craig, Michael Driscoll, Steve Humphreys, Hilary Kilpatrick, Yaacov Lev, Alexander Martin, Megan Montague, Carl Petry, Nasser Rabbat, Warren Schultz, Daniella Talmon-Heller and Cristina Tonghini. My parents and siblings provided the usual chorus of warm approval. The people at Penguin made the writing of the book a true pleasure, especially Charlene Davis at the very beginning and Mariateresa Boffo, Elisabeth Merriman and Monica Schmoller at the very end.

I also thank the publisher Taylor and Francis for granting

me permission to print slightly amended versions of translations that originally appeared in two articles by me: 'Usama ibn Munqidh's *Book of the Staff (Kitab al-'Asa)*: Autobiographical and Historical Excerpts', *Al-Masaq: Islam and the Medieval Mediterranean* 17 (2005), pp. 109–23, and 'Usama ibn Munqidh's *Kernels of Refinement (Lubab al-Adab)*: Autobiographical and Historical Excerpts', *Al-Masaq: Islam and the Medieval Mediterranean* 18 (2006), pp. 67–78. For further details see www.informaworld.com. The family tree of the Banu Munqidh included in this book is based upon that found in André Miquel's translation, *Des Enseignements de la Vie* (Paris, 1983), pp. 78–9, with some emendations.

A few people gave me special gifts. David Nicolle kept me honest about my translations of medieval military technical terms and helped me crack the vexing mystery of the 'chisel-headed' arrow. Qasim al-Samarrai, in a gesture that Usama would have found *min al-'aja'ib*, sent me from Leiden his personal copy of his hard-to-find edition of the *Kitab al-I'tibar* so that I might make my own copy for use in this translation. Ella Almagor greatly helped this translation through gentle correction over the years and sheer inspiration as we spent a memorable Jerusalem evening swapping stories like a couple of old Munqidhites. Her own labour of love, a Hebrew translation of Usama's work, is eagerly expected. Finally, L. M. Harteker waited with beauty, wit and patience while I finally found the good sense to dedicate a book to her.

List of Abbreviations

Cobb   Paul M. Cobb, *Usama ibn Munqidh: Warrior-Poet of the Age of Crusades* (Oxford: Oneworld, 2005).

Dussaud   René Dussaud, *Topographie historique de la Syrie antique et médiévale* (Paris: Librairie Orientaliste Paul Geuthner, 1927).

EI2   *Encyclopaedia of Islam*, 2nd edn (Leiden: E. J. Brill, 1954–2001).

Gibb   H. A. R. Gibb, book review of Philip K. Hitti, *An Arab-Syrian Gentleman and Warrior in the Period of the Crusades*, *Bulletin of the School of Oriental and African Studies* 6 (1943), pp. 1003–11.

Hitti   Usama ibn Munqidh, *Kitab al-I'tibar*, ed. Philip K. Hitti (Princeton: Princeton University Press, 1930).

Hitti, *Memoirs*   Philip K. Hitti, *An Arab-Syrian Gentleman and Warrior in the Period of the Crusades: Memoirs of Usama Ibn Munqidh* (New York: Columbia University Press, 1929).

Kamil   Ibn al-Athir, *al-Kamil*, ed. C. J. Tornberg (Beirut: Dar Sadir reprint, 1966), 14 vols.

Lubab   Usama ibn Munqidh, *Lubab al-Adab* (Beirut: Dar al-Kutub al-'Ilmiya, 1980).

Miquel   André Miquel, *Des Enseignements de la Vie: Souvenirs d'un gentilhomme syrien du temps des Croisades* (Paris: Collection Orientale de l'Imprimerie Nationale, 1983).

Rotter | Gernor Rotter, *Ein Leben im Kampf gegen Kreutzritterheere* (Tübingen: Horst Erdmann, 1978).

Samarrai | Usama ibn Munqidh, *Kitab al-I'tibar*, ed. Qasim al-Samarra'i (Riyadh: Dar al-Asala, 1987).

Siyar | Shams al-Din al-Dhahabi, *Siyar a'lam al-nubala'*, ed. Bashshar Ma'ruf, 28 vols. (Beirut: Mu'asasat al-Risala, 1996).

Smith | G. Rex Smith, 'A New Translation of Certain Passages of the Hunting Section of Usama ibn Munqidh's *I'tibar*', *Journal of Semitic Studies* 26 (1981), pp. 235–55.

Ta'rikh | Ibn al-Qalanisi, *Ta'rikh Dimashq*, ed. Suhayl Zakkar (Damascus: Dar Hassan, 1983).

Vie | Hartwig Derenbourg, *Ousâma ibn Mounkidh: Un Émir syrien au premier siècle des Croisades (1095–1188). Tome Premier: Vie d'Ousâma* (Paris: Ernest Leroux, 1889).

Chronology of Events in the Life of Usama ibn Munqidh

1095 *4 July* Usama born at Shayzar; *27 November* Pope Urban II calls for the First Crusade at Clermont.

1098 Usama's uncle Nasr dies; his uncle Sultan rules as lord of Shayzar; *9 March* County of Edessa founded by Baldwin of Boulogne; *3 June* Antioch taken by First Crusade.

1099 *15 July* Jerusalem taken by First Crusade.

1101 Baldwin I, King of Jerusalem; Bohemund I of Antioch taken prisoner; Tancred regent at Antioch.

1103–5 Second reign of Bohemund at Antioch; he then departs for Europe.

1104 Muslim offensive against the Franks in northern Syria; *May* Franks capture Acre.

1105–8 Second regency of Tancred at Antioch.

1105 Frankish counter-offensive in northern Syria led by Tancred.

1108–12 Tancred, Prince of Antioch.

1109 *12 July* Franks capture Tripoli.

1110 *May* Edessa besieged by Mawdud of Mosul; *5 December* Baldwin I captures Sidon.

1112 *12 December* death of Tancred; Roger of Salerno succeeds him at Antioch.

1113 *June* failed Frankish attempt on Damascus.

1114 *March* Nizari assault on Shayzar.

1115 *June* Frankish offensive in northern Syria thwarted; *15 September* Frankish victory at Danith; Muslim counter-offensive led by Bursuq of Hamadhan thwarted.

1118 Baldwin II, King of Jerusalem.

1119 *28 June* Muslim victory under Il-Ghazi at al-Balat, 'The

Field of Blood'; death of Roger of Salerno; Baldwin II of Jerusalem rules as regent in Antioch; *14 August* victory of Baldwin II over Il-Ghazi at Danith; *September* Joscelin I Count of Edessa.

1119/20 Templars founded.

1123 Baldwin II taken captive in Aleppo.

1124 *19 June* Baldwin II a hostage at Shayzar; *7 July* Franks capture Tyre; *30 August* Baldwin II is released.

1126 *October* Bohemund II arrives from Italy and takes over as Prince of Antioch.

1127 *September* Zangi made atabeg of Mosul.

1128 *January* Zangi captures Aleppo.

1129 *November* failed Damascus Crusade of Baldwin II.

1130 *February* Bohemund II killed in Cilicia; Baldwin II regent again at Antioch.

1131 Joscelin II Count of Edessa; *6 June* Usama exiled from Shayzar; *31 August* Fulk V of Anjou, King of Jerusalem; *3 September* Zangi attacks Hama and Homs; Usama enters his service; *November* Usama in Mosul.

1132 Zangi (with Usama) at Tikrit; Zangi (with Usama) campaigns against the caliph al-Mustarshid near Baghdad.

1134 Usama with Zangi on campaign against Artuqids near Amid.

1135 Failed campaign against Damascus by Zangi, followed by raids on Antioch.

1136 Raymond of Poitiers Prince of Antioch.

1137 Campaign of Zangi against Homs; *11 July* Usama with Zangi against the Franks at Ba'rin/Rafaniya; Raymond II Count of Tripoli; *30 May* death of Usama's father.

1138 Zangi (with Usama) in battle against the Franks near Qinnasrin; *April–May* Byzantine-Frankish siege of Shayzar; Usama arrives at Burid court in Damascus; *8 September* Usama on pilgrimage to Jerusalem.

1139 Usama meets Ridwan, exiled vizier of Egypt; Ridwan imprisoned in Egypt; *10 October* Zangi conquers Baalbek.

1140–43 Voyages of Usama and Mu'in al-Din to Latin Kingdom of Jerusalem.

1143 *10 November* death of Fulk V, King of Jerusalem.

1144 Edessa recaptured by Zangi; *30 November* Usama arrives in Cairo.

1146 *14 September* death of Zangi; succeeded by Nur al-Din at Aleppo; Joscelin II's failed attempt to retake Edessa; Nur al-Din sacks the city.

1147–8 Nur al-Din campaigns against Antioch.

1148 Ridwan escapes from prison and attempts to seize power in Cairo; he is killed; *July* armies of the Second Crusade fail at Damascus.

1149 *30 August* death of Mu'in al-Din in Damascus; renewed campaigns by Nur al-Din against Antioch; *29 June* defeat and death of Raymond of Poitiers; *10 October* death of Fatimid caliph al-Hafiz in Egypt; al-Zafir succeeds him; Cairo seethes.

1150 *January* failed assassination plot on Ibn al-Sallar; *May* Usama, on a mission from Cairo, meets with Nur al-Din outside Damascus; *end of year* Usama in Ascalon, raids Franks in the vicinity.

1152 Usama returns to Cairo; Raymond II, Count of Tripoli, assassinated; Raymond III succeeds him.

1153 Usama with the Fatimid army defending Bilbays; *3 April* Ibn al-Sallar assassinated; *22 August* Ascalon captured by Franks; Reynald of Châtillon regent at Antioch.

1154 *15 April* al-Zafir, Fatimid caliph, assassinated in Cairo; al-Fa'iz succeeds him; military revolt in Cairo; *26 April* Nur al-Din captures Damascus; *30 May* Usama flees Egypt; *19 June* he arrives at Damascus.

1155 Usama on campaign with Nur al-Din in Anatolia.

1157 *August* massive earthquake in Syria; Shayzar destroyed; brief Frankish occupation.

1158 *February* Franks besiege Harim; *April* Egyptian campaigns against Ascalon.

1160 *23 July* death of Fatimid caliph al-Fa'iz; al-'Adid succeeds him; *December* Usama visits Aleppo and Mosul, then proceeds on pilgrimage to Mecca.

1163 *10 February* death of Baldwin III; Amalric I, King of Jerusalem, campaigns against Egypt; Nur al-Din (with Usama) on campaign against Antioch; Nur al-Din thwarted against Tripoli.

1164 *12 August* Nur al-Din recaptures Harim; Bohemund III and Raymond III are captured; *end of the year* Usama moves to Hisn Kayfa in service to Qara Arslan.

1166–7 Residence and travels of Usama in Upper Mesopotamia.

1169 *26 March* Saladin named vizier in Egypt.

1170 Usama visits Mosul.

1171 *13 September* Fatimid caliph al-'Adid dies; end of Fatimid dynasty; Saladin seizes power in Egypt for Nur al-Din.

1171/2 Usama composes his *Book of the Staff* and (about this time) his *Dwellings and Abodes*.

1174 *15 May* Nur al-Din dies at Damascus; *11 July* death of Amalric; Baldwin IV, King of Jerusalem; *28 October* Saladin enters Damascus; Usama arrives shortly thereafter; he completes his *Creator of High Style* (about this time).

1176 Saladin (possibly with Usama) on campaign in north Syria.

1183 Saladin captures Aleppo; Usama completes his *Kernels of Refinement* and (about this time) his *Book of Contemplation*.

1185 Death of Baldwin IV, King of Jerusalem; Baldwin V succeeds him, with Raymond III of Tripoli as regent.

1186 Death of Baldwin V; Saladin lord of Mosul.

1187 Death of Raymond III of Tripoli; *2 October* Saladin recaptures Jerusalem.

1188 Saladin captures Latakia; *15 November* death of Usama in Damascus.

Introduction

Usama ibn Munqidh, the author of our texts, was born at his family's castle at Shayzar in northern Syria on Wednesday, 4 July 1095. Later that same year, on Tuesday, 27 November, Pope Urban II gave a speech thousands of miles away to an assembled crowd at Clermont in the Auvergne in France that ultimately led to the First Crusade and to thousands of European Christians marching from their homelands towards Jerusalem in Palestine, some passing in the very shadow of Usama's home. This, of course, was only the first of many crusades to the Near East, the genesis of a centuries-long sequence of expeditions that intensified the encounter between the Islamic world and the West. Usama, a witness present at the creation, provides through his writings a moving and memorable record of one Muslim's experience of that long encounter.

Usama was known among his contemporaries as a warrior, courtier and distinguished man of letters. He was celebrated not just for his own original creations, but also for his prodigious grasp of the vast and venerated body of older classical Arabic poetry. Although only a few of his works have survived, it seems clear that Usama specialized in topical anthologies – collections of poems and anecdotes grouped around a particular theme. The last texts translated in this book come from two such anthologies, one on walking-sticks – the *Book of the Staff* – and another on refined conduct – *Kernels of Refinement*. In these two works, as perhaps with others now lost, Usama included anecdotes from his own chequered life that are as informative for students of the medieval Near East as they are entertaining for any curious reader.

But it is through the work that forms the bulk of the present book that Usama has rightly achieved his greatest fame. This is his collection devoted to the inevitability of Fate, called the *Kitab al-I'tibar* or *The Book of Contemplation*. Unlike his other works, *The Book of Contemplation* includes only scant samples of poetry, relying instead on narrative anecdotes to illustrate the inscrutability of God's will in our lives. Remarkably for his day, Usama chose anecdotes that are heavily autobiographical, featuring chatty tales in often informal language about himself, his family, or the people he encountered over the course of his many adventures. These extend from his early years at Shayzar to his service with various Muslim lords in the Near East, including the leaders of the Muslim 'counter-crusade': the war-lord Zangi, his son Nur al-Din and the mighty sultan Saladin. Most famously, his recollections also include his interactions with the Crusaders and European settlers who were his neigh-bours (known collectively as 'Franks', despite their varied origins) and his exasperated observations of their curious ways. Written at the end of his long life, *The Book of Contemplation* is shot through with precious detail, sharp wit, deep melancholy and, as with all autobiography, gilded artifice. It is, by any token, a remarkable record of one man's vision of his times. Taken together, the writings presented in this book are not just curious samples of medieval Arabic prose and autobiography. They are in fact among the most complete and human examples of Islamic perspectives on the crusades and a window into the new world that was formed after those 'marked with the cross' first arrived at the close of the eleventh century.

Usama's World

The Islamic world in which both the first crusaders and Usama found themselves was a divided one. As in Christendom, there had been political and theological divisions within the Islamic community from an early period. In the first Islamic centuries, Islamic lands were unified in theory by the caliph, who was held to be the sole ruler of the entire Muslim community, a successor for the Prophet Muhammad (d. 632), Islam's founder, though not a prophet himself. In practice, many Muslims disputed the claims of certain individuals or lineages to hold the office of caliph. The most notable such dispute over a claimant involved the Prophet's cousin 'Ali, whose followers felt he and his descendants were the only legitimate successors to the Prophet, and so venerated them as their religious leaders or *imams* (though all Muslims hold 'Ali in high regard). Over time, slightly different attitudes towards Islamic law, theology and practice developed between the minority of Muslims who revered 'Ali and his kin as imams and the majority who did not, and the two groups coalesced into sects – the former known as Shi'ites, the latter known as Sunnis. Whereas Shi'ites took a sceptical view of the claims of Sunni rulers to be the heirs of the Prophet's right to rule the Muslim community, most Sunni Muslims simply acquiesced to the political realities of the day and recognized as legitimate the various groups and dynasties that held the caliphate. Since 750, the 'Abbasid dynasty held the office of caliph, and they would stand as the very emblem of Sunni religious authority for most of the Middle Ages. The 'Abbasid caliphs chose Iraq as their central province, founding Baghdad as their capital. And so it remained, even as, by the tenth century, the central authority of the caliphs waned and province after province became the domain of independent successor-states, some loyal to Baghdad, some not so loyal.

Throughout these formative centuries, Shi'ism only occasionally posed a serious political threat to the caliphate and Shi'ites settled down tensely but tolerantly with their Sunni neighbours, holding to their differences from the religious mainstream, but remaining politically quiescent. However, towards the end of the tenth century, all this changed when Shi'ism was embraced by a number of provincial successor dynasties, in Iran, Syria, and even in the 'Abbasid heartland of Iraq.

Foremost among these new Shi'ite states was the Fatimid caliphate of Egypt and Syria. The Fatimids came to power first in North Africa and then, in 969, captured Egypt and founded their capital city, Cairo. The Fatimid rulers adopted the title of caliph and made it perfectly clear that one of their top priorities was to eradicate their Sunni 'Abbasid rivals. At various times, the Fatimid caliphs controlled Egypt, Syria and Palestine, Sicily, and the coastal lands of the Red Sea in Africa and Arabia. A Fatimid agent had once even infiltrated Baghdad. Nevertheless, by Usama's day, the Fatimids had long settled into their role as a major Muslim power, and they were experiencing the ill effects of that complacency. Although the Fatimid caliph was the titular head of state in his realm, real power came to be held by a string of mighty viziers, who controlled not just the administration, but also Egypt's large and diverse military.

The Fatimids embraced a form of Shi'ism that was itself an offshoot from mainstream Shi'ism, called Isma'ili Shi'ism. Isma'ili Shi'ism, in its turn, experienced its own share of fissures, most notably in 1094, when Nizar, a prince of the Fatimid dynasty, was passed over in the succession to rule his family's Shi'ite caliphate and rebelled. When Nizar was defeated and killed, some members of the Isma'ili community broke away and founded their own Nizari sect loyal to the line of the slain prince. By the early twelfth century, the Nizaris had spread their teaching among the Isma'ili community already present in Syria, and made northern Syria and the mountains near Usama's home of Shayzar their favoured local refuge. In the process, they now found themselves in open conflict with fellow Shi'ites as well as with Sunnis. Outnumbered and persecuted, the Nizaris preferred to base themselves in remote locations or mountain fortresses and, unable to send vast armies to confront their foes, they chose the craftier and psychologically effective method of selectively and unpredictably murdering the leaders of their enemies. Contemporaries attributed all manner of strange beliefs and practices to the Nizaris, and explained their unwavering faith by claiming their agents worked under hashish-soaked delusions. As a result, the Arabic word for hashish-eaters, *hashishiyin*, entered into Western lexicons as 'Assassins' as the name for this sect and anyone else who employed their tactics. In Usama's world, the Nizaris found their victims among the Franks, local Muslims, and even Usama's household.

The Nizaris had felt the need to move into Syria largely because Iran, their original home-base, had become the heartland of a new and muscular Sunni political force: the Seljuk Turks. By the middle of the eleventh century, a confederation of nomadic Turkoman tribesmen known as the Oghuz, under the leadership of the Seljuk (or Saljuq) family, had migrated from Central Asia into north-eastern Iran and taken over much of the region from local rulers. In 1055, the Seljuks entered Iraq and crushed the local Shi'ite dynasty then dominating the 'Abbasid caliphs in Baghdad, a clear message to the Shi'ite Fatimids in Egypt. The 'Abbasid caliph granted the Seljuk rulers the title of 'sultan', in recognition of the fact that they wielded effective power in the region, possessed seemingly limitless military might and rendered timely services for the caliphate and for Sunnism in general. Over the next few decades, the Seljuk sultans extended their control over Iran, Iraq, and most of Syria–Palestine.

The Seljuks governed their far-flung territories as a collection of provinces ruled by kinsmen, vassals and trusted commanders (known as *amir*s or emirs) rather than as a centralized empire, and this certainly contributed to the divisions already apparent in the region. To help them govern, the Seljuks used a combination of tribal armies of nomadic Turkomans and, like many dynasties before them, a standing army of (usually) Turkish slave-troops called *mamluks*. The Seljuks liked to prepare their princes for their future political careers by giving them governorates as children, sending with them a trusted commander to rule for them and to act as a tutor and adviser. These men were known as atabegs. Like many rulers before them, the Seljuk sultans and their men cultivated strong ties with scholars of Islamic law and men of religion to bolster their Sunni credentials; they also relied upon their city's locally chosen headman or chief (*ra'is*) to serve as interlocutor with their local subjects. These strategies of rule, a mixture of 'Abbasid precedent and Seljuk innovation, became the standard tools for organizing Islamic states throughout the Middle Ages. For Usama, the Seljuk sultans were distant lords, and it was their semi-autonomous representatives, the atabegs, amirs and chiefs of the cities of Syria and Iraq, that most concretely constituted Seljuk power for him.

These Seljuk sultans are often referred to as the 'Great Seljuks' to distinguish them from another enterprising branch of
the family that had left its kin behind in Iran and forged ahead
with their own Turkoman troops into Anatolia – the first Turks
to settle in what is now known as Turkey. Anatolia had for
centuries stood as the core province of the Byzantine, or eastern
Roman, empire. As a result, for Muslims Anatolia came to
epitomize the empire as a whole and was known as 'The Land
of the Romans', *Bilad al-Rum*, or just *al-Rum* for short. The
members of the branch of the Seljuks that conquered it were
therefore known as the Seljuks of Rum. Despite the proximity
of Anatolia to northern Syria, Usama had only limited inter-
action with the Seljuks of Rum, as when he fought them as the
foes of the many local lords he served.

Beyond the Seljuks of Rum, at the horizon of Usama's world,
stood Constantinople, the redoubtable and venerable capital of
the Christian, Greek-speaking Byzantine empire. Ever since the
arrival of the Turks in Anatolia, the Byzantines had been on
the defensive, trying, but never effectively succeeding, to hold
on to their lands there. In Usama's infancy, the Byzantines were
experiencing something of a revival of fortune under an active
new emperor, Alexius Comnenus. He and his successors felt
keenly the pressures that Muslim expansion placed on their
borders in Anatolia, and they never lost sight of the fact that
Syria, including Usama's homeland, had once been Byzantine
territory.

It was into this frontier, the fractured meeting-ground of
Shi'ite Fatimids, Sunni Seljuks and Christian Byzantines, that
the first crusaders plunged. The Byzantine emperor Alexius had
hoped he might be able to channel the military capabilities of
the first crusaders to reconquer formerly Byzantine lands in
Anatolia and Syria. In fact, the Byzantines gained very little
from the affair; instead, the Franks wrested control of large
swathes of land in the region for themselves and made them the
basis for four Latin states. The first of these to be created was
the County of Edessa, in Upper Mesopotamia, founded in 1098,
followed by the Principality of Antioch (later in 1098), the
Kingdom of Jerusalem (in 1099) and the County of Tripoli

(1109). From these lands, the armies of the Latin settlers ranged throughout Syria and Palestine and as far afield as Egypt, Jordan, Anatolia and northern Iraq.

This Frankish threat elicited only modest concern from the sultans in the East. From the point of view of the Great Seljuk sultans, who were usually (when not on campaign) based in Baghdad or Isfahan in Iran, Syria was an impoverished outlier of the Seljuk world. The sultans only occasionally made defending Syria a priority; more often, it was an arena for ambitious atabegs, amirs, princelings and local native vassals like Usama's family, the Banu Munqidh. By the time Usama was born, the Banu Munqidh had established themselves as a native Arab household of consequence, having been involved in the politics of Aleppo and northern Syria for some decades. Their domain was centred on the castle of Shayzar, which sat, as it does today, nearly impregnable, on a hairpin bend in the Orontes River at a crucial bridge and crossing-point, over-looking Shayzar town. Although some members of the family had served the Fatimids in Cairo, the lords of Shayzar became vassals of the Great Seljuks shortly before Usama's birth. Wedged between the borders of its Frankish and Muslim neigh-bours, Shayzar in northern Syria sat on a frontier in a region that was itself a frontier. This made for interesting times at Shayzar, and perhaps contributed to Usama's penchant for acute observations of the mysteries of God's plan and the varieties of human nature.

Usama's world was but a smaller part of the world of Islam, specifically that experienced by its warrior elites. Like his Muslim contemporaries, Usama strove to live his life in a way that was most pleasing to God, and he received guidance on how to do so from the teachings of the Qur'an and the injunc-tions of Islamic law. He worked for both Fatimid and Seljuk (or Seljuk-allied) regimes, and it is still an open question as to whether he considered himself a Shi'ite or a Sunni (probably the latter). That this is so is largely because the record of his own religious practice in his writings is rather generic, devoid of any doctrinal red flags. What his writings do provide, though, is a record of the private practice of a family of medieval

Muslims, as opposed to the institutional or public displays of
religious belief that one typically finds in the sources. For
example, Islamic mysticism, or Sufism, does not feature much
in Usama's religious landscape. Indeed, he did not encounter
any organized Sufi brotherhoods until late in life. Rather,
Usama seems to have occupied himself with more individual
expressions of devotion, inflected by popular asceticism: praying, fasting, giving alms, pilgrimage to Mecca and Jerusalem,
rescuing prisoners, reciting the Qur'an, and so on. He praises
in others the related virtue of engaging in jihad, meaning (in
this case) holy war against the Franks. Significantly, however,
he does not describe his own military experiences in this way,
much as we might think this would have suited the men he
served, a fact which reveals something of Usama's character
and the limits of jihad-speak, even during the counter-crusade.
Usama also had a particular, but quite ordinary, fondness for
visiting holy places and holy men – if the latter should be living
exemplars of piety, so much the better. Indeed, Usama devotes a
separate appendix in *The Book of Contemplation* to miraculous
deeds associated with such holy men. These stories are set
alongside tales of remarkable cures, which are related to the
feats of holy men by the way in which accidental remedies
brought on by dream-visions or certain diets give proof to the
vagaries of God's will.

In tandem with Usama's refined code of honour and politesse,
Islam further structured Usama's relationship with other men
and, of course, other women. In Usama's world, it was taken
for granted that the affairs of men overshadowed those of
women, who were seen as the building-blocks of the family and
of society, and whose chastity, therefore, men must anxiously
guard. As a result, the domestic seclusion of women was normal, and their lives, even their names, are only sparsely mentioned in the sources. It is thus all the more delightful that
Usama has left us precious (though discreet) glimpses into this
aspect of his world.

Usama's world was crowded with human variety. The men
and women he encountered included groups that we would
nowadays call Arabs, Turks, Kurds, Armenians, Africans,

Greeks and Europeans. The people were Muslims of various kinds, of course, but also Latin Christians loyal to Rome, Greek Christians and Melkites loyal to Constantinople, and other native Near Eastern Christians, whether Copts in Egypt or Syrian Orthodox Christians in Syria, Iraq and Upper Mesopotamia, to name only the largest groups. Usama alludes (possibly) to Druze communities in the mountains, and the larger cities of the region always included ancient and active Jewish communities. At Shayzar itself, Usama's kin were of course central to his life. These included his father Murshid, but also his domineering uncle Sultan, who was lord of Shayzar for most of Usama's life. His family also included a dizzying array of uncles, cousins and nephews, as well as their women and children. Finally, it also embraced, like the households of sultans and atabegs, servants and slaves of various kinds, including concubines and soldiers, but also domestic help, nannies, physicians, craftsmen, grooms, huntsmen, animal-keepers, and so on, most referred to generically as *ghilman* (singular *ghulam*), often translated here with equal vagueness as 'attendant'. The Banu Munqidh were a clan composed of many families, and so Shayzar was, quite literally, a house of many mansions.

Then there are the Franks. Usama is most famous today for his observations on the manners and customs of the Latin settlers who inhabited his part of the world, and he is certainly the most cherished of all the Muslim eyewitnesses of the crusades. This is due, no doubt, to his marvellous eye for detail and human portraiture. And it helps that his stories are also rather funny and a bit risqué too. But as it happens, despite his personal interactions with the Franks, Usama generally indulged in the stereotypes about Franks that were already commonplace in his day – their lack of refinement, their low intelligence, their animal qualities, and so on – and his own contribution to our general knowledge of the culture of the European settlers in the Levant should not be exaggerated. Nevertheless, Usama's writings concerning the Franks are undeniably valuable in two specific areas: regional politics, where he provides a localized and personal glimpse of some of the key events, people and practices of the day; and social relations, where he shines as a decidedly non-detached ethnographic participant-observer of, *inter alia*, Frankish mores, medicine, law and religion. Usama's works would still be valuable and moving without his accounts of the Franks, but we would have very little sense of what the crusades truly meant to medieval Muslims without them.

Humans, Franks grudgingly included, were only the loudest inhabitants of Usama's world, which was also home to animal species so multifarious that it startles readers who think of the Near East solely as a place of desolate landscapes and camels (winsome as they may be). Songbirds, cats, dogs, mice, flies, cattle, gazelles, wild asses, wild boar, deer, hares, waterfowl, horses, hawks, falcons, serpents, hyenas, cheetahs, leopards and, most importantly, lions are just some of the animals that appear in his writings. Usama, whose name indeed means 'lion', was a keen observer of the natural world, a fact which was an advantage for him as a poet and an absolute necessity for him as a hunter. Like many men of the upper strata of medieval Islamic society, Usama found hunting to be an absorbing pastime, one pursued more for sport than for acquiring food. At Shayzar, hunting was pursued passionately, one might even say pathologically in the case of Usama's father, who seems to have spent most of his free time on the chase. Usama's writings abound with references to hunting practices, especially his *Book of Contemplation*, to which he even added an appendix devoted to hunting-stories. His days spent hunting were pleasant times, and, as one reads his tales of the hunt, one gets a vivid sense of the landscape around Shayzar and a palpable sense of an elderly man's nostalgia for endless days of youth spent with long-passed friends and kin running game to ground amidst the liquorice-bushes, cane-brakes and asphodel of home.

The Author

When Usama was born in 1095, it may well have been expected that he would in time become lord of Shayzar himself, and he seems to have harboured this ambition in his later life. After the death of his uncle Nasr in 1098, his father Murshid and his

uncle Sultan were the leading men of the Banu Munqidh (see
Family Tree, pp. 272–3). Usama's father found that politics did
not agree with his religious scruples or his ascetic bent (or his
preoccupation with hunting) and so he withdrew, leaving Sultan to become lord of Shayzar. Sultan had no male children at
the time and so the young Usama must have been raised to
think that Shayzar would one day be his. He certainly acted
that way, hunting, fighting and helping to administer the lands
of his family's domains. Usama had no formal education as we
would call it today, but instead studied under tutors who were
retained in his father's household. From these men, some of
them refugees from the Frankish invasions, he learned rhetoric,
grammar and poetry – the literary arts any future prince should
know, and which he came to embody.

He witnessed combat, beginning in his teens, and honed his
skills fighting Shayzar's local Muslim rivals. He also had his
share of experience with the Franks, particularly those from
Antioch or Tripoli, who made frequent raids to pillage the
countryside and rustle livestock. But then prolonged engagements were often sealed with treaties and even festivities, and
this allowed Usama the opportunity to study the Franks at his
ease. An even closer study was made possible in 1124, when
the captive Baldwin II, King of Jerusalem, resided at Shayzar as
a guest of his uncle Sultan while the details of a prisoner
exchange were worked out. It was a kindness that put Usama
and the Banu Munqidh in good standing with the Franks.

Family, poetry, hunting and fighting: life at Shayzar for a
young man like Usama was a dream. The rude awakening came
in 1131. By then, Usama's uncle Sultan had managed to have a
son, Muhammad, a fact which made the continued presence of
Usama at Shayzar rather troubling for him. After all, Usama's
father had refused the lordship of Shayzar and as he grew old
and infirm his brother Sultan was increasingly the sole figure of
authority left at Shayzar. Why shouldn't the amirate pass down
to Sultan's own son, Muhammad, instead of the sons of his
brother, especially the precious Usama? One night, according
to Usama, Sultan had a fevered conversation with him and
demanded that he collect his belongings and leave home. In

June of 1131, Usama solemnly embraced this exile, his first of many, and left Shayzar.

With Shayzar behind him, Usama sought service in the nearby principality of Homs, which was just then under siege by Zangi, the ambitious atabeg of Mosul and lord of Aleppo. When Homs finally fell to Zangi, Usama was captured and, it appears, entered the atabeg's service, residing in Mosul in Upper Mesopotamia, where he hunted, campaigned and held literary gatherings. In 1132, Zangi was on campaign again in Syria, and Usama was posted to the city of Hama under Zangi's trusted general, al-Yaghisiyani. He may well have visited Shayzar in 1137 when his father died, and he certainly was there by the spring of 1138 when, contrary to Zangi's command, he left Hama to assist in the defence of his home against a joint Frankish-Byzantine siege. As a result of this infraction, when the siege was lifted Usama found himself now abandoned by his commander yet still unwelcome in his ancestral home. He tightened his belt and sought service in Damascus.

Damascus was the capital of a petty Turkish dynasty of Seljuk vassals called the Burids, but the Burid princes were at the time mere figureheads who deferred to their powerful Rasputin, the atabeg Mu'in al-Din Unur. Faced with Zangi's unambiguous goal of conquering their city, the Burids under Mu'in al-Din sought to enlist the support of al-Afdal Ridwan, a former Fatimid vizier who was in Syria hiding out from his enemies. Usama was sent on a diplomatic mission to seal the deal, and he almost succeeded, had Ridwan not skived off back to Egypt, where he was captured and imprisoned. After this setback, Damascus was now obliged to make common cause with their Frankish neighbours in the Latin Kingdom of Jerusalem, so both Mu'in al-Din and Usama travelled to Frankish territory on numerous occasions between 1140 and 1143, visiting (at least) the Frankish-controlled towns of Jerusalem, Acre, Nablus, Sebaste, Haifa and Tiberias, meeting and treating with various Frankish leaders and their subjects. It is these visits that provide the setting for many of his observations of Frankish customs related in this volume. The treaty settled, he seems to have spent the rest of his tenure with the Burids getting into trouble. Indeed, by 1144 his political intrigues in Damascus had so vexed the local *ra'is* that the man refused to return to the city until Mu'in al-Din had expelled Usama, his family and his followers. His welcome overstayed, Usama took the hint and arrived in Cairo, the capital of the Fatimid caliphate of Egypt, later that year.

In Cairo, the reigning caliph, al-Hafiz, was in need of seasoned commanders, so Usama found a ready welcome for his talents as a warrior and courtier. He also found Egypt a tempting laboratory for his own personal ambitions. Even though he would later tell the story as a cautionary tale about testing fate, Usama may have been inspired by what he saw of the politically fluid situation in Egypt during the attempted coup of al-Afdal Ridwan, the once-exiled vizier whom he had tried to enlist for the Burids against Zangi. In 1148, al-Afdal Ridwan escaped from his confinement in Egypt and rallied sufficient troops to contest the caliph, but he failed, spectacularly so, and was killed. Usama's own involvement was ambiguous. By 1149, much of Usama's old life was behind him and he was facing an acute crisis of patronage: his first patron Zangi had died in 1146; Mu'in al-Din the Burid was gone too, having died after the failed Frankish siege of Damascus during the Second Crusade (1148); and now in Egypt the ageing caliph al-Hafiz was ill and weakened. In this setting, Usama decided to take steps to secure his future.

The next years in Egypt were ones of plot and counter-plot, and given Usama's reticence about his involvement in the disasters that resulted, the scene deserves a careful outline here. Usama found the security that he sought, or so he thought, in an unexpected quarter. The Fatimid caliph al-Hafiz died in October of 1149 and was succeeded by his teenage son, al-Zafir. For his vizier, al-Zafir was forced to recognize the commander Ibn al-Sallar, who seized power upon the succession. Ibn al-Sallar brought with him his impetuous stepson, the amir 'Abbas, who would later follow cataclysmically in his stepfather's footsteps. Both Ibn al-Sallar and 'Abbas profited from the counsel and experience of Usama, even as the resentful caliph al-Zafir hatched his plans for revenge. Having settled into power as vizier, Ibn al-Sallar was keen to wage war on the Franks, but he needed outside help to do so. And so he concocted a plan to make an alliance with the rising power in Syria, the son of Zangi, named Nur al-Din, and turned to his trusted Syrian amir Usama to see to it. Ibn al-Sallar hoped Usama could persuade Nur al-Din to join him against the Franks, who were threatening Ascalon, the Fatimid foothold in Palestine. After a series of tribulations, Usama eventually made it to Syria, but was unable to forge the necessary alliance. Nur al-Din had his own plans, which did not (yet) include involving himself in Egyptian affairs. Usama gathered what troops he could and returned to Cairo, pausing in Ascalon to participate in various small campaigns against the Franks.

Returning to Cairo, Usama threw himself again into the poisonous polygonal relationship of the caliph al-Zafir, Ibn al-Sallar, his stepson 'Abbas and the latter's young son, Nasr. In 1153, Ibn al-Sallar was the first to go, assassinated in a plot hatched by al-Zafir, 'Abbas and Nasr and, some sources say, egged on by Usama, who was never known to ignore the knock of a Machiavellian opportunity. The next to go, in 1154, was the caliph himself, al-Zafir, whom 'Abbas had brutally rubbed out, putting an infant on the throne as his successor. Cairo exploded, and a new vizier seized power, named Ibn Ruzzik. Arriving in Cairo, the latter forced the triumvirate of 'Abbas, Nasr and Usama to abandon Egypt. Usama, who was now an expert at burning bridges, had very little choice of a destination. The three fled to Syria, facing en route a series of misadventures and conflicts with Franks and Bedouin so dire that only Usama and his men survived to reach Damascus, the newly conquered capital of Nur al-Din's Syrian domain.

Under Nur al-Din's patronage, Usama tried to reconstruct his life in Syria as best he could, fully conscious of his proximity to his old home, Shayzar. He arranged to have his family sent from Egypt, though the boat was attacked by Franks and he lost much of his property and, more tragically, his personal library. His family reconstituted, he could now turn his attentions to Shayzar. As his uncle Sultan had recently died, Usama saw his opportunity to make amends with his cousin Muhammad, the new lord of Shayzar, but it was all in vain. For in

August 1157, an earthquake struck, levelling cities throughout northern Syria. At Shayzar, where Usama's cousin had gathered most of the family to celebrate the circumcision of his young son, the earthquake had been indiscriminate and destroyed the castle and nearly all who were in it. Virtually all of Usama's relatives were wiped out in one blow. In just one of the twists in Usama's fate-struck life, he, alone in Damascus, was saved from the calamity at Shayzar by the very exile he so resented.

Usama spent the next decades as a dutiful courtier in Nur al-Din's Syria and then, in 1164, he entered the service of one of Nur al-Din's vassals, Qara Arslan of the Artuqid dynasty of Hisn Kayfa, far off in the province of Diyar Bakr in the upper reaches of the Tigris River. His decade in Diyar Bakr is especially vague to us, though he seems to have slowed down and taken to writing. For it is in Diyar Bakr where he did much of the work for which he was known, including the *Book of the Staff*, excerpted in the present volume.

In 1174, Usama was delighted to be asked to join the court of the new ruler of Damascus. This was the mighty sultan Saladin, a former commander for Nur al-Din, who, now that Nur al-Din had died, was well on his way towards building a new and powerful state that united Egypt, Syria and Upper Mesopotamia, whether his Frankish or Muslim rivals liked it or not. Saladin accorded the old warrior and diplomat a certain amount of respect while he used Damascus as his base for further conquests in Syria and Palestine. According to one source, he would even meet with Usama for advice on warfare and proper conduct. Usama's advanced age kept him confined at home, where he composed and polished his works. Among the books he finished in Damascus were the autobiographical *Book of Contemplation*, translated here, and his guide to ideal conduct, *Kernels of Refinement*, which has provided some excerpts in the present volume. He also compiled his *Diwan*, a collection of his own poetry, which was said to be a favourite of Saladin's.

Indeed, it was for his literary works, not his political career, that Usama's peers most admired him. 'Usama was, in the power of his poetry and prose, like his name ["lion"],' as one admirer put it. Another called him 'one of the poets of the age, holding the reins of both poetry and prose'. Usama was held to be an *adib*, that is, a master of *adab*, a term which has come to mean 'literature' in a general sense, but in Usama's day embraced 'refinement' in various modes. This could suggest refinement in the meaning of an author's message – in its moral and social lessons, its witty entertainment value or its intellectual stimulation. But just as often it indicated refinement in its medium – in the high style and cultivated vocabulary of an author's verse and prose offerings.

Refined works like these were intended for refined audiences. Medieval Islamic society was a highly literate one, but Usama wrote for a small elite audience, even had there been a mass market to welcome him. Thanks to the abundance of parchment, paper and copyists, books were relatively inexpensive to produce, but they were nonetheless luxury items. The sorts of books Usama wrote might find their way to the book-markets, but they were far more likely to be granted as gifts to other elite readers, whether patrons or colleagues. In Usama's case, for example, the long excursus of praise for the sultan Saladin in *The Book of Contemplation* is a clear indicator of the book's intended recipient, and an artfully crafted 'thank you' note from one of Usama's colleagues testifies to one reader who got his advance copy of the *Book of the Staff*. Others of his titles were intended for family members.

The patron was, as in so many things, the key: he funded and sometimes inspired a book, he received it and retained it as a gift and, if it became popular in the right circles, ensured its long life by inspiring more copies or, at least, quotations in other books. Usama had a sterling literary reputation in his day, but given the vagaries of manuscript preservation over the centuries it is hard to judge how he fared thereafter. All in all, posterity seems to have treated him fairly well, even if his audience and range were limited: his works do not seem to have been copied or quoted much beyond the fourteenth-century Near East. Perhaps he will now receive the broader readership he deserves.

His favoured genre, the topical anthology, was a tried and

true one for Arab writers working in the *adab* mode, resulting in collections of poetry or of poetry and prose combined. Usama's most illustrious predecessor in this vein, and in many others, was the polymath al-Jahiz (d. 868), who wrote anthologies on a wide range of subjects, including (among many others) rhetoric, animals, nostalgia, passion, secrets and envy. Al-Jahiz often employed a dialectical technique whereby he alternated between highlighting a subject's virtues and exposing its faults, a technique that seems perverse to modern readers, but was adopted by many writers, including Usama. A good anthologist was sensitive to reader fatigue, so anthologists intentionally flit about from subject to subject or insert humour when the tone gets too heavy. Usama also used these techniques. This 'rambling' mode is often depicted as a product of Usama's old age, but in fact he is keeping to the rules of his genre. Jahizian foundations aside, Usama's most direct inspiration was undoubtedly al-Tha'alibi (d. 1038), a towering figure wholly underestimated today, who wrote nearly a hundred works, of which about half seem to have survived, and only a quarter to have been published. His anthological interests were Jahizian in scope, but it was his great masterpiece, a geographically arranged sampler entitled *Yatimat al-dahr* (*Unique Pearl of the Age*), that Usama mined in his works for snippets of exquisite and ancient poetry and (less often) prose. And there were very few writers in Usama's time who did not turn to al-Tha'alibi in this way. Indeed, like others of his peers, Usama is credited with composing a continuation of the *Yatimat*, updating it to his own era.

Like al-Jahiz and al-Tha'alibi, Usama composed works devoted to an admirable variety of subjects, including the three works included or sampled in the present volume (discussed below). It was only a matter of time before a respected *adib* like Usama would decide to compose a work on rhetoric and eloquence, and his *al-Badi' fi'l-Badi'* (*Creator of High Style*) was his answer. It is devoted to the standard rhetorical figures used in poetry, such as antithesis, double entendre or pun, each decked out with examples selected from the finest poets. Usama admits in his introduction to the work that it is more of a

distillation of older treatises than a work of originality. His
model seems to have been the great rhetorician Ibn al-Mu'tazz
(d. 908), who wrote a similar work on rhetorical figures. The
baroque deployment of these figures was the hallmark of the
'modern' poets that many of Usama's peers sought to emulate,
as opposed to the allegedly natural and conservative style of
the 'ancient' poets of the pre-Islamic and early Islamic eras. To
judge from the evidence of his own poetry, Usama put himself
in the modernist camp, but he possessed an aficionado's love
for the ancients, taking every opportunity to show off his knowledge of them by allusion and quotation.

This is most evident in his *Kitab al-Manazil wa'l-Diyar* (*Book
of Dwellings and Abodes*). It is a masterful analysis of the
conventions used in the preludes of classical Arabic odes, and
the images of campsites and dwellings they employed. It is also
a very personal work. Composed in distant Diyar Bakr, what
he called 'a forsaken corner of the world', Usama, a restless
and now ageing exile, one of the few survivors of his devastated
house, passed his idle moments compiling a book about the
longing of poets for their Time-effaced homes. Whatever his
faults, to know this is to know much about Usama and the
sympathy he elicits.

Usama extended his interest to other realms. One early work
was devoted to youth and old age, and was written for his
father; another seems to have been a collection of political
wisdom or a 'mirror for princes' for the ruler of Diyar Bakr;
still others were devoted to castles and fortresses, rivers, dream
visions, consolation, bearing loss, notable women, and other
matters. For those who know Usama's penchant for juicy anecdotes, this list is both thrilling and mournful: not a single word
of these works survives.

Usama ibn Munqidh died in Damascus on Tuesday,
15 November 1188, at the astonishing age of ninety-three, just
over a year after his lord Saladin recaptured Jerusalem from
the Franks and turned the tide of the invasion from Europe that
had begun in Usama's infancy. He was buried in a mausoleum
on the north bank of the Yazid River, on the east side of Mount
Qasiyun, which looms over the city now as it did then. Usama's

tomb did not last through the centuries and it is lost. All that
remains of the man are his works, only some of which comprise
the present volume.

The Works

The last two of the three works treated in this volume are quite
typical of the thematic anthology genre discussed above, though
only their longer prose anecdotes have been included here. The
first of these, the *Kitab al-'Asa* or *Book of the Staff*, is devoted
to the subject of famous staves and walking-sticks. The reader
may well wonder how many of these there could possibly be,
but Usama had no trouble rounding out what is in fact a
delightful sampling of poetry, stories, history, proverbs,
exegesis, tradition and random lexicographical detours. The
poetry includes selections from every era of Arabic poetry,
ancients and moderns, including poetry by Usama and other
members of his family. The prose includes some well-worn tales
about, for example, the staff of Moses, but also anecdotes from
Usama's own day, as vivid and autobiographical as any to be
found in his more famous *Book of Contemplation*. The book
was composed in 1171 or 1172 in Diyar Bakr. Of particular
note among the excerpts from the book included here is
Usama's introduction to the text, which vividly illustrates the
place of books in medieval Islamic society (and the sort of
characters that associate with them). Other anecdotes reveal
much about the religious setting of Usama's world, such as his
account of pilgrimage to Jerusalem, of a miraculous staff which
saves a man from the Franks and of Usama's visit to the tomb
of St John the Baptist. This last account, thanks to Derenbourg's
early and admittedly speculative readings, has long been read
as a description of the Hospitallers; the present translation
offers a slightly different reading.

The second of these texts, the *Lubab al-Adab* or *Kernels of
Refinement*, is, as its title suggests, a collection of examples
(the 'kernels') to guide the reader to refined social conduct. A
manuscript of the work is dated to 1183 and was presented to
Usama's son Murhaf in 1186, and so it would have been

composed during Usama's last years under Saladin in Damascus. Like the *Book of the Staff*, it consists of varied selections of Arabic poetry, including some by Usama, pungent narratives, bits of wisdom, Qur'anic commentary, traditions of the Prophet and, luckily for us, some meandering autobiographical accounts. The book is divided into chapters devoted to those features that Usama thought were absolute requirements for readers seeking refinement and courtly poise – in short, *adab*: political wisdom, generosity, courage, flawless manners, eloquence, literacy and wit, and so on. The book is not just an etiquette manual, but a blueprint for how to become the ideal Muslim courtier in the age of the Crusades. As such, it deserves much greater attention from historians of the period than it has so far received. Among the few excerpts included here, of particular interest is Usama's account of the sequel to the First Crusade in northern Syria, his only reference to those events that is known to have survived.

Finally, the text which makes up the bulk of this book is Usama's famous *Kitab al-I'tibar* or *The Book of Contemplation*, composed, as the author states, perhaps with some inaccuracy, in his ninetieth Muslim year, or *c.* 1183. Given the long encomium that ends the work, it seems likely that it was Usama's patron, the mighty Saladin, who was the work's intended recipient.

Because of the book's heavily autobiographical nature, it is often referred to as Usama's 'memoirs', but that is not really an acceptable label. Usama certainly filled the book with accounts about himself and about people and events from his own long life. But it is not intended to be a narrative of his life, still less a soul-searching reflection upon his contribution to history. The focus of the book, evident in its Arabic title, if not in all of its many English approximations, is rather different.[1] The *i'tibar* promised in the title is not just learning or reflection, but the gaining of knowledge by contemplation of *'ibar* (singular *'ibra*), instructive examples or proofs of divine omnipotence. The term is Qur'anic: the story of Joseph, for example, ends with the statement, 'There is a lesson [*'ibra*] in the stories of such people for those who understand.'[2] The Qur'an frequently exhorts its audience to learn from the fate of hard-hearted pagans and the ruins of their once-proud civilizations. Usama makes use of this theme or its variants throughout his own work. Contemplation of the passing of what had once been was also something of a sub-genre in Arabic literature, from the belles-lettrist al-Jahiz (d. 868) to the philosopher of history Ibn Khaldun (d. 1406). Usama's *Book of Contemplation*, then, is a meditation upon the basic fact that God works in mysterious ways, and nothing we can do will hasten or slow the fate that He has decreed for us. Readers are surely grateful that most of the richly detailed examples he adduces to demonstrate this fact come from his own fateful life, but Usama is not the hero of the book – God is.

Usama, his family, the Franks, Egyptians, Syrians, men, women, friends, foes, creatures natural and supernatural all populate the pages of this remarkable book and provide fodder for our contemplation. No matter the person (or beast) or the context, God alone chooses the moment to effect His will and to cause success or failure, often with utter disregard of our own expectations. A mighty warrior cannot overcome his fate, but even the lowliest person can survive lethal blows if their time has not yet come. A hornet sting may kill one man if God so decides, but a dog might save another man from a vicious lion. A Frank might wound one of Usama's kinsmen but, then again, that Frank might just as easily be eaten by a leopard. Repeatedly, we see the marvels of God's creation, in the bizarre behaviour of barbarians like the Franks, in remarkable cures for ailments, in the miracles of holy men and in the strength of character in unexpected quarters: in women, slaves and even animals.

The Book of Contemplation consists of individual anecdotes strung together, usually grouped in clusters of sub-themes, like 'pearls on a necklace', to use an image beloved of the medieval anthologists. It is grouped into two parts, each one (to judge from the surviving complete parts) beginning and ending with an ornate narrative envelope affirming the specific topic of each section. The introduction of Part I is lost, but thanks to a quotation preserved by a later author (see Other Excerpts

below) Usama's introductory paragraph and description of
its contents has been preserved. From this evidence, it is clear
that Part I was intended to provide examples from battles in
which Usama himself participated and the 'great events' and
'calamities' that he witnessed at Shayzar and during his long
career serving other lords. The surviving manuscript, which is
badly damaged, begins close to the end of Part I, just before
Usama leaves the service of the Atabeg Zangi. It passes rather
rapidly through his stay with the Burids of Damascus, proceeds
to his Egyptian imbroglio and concludes with him entering the
service of Nur al-Din.

Part II, the bulk of the surviving text, is clearly indicated by
a new page in the manuscript and a shift of focus. This part also
deals with military examples, 'Wonders of Warfare, Against
Infidels and Muslims', but in fact treats a whole range of sub-
topics, and is not simply limited to Usama's own experience,
but also includes stories told to him by others, indicated by an
isnad, a long chain of authorities (e.g., 'I heard from my father
that the lord of Damascus told him that someone told him the
following tale'), or Usama's recollection of events in which he
was not actually involved. It is in this section, for example, that
we find his reflections on the Frankish character, on bravery,
on admirable women, remarkable animals, and so on. After a
rather mournful monologue of despair at his weakness and old
age, this part – and with it the book proper – ends with an
encomium to Saladin. However, the text does not end here,
for Usama has appended two short sections to *The Book of
Contemplation*, at least to this manuscript. One is devoted to
'Curious Tales' of holy men and healers, the other to tales of
hunting. These are clearly and explicitly later additions to *The
Book of Contemplation*, and while they do not form an integral
part of that book, they nevertheless share its major goal of
providing examples of Fortune's fickle tides for the reader to
ponder.

The most notable feature of *The Book of Contemplation*,
and the one for which it is suitably famous, is the ambidextrous
nature of Usama's style and language. On the one hand, there
are long introductory and hortatory passages written in the

baroque high style that Usama loved, usually in the form of rhymed prose called *saj'*. On the other, there is the rest of the book, written in a style so informal as to have been a little shocking at the time. The anecdotes certainly make refreshing reading when compared, say, to the stylistic fireworks that al-Jahiz uses in his writing. One gets the sense that one is listening to Usama quietly reminiscing, not reading the carefully crafted cautionary tales of a master of rhetoric and high style. But, of course, therein lies his mastery: he makes his artifice seem natural.

Behind this informality, there is also a sort of linguistic optical illusion at work. For Usama chose to write most of this work not in the formal and cultivated classical Arabic of his *literati* peers, but rather in an Arabic that, though founded in classical Arabic, in fact contains forms of what scholars have come to call Middle Arabic. It is certainly not 'pure' classical Arabic, to judge from the number of words of Turkish, Persian and even Old French origin. For the latter, Usama usually supplies an explanatory aside, and so I have put these words into their modern French equivalents to retain their foreignness in this English translation. Vocabulary aside, Middle Arabic is emphatically not, as is sometimes believed, a degraded version of classical Arabic – they are both roughly parallel outgrowths of the Arabic of north Arabia. Middle Arabic simply possesses a distinctive and less rigid grammar, syntax and morphology that are at odds with those of classical Arabic. For Usama, Middle Arabic forms were modern and were what came to mind; classical Arabic was more 'literary' and required a certain amount of forethought. *The Book of Contemplation* is one of the very few Islamic texts to preserve Middle Arabic forms from this period, and so is doubly precious in this regard. Moreover, the evidence of Usama's occasional 'slips' into Middle Arabic suggests something about his working method, i.e., that this work was dictated and copied down, rather than written by Usama himself (although he may have used notes). The copyist, or a copyist, seems further to have tried to 'clean up' Usama's Middle Arabic a bit by 'classicizing' some of the offending expressions. In Arabic, the result reads a bit like thieves' cant spoken by the Queen, but for translators it allows for a text that is marvellously conversational and diverting.[3]

Translating Usama

Because of its wide popularity, *The Book of Contemplation* has been translated into most major European languages including, as of this writing, Danish, French (twice), German (twice), Russian, Spanish, Polish and Serbian. The present translation is the second translation of the Arabic text into English, having been preceded by Philip Hitti's popular 1929 translation.[4] For specialists unaware of the text's genealogy, a brief review of some of the past editions may prove illuminating, particularly given the warm welcome Hitti's translation often receives.

It was the French Orientalist Hartwig Derenbourg (d. 1908) who rediscovered and reconstructed the manuscript of *The Book of Contemplation* in the sweltering summer of 1880 in the Escorial Library, near Madrid. He was also the first to attempt an edition of the Arabic text, which he published in 1886, followed by a massive biography and study of Usama's life and times in 1889; this remains the indispensable point of reference for the subject. He published his French translation, the first in any language, in 1895.[5] His own account of the discovery of the manuscript is a ripping yarn of philological derring-do worthy of Usama,[6] and he deserves the credit for essentially creating Usama as a subject of historical and literary interest in modern times. That said, pathfinders are always awarded the privilege of making the most mistakes, and both his Arabic edition and translation have been largely superseded by now, even if his biography remains a monument to the 'pure scholarship' of classic French Orientalism.

In 1930, the Lebanese-born scholar Philip K. Hitti (d. 1978), then a professor at Princeton University, published an entirely new edition of the Arabic text, based upon a fresh and thorough examination of the manuscript.[7] The result was a great improvement on Derenbourg's pioneering attempt, the product of a native-speaker's instinct and great philological skill. The Arabic edition further encouraged other later translations, including two German translations, the best by Gernot Rotter, and a superb French translation by André Miquel, which some would say is even better than Usama's original.[8] Since Hitti was unkind enough to castigate Derenbourg for his early errors, though, it must in all fairness be said that even Hitti's edition has its share of flaws. It could hardly be otherwise, given that we are dealing with a single unique manuscript that is, on the one hand, badly damaged and, on the other, written for the most part without the diacritical points by which one distinguishes individual Arabic letters. As a result, the Iraqi-born scholar Qasim al-Samarrai felt justified in producing his own new edition in 1987.[9] Of these two most recent editions, Hitti's remains the standard if only because of its availability, and it is the text upon which the present translation has been based. Nevertheless, Samarrai's edition provides many crucial clarifications and is an indispensable ally in understanding Usama's text.

Hitti's English translation, the first ever produced, was based upon his edition of the Arabic, though by a quirk of publication schedules it was published one year before the Arabic text was produced.[10] The translation is at once accurate and insightful, but prose like a lion it isn't. Perhaps the Arabist H. A. R. Gibb, something of a warrior-poet himself, put it best in his long review of the book:[11]

> It is no reflection upon Dr. Hitti that precisely the same factors which give him exceptional qualifications as an editor of the text render him but an indifferent translator of it. To steer as happily and as surely as Usama does between the stilted and the slangy demands a trained ear for English and a pen that instinctively recoils from such sentences as 'I told thee that there wasn't a thing I could do for thee.'

In attempting to convey the 'medievalness' of this text to his readers with twee archaisms in this way, Hitti did a real injustice to the spirit of the original. For, if anything, Usama's famous colloquial style would have been received as strikingly, even annoyingly, contemporary by his bookish peers: Hitti's direction was precisely the wrong one to take.

Hitti's translation has smaller issues, too, mostly issues of word choice, but also concerns of a slightly more technical character. In 1981, for example, G. Rex Smith decoded much of Usama's use of what Joyce called 'the subtle and curious jargon' of falconry, revealing nuances that Hitti – no great huntsman he – simply missed.[12] The same might also be said of Hitti's understanding of Shayzari topography, military terminology, metrology, and so on. Moreover, the fields of Crusades studies and Islamic history have grown at a staggering pace in recent years, and we simply know more about Usama's world than we did decades ago – Hitti's annotations are no longer even a fair guide. My many differences with Hitti (and other translators) sometimes make it into the Notes on this text, but for the most part I have made my choices quietly so as not to overburden the reader, even the reader of endnotes, with technical philological diversions.

In the present translation, I have tried to improve upon the genuine achievements of Hitti (and his predecessors) in a few concrete ways, though my peers may well argue that I have committed a few philological sins of my own. I have, for example, tried to steer between 'the stilted and the slangy' as Usama would have had he written in English. I have also tried to keep Usama's status as a poet ever in mind. For example, like many translators of Arabic, Hitti chose the better part of valour when it came to rendering the rhyme of Usama's florid rhymed prose: he didn't. The result for Hitti was a fairly straightforward and clear unrhymed English prose, but this has added to the book's (mis)identification as mere 'memoirs' by diluting the baroque quality of the original *adab* style. In this translation, I have put these sections in rhyme as appropriate, though at the risk of having produced passages reminiscent of Dr Seuss. With regard to rhyme in verse, I have tried, for example, to represent the differences in style between the venerated classical Arabic poetry that Usama quotes and his own 'modern' verses by putting the former in rhyme and the latter in a more 'contemporary'-sounding blank, unmetred verse, even though both styles rhyme in the original Arabic.

Usama's intent in writing *The Book of Contemplation* was

to urge us to temper our pride by mulling over the fates of those who went before us, just as surely and ineluctably as we one day will go. As a faltering translator – and reader – I can hardly take leave of that book and the other texts included here without acknowledging the heavy debt I owe to these other translators and scholars who came before me. As with the delightful and moving tales that Usama has given us in this book, there is an *'ibra* in the stories of these people for those who understand.

NOTES

1. The book has been variously called *Memoirs*, *Autobiography*, the *Book of Learning by Example*, *Life's Examples*, *Life's Lessons* and *Reflections* to name only a few choices. The title used here, *The Book of Contemplation*, is no great improvement.

2. Qur'an 12:111.

3. On Usama's use of Middle Arabic, the technical study by Schen is fundamental: I. Schen, 'Usama ibn Munqidh's Memoirs: Some Further Light on Muslim Middle Arabic, Part I', *Journal of Semitic Studies* 17 (1972), pp. 218–36; and 'Part II', *Journal of Semitic Studies* 18 (1973), pp. 64–97.

4. Philip K. Hitti, *An Arab-Syrian Gentleman and Warrior in the Period of the Crusades: Memoirs of Usama Ibn Munqidh* (New York: Columbia University Press, 1929). Here I do not reckon the rendering of George R. Potter, *The Autobiography of Ousama* (London: Routledge, 1929), which is simply an English translation of Derenbourg's French (see note 5). For the same reason, I exclude Georg Schumann's German rendering, *Usama Ibn Munkidh, Memoiren eines syrischen Emirs aus der Zeit der Kreuzzüge* (Innsbruck: Wagner'schen Universitäts-Buchhandlung, 1905) and the Russian rendering of M. A. Salier, *Kniga nazidaniia* (Petrograd: Gosudarstvennoe Izdatel'stvo, 1922).

5. Hartwig Derenbourg, *Ousâma ibn Mounkidh: Un Émir syrien au premier siècle des Croisades (1095–1188). Texte arabe de l'Autobiographie d'Ousâma publié d'après le manuscrit de l'Escurial* (Paris and Leiden: Ernest Leroux, 1886); *idem, Ousâma ibn Mounkidh: Un Émir syrien au premier siècle des Croisades (1095–1188), Tome Premier: Vie d'Ousâma* (Paris:

Ernest Leroux, 1889); *idem, Souvenirs historiques et récits de chasse par un émir syrien du douzième siècle. Autobiographie d'Ousâma Ibn Mounkidh intitulée «L'instruction par les exemples»* (Paris: Ernest Leroux, 1895).

6. Hartwig Derenbourg, 'Comment j'ai découvert en 1880 à l'Escurial le manuscrit arabe contenant l'Autobiographie d'Ousâma Ibn Mounkidh (1095–1188)', preface to Schumann, *Memoiren*, pp. v–ix.

7. Usama ibn Munqidh, *Kitab al-I'tibar*, ed. Philip Khuri Hitti (Princeton: Princeton University Press, 1930).

8. André Miquel, *Des Enseignements de la Vie: Souvenirs d'un gentilhomme syrien du temps des Croisades* (Paris: Collection Orientale de l'Imprimerie Nationale, 1983); Gernot Rotter, *Ein Leben im Kampf gegen Kreutzritterheere* (Tübingen: Horst Erdmann, 1978); Holger Preissler, *Die Erlebnisse des syrischen Ritters Usama ibn Munqid* (Leipzig: Gustav Kiepenheuer, 1981).

9. Usama ibn Munqidh, *Kitab al-I'tibar*, ed. Qasim al-Samarra'i (Riyadh: Dar al-Asala, 1987).

10. Hitti, *Memoirs*.

11. H. A. R. Gibb, book review of Philip K. Hitti, *An Arab-Syrian Gentleman and Warrior in the Period of the Crusades*, Bulletin of the School of Oriental and African Studies 6 (1943), pp. 1003–11.

12. G. Rex Smith, 'A New Translation of Certain Passages of the Hunting Section of Usama ibn Munqidh's *I'tibar*', *Journal of Semitic Studies* 26 (1981), pp. 235–55.

Further Reading

Editions

Derenbourg, Hartwig, *Ousâma ibn Mounkidh: Un Émir syrien au premier siècle des Croisades (1095–1188). Texte arabe de l'Autobiographie d'Ousâma publié d'après le manuscrit de l'Escurial* (Paris and Leiden: Ernest Leroux, 1886). The first scholarly edition of *The Book of Contemplation*.

Usama ibn Munqidh, *Kitab al-'Asa*, ed. Hasan 'Abbas (Alexandria: al-Hay'a al-Misriya al-'Amma li'l-Kitab, 1978). The first complete scholarly edition of the *Book of the Staff*, which provides some excerpts in the present volume.

——, *Kitab al-I'tibar*, ed. Philip K. Hitti (Princeton: Princeton University Press, 1930). The standard edition of *The Book of Contemplation*, greatly improves upon Derenbourg. The basis for the present translation.

——, *Kitab al-I'tibar*, ed. al-Qasim al-Samarra'i (Riyadh: Dar al-Asala, 1987). The most recent edition of *The Book of Contemplation*, with some important readings at variance with the standard Hitti edition.

——, *Lubab al-Adab*, ed. A. M. Shakir (Cairo: Maktabat Luwis Sarkis, 1935). The first edition of the *Kernels of Refinement*, which provides some excerpts in the present volume.

Usama

Cobb, Paul M., *Usama ibn Munqidh: Warrior-Poet of the Age of Crusades* (Oxford: Oneworld, 2005). A short, up-to-date and accessible biography of Usama.

——, 'Usama ibn Munqidh's *Book of the Staff (Kitab al-'Asa)*:

Autobiographical and Historical Excerpts', *Al-Masaq: Islam and the Medieval Mediterranean* 17 (2005), pp. 109–23.

——, 'Usama ibn Munqidh's *Kernels of Refinement (Lubab al-Adab)*: Autobiographical and Historical Excerpts', *Al-Masaq: Islam and the Medieval Mediterranean* 18 (2006), pp. 67–78.

Derenbourg, Hartwig, *Ousâma ibn Mounkidh: Un Émir syrien au premier siècle des Croisades (1095–1188). Tome Premier: Vie d'Ousâma* (Paris: Ernest Leroux, 1889). The classic biography of Usama and the starting point for serious research on him.

Irwin, Robert, 'Usamah ibn Munqidh: An Arab-Syrian Gentleman at the Time of the Crusades Reconsidered', in *The Crusades and Their Sources: Essays Presented to Bernard Hamilton*, ed. J. France and W. G. Zajac (Aldershot: Ashgate, 1998), pp. 71–87. A sensitive sketch of Usama in his literary context.

Medieval Islam

Allsen, Thomas T., *The Royal Hunt in Eurasian History* (Philadelphia: University of Pennsylvania Press, 2006). A clear and stimulating global view of one of the most important pastimes in Usama's world.

Berkey, Jonathan, *The Formation of Islam: Religion and Society in the Near East, 600–1800* (Cambridge: Cambridge University Press, 2003). A survey of religious and social developments in the medieval Islamic world.

Irwin, Robert, *Night and Horses and the Desert* (Woodstock: Overlook Press, 2000). A collection of medieval Arabic literature of the sort Usama would have been steeped in – a modern *adab*-anthology as it were.

Lapidus, Ira, *A History of Islamic Societies*, 2nd edn (Cambridge: Cambridge University Press, 2002). A massive survey of Islamic history from late Antiquity to the present.

Nicolle, David, *Saracen Faris, AD 1050–1250* (Botley: Osprey, 1994). A richly illustrated reconstruction of the military and material world of men of Usama's social class.

The Crusades

Hillenbrand, Carole, *The Crusades: Islamic Perspectives* (London: Routledge, 2000). A fundamental survey of Islamic understanding of the Crusades and Frankish society.

Holt, P. M., *The Age of the Crusades: The Near East from the Eleventh Century to 1517* (London: Longman, 1986). A more technical survey of Islamic history, c. 1070–1517.

Riley-Smith, Jonathan, *The Crusades: A Short History*, 2nd edn (New Haven: Yale University Press, 2005). The standard survey of the history of the Crusades.

Tyerman, Christopher, *God's War: A New History of the Crusades* (Cambridge, Mass.: Belknap/Harvard, 2006). A new and thoughtful survey of the history of the Crusades in all their manifestations.

A Note on the Texts

To make the texts in this book more accessible to non-specialists, I have taken one especially drastic step. Medieval Arabic names are famously complex and repetitive, and one individual might be referred to in five different ways in the course of the same paragraph. When combined with the heavy use of pronouns in the original, it is no wonder that even the best-prepared readers lose their way. I have therefore regularized all the names in the texts (and have often spelled out pronouns). That is, I have chosen one distinctive form and have almost always retained it whenever Usama refers to that person, regardless of the form actually used in the text itself. Usama does not play with names in any complicated way, so this step has I hope made the text easier to follow without adversely affecting our author's literary intentions. Readers who really want to know the specific name-forms will usually have enough Arabic to go to the original. Thus, the commander Salah al-Din Muhammad al-Yaghisiyani is known throughout simply as 'al-Yaghisiyani' so as to avoid any confusion with anyone else who bears the title Salah al-Din (there are many) or the name Muhammad (even more).

I have dispensed with all diacritical marks – the dots and dashes that scholars often add to letters to render the sounds of Arabic into our alphabet; my assumption has been that non-specialists won't miss these and that specialists won't need them. The exceptions are the Arabic letters *'ayn*, which represents a distinctive constricting at the back of the throat, and *hamza*, a glottal-stop. These are indicated by single opening and closing quotations marks, respectively. I have taken a similar

approach with calendrical matters. Usama of course reckoned
time according to the Muslim calendar, which is lunar. As a
result, relative to the Common Era calendar used by most
readers today, the months do not have solid equivalents to solar
months and Muslim holidays are movable feasts. I have retained
the Muslim dates as Usama expressed them, but they are followed immediately by their equivalent in Common Era dates
in parentheses. All references to the Qur'an refer to the translation of M. A. S. Abdel-Haleem, *The Qur'an* (Oxford: Oxford
University Press, 2004).

Finally, it was customary in Usama's day to include conventionalized parenthetical blessings when mentioning certain
figures like God, the Prophet, or, most commonly, any dearly
departed acquaintance or kinsman ('may God have mercy upon
him' or the like). There were conventionalized curses, too, for
the damned (like the Franks). I have retained all of these, despite
their repetitive nature, lest, after all my concessions to read-
ability, I receive my own parenthetical curses from my peers.

The Book of Contemplation

The Book of Contemplation survives in only one badly damaged manuscript held at the Escorial (#1947). The first twenty-
one folios of the work (roughly sixty pages or 25 per cent of
Hitti's printed Arabic edition) have been lost, so the text begins
in mid-sentence. Some later medieval sources give quotations
from this lost portion, and some of these have been collected
and translated here alongside the excerpts from the *Book of
the Staff* and *Kernels of Refinement*. The present translation
is a fresh translation based upon the 1930 Arabic text of
Hitti, although I have made different readings when warranted.
Numbers appearing in square brackets in the text indicate the
page numbers of Hitti's edition. Students of the Arabic will find
this helpful, as the pagination in Hitti's old translation refers
to the original Arabic manuscript, not to the published edition.

The original manuscript provides few clues with regard to
paragraphing. Most section headings and divisions in Hitti's
edition and translation are entirely of his invention. With some

reluctance, but for the sake of the reader, I have included my own headings, creating sections according to themes that are occasionally different from Hitti's but that seem to me to be what Usama had in mind as his organizing principle. The Guide to Contents of *The Book of Contemplation* is likewise my own creation.

Other Excerpts

The other excerpts included in this book are autobiographical or historical anecdotes by Usama which are not already included in the surviving text of *The Book of Contemplation*. As with my translation of that text, the headings and Guide to Contents for these excerpts are of my own devising. The excerpts fall into three groups. The first are passages that are almost certainly from the lost twenty-one folios of Part I of *The Book of Contemplation*, quoted by other medieval authors. These fragments were collected by Qasim al-Samarrai in his edition of the Arabic text of *The Book of Contemplation* (pp. 15–23), but I include here only those passages which are explicitly said to be in Usama's own words. In this first group, numbers in square brackets in the texts of the translation indicate the pagination of al-Samarrai's edition, not the original source.

The second and third groups are anecdotes extracted from two other works, the *Book of the Staff* and *Kernels of Refinement*, respectively. These anecdotes have already appeared in translation elsewhere, but their presentation here allows me the chance to correct a few gaffes of my own in those earlier versions. In these latter two groups, numbers in square brackets represent the pagination of the original Arabic edition.

THE BOOK OF
CONTEMPLATION

Guide to Contents

In the Service of Nur al-Din

PART II: WONDERS OF WARFARE, AGAINST INFIDELS AND MUSLIMS

PART III: CURIOUS TALES: HOLY MEN
AND HEALERS

PART IV: EPISODES OF HUNTING

PART I

GREAT EVENTS AND CALAMITIES DURING MY LIFE

IN THE SERVICE OF THE ATABEG ZANGI

§ *A Battle with the Franks (fragment)*

... there were not many Muslim casualties in that battle.[1] However, a messenger named Ibn Bishr had arrived earlier from the caliph al-Rashid,[2] son of al-Mustarshid (may God have mercy upon them both), in order to summon the atabeg[3] before him, and so he took part in that battle too. He happened to be wearing a gilded cuirass,[4] so a Frankish knight, named Ibn al-Daqiq,[5] thrust him through [2] the chest with his spear such that it stuck out through his back (may God have mercy upon him). But a large number of Franks were killed. The atabeg (may God have mercy upon him) ordered that their heads be collected in a field opposite the fortress: they totalled three thousand.

§ *Shayzar under Siege*

After this, in the year 532 (1138), the king of the Romans[6] went out again into our lands. He and the Franks (may God forsake them) made an alliance agreeing to march on Shayzar together and besiege it.

Al-Yaghisiyani[7] said to me, 'Now what do you think about what this mother-bereaving boy has done?' By this he meant his own son, Shihab al-Din Ahmad.

'And what has he done?' I asked.

He said, 'He sent a messenger to me saying, "You'd better find someone else to take charge of your lands."'[8]

'So what did you do?' I asked.

'I sent a messenger to the atabeg,' he replied, 'and said, "I give the place back to you."'

'What a frightful thing you've done!' I said. 'Won't the atabeg now just say to you, "When it was meat you ate of it, but when it was bone you threw it back to me"?'

'So what should I do?' he asked.

'I will go set myself up in Shayzar,' I replied. 'If God (may He be exalted) should rescue it, then it will be because of your good fortune, and this will redound to your glory before your lord; and if the place is taken and we are slain, it will merely be our just fate, and you will not be blamed.'

He said, 'You are the only one who has ever said such a thing to me.'

I assumed that he would keep to this plan, so I gathered together sheep, a large amount of flour, butter and whatever someone under siege might need. However, at sunset, while I was in my house, his messenger came to me and said, 'Al-Yaghisiyani says to you: "After daybreak we leave for Mosul,[9] so prepare your things for travel."'

At this, I was overcome with anxiety, and I said, 'Shall I travel to Mosul and leave my sons and brothers and household to be put under siege?'

The next morning, I rose and rode to al-Yaghisiyani at [3] his tent and asked his permission to return to Shayzar to collect some supplies and money that we would need on the road. He permitted this, but said, 'Don't take too long.' So I rode out and reached Shayzar.[10] But in the meantime he did something that broke my heart and inflamed my suspicion: he moved quickly and sent men to my house and took up all the tents, weapons and baggage that were there, seized most of those beloved to me and tracked down my companions. It was an immense and frightful disaster.[4]

IN THE SERVICE OF THE BURIDS
OF DAMASCUS

§ *Usama Moves to Damascus*

And so the situation required that I move to Damascus. The messengers of the atabeg, meanwhile, came repeatedly to the lord of Damascus[11] demanding that I return. But I remained in Damascus for eight years, during which time I was involved in numerous battles.[12] The lord of Damascus (may God have mercy upon him) granted me a lavish stipend and fiefs,[13] and distinguished me by making me one of his close associates and by extending to me every kindness – all this in addition to the fact that the commander Mu'in al-Din[14] (may God have mercy upon him) honoured me, made me his constant companion and looked after all my needs.

§ *Usama Takes his Leave of Damascus*

Then certain things came to pass[15] that necessitated my re-location to Cairo. I was obliged to leave behind any household belongings or weapons that I could not carry, and what I lost on my estates amounted to yet another disaster. Despite all of this, the commander Mu'in al-Din (may God have mercy upon him) was benevolent and kind, full of sorrow at our separation, and he acknowledged his inability to alleviate my situation.

He even sent me his scribe, the chamberlain Mahmud al-Mustarshidi (may God have mercy upon him), through whom he said: 'By God, if I had only half the people with me, I would crush the other half with them, and even if I had only a third of them, I would crush with them the remaining two thirds, rather than be separated from you. But the populace in its entirety has amassed against me and I am powerless. Wherever you may be, the friendship between us will always be at its best.'

Concerning this, I say:[16]

[5] Mu'in al-Din, how many necklaces have you bestowed,
   Like the rings of a dove, upon my neck?

Benevolence has enthralled me to you in obedience;
    For to the noble, in benevolence lies bondage.
I find myself tracing my lineage back to your friendship,
    Even though I was once of glorious ancestors,
       self-ennobled.
Don't you know that, just because I trace my kinship
    To you, everyone who can hurls shafts at my heart?
Were it not for your sake, my unruliness would not have
      been restrained
    In the face of abuse, without my blade making its mark.
But I was afraid that the flames of the enemy would burn
      you
    And so instead I quenched their fuel.

IN THE SERVICE OF THE FATIMIDS
OF CAIRO

§ *Usama Arrives in Cairo*

[6] My arrival in Egypt fell on Thursday, 2 Jumada al-Akhira
of the year 539 (30 November 1144). The moment I arrived,
the caliph al-Hafiz[17] took me into his service. He invested me
with a robe of honour in his presence, and gave me a wardrobe
full of clothes along with one hundred dinars.[18] He also granted
me the right to use his baths. He settled me in one of the
residences of al-Afdal ibn Amir al-Juyush[19] – an extremely fine
one too, complete with carpets, furnishings, a large reception-
room and utensils all of brass – all of this with the understanding that I would never be asked to return any of it. I remained
there for a period of residence, the recipient of honour, respect,
uninterrupted favours, and a fief, the revenues of which were
easy to collect.

§ *Factional Fighting among the Black Troops*

Bad blood and dissension broke out among the black troops,[20]
who comprised a large body of men. On one side were the
Rayhaniya, who were the slaves of al-Hafiz. On the other side

were the Juyushiya, Iskandraniya and Farahiya regiments. So
the Rayhaniya were on one side and all of these other regiments
were on the other side, allied against the Rayhaniya. A group
of the royal bodyguard also joined the Rayhaniya. Both factions
assembled a large body of men. Al-Hafiz was overwhelmed by
all this,[21] and his messengers went back and forth between
them, for he was eager [7] to reconcile them. But the troops,
who were in the same part of town as he was, would not agree
to this. The next morning, the two sides fought in Cairo, and
the Juyushiya and their companions were victorious over the
Rayhaniya. Of this latter group a thousand men were killed in
the market of Amir al-Juyush; their corpses blocked up the
market street. As for us, we stayed armed night and day for
fear the troops might turn against us – for they had done just
such a thing before I came up to Egypt.

After the Rayhaniya were massacred, the populace assumed
that al-Hafiz would condemn the action and set upon their
murderers, but he was ill, on the verge of death. He died (may
God have mercy upon him) two days later, and as a result not
even two goats locked horns over it all.[22]

§ Al-Zafir as Caliph and the Coup of Ibn al-Sallar

Al-Zafir, al-Hafiz's youngest child, took the throne after al-
Hafiz. He chose as his vizier Ibn Masal,[23] who was an old man
of some stature. At that particular time, the amir Ibn al-Sallar[24]
(may God have mercy upon him) was off in his province. There,
he mustered troops, gathered them together and set off for
Cairo, sending word ahead to his residence there.

Al-Zafir called a meeting of all his amirs in the Vizierate
Assembly-Hall, sending to us the chief prefect, who said:
'Amirs, this Ibn Masal is my vizier and my deputy. Let he who
obeys me obey him also and follow his orders.'

The amirs responded: 'We are the slaves of our lord, hearing,
obeying.' The prefect returned to the palace with this response.

At that, one of the amirs, an old man called Lakrun, said,
'Amirs, are we to abandon Ibn al-Sallar to be murdered?'

They replied, 'No, by God!'

'Then get up!' he said.

At this, they all rushed out of the palace, saddled up their horses and mules and left to give aid to Ibn al-Sallar. When al-Zafir saw that, and it became clear that he could not resist him, he gave a large sum of money to Ibn Masal, saying, 'Go out to al-Hawf,[25] collect men, muster troops, distribute cash among them and repulse Ibn al-Sallar!' And so Ibn Masal went to do just that.

[8] Meanwhile, Ibn al-Sallar arrived in Cairo and entered the Vizierate Palace. The garrison agreed to follow him and he treated them well. He ordered me and my companions to lodge in his residence, and set aside a part of it for my own private use. Ibn Masal was in al-Hawf, where he assembled a large host of Lawata,[26] men from the Egyptian garrison, black troops and Bedouin. In the meantime, 'Abbas (a stepson of Ibn al-Sallar)[27] went out and set up camp on the outskirts of the city. The next morning, a band of Lawata tribesmen led by a relative of Ibn Masal headed out for 'Abbas's camp. A portion of 'Abbas's Egyptian troops deserted him, but he, his bodyguard and those from the garrison who remained loyal to him stayed fighting through the night of this treacherous ruse.

News of this reached Ibn al-Sallar, who summoned me that night as I was staying with him in his residence. 'Those dogs', he said (meaning the Egyptian troops), 'kept the amir (meaning 'Abbas) busy with nonsense so that a group of Lawata could swim across to him. Then they deserted him, some of them even going back to their homes in Cairo, and the amir was left fighting!'

I said, 'My lord, we will ride out against them at dawn. By the time the sun has risen, we will be done with them, if God the Exalted so wills it.'

'Right!' he said. 'Start out early on your ride.'

So we set out against them early the next morning; none escaped except for those who swam across the Nile with their horses. The relative of Ibn Masal was captured and executed.

The army then joined forces with 'Abbas, and he sent it against Ibn Masal. He met the enemy near Dalas[28] and shattered them, killing Ibn Masal. Seventeen thousand black troops and others were killed. They carried the head of Ibn Masal back to

Cairo. No one remained to oppose or contend with Ibn al-Sallar. Al-Zafir invested him with the robes of the vizierate and granted him the title 'al-Malik al-'Adil',[29] and he now had full charge of affairs.

§§ Al-Zafir's Plot against Ibn al-Sallar

[9] Mind you, as al-Zafir did this he was all the while turned against Ibn al-Sallar in loathing, secretly wishing him evil. Al-Zafir decided to murder him and so hatched a plot with a group of the caliphal bodyguard and others whom he won over with bribes, ordering that they besiege Ibn al-Sallar's palace and kill him. It was the month of Ramadan, and the group of plotters had assembled in a house near Ibn al-Sallar's palace, biding their time until midnight when his companions would be dispersed.

I happened to be with him that night.[30] One of the conspirators had informed Ibn al-Sallar of the plot, so after his guests had finished with dinner and had gone, he summoned two of his attendants and ordered them to attack the house in which the conspirators were assembled. This house, since God desired some to be spared, had two doors: one close to the palace of Ibn al-Sallar, the other further away. The first group of Ibn al-Sallar's men attacked the nearer door before their companions had reached the other door, so the conspirators fled, escaping through that door. Of these, about ten of the caliphal bodyguard who were friends of my attendants came to me that night and we hid them. The town awoke the next morning in the midst of a search for those who had fled; whoever was caught was killed.

§§ Aftermath: Two Examples of Fate's Inscrutability

One amazing thing that I saw that day was a man from the cohort of black troops involved in the conspiracy who fled to the roof of my house, with men wielding swords right behind him. He looked down into the courtyard from that great height. In the yard there was a tall lote tree.[31] So he jumped from the roof onto that tree, steadied himself on it, then climbed down and went via a passageway into a nearby sitting-room where he knocked over a brass candle-holder and broke it, then went on further to a spot behind a load of baggage that was in the sitting-room and hid himself there. The men pursuing him were looking down from above, so I yelled at them and sent up [10] my attendants to confront them and they drove them away. I then went inside to see the black soldier.

He threw off a cloak he had with him, saying, 'Take it. It's yours.'

To this I replied, 'May God increase your bounty: I have no need of it.' And so I sent him out, accompanied by a group of my attendants, and he was saved.

I sat down on a stone bench in the vestibule of my house, when a young man entered, greeted me and sat down. I found him to be well spoken and a charming conversationalist. But as he was conversing, a man came calling for him and so he went away with him. I therefore sent an attendant of mine after him to find out why he was called away (I was then living near the palace of Ibn al-Sallar). The moment that young man presented himself before Ibn al-Sallar, the latter ordered his head to be cut off, and so he was killed. My attendant came back. He had inquired into the young man's crime and he was told that he used to issue forged documents. Glory be to He who determines the length of our days and fixes the moment of our death! During this period of strife, a number of Egyptian and black troops were killed.

§ A Mission to Syria and Starving Bedouin at al-Jafr

Ibn al-Sallar (may God have mercy upon him) ordered me to prepare for a journey to Nur al-Din[32] (may God have mercy upon him). He said, 'You will take with you treasure and go to him to persuade him to besiege Tiberias[33] and keep the Franks occupied so that we can set out from here and lay waste to Gaza.'[34]

The Franks (may God confound them) had just started to rebuild Gaza so that they might blockade Ascalon.[35]

I said, 'My lord, if he refuses your request or if he has other pressing concerns that prevent him from doing so, what are your orders?'

He replied, 'If he lays siege to Tiberias, then give him the treasure that you have with you. But if there is something that prevents him, then enlist as many soldiers as you can from his army and go up to Ascalon, establishing yourself there to combat the Franks. Once you arrive, write to me and I will send you orders about what you should do next.'

He then gave me six thousand Egyptian dinars and a camel-load of clothes of [11] Dabiqi cloth, ciclatoun, squirrel-fur, Dimyati brocade and turbans.[36] He also assigned a group of Bedouin to me to act as guides. And so I set out, he having dispelled all obstacles to my travel by seeing to all my needs, great or small.

As we approached al-Jafr,[37] my guides said to me, 'This place is rarely free of Franks.'

So I ordered two of the guides riding Mahri camels[38] to go ahead of us to al-Jafr. Yet no sooner had they departed than they returned, their Mahri camels flying, saying, 'The Franks are at al-Jafr!'

So, I stopped, assembled the camels that were carrying my luggage and certain members of the party travelling with me and sent them back westward.

I then chose six horsemen from my *mamluk*-troops[39] and said, 'You go ahead of us and I'll be right behind you.' So they went galloping off while I went behind them.

One of them returned to me and said, 'There isn't anyone at al-Jafr. Maybe what they had seen were Bedouin.' He and the guides then began arguing. I sent someone to go and collect the camels and continued on my way.

When I arrived at al-Jafr (where there is water, green herbage and trees), there appeared from the undergrowth a man wearing a black outer-garment. We captured him and my companions then fanned out and captured another man, two women and some youngsters. One of the women came forward and grabbed my garment and said, 'Sheikh, I am at your mercy!'

I said, 'You are free. What is the matter with you?'

'Your companions', she replied, 'have taken of mine a garment, a brayer, a barker and a bead.'[40]

I said to my attendants, 'Whoever has taken anything, give it back.'

[12] So an attendant came and presented a piece of cloth of maybe two cubits in length.

'That's the garment,' she said.

Another one came and presented a piece of sandarach resin.[41] 'That's the bead,' she said.

'What about the donkey and the dog?' I asked.

As for the donkey, they said that they had tied up his forelegs and hind legs, and had thrown him to the ground on the grass. As for the dog, it was loose, running around from place to place.

I then called all these people together and saw that they were in a truly deplorable state: their skin had dried up around their bones. 'So,' I asked them, 'who are you then?'[42]

They said, 'We are of the Banu Ubayy.'

The Banu Ubayy are an Arab clan from the tribe of Tayyi'. They only eat carrion[43] yet go around saying, 'We are the finest of all the Arabs. You won't find among us anyone with elephantiasis, leprosy, blindness or any chronic disease.' And if a guest stays with them, they slaughter an animal for him and feed him with food other than what they eat.

I asked them, 'What brings you out here?'

They replied, 'We have heaps of corn buried in the ground in the Hisma,[44] and we have come to collect it.'

'And how long have you been here?' I asked.

'Since the feast of Ramadan',[45] they replied, 'we have been out here, without setting eyes on any food.'

'So what do you live on?' I said.

'On carrion,' they replied (meaning dried-up, thrown-away bones), 'we crush them and mix them with water and orach leaves[46] (a plant common to those parts) and we survive on that.'

'And your dogs and donkeys?' I asked.

They said, 'The dogs we feed with our own food and the donkeys eat hay.'

'So why', I pressed, 'don't you go into Damascus?'

They said, 'We were afraid of the plague.'

Yet there is no plague greater than the one afflicting them! This took place after the Feast of Sacrifice.[47] We stopped there until our camels came back and I gave them some of the extra provisions we had with us. I also cut up a cloth I had been wearing on my head and gave it to the two women. They almost lost their minds with joy on account of the food. I warned them, 'Don't stay here or else the Franks will capture you.'

§§ A Vigilant Arab Guide

[13] One of the amazing things that happened to me during that trip was the following. One night I dismounted to pray the sunset and dusk prayers (abridged and combined), when the camels ran off.[48] So I stood on a bit of raised ground and said to my attendants, 'Go spread out in search of the camels, and then come back to me. I won't move from my place.'

They spread out and galloped about this way and that and never laid eyes on the camels. Then they all came back to me saying, 'We didn't find them, and we don't know which way they went.'

So I said, 'We'll seek assistance from God (may He be exalted) and travel using the stars to guide us.'

And so we set out, even though, separated in the desert from our camels as we were, we risked meeting a grim fate indeed.

Now, among our guides was a man called Jazziya, a man of vigilance and savvy. When he became aware of our tardiness, he realized that we had strayed off from the rest of the party. So he, while still sitting on his camel, took out his flint-and-steel and began striking them, the sparks from the flintstone flying this way and that. As a result, we saw him from far away and headed off in the direction of the fire until we caught up with the party. Had it not been for God's kindness and the inspiration He gave to that man, we would have perished.

§§ A Felonious Mule

Another thing that took place during that trip was the following. Ibn al-Sallar (may God have mercy upon him) had told me, 'Don't let the guides who are with you know about the treasure.'

So I put four thousand dinars in a saddle-bag on a saddle-mule being led alongside me and handed him over to an attendant. I also put two thousand dinars, along with my own petty cash, a bridle and some Maghribi dinars[49] in another saddle-bag on a horse being led alongside me, and I handed it off to another attendant. Whenever we stopped to camp, I would put the saddle-bags in the middle of a carpet, fold up its edges on top of them, spread another carpet over it and sleep on top of the saddle-bags, rising before my companions when it was time to go. The two attendants who were responsible for the saddle-bags would then come [14] and take charge of them. As soon as they had them tied onto the two animals alongside me, I would mount up and rouse the rest of my companions and we would busy ourselves about the departure.

One night, we stopped to camp in the Wilderness of the Children of Israel.[50] When I rose to depart, the attendant in charge of the mule being led alongside me took his saddle-bag, threw it onto the back of the mule and turned around intending to tighten it down with its strap. But the mule started and then galloped off with the saddle-bag still on it. At this, I mounted my horse, which the groom had just brought to me, and shouted to one of my attendants, 'Saddle up! Saddle up!'

I galloped off in pursuit of the mule but I didn't catch up with it, since it was going like a wild ass. My horse was already exhausted because of the pursuit when my attendant caught up with me. So I said, 'Follow the mule that way!'

He left and returned saying, 'By God, my lord, I didn't see the mule! But I did find this saddle-bag, which I picked up.'

'It was the saddle-bag that I was looking for,' I replied. 'The mule is no big loss.'

So I went back to the camp and what do you know, but the mule had come galloping back, made its way into the horses' picket-line and stopped, as if it had wanted to do nothing else except lose four thousand dinars!

§§ *Meeting with Nur al-Din*

By that route of ours we arrived at Bosra,[51] where we found that Nur al-Din (may God have mercy upon him) was encamped against Damascus. It happened that the amir Asad al-Din Shirkuh[52] (may God have mercy upon him) had already arrived in Bosra, so I went with him to the army. We arrived on Sunday night.[53] I awoke the next morning to discuss my mission with Nur al-Din. He said, addressing yours truly,[54] 'The people of Damascus are my enemies. The Franks are my enemies. I don't trust either of them enough to get between them.'

'Then', I asked him, 'will you permit me to enlist a body of troops from the soldiers rejected for service in your army? I will take them and return, and you can send along with me one of your companions at the head of thirty horsemen so that it can be said to have been carried out in your name.'

'Make it so,' he said.

By the following Monday, I had recruited 860 horsemen. I took them [15] and set out into the very heart of Frankish territory,[55] stopping and starting out again at the sound of the bugle. Nur al-Din sent with me the amir 'Ayn al-Dawla al-Yaruqi[56] at the head of thirty horsemen.

§§ *At the Cave of the Seven Sleepers*

My route took me by the Cave of the Seven Sleepers.[57] So I stopped there and went in to pray at the mosque, but I did not go through the narrow passage that one finds there. One of the amirs of the Turks who were with me, called Barshak, came, wanting to enter by that narrow cleft.

I said, 'What are you doing that for? Come and pray outside.'

'There is no God but God,' he replied. 'I must be a bastard then if I can't get through that narrow cleft!'

'What are you talking about?' I asked.

He said, 'This is a place that no son of adultery can pass through – he cannot enter.'

What he said forced me to get up, enter by that spot, pray and come out again without – God knows – believing what he said. Indeed, most of the troops came and entered and prayed.

Yet, in the army with me was Baraq al-Zubaydi, who had with him a slave of his, a black man – devout fellow, taken to praying a lot, and one of the tallest and leanest people. He came to that spot and tried with all his might to enter, but he could not get through. The poor fellow wept, moaning and sighing over and over, and then left after failing to enter.

§§ At Ascalon: Fighting the Franks

When we arrived at Ascalon, dawn had broken. We unloaded our baggage in the public prayer-space. At sunrise, the Franks came to pay us a little good-morning visit.[58]

So Nasir al-Dawla Yaqut, the governor of Ascalon, came out to us crying, 'Your baggage: pick it up! Pick it up!'

I said, 'What, are you afraid the Franks will take it from us?'

'Yes!' he said.

'Well, now, don't worry,' I said. 'They've been watching us in the desert [16] and keeping us company all the way to Ascalon, and we haven't been afraid of them yet. Are we supposed to be scared of them now, while we're in our own city?'

The Franks stood off from us at a distance for a while. Then they went back to their territory, mustered more troops and came at us with cavalry, infantry and tents, clearly intending to put Ascalon to siege. So we went out against them, the infantry of Ascalon having already set out.

I circled around our detachment of infantry and said, 'Comrades! Go back and man your walls, and leave these men to us! If we are victorious over them, then you can join us; if they are victorious over us, then you will be safe behind your city walls.'

But they refused to go back. So I left them and continued on towards the Franks, who had just unloaded their tents in order to pitch them. We surrounded them, pressing them so that they weren't able to fold up their tents. So they threw them away just as they were, all spread out, and went away in retreat. After they had withdrawn some distance from the town, a group of those defenceless, useless fools[59] followed them. So the Franks turned back and bore down upon them and killed a few of them. As a result, the infantry, whom I had told to go back but who refused, were routed and threw down their shields. We then encountered the Franks and drove them back. They then returned to their own territory, which was close to Ascalon.

Those infantrymen whom the Franks had routed came back, blaming one another and saying, 'Ibn Munqidh knew better than we did. He told us "Go back!" but no, we didn't do it; now we've been routed and disgraced!'

My brother, 'Izz al-Dawla 'Ali (may God have mercy upon him), was in the group that left with me from Damascus, he and his companions, for Ascalon.[60] He (may God have mercy upon him) was one of the great cavaliers of the Muslims, who fought for religion, not for worldly matters. One day we went out from Ascalon to make a foray [17] on Bayt Jibril[61] and raid it. So we went and attacked them. I noticed, as we set off to leave the town, that there were some large heaps of grain there. So I stopped with my comrades and started a fire and set the threshing floors alight. We then went from one place to another in this fashion, while the army itself had gone on ahead of me. Meanwhile, the Franks (God curse them) assembled from their fortresses. These are close to one another and house large numbers of cavalry so that the Franks can attack Ascalon day or night. But now the Franks made a sortie against our comrades.

One of our horsemen came to me at full gallop and cried, 'The Franks have come!'

So I set off for our comrades; the vanguard of the Franks had already arrived. The Franks (God curse them) are the most cautious of all men in war. They climbed up a hill and stayed there, and we climbed a hill directly across from them. Between these two hills was an open space where our comrades who had been separated from us and those who led the extra horses crossed right beneath them. The Franks didn't even send one horseman down against them for fear of some ambush or trick. If the Franks had just come down, they would have captured our comrades down to the last man. And we, all the while, stood right across from them, inferior in numbers, with our main troops gone ahead of us, routed. But the Franks remained stationed on that hill until our comrades' crossing was finished – then they set out against us. As we fought, we withdrew before them, and they did not renew their pursuit. But whoever stopped his horse, they killed, and whoever fell from his mount, they captured. Then they turned back from us. Thus God (Glory be to Him) decreed that we would be safe thanks to their exaggerated sense of caution. If we had been as numerous as they were and had been as victorious over them as they had been over us, we would have wiped them out.

I spent four months in Ascalon fighting the Franks. During this period, we made an assault on Yubna,[62] in which we killed about a hundred souls and captured some prisoners. After that period, a letter came to me from Ibn al-Sallar (may God have mercy upon him), summoning me back. [18] So I set out for Egypt while my brother, 'Izz al-Dawla 'Ali (may God have mercy upon him), remained behind in Ascalon. The army there set out and made an attack on Gaza, during which he achieved martyrdom (may God have mercy upon him). He was a genuine scholar, a real cavalier and a truly devout Muslim.

§ 'Abbas as Vizier and the Murder of Ibn al-Sallar

As for the unrest in which Ibn al-Sallar was killed (may God have mercy upon him), it happened like this.[63] Ibn al-Sallar had prepared an army to send to Bilbays to defend the country from the Franks;[64] it was commanded by his stepson, 'Abbas, who brought with him his own son, Nasr (may God have mercy upon him). Nasr stayed with his father among the troops for a few days, but then returned to Cairo without permission or leave from Ibn al-Sallar. Ibn al-Sallar objected to this and ordered him to return to the army, since he thought Nasr had gone to Cairo just for fun and games because of the hardships of army life.

But meanwhile, Nasr had hatched a plot with al-Zafir. The caliph got a group of his attendants, with Nasr at their head. Their plan was to use them to attack and kill Ibn al-Sallar in his palace while he spent the evening in the private quarters and slept. Nasr arranged with one of Ibn al-Sallar's household managers[65] to inform Nasr when his master had gone to sleep. It also happened that the owner of the palace, Ibn al-Sallar's wife, was Nasr's grandmother, so he was free to enter it without asking permission. And so, when Ibn al-Sallar fell asleep, the manager informed Nasr of it, and he, with six of his attendants, attacked Ibn al-Sallar in the chamber where he slept and killed him (may God have mercy upon him). Nasr cut off his head and brought it to al-Zafir. That happened on Thursday, 6 Muharram in the year 548 (3 April 1153). Now, in Ibn al-Sallar's palace there were about a thousand men drawn from his *mamluks* and sentries. But they were in the public chambers while he was killed in the private quarters.[66] Ibn al-Sallar's men left the palace and a fight broke out between them and the followers of Nasr and al-Zafir until Ibn al-Sallar's head was raised up on a spear. As soon as Ibn al-Sallar's men saw that, they split into two groups: one group [19] that left through the Cairo Gate and went to Nasr's father, 'Abbas, to offer their service and loyalty, and another group that threw down their weapons and came to Nasr himself, kissed the ground before him and entered into his service.

Nasr's father, 'Abbas, arose the next morning, entered Cairo and took his seat in the Vizierate Palace. The caliph al-Zafir invested him with robes of honour and handed over to him the affairs of state. Meanwhile, Nasr became the caliph's constant companion and his intimate friend. His father, 'Abbas, came to loathe Nasr[67] for that, suspicious even of his own son, knowing as he did the way in which some people could turn one group against another so that they destroy one another and be rid of them both and take possession of everything they owned. One night, the two of them, father and son, summoned me to their presence. They were alone in a private place, hurling accusations at each other, 'Abbas barraging him with words while his son kept his head lowered as if he were a leopard, rebutting him word for word, which only infuriated 'Abbas and made him blame him and vilify him all the more.

So I said to 'Abbas, 'My lord 'Abbas, how much more blame and reproach are you going to hurl at my lord Nasr, while he remains silent? You should really point the blame at me. For I have been with him in everything he does and I do not claim to be innocent of his deeds, bad or good. What then has he done wrong? He has not mistreated any of your companions, nor has he frittered away any of your money, nor has he criticized your regime. Indeed, he has risked his life so that you might attain this position. He has therefore done nothing to merit blame from you.'

And so the father relented and the son held me in high regard.

§§ Al-Zafir's Plot against 'Abbas

Al-Zafir now concocted a plan with Nasr, convincing him that, if Nasr killed his father, al-Zafir would appoint him to the vizierate in his place. He also sent him generous gifts. One day I was in Nasr's presence when he received twenty silver trays holding twenty thousand dinars – a gift from the caliph. Then the caliph ignored him for a few days, only to send him every variety of clothing, the likes of which I had never seen before in one collection. Then he ignored him again for a few days, later sending him fifty silver trays holding fifty thousand dinars. And then he ignored him yet again for a few days, later sending him thirty baggage mules and forty camels with all their tack, bags and ropes.[68] [20] The one who used to act as go-between for them was a man named Murtafa' ibn Fahl. During this whole period, I was with Nasr all the time. He wouldn't permit me to be absent night or day; I used to sleep with my head at the end of his pillow.

I was with him one night at the Shabura Palace, when that Murtafa' ibn Fahl came and talked with him through the first third of the night. I kept away. Murtafa' then withdrew and Nasr called me to him and asked, 'Where have you been?'

'By the window,' I replied, 'reading the Qur'an. I really didn't have time to read from it all day.'

He then began to open up to me about what he was planning, so that he might get a sense of where I stood on the matter, hoping I would strengthen his resolve to do the evil deed that al-Zafir had persuaded him to do.

So I said to him, 'My lord, let not Satan make you stray, and be not beguiled by him who would delude you! For killing your father is not like killing Ibn al-Sallar. Do not do anything that will leave you damned until the Day of Judgment.'[69]

At this, he lowered his head, cut short our conversation and we went to sleep. He later acquainted his father with the whole

affair. So the latter behaved kindly towards him, won him over
– and plotted with him to murder al-Zafir.

§§ 'Abbas and Son Murder al-Zafir

Al-Zafir and Nasr were the same age, and they used to go out
together at night in disguise. So Nasr invited the caliph over to
his house, which was by the Sword-Makers' Market, having set
up a band of his companions in one side of the house. As soon
as the caliph was all settled in the sitting-room, Nasr's men
rushed out at him and killed him. That was Wednesday night,
the last day of Muharram of the year 549 (15 April 1154).
They threw him into a deep well in Nasr's house. A black
servant of the caliph's had accompanied him, a man called Sa'id
al-Dawla, who never used to leave his side. They killed him
too.

The next morning, Thursday, 'Abbas went to the palace as
usual to give his greetings and took a seat in a side-chamber in
the Vizierate Assembly-Hall as if he were waiting for al-Zafir
to come and hold audience and receive greetings. When the
time during which the caliph usually held audience had elapsed,
'Abbas summoned the chief prefect and said, 'Why has our lord
not held audience to receive the customary greetings?'

The prefect was at a loss to reply.

'Abbas shouted at him, 'What's with you that you don't
answer me?'

The prefect replied, 'My lord, we don't know where our lord
is!'

'Would someone like our lord just go missing?' 'Abbas coun-
tered. 'Go back and see what's going on.'

So he left, then came back and told him, 'We couldn't find
our lord.'

At this 'Abbas said, 'The [21] people cannot remain without
a caliph. Go in to the lords, his brothers, and bring out one of
them so we can pledge our allegiance to him.'

So the prefect left, then came back and said, 'The lords say
to you, "We have nothing to say about the matter of the caliphal
office. Al-Zafir's father cut us out of it, and established it with
al-Zafir, and so the office belongs to his son after him."'

'Abbas replied, 'Then bring him out so that we can pledge our allegiance.'

'Abbas, having murdered al-Zafir, decided to claim that the caliph's own brothers had killed him and to have them killed because of it. The son of al-Zafir[70] now appeared, a mere infant, carried on the shoulders of one of the household managers of the palace. 'Abbas took him up and carried him, as the people wept. Carrying him, he went inside with him, to the boy's father's audience-chamber, where now stood the sons of al-Hafiz:[71] the amir Yusuf, the amir Jibril and their nephew, the amir Abu al-Baqa. We were sitting in the portico, with more than a thousand Egyptian troops in the palace, when we were surprised to see a bunch of men burst out of the audience-chamber into the hall, and then to hear the sounds of swords striking someone. So I said to one of the attendants, an Armenian, 'Go and see who was killed.' And off he went.

When he came back he told me, 'Those men are no Muslims! That was my lord Abu al-Amana they just killed (meaning the amir Jibril)! One of them cut open his stomach and was yanking out his intestines!'

Then 'Abbas came out, dragging the amir Yusuf, the latter's naked head clenched under his armpit. He had already struck Yusuf with a sword, for blood was pouring out of him.[72] Abu al-Baqa, his nephew, was in the hands of Nasr, so they brought the two of them into a side-chamber in the palace and killed them there.[73] And yet all this occurred while there were a thousand swords unsheathed in the palace. That day was one of the most disquieting days I have ever lived through, given all the hideous injustices that occurred, injustices condemned by God (may He be Exalted) and all His creatures.

§§ An Amazing Thing: The Dead Steward

[22] One of the amazing things that happened on that day was this: 'Abbas, when he tried to go into the audience-chamber, found that its door was locked from inside. The man whose job it was to open and close the audience-chamber was an old steward called Amin al-Mulk. They tried the door various ways

and finally opened it. When they went in, they found that steward behind the door, dead, the keys still in his hand.

§ A Military Revolt against 'Abbas

As for the unrest that broke out in Egypt and the victory of 'Abbas over the Egyptian army during it, it happened like this. Once he had done what he did to the sons of al-Hafiz (may God have mercy upon him), the hearts of the people were hardened against him and they nursed in them hostility and spite. So now those daughters of al-Hafiz remaining in the palace wrote to that cavalier of the Muslims, Ibn Ruzzik[74] (may God have mercy upon him), urging him to assist them. So he assembled his troops and set out from his province, making for Cairo. By the order of 'Abbas, the fleet was repaired and stocked with provisions, weapons and cash. He then took charge of the troops, ordering them to mount up and march with him. That was on Thursday, 10 Safar in the year '49 (26 April 1154). He ordered his son Nasr to remain in Cairo, and told me, 'You stay with him.'

When 'Abbas had left his palace, on his way to confront Ibn Ruzzik, the army conspired against him and bolted the gates of Cairo shut. The combat between us and them took place in the streets and alleyways: their cavalry would fight us in the high-street, their infantry peppering us with arrows and stones from the roof-tops. Women and children threw stones at us from windows. The fighting between us lasted from early morning until late in the afternoon. In the end, 'Abbas was victorious over the Egyptian troops, and they opened the gates of Cairo and fled. But 'Abbas pursued them into the hinterland and killed those he could. He then returned to his palace and regained command of things.[75]

[23] He also ordered the quarter of Barqiya[76] to be razed, because it was where many of the soldiers' houses were located. But I managed to calm him down about that and said, 'My lord, if you set a fire, you will burn both what you want burned and what you don't want burned, and you won't know how to put it out.' In this way, I changed his mind about it. I also

secured safe-conduct from him for the amir al-Mu'taman ibn
Abi Ramada after he had ordered his death. I conveyed an
apology for him, and 'Abbas pardoned his crime.

And so that outburst of unrest was quieted. But the whole
incident had surprised 'Abbas, and made him clearly aware of
the hostility of the army and the amirs towards him, and that
he could no longer live among them. So he made up his mind
to leave Egypt and head for Syria to Nur al-Din (may God have
mercy upon him) to ask him for assistance.

Messengers now shuttled back and forth between those who
were in the palace and Ibn Ruzzik. Ever since I arrived in Egypt,
there had been a warm friendship and intimate fellowship
between me and Ibn Ruzzik (may God have mercy upon him).
So he sent a messenger to me to say, ''Abbas can no longer
remain in Egypt. He'll go instead to Syria, so I now rule the
country. You know what there is between me and you, so don't
go with him. For he will need you in Syria, and he will want
you and try to take you with him. I beg you, for God's sake,
please do not accompany him. You are my partner in everything
good that I might be granted.'

And yet, it was as if demons had whispered to 'Abbas what
he said, or else he suspected it anyway because of what he knew
of the friendship between me and Ibn Ruzzik.

§ Civil Strife: 'Abbas Abandons Egypt to
Ibn Ruzzik

As for the unrest during which 'Abbas left Egypt and the Franks
killed him, it happened this way. Once he began to suspect
whatever it was he suspected was going on between me and Ibn
Ruzzik (or perhaps someone told him), he summoned me to his
presence and demanded that I swear by forcible oaths from
which there is no escape that I would leave with him and
accompany him. But he was not satisfied even then, so he sent
one of his household managers under cover of night to go into
the private quarters and take my household, my mother and
my sons to his palace, saying to me, 'I'll cover all their expenses
on the road and transport them with Nasr's mother.'

[24] 'Abbas then set about making the arrangements for his

journey, preparing his horses, camels and mules. He brought
two hundred horses and mares led by bridles held by men on
foot (as is their custom in Egypt), two hundred pack mules and
four hundred camels carrying his baggage. He was a real devotee of astrology and was convinced by the horoscope to set out
on Saturday, 15 Rabi' al-Awwal of that year (30 May 1154).

I happened to be with him when an attendant of his called
'Antar the Elder came to see him. This 'Antar was in charge of
all his affairs, great or small. He said, 'My lord, what is to be
hoped for if we go to Syria? Take instead your treasure, your
household, your attendants and your followers and go to Alexandria, where we can muster and assemble troops and go back
and fight Ibn Ruzzik and his comrades. That way, if we are
victorious, you can return to your palace and your kingdom; if
we fail, then we can return to Alexandria, to a city where we
are protected and defended from our enemies.' At that, 'Abbas
chided him and said his plan would be a mistake – yet it was
the right one.

The next day, 'Abbas summoned me early in the morning.
When I came before him, I said, 'My lord, if I am going to be
with you from dawn to dusk, when will I make the preparations
for my journey?'

He replied, 'We have with us some messengers from
Damascus. Send them on their way and then go make your
preparations.'

Prior to this, he had summoned to his presence a group of
amirs whom he made swear oaths that they would not betray
him or plot against him. He also summoned a group of Arab
tribal leaders from the tribes of Darma', Zurayq, Judham,
Sinbis, Talha, Ja'far and Lawata and made them swear similar
oaths, on the Qur'an itself, and vowing to divorce their wives
if they broke it. So we were naturally surprised (I being with
him that early Friday morning) that the troops had donned
weapons and were marching against us – and their leaders were
those very amirs whom he had made swear their oaths just the
day before. 'Abbas ordered his mounts to be saddled, and once
that was done they were stationed at his palace gate. They were
like a barrier between us and the Egyptian troops, who were

not able to get to us because of the multitude of animals outside.

At this, his attendant, 'Antar the Elder – the one who had just suggested to 'Abbas that plan, and who was [25] in charge of the men there – went out and screamed and cursed at his men, saying, 'Go back to your homes!' So they abandoned the animals and went away, grooms, muleteers and camel-drivers. The animals were thus left unattended and were given up to plunder. At this, 'Abbas said to me, 'Go and summon the Turks – they're stationed at the Victory Gate[77] – the scribes will make sure they get paid.' But when I went and summoned them, they rode off – all of them, about eight hundred horsemen – and rushed out of the Cairo Gate fleeing from the fighting. The *mamluks* rode off, too – there were even more of them than the Turks – and they also went out through the Victory Gate. So I returned to 'Abbas and let him know what had happened. Then I busied myself with removing my household, whom 'Abbas had transported to his palace. I got them out along with the wives of 'Abbas. Finally, when the road was clear and the animals had been plundered down to the last one, the Egyptian troops arrived to expel us. We were but a tiny group and they a massive host.

Once we had left through the Victory Gate, they came and locked the gates, returned to our homes and plundered them. They took from the hall of my home forty of those large camel-bags, all sewn up and filled with silver, gold and cloth. From my stables, they took thirty-six horses and saddle-mules with their saddles and their full tack and twenty-five camels. From my fief at Kum Afshin, they took two hundred head of cattle belonging to the residents, a thousand sheep and a granary full of grain.[78]

§§ *Attacked by Arab Tribes*

Once we had left the Victory Gate behind us, the Arab tribes whom 'Abbas had made to swear oaths came together and they fought us from the early morning hours of Friday[79] until Thursday, [26] 20 of Rabi' al-Awwal (29 May–4 June 1154). They spent every daylight hour fighting us. Once night fell and we encamped, they let us be so that we could sleep, then they would ride at us with a hundred horsemen, pressing at us with their horses from all sides, raising their voices in shouts. If any of our horses were startled and ran out to them, they took it.

One day, I withdrew from my comrades. I was riding a white horse – one of my worst. The groom had saddled him without knowing what would happen, and I had no weapons with me except my sword. Suddenly, the Arabs attacked me, and there I was: I couldn't find any way to repulse them, my horse couldn't help me escape and their arrows started falling on me. I thought to myself, 'Jump off the horse, draw your sword, and have at them.' But as I gathered myself to jump, my horse stumbled and I fell onto some stones and a patch of rough ground. A piece of skin from my head was ripped off and I became so dizzy that I didn't know where I was. A group of Arabs gathered around me, while I just sat there, bare-headed, clueless, my sword lying in its scabbard.

One of them struck me twice with his sword, saying, 'Hand over the dosh!' but I didn't know what he was saying. So they took my horse and my sword.

The Turks caught sight of me and doubled back. Nasr sent me a horse and a sword, and I set off without having even a bandage to dress my wounds. Glory be to He whose kingdom lasts forever!

We travelled on, and not one of us carried even a handful of provisions. Whenever I wanted to drink some water, I would dismount and drink from my hand. Yet just the night before, I had been sitting on a chair in one of the antechambers of my house, while some people offered me sixteen camels for transporting water and however many water-skins and bags God (glory be to Him) had willed. In the end, I was unable to transport my household, so at Bilbays I sent everyone back to stay with Ibn Ruzzik (may God have mercy upon him). He treated them well, let them stay in a house, [27] and granted them a stipend to cover their needs. Finally, when the Arabs who were fighting us wanted to go back, they came to us and extracted a pardon from us should we ever return.

§§ *Franks at al-Muwaylih. Bedouin Attacks and a Bedouin Rescue*

I continued on with our company until Sunday, 23 Rabi' al-Awwal (7 June 1154). We were surprised the next morning by a party of Franks at al-Muwaylih,[80] who killed 'Abbas and his son Husam al-Mulk, took his son Nasr captive and made off with his treasure and his wives. They killed anyone whom they could, and took my own brother, Muhammad (may God have mercy upon him), as prisoner. We had taken refuge in the hills, so the Franks left us and went back.

Under conditions worse than death – without provisions for the men or fodder for the horses – we continued on through Frankish territory until we reached the mountains of the Banu Fuhayd (may God curse them), in Wadi Musa.[81] We climbed through narrow and treacherous paths that led to a wide, desolate plain, full of men and stone-pelted devils.[82] The Banu Fuhayd killed anyone who got separated from the main party straight away.

Now, that region always has a few men from the Banu Rabi'a there, the amirs of the Tayyi' tribe. So I asked, 'Which of the Banu Rabi'a amirs is here now?'

'Mansur ibn Ghidfal,' they told me.

As it happens, he was a friend of mine. So I passed two dinars to one of them and said, 'Go find Mansur and tell him, "Your friend Ibn Munqidh greets you and tells you to come to him early in the morning."' We spent a miserable night, terrified of the Arabs there.

When first light broke, they took all their equipment and stationed themselves at the spring, saying, 'We're not going to let you [28] drink our water while we die of thirst.' Mind you, this spring provided enough water to supply Rabi'a and Mudar,[83] and there were many more in their territory just like it. They just wanted to stir up trouble between us so that they could kidnap us.

And so there we were when Mansur ibn Ghidfal finally arrived. He screamed at the Arab tribesmen and cursed them, so they dispersed. 'Mount up!' he said, and so we did, and we went down the mountain on a road even more narrow and treacherous than the one we took on the way up. We came down to flat ground safe and sound, though we almost didn't make it. I collected one thousand Egyptian dinars for the amir Mansur and gave them to him, and he went back home.

We continued on, those of us who survived the Franks and the Banu Fuhayd, reaching the city of Damascus on Friday, 5 Rabi' al-Akhir of that year (19 June 1154). The fact that we arrived safely at all after that journey is a proof of the power of God, the Mighty and Majestic, and of His excellent protection.

§§ The Story of Usama's Saddle

One of the curious things that happened to me during that battle with the Franks[84] happened like this. Al-Zafir had once sent Nasr a small, handsome Frankish ambler horse. One day, I went out to a village of mine, while my son, Abu al-Fawaris Murhaf, stayed with Nasr.

The latter said, 'We need a nice handsome saddle for this ambler, like the saddles they make in Gaza.'

So my son said, 'I have already found one, my lord, and it surpasses any you could desire.'

'Then where is it?' he asked.

'In the house of your servant, my father,' he replied, 'for he has a lovely saddle from Gaza.'

'Go and bring it here,' Nasr commanded. So he sent a messenger to my house, who took the saddle. It pleased Nasr, so he strapped it onto the ambler. That saddle came with me from Syria on one of those horses that is led alongside. Its saddle-cloth was quilted, fringed in black and exceedingly handsome. It weighed 130 mithqals.[85]

[29] When I came back from my fief, Nasr said to me, 'We took the liberty to take this saddle from your house.'

So I said, 'My lord, I am happy to be of service to you.'

When the Franks attacked us at al-Muwaylih, I had five of my mamluks with me on camels, the Arabs having taken their horses earlier. After the Franks attacked, some of the horses were left behind, roaming at will. So the attendants dismounted from their camels, intercepted the horses and took however many they needed to ride. And on one of those horses that they seized was my golden saddle that Nasr had taken.

Husam al-Mulk[86] (the nephew of 'Abbas) and a brother of 'Abbas who was a son of Ibn al-Sallar were both among those with us who survived that battle. Husam al-Mulk had heard the story of the saddle and said (and I heard him say this), 'Everything that belonged to the poor wretch (meaning Nasr) was pillaged, some of it by the Franks, some of it by his own comrades.'

So I said, 'Perhaps you are referring to the golden saddle?'

'Indeed,' he said.

So I ordered that the saddle be brought forth and I said to him, 'Read what is on the saddle-cloth. Is it the name of 'Abbas and the name of his son, or is it my name? Who was there in all of Egypt but I who was able to ride in a golden saddle in the days of al-Hafiz?' My name was written along the border of the saddle-cloth in black, and its centre was quilted.

When he read what was on it, he apologized and kept silent.[87]

§§ Digression: The Lesson of Ridwan. The Case of Qatr al-Nada

Even if the divine will had not been executed on 'Abbas and his son, and even if they had not suffered the consequences that they did for their injustice and ingratitude, 'Abbas might still have learned a lesson from what had happened before his time to al-Afdal Ridwan[88] (may God have mercy upon him). Ridwan had once served as vizier when the troops rose against him at the bidding of al-Hafiz, just as they rose against 'Abbas, so he fled from Egypt to Syria. Meanwhile, his palace and private quarters were given up to the most thorough pillage. Indeed, a man known as Commander Muqbil saw a serving-girl with the black troops, so he bought her from them and sent her to his house. Now, he had a righteous wife and she took the serving-girl up to a room in the highest part of the house.

There she heard the girl say, 'Perhaps [30] God will make us prevail over those who treat us so unjustly and who are so ungrateful for our acts of kindness.'[89]

So the wife asked her, 'Who are you?'

She replied, 'I am Qatr al-Nada, daughter of Ridwan.' The wife then sent a message to her husband, Commander Muqbil, who was on duty at the palace gate, summoning him home. She informed him of the girl's status. In turn, he wrote a report to al-Hafiz and informed him about it. Al-Hafiz then sent one of the palace servants, who took her from Muqbil's house and restored her to the palace.

§§ Digression: Courting Ridwan's Help. He is Captured in Egypt

After that, Ridwan arrived in Salkhad,[90] where Amin al-Dawla Gumushtagin al-Atabaki[91] was staying (may God have mercy upon him). Gumushtagin received his guest generously, settled him in a house there and put his services at his disposal. At the time, the King of Amirs, the atabeg Zangi (may God have mercy upon him), was at Baalbek, putting it to siege.[92] He wrote to Ridwan and it was decided that Ridwan would join him.

Ridwan was a perfect man: magnanimous, brave, a writer and scholar. The troops were especially fond of him because of his greatness of heart. So the amir Mu'in al-Din[93] (may God be pleased with him), said to me, 'If this man joins forces with Zangi, he will cause us a great deal of harm.'

'So what do you plan to do about it?' I asked.

He said, 'You will go to him, and maybe you can change his mind about joining Zangi, and he will come to Damascus instead. Use your own judgment in how you carry this out.'

So I went to see Ridwan at Salkhad, where I met with him and his brother, al-Awhad, and spoke with them. Ridwan said to me, 'The matter is out of my hands. I have made a vow to this sultan to join him, and I must fulfil it.'

'May God lead you to your reward!' I said. 'I'll just go back to my lord, then, since he cannot do without me. But before I go, I wanted to let you know what was on my mind.'

'So tell me,' he said.

'If you go and join the atabeg Zangi,' I asked, 'would he have enough troops so that he could send half with you to return to Egypt, and still keep half for himself to besiege us?'

'No,' he said.

'Alright then,' I said, 'when he camps before Damascus to besiege and capture it, after a long period – with his troops weakened, [31] their provisions exhausted and their march prolonged – would he then be able to go with you to Egypt before he renewed his equipment and strengthened his troops?'

'No,' he admitted.

I continued, 'It is at just that time that he will say to you, "Let's go to Aleppo so that we can renew the equipment we need for our march." But when you arrive at Aleppo, he will say, "Let's just head over to the Euphrates to enlist the Turkomans." And when you have encamped on the Euphrates, he will say, "If we don't cross the Euphrates, the Turkomans won't join us." And so, when you have finally crossed over, he will flaunt you like a trophy and boast before the sultans of the East, saying, "Look! This is the ruler of Egypt[94] I have in my service!" When that happens, you'll wish you could see just one stone from Syria, but you won't be able to. That's when you'll remember my words and say, "He gave me advice, but I ignored it."'

At that Ridwan lowered his head in thought, not knowing what to say. He then turned to me and asked, 'What then should I do, if you are so eager to return?'

'If, by staying here a bit longer,' I replied, 'I can assist our cause, then I will stay.'

'Do so,' he said. So I stayed.

The negotiations continued between us, back and forth. He finally agreed to come to Damascus provided that he be given thirty thousand dinars, half in cash, half in fief, that he be given the 'Aqiqi Palace and that his companions be granted stipends. Ridwan wrote out these conditions for me himself – he had a superb hand. He then said, 'If you like, I'll go with you.'

To this I replied, 'No. I'll go and take the messenger-pigeons from here with me. When I have arrived and cleaned out your house and got all your affairs ready, I will let the pigeons fly back to you and, at the same time, I'll head out and meet you halfway and enter the city in your company.' He agreed to that and I then took my leave and departed.

Now, Amin al-Dawla[95] was eager to hasten Ridwan's departure for Egypt, given all that Ridwan had promised him and all that he hoped to gain from it. He thus assembled all the men he had with him that he could, and sent them out with him after my departure. But once Ridwan had crossed the borders of Egypt, the Turkish soldiers that were with him turned against him and pillaged his baggage. He took refuge in one of the Arab encampments, sent messengers to al-Hafiz demanding safe-conduct and eventually returned to Cairo. But the moment he arrived in Cairo, al-Hafiz had him arrested and thrown into prison – him and his son.

§§ Digression: Ridwan's Escape from Prison

[32] It happened that when I first arrived in Cairo,[96] he was still in prison in a house next to the palace. By using an iron spike, he managed to dig a tunnel fourteen cubits long and escape on Wednesday night.[97] One of the amirs, a relative, knew of his plan. This amir and a henchman of his from the Lawata tribe were waiting for him by the palace. They all then went towards the Nile and crossed over into Giza.[98] Cairo was all in tumult at his escape. The next morning, Ridwan appeared in a belvedere in Giza, where the troops assembled before him. Meanwhile, the Egyptian troops prepared to fight him. Then, early on Friday morning, he awoke and crossed into Cairo. The Egyptian army was armed and ready for battle, commanded by Qaymaz, Master of the Gate.[99] When they met, Ridwan routed them and then he entered Cairo.

I had already ridden to the palace gate with my companions before he entered the city. I found that the gates of the palace were locked and no one was guarding them. So I returned to my house and stayed there. Ridwan set himself up in the al-Aqmar Mosque.[100] Various amirs came and joined him, bringing him food and cash. But al-Hafiz had assembled a group of black troops in the palace, who started drinking and soon became drunk. He had the palace gate opened for them and they rushed out seeking Ridwan. When the screams of these black troops reached them, all of the amirs with Ridwan rode off and scattered. Ridwan went out of the mosque only to find that his groom had stolen his horse and fled. As a result, one of the men

of the caliphal bodyguard saw Ridwan standing there at the
door to the mosque and said, 'My lord, why don't you take my
horse?'

'Indeed,' Ridwan replied. So the young guardsman galloped
up to him, sword in hand. Then, making as if he was leaning
over to dismount, the guardsman struck Ridwan with his sword
and Ridwan fell. Soon, the black troops arrived and killed him.
The Egyptians divided up his flesh and ate it in order to acquire
his valour.[101] Thus his story serves as a warning and a lesson
from which to learn by example, even if the divine decree had
not been executed.[102]

§§ *Bleeding Saves a Soldier at al-Muwaylih*

[33] On that day,[103] one of our Syrian companions suffered
from multiple wounds. His brother came to me and said, 'My
brother is as good as dead. He's been wounded by so many
blows, this way and that from swords and other weapons, that
he has fallen unconscious and won't come round.'

'Go back and bleed him,' I told him.

'But', he exclaimed, 'he has already lost twenty *ratls* of
blood!'[104]

'Go back and bleed him!' I said. 'I am more experienced than
you are about wounds. There is no other cure for them than
bleeding.'

So he went and took himself off for two hours, then returned
obviously overjoyed and said, 'I bled him and he's now conscious, sitting up, eating and drinking. The illness has gone
from him.'

'Praise be to God!' I said. 'If I hadn't tried this out a million
times on myself, I wouldn't have suggested it to you.'

IN THE SERVICE OF NUR AL-DIN

§ *Usama's Family Delivered. The Franks Seize*
his Property

[34] I then entered the service of Nur al-Din[105] (may God have mercy upon him). He corresponded with Ibn Ruzzik about transporting my household and sons who had been left behind in Egypt, and who, I might add, had been treated very well. But Ibn Ruzzik sent the messenger back and begged off, claiming that he feared for their safety because of the Franks. He wrote to me, saying, 'Come back to Egypt: you know what our relationship is like. If you are expecting any ill-will from the palace staff, then you can go to Mecca where I will send you a document granting you the city of Aswan,[106] and I will send you all the reinforcements you need to combat the Abyssinians (for Aswan is one of the frontier-fortresses of the Muslims). Then I will let your household and sons come to join you.'

So I consulted with Nur al-Din, seeking his advice on the matter. He said, 'You are not seriously considering, having just left behind Egypt and all her troubles, going back there! Life is too short for that! I'll send a messenger to the king of the Franks[107] to obtain safe-passage for your household, and I'll also send someone along to conduct them here.' And so he (may God have mercy upon him) sent a messenger and obtained the safe-passage from the king, with his cross right on it,[108] good for both land- and sea-travel.

So I sent along the safe-passage with a servant of mine, as well as a letter from Nur al-Din and my own letter for Ibn Ruzzik. Ibn Ruzzik then sent my family on to Damietta in one of his own personal launches, along with all the provisions and cash they would need, and his own letter of protection. From Damietta, they sailed in a Frankish ship. As they approached Acre, where the king was (may God *not* [35] have mercy upon him), the king sent out a group of men in a small boat to sink the ship with axes, as my own companions looked on. The king rode out on his horse, stopped at the shore and took as pillage everything that was in the ship.

A servant of mine swam across to him, holding the safe-passage document, and said to him, 'My lord king, is this not your document of safe-passage?'

'Indeed it is,' he said. 'But this is the procedure among the Muslims: if one of their ships is wrecked off one of their towns, then the inhabitants of that town get to pillage it.'

My servant then asked, 'So you are going to take us prisoner?' 'No,' the king replied, and he had my family (may God curse him) brought to a building, where he had the women searched and took everything they had with them. In the ship there had been jewellery that had been entrusted to the women, along with cloth and gems, swords and other weapons, and gold and silver amounting to something like thirty thousand dinars. The Franks took it all and then sent my household five hundred dinars, saying, 'You can get to your country on this,' even though the party totalled some fifty men and women.

As for me, I was at that very moment with Nur al-Din in the land of the king Mas'ud, in the region of Ra'ban and Kaysun.[109] The news that my children and my brother's children and our women were safe made it easier to take the news about all the wealth that was lost. Except for my books: they totalled four thousand bound volumes of the most precious tomes. Their loss was for me a heartache that lasted all my life.

§ Conclusion

These, then, are the kinds of calamities that can the tallest mountain shake, and the most precious fortune cruelly break. But God (glory be to Him) recompenses us in His mercy and concludes all things in His kindness and forgiveness. These were the great events that I witnessed, in addition to the calamities that I endured, but out of which I emerged safely, according to the timing as Fate wishes, though I was ruined by the loss of my riches.

PART II
WONDERS OF WARFARE, AGAINST INFIDELS AND MUSLIMS

§ Introduction

[36] In the midst of these events, there were periods when I saw countless battles against infidels and against Muslims. Of the wonders that I witnessed and experienced in these various wars, I will mention here only those that come to mind. For forgetfulness is not to be disparaged in someone who has seen time pass without cease; it is indeed a legacy of all sons of Adam passed on from their father (God's blessing be upon him, and peace).

§ The Haughtiness of Horsemen

One such wonder is what I witnessed of the haughtiness of horsemen and the way they oblige themselves to face dangers. We were engaged in battle with Mahmud ibn Qaraja,[1] the lord of Hama at the time, and the fighting between us was having no result,[2] the contingents of infantry standing at the ready while the melee carried on between the fast cavalry.

One of our men came up to me, a celebrated soldier and horseman called Jum'a, of the Banu Numayr tribe, and he was crying. So I asked him, 'What's the matter with you, Jum'a? Is this really the time to be crying?'

He replied, 'Sarhank ibn Abi Mansur stabbed me with his spear!'

'What if Sarhank did stab you,' I asked, 'so what?'

'So nothing,' he said, 'except for being hit by someone like Sarhank! By God, death would be easier for me than to have been hit by him! But he tricked me and took me by surprise.'

I then started to quieten him down and make light of the

matter to him, but he turned the head of his horse around and headed back towards the melee.

'Where are you going, Jum'a?' I asked.

'To Sarhank!' he replied. 'By God, I'll stab him good or die trying!'

He disappeared for a time, while I was busy with the enemy facing me. Then he came back laughing, so I asked him, 'What [37] did you do?'

'I stabbed him!' he replied. 'And, by God, if I hadn't stabbed him, my soul would have withered.'

He had attacked him while Sarhank was with a group of his companions, and then he came back. It is as if the poet had Sarhank and Jum'a in mind when he said:

> You do not even think, so great is your benevolence,
>   Of the thirsty avenger who is conscious of his
>   inheritance.
> Indeed, you doze yourself and awaken further his ire
>   For he slept not; how could he, given his desire?
> Now, one day, it may be Time's pleasure
>   To let him mete out to *you* an extra measure.[3]

This Sarhank was a noteworthy horseman, a leader among the Kurds. But he was just a youngster, whereas Jum'a was a mature man, distinguished by his age and his experience in acts of courage.

§ *Malik al-Ashtar and Abu Musayka*

I am reminded by the case of Sarhank of something Malik ibn al-Harith al-Ashtar[4] did (may God have mercy upon him) to Abu Musayka al-Iyadi. It happened like this: when the Arab tribesmen apostatized in the days of Abu Bakr al-Siddiq[5] (may God grant him favour) and God (glory be to Him) made him decide to fight them, Abu Bakr got the troops ready to march upon the apostate Arab tribes. Abu Musayka al-Iyadi was with the Banu Hanifa, who were the most powerful Arab tribe, and Malik al-Ashtar was in the army of Abu Bakr (may God have mercy upon him).

As the troops stood at the ready, Malik came forward in

challenge between the two ranks and shouted, 'Abu Musayka!' So he too stepped forward.

Malik said to him, 'Bah! Abu Musayka! After converting to Islam and reciting the Qur'an, you return to unbelief?'

'Get away from me, Malik!' said Abu Musayka. 'The Muslims forbid wine, and I cannot do without it.'

'Well then,' said Malik, 'do you agree to a duel?'

'I do,' replied Abu Musayka.

And so they fought with spears and they fought with swords. Abu Musayka struck Malik with a blow that split his head open and caused his eyelids to droop; because of that blow, Malik was named 'the Droopy-Eyed'.

Malik retreated to his camp, holding tight to the neck of his horse. A group of his kinsmen and friends gathered around him, crying. Malik said to one of them, 'Put your hand in my mouth.'

The man put his finger in [38] Malik's mouth, and he bit down on it. The man writhed in pain.

So Malik said, 'Nothing wrong with your man. "Sound teeth, sound head", it's been said. Just pack it (meaning the wound) with flour and wrap it with a turban-cloth.'

Once they had packed it and wrapped it up, he said, 'Get my horse.'

'Where are you going?' they asked.

'To Abu Musayka,' he replied.

Malik then stepped forward in challenge between the two ranks and shouted, 'Abu Musayka!' And Abu Musayka shot towards him like an arrow. But Malik struck him on his shoulder with his sword, splitting him in two down to his saddle, killing him. Malik then returned to his camp and remained there for forty days, unable to move. But then he recovered and was healed of his wound.

§ A 'Master's Blow' is Not what it Seems

Another case that I witnessed of the recovery of someone who had been stabbed, and who had been expected to die, happened as follows. We encountered the advance cavalry of Mahmud ibn Qaraja, who had come into our territory and set up an

ambush against us. Once our infantry and his were drawn up
at the ready, our cavalry dispersed.

A horseman from our army called 'Ali ibn Sallam al-Numayri
came up to me and said, 'Our companions have dispersed. If
the enemy attacks them, they will annihilate them.'

'Hold back my brothers and cousins,' I offered, 'so that I can
bring the men back alone.'

So he told them, 'Amirs, let this man bring the horsemen
back, and do not follow him. For if you do, the enemy will
attack them and dislodge them.'

'Go ahead,' they replied and I galloped off on my horse to
bring them back. The enemy were keeping away from them in
order to draw them further out and then overpower them.

When the enemy saw that I was bringing the horsemen back,
they attacked us. Their ambush-party also came out against us,
while I remained behind some distance from my companions.
So I turned back to confront the ambush-party, wanting to
defend the rear of my companions. But I found that my cousin,
Layth al-Dawla Yahya (may God have mercy upon him), had
already circled back behind his companions from the southern
side of the road while I was to its north. So we went at them.

Now one of their horsemen, called Faris ibn Zimam, who
was an Arab and a renowned cavalier, rushed past us wanting
to put his spear [39] into our companions. But my cousin beat
me to him and thrust his spear at him. Both Faris and his horse
fell to the ground and my cousin's spear exploded with such a
loud noise that I and everyone else could hear it.

Now, my father (may God have mercy upon him) had earlier
sent a messenger to Mahmud ibn Qaraja, and Mahmud brought
the messenger with him when he set out to attack us. And so,
when Faris ibn Zimam was speared, and Mahmud did not get
what he wanted from us, he sent that messenger from where he
was with an answer to the message that my father had sent him
to deliver in the first place, and returned to Hama.[6] So I asked
the messenger, 'Did Faris ibn Zimam die?'

'No,' he replied. 'By God, he wasn't even wounded! Layth
al-Dawla thrust his spear at him – and I saw him do it – and
threw Faris and his horse to the ground. And I heard the noise

of the spear breaking, too. But what happened was that when Layth al-Dawla struck at him from the left, Faris inclined to the right side, his *quntariya*-spear[7] gripped in his hand. As a result, his horse fell upon his *quntariya*-spear, while the spear happened to be poised spanning a ditch, and it snapped. Layth al-Dawla tried to hit Faris from behind with his spear, but it fell from his hand. So what you heard was the noise from the *quntariya*-spear of Faris ibn Zimam. As for the spear of Layth al-Dawla, they brought it before Mahmud ibn Qaraja while I was present, and it was completely intact, not a scratch on it, and Faris hadn't even a wound on him.'

I was amazed that he was safe at all. That spear-thrust was like the 'master's blow' that 'Antara speaks of:

> The horsemen and even the horses know
>> That I smote their host with a master's blow.

The entire enemy contingent, including the ambush-party, retreated without having accomplished anything they had wanted. The verse I just quoted above is from some verses by 'Antara ibn Shaddad,[8] who says in them:

> I am a man, one part from 'Abs's line nobly made,
>> The other part, this I protect with my naked blade.
> When the war-band looks about and makes to run and hide,
>> I best those men who in all their uncles take such pride.
> If Death could be depicted, it would wear my face,
>> Should those men ever find themselves in a hard, tight place.
> The horsemen and even the horses know
>> That I smote their host with a master's blow.
> They challenged me to dismount – I was the first to land:
>> For why would I ride a horse if I could never stand?

§ Usama Deals a Deceptive Blow

[40] A similar thing happened to me during an attack against Apamea.[9] Il-Ghazi[10] (may God have mercy upon him) had just defeated the Franks at al-Balat – that was on Friday, 5 Jumada

al-Ula, in the year 513[11] (14 August 1119). He annihilated them and killed Roger,[12] lord of Antioch, and all his horsemen. So my uncle Sultan (may God have mercy upon him) went to join Il-Ghazi. My father (may God have mercy upon him) remained behind in the castle at Shayzar, he having been told to send me to Apamea at the head of the troops that were with me at Shayzar, and to call to muster the troops and the Arab tribesmen to go pillage the crops there (for a large host of Arab tribesmen had just joined us).

A few days after my uncle's departure, the town crier called us to arms. I set out at the head of a small group, barely amounting to twenty horsemen, all of us convinced that Apamea had no cavalry stationed in it. I also brought along a large body of pillagers and Bedouin. But as soon as we arrived at Wadi Abu al-Maymun and the pillagers[13] and Arab tribesmen had scattered over the fields, a large contingent of Franks came out and attacked us. For, that very night, there had arrived in Apamea sixty horsemen and sixty infantrymen! They cleared us out of the valley, pushing us back before them until we reached our men who were already in the fields pillaging them, and who were now raising a loud tumult. Death seemed preferable to me compared to the destruction of that crowd of people who had come with me. So I turned to confront a horseman in the Frankish vanguard who, in order to pass swiftly before us, had taken off his hauberk[14] and lightened his gear. I thrust my spear into his chest and he flew off his saddle, dead. [41] Then I confronted their cavalry who followed him, and they took flight even though I was completely green to combat, never having taken part in a battle before that day. With a horse beneath me as fleet as a bird, I continued on the heels of my enemies, sometimes attacking with my spear, sometimes manoeuvring away from them for cover.

In the Frankish rearguard was a horseman on a black horse, big as a camel. He was wearing a mail hauberk and a gambeson.[15] I was afraid of him, thinking he might be trying to lure me further along so that he could turn on me and attack, until I saw him spur his horse onward and it twitched its tail. I knew then that it had become exhausted, so I attacked, running my spear through him such that it stuck out nearly a cubit in front of him. Thanks to the lightness of my body, the force of the spear-thrust and the speed of the horse, I was bumped backwards from the seat of my saddle.[16] Turning back, I pulled my spear from him, assuming I had killed him. I then assembled my comrades and found them safe and sound.

Now, there was with me a young *mamluk* who was leading a black mare alongside me. Under him was a fine-looking saddle-mule, sporting a thick silver saddle-blanket.[17] The *mamluk* dismounted, left the mule on its own, mounted the mare and flew off back to Shayzar. As soon as I had rejoined my comrades, who had caught hold of the mule, I asked after the *mamluk*, but they said, 'He left.' I realized then that he would reach Shayzar and worry my father (may God have mercy upon him). So I called for one of the soldiers and told him, 'Go quickly back to Shayzar and let my father know what has happened.'

Sure enough, the young servant, having returned to Shayzar, was summoned before my father, who asked him, 'What did you meet with?'

He replied, 'My lord, a thousand Franks came out and attacked us! I doubt if anyone has escaped, except my master!'

'And how', my father asked, 'would your master, alone of all the people, escape?'

The boy replied, 'I saw him in full armour, riding the dark mare[18] . . .', and continued his account, when that soldier I sent after him finally arrived and informed my father of the truth of the matter. I came in after him, so my father (may God have mercy upon him) asked me to tell him what happened.

'My lord,' I told him, 'this was the first battle in which I ever took part. But when I saw that the Franks had reached our men, death seemed preferable to me. So I turned to confront the Franks, either to be killed or to defend that crowd.'

And he spoke (may God have mercy upon him), quoting this verse as illustration:

The coward of the tribe will flee to save his own head
But the brave will stay to defend a stranger instead.

After a few days, my uncle (may God have mercy upon him)
returned from his visit to Il-Ghazi (may God have mercy upon
him). His messenger came to summon me at a time that was
not his usual time for such a meeting. So I went to him [42] and
who should I see with him but some Frankish man. My uncle
said, 'This horseman has come from Apamea wishing to set
eyes on the cavalier who speared the horseman Philip. For the
Franks are amazed by that spear-thrust, which pierced two
layers of the horseman's armour, and yet he survived.'

'But how', I cried, 'could he have survived?'

'That blow', the Frankish knight explained, 'only pierced the
skin at his waist.'

'Fate is indeed an impregnable fortress,' I replied, for it
seemed unimaginable to me that he could have survived that
spear-thrust.

Thus I say that whoever is about to thrust a spear should
clasp it tightly to his side with his hand and his forearm, and
let his horse do what it does in such a situation. For if he should
move his hand with the spear or extend out with it, then his
thrust will have no effect and do no damage.[19]

§ *Varieties of God's Will: The Opposing Fates
of a Warrior and an Artisan*

Once, when we had an encounter with the Franks, I witnessed
a horseman of ours called Badi ibn Talil al-Qushayri, one of
our bravest men, fighting without any armour except for two
cloth garments. A Frankish horseman thrust his spear through
his chest and cut through that little bone that is in one's chest,[20]
the spear sticking out through his side. So he withdrew and we
did not think he would make it back to his home alive. But
God (glory be to Him) decreed that he should be saved, and
he recovered from his wound. But for a year afterwards, it
remained the case that whenever he slept on his back, he could
not sit up unless someone set him up by his shoulders. Then his
ailment passed from him completely and he went back to living
and riding as he used to do.

Thus, I say that glory belongs to He who executes His will
upon His creations, bestowing life and sending death, He who

THE BOOK OF CONTEMPLATION: PART II

lives and never dies! With His hand all goodness He brings: He has power over all things.[21]

We also had with us an artisan, called 'Attab, the stoutest, tallest man there ever was. He went into his house one day and, as he was sitting down, he leaned his hand against a garment [43] lying there, which happened to have a needle in it. The needle went into the palm of his hand and he died from it. By God, he would moan over his wound down in the city and his moans could be heard up in the citadel, so bulky was his body and loud his voice. So he gets a pin-prick and dies, while this al-Qushayri has a *quntariya*-spear thrust through his chest and exit out his side without any harm coming to him!

§ Thief-Stories: The Bandit al-Zamarrakal Belittles his Wounds

One year, the lord of Antioch (may God curse him) marched against us at the head of his cavalry, infantry and baggage. So we rode out to meet them, thinking they would fight us. But they came and set up camp in the place where they were used to do so, and settled down in their tents. So we went back to our side of the river. Then, later, we rode out thinking they would fight us, but they did not ride out from their camp.

Now, my cousin Layth al-Dawla Yahya happened to have a crop of grain that had been harvested not far from where the Franks were, so he assembled some pack-animals intending to go over to the crop and carry it off. Numbering twenty fully equipped horsemen, we went out with him and positioned ourselves between him and the Franks until he loaded up the crop and left. Then, with a man born to our household,[22] named Husam al-Dawla Musafir (may God have mercy upon him), I turned off towards a vineyard where we could see some shapes along the bank of the river. When we approached these shapes that we had seen, just as the sun was setting, we saw that they were an old man wearing a woman's get-up[23] and another man who was with him. So Husam al-Dawla (may God have mercy upon him), who was a great fellow and loved a bit of fun, asked him, 'Tell me, old man, what are you doing here?'

'I am waiting for nightfall,' the old man confided, 'and then

I will ask God the Exalted to supply me with the horses of those infidels.'[24]

'And I suppose, old man,' Husam al-Dawla continued, 'that you will just chew through the horses' tethers with your teeth to get them?'

'No,' he said, 'with this knife.' And he drew out from inside his clothing a knife fastened by a string and shining like a tongue of flame. He wasn't wearing any trousers,[25] either. So we left him there and withdrew.

The next morning I woke early and rode out to wait for whatever the Franks were going to do, when who should I see but that old man [44] sitting on a rock in my way, with coagulated blood all over his leg and foot.

'May your safety bring you health!' I said. 'What have you done?'

He said, 'I took a horse, a shield and a spear from them, but one of their infantrymen caught up with me while I was on my way out, in the middle of their troops. He jabbed at me and the *quntariya*-spear went into my thigh. But I still made off with the horse, shield and spear.' And he made light of his wound as if it had happened to someone else. That man, who was called al-Zamarrakal, was one devil of a brigand.

§§ Mu'in al-Din's Tale concerning al-Zamarrakal

The amir Mu'in al-Din[26] (may God have mercy upon him) told me another story about al-Zamarrakal. He said:

Once, during the time I was posted to Homs, I made a raid on Shayzar. At the end of the day, I returned and encamped at a village in the hinterland of Hama; at the time I was an enemy of Hama's lord.[27] A detachment of my men came to me, bringing with them an old man. He had aroused their suspicions and so they captured him and brought him before me. I said, 'So, old man, who are you then?' 'My lord,' he protested, 'I am just a poor old palsied beggar (at this he held out his hand, which was indeed palsied). The soldiers took two goats from me, so I went along behind them hoping they would grant them to me for pity's sake.'[28]

I said to some soldiers in my bodyguard,[29] 'Keep him in custody until tomorrow.' So they sat him down between them while they sat on the sleeves of the camel-hair garment he was wearing. But during the night, why, he took advantage of their carelessness and slipped out of the garment and, leaving it under them, flew the coop. They caught on to his trail, but he outpaced them and got away.

'Prior to this,' Mu'in al-Din continued, 'I had sent some of my companions out on business. They now came back to me, and among them was a guardsman named Sawman, who used to live at Shayzar. So I told him the story of the old man and he cried, "What a pity I missed him! If I had got my hands on him, I would have drunk his blood. That was al-Zamarrakal!" So I said, "Well, what is there between you two?" Sawman began:

One day, the Frankish army encamped against Shayzar, so I went out and circled around them, hoping maybe to steal a horse from them. When darkness fell, I walked up to the horses' picket-line, right in front of me, when who should I find but this fellow sitting right there. So he asked me, [45] 'Where are you headed?' And I said, 'I'm going to grab a horse from this picket-line.' And he said, 'Right, like I've been here since suppertime keeping an eye on the place just so *you* can steal the horses!' 'Don't talk nonsense,' I said. 'And you, don't kid yourself!' he retorted. 'By God, I am not about to let you take anything!' But I ignored his threat and made for the picket-line, so he stood up and started shouting at the top of his lungs, 'O poor me! What a disappointment! And after all my hard work and vigilance!' And he kept at it until the Franks came out at me. As for him, he took off. The Franks chased after me until I threw myself in the river, and I really didn't think I would escape from them. If I had just got my hands on that one, I would have drunk his blood. He is a great brigand, and if he was following along after the soldiers, then he was only doing it to steal something.

People who knew that al-Zamarrakal used to say of him, 'That guy would steal a loaf of bread from his own house.'

§§ A Prized Horse is Stolen and then Given Away

Here's an amazing example concerning stealing. There used to be a man in my service named 'Ali ibn al-Dudawayhi, a native of Mudhkin.[30] One day, the Franks (may God curse them) encamped against Kafartab,[31] which at the time was controlled by al-Yaghisiyani[32] (may God have mercy upon him). This 'Ali ibn al-Dudawayhi went out and circled around the Franks and, taking one of their horses, mounted it and rode it out of their camp at a gallop. But he heard a noise behind him and thought that some of the enemy had ridden out to get him. So he redoubled his galloping but the noise kept on behind him – even after two farsakhs[33] at full gallop it still followed. Finally, he turned around to see what was following him in the dark, and what should he find but a female mule that used to keep that horse company – it had broken its tether and was following along. So 'Ali stopped in order to fasten his kerchief around the mule's neck and took it with him. He was with me the next morning in Hama with the horse and the mule. That was one of the noblest horses, exceedingly handsome and fast.

[46] Now, one day I was with the atabeg while he was besieging Rafaniya.[34] He had summoned yours truly and asked, 'So what's the deal with that horse you've got ferreted away?' He had been told the story of the horse, you see.

'By God, my lord, I don't have a horse hidden away,' I protested. 'No, all my horses are with the army.'

'And that Frankish horse?' he asked.

'At the ready,' I replied.

'Send someone to bring it here,' he demanded.

So I sent someone to bring the horse and then told the servant, 'Now go take it back to my stables.'

At this the atabeg interjected, 'Leave it here with me for a while.'

The next morning, he raced the horse and won, and returned it to my stables. But then he again called for it to be brought from town,[35] raced it and won. At that, I just sent it off to his stables.

§ A Soldier Killed by a Chisel-Headed Arrow

In the battle that occurred at the end of this particular period,[36] I witnessed the following:

We had with us in the army a man called Rafi' al-Kilabi, a famous horseman. We and the Banu Qaraja had met to fight one another. The enemy had assembled and mustered a host of Turkomans and others against us, so we went and rolled out the red carpet for them[37] at an open plain outside of town. But it became clear that they were too numerous for us, so we retreated, with some of us holding back to defend the others. This soldier Rafi' was among the ones who defended the rearguard. He was wearing a *kazaghand* and, on his head, a helmet without an aventail.[38] But he turned around to see if he might have a chance to attack the enemy, and a chisel-headed arrow[39] struck him in his throat, slaughtering him. He fell on the spot, dead.

§ A Warlord Killed by a Trifling Wound

I witnessed a similar thing with regard to Mahmud ibn Qaraja. The conflict between him and us having been settled, he had sent a message to my uncle saying, 'Tell Usama [47] to meet me with one horseman at Kar'a,[40] so that we can go and look for a place where we can lie in ambush against Apamea, and then we can make an attack on it.' My uncle told me, so I rode out and met Mahmud and reconnoitred the various spots.

Then we combined his army and ours, with me leading the army of Shayzar and Mahmud ibn Qaraja at the head of his army, and we set out for Apamea. We encountered the enemy cavalry and infantry in the ruins near the city. It is a place where horses cannot easily move because of all the blocks and columns and ruined foundations, so we were unable to dislodge them from the area. But then one of our soldiers asked me, 'Do you want to rout them?'

'Yes, I do,' I replied.

'Then lead us off towards the gate of the citadel,' he said.

'Let's go,' I said.

But the soldier who had made this suggestion soon regretted it when he realized that the enemy would be able to charge through us and beat us to the citadel. He tried to dissuade me from going, but I refused and set off for the gate.

The moment the Franks saw us heading for the gate, their cavalry and infantry turned back towards us, charged through us and beat us there. The horsemen dismounted inside the gate of the citadel, sent their mounts further up into it and lined up the points of their *quntariya*-spears in a row across the gate. Meanwhile, I, with a comrade of mine – one of my father's *mamluks* (may God have mercy upon him), whose name was Rafi' ibn Sutakin – was standing under the wall across from the gate, with quite a lot of stones and arrows raining down upon us. Mahmud ibn Qaraja, for his part, out of fear of the Kurds,[41] was positioned far from the Franks at the head of a war-band. One of our comrades, called Haritha al-Numayri, a relative of Jum'a,[42] received a spear-thrust crossways clear through the chest of his horse. The *quntariya*-spear stuck into the horse, which struggled until the spear fell out. The skin from the horse's chest fell forwards and stayed there, hanging on its forelegs.

As for Mahmud ibn Qaraja, he was far removed from the combat, but an arrow flew from the citadel and struck him on the side of his forearm-bone, yet it did not pierce the arm-bone so much as the length of a barley-grain. So [48] his messenger came to me to tell me on his behalf, 'Maintain your position until you can assemble all our men who are scattered across the area. I am wounded and feel as if the wound were in my heart. I am withdrawing, so it is up to you to protect the men.' And so he withdrew while I led the men away and encamped at Burj al-Khurayba.[43] The Franks used to station a sentinel there to be able to spot us whenever we made a raid on Apamea. Late that afternoon, I arrived at Shayzar and Mahmud ibn Qaraja was in my father's residence, trying to unwrap his wound to treat it, but my uncle forbade him to do so saying,

'By God, do not unwrap your wound until you get to your own house.'

'But I am in the home of my father,'[44] he protested, meaning my own father (may God have mercy upon him).

'Yes, well,' my uncle replied, 'when you've got back to your house and your wound has healed, then the home of your father will be at your disposal.'

And so at sunset, Mahmud ibn Qaraja rode off to Hama. He remained there the next day and the day after, but then his hand turned black, he lost consciousness and died. This all happened to him simply because his time had come.

§ A Spectacular Spear-Thrust

One of the most spectacular spear-thrusts that I witnessed was inflicted by a horseman from the Franks (may God confound them) on a horseman from our troops, called Sabah ibn Qunayb – from the Kilab tribe. It cut through three rib-bones on his left side and then through three on his right.[45] Finally, the sharp edge of the spear-head struck his elbow-joint, splitting it in two just like a butcher does with a joint of meat. He died instantly.

§ A Warrior's Wedding Garb Proves Fatal

A Kurdish soldier of ours, called Mayyah, once speared a Frankish horseman, forcing a ring of his mail hauberk into his abdomen and killing him. A few days later, the Franks made an attack against us. Now, Mayyah had just got himself married, so he went out to fight wearing over his hauberk a red robe, one of his nuptial garments, [49] which made him conspicuous. As a result, a Frankish horseman thrust his spear at him and killed him (may God have mercy upon him). How close the funeral to the wedding![46]

This story reminds me of an account about the Prophet (may God's blessing and peace be upon him). Someone recited this verse to him by Qays ibn al-Khatim:[47]

On the day of the defence I fought in a state of undress
　　Toying with the sword in my hand as if I was playing at
　　　　chess.

So the Prophet (may God's blessing and peace be upon him) asked those of the Ansar[48] who were present (may God be pleased with them), 'Were any of you present at the Battle of al-Hadiqa?'[49]

'Messenger of God, may God's blessing and peace be upon you,' replied one of the men. 'I was present, and so was Qays ibn al-Khatim. Being newly married, he wore a red mantle and, by Him who sent you to bring Truth, Qays fought exactly as he said he did.'

§ An Aged Retainer Strikes a Devastating Blow

One of the most amazing spear-thrusts occurred with a Kurdish soldier called Hamadat, a long-time comrade who had travelled with my father (may God have mercy upon him) to Isfahan to the court of the sultan Malikshah.[50] But now he had grown old, raised children, and his eyesight was weak.

My uncle Sultan (may God have mercy upon him) said to him, 'Hamadat, you have become old and feeble, and we owe you many favours as you have served us well. If you retire to your mosque (for he had a mosque by the door to his house) and let us register your children in the stipend-list, then you will get two dinars every month and a load of flour, so long as you stick to your mosque.'

'I'll do it, sir,' he said.

But the deal only lasted a short time. For he later came to my uncle and said, 'Sir, by God, I can't get used to just sitting [50] around the house. I would rather be killed on my horse than die in my bed.'

'It's up to you,' my uncle replied, and gave orders that his name be registered like it used to be.

Only a few days passed before the Cerdagnais,[51] the lord of Tripoli attacked us. The soldiers rushed to confront them, and Hamadat was among the most courageous group. He positioned himself on some raised ground, facing south, but a Frankish horseman attacked him from the west. One of our comrades shouted at him, 'Hamadat!' so he turned and saw the horseman headed for him. He pointed the head of his horse northward, hefted his spear in his hand and thrust it straight into the chest of the Frank, the spear piercing him right through. The Frank retreated clasping his horse's neck, breathing his last.

When the fighting ended, Hamadat said to my uncle, 'Tell me, sir: if Hamadat had kept to his mosque, who would have struck that blow?'

This reminds me of the verse of al-Find al-Zimmani:[52]

> Behold the blow of an old man, ground down and worn,
> While my peers shun weapons, this makes me feel
> reborn!

This al-Find was already an old man when he went to battle and struck with his spear two approaching horsemen and killed them both together.

§ Two Horsemen Felled with one Blow

Indeed, something like that had happened just previously. A peasant farmer from al-'Ala[53] came galloping to my father and uncle (may God have mercy upon them both), and told them, 'I saw a detachment of Franks coming from the direction of the desert – they've lost their way. If you march out against them, you'll be able to take them.'

So my father and my two uncles departed at the head of a body of troops to confront that lost detachment, and who should it be but the Cerdagnais, the lord of Tripoli, at the head [51] of three hundred horsemen and two hundred Turcopoles[54] (those are archers for the Franks). Once they saw our comrades, they mounted their horses, charged at our comrades and routed them. They then stuck to their trail. A *mamluk* belonging to my father, called Yaqut the Tall, circled back around towards them while my father and uncle (may God have mercy upon them both) watched him. He thrust his spear at one of their horsemen who was alongside another of their knights (for they were both pursuing our comrades), and struck down both horses and horsemen at the same time. Now, this Yaqut was always mixed up in crimes and wrong-doings, and he had done one deed for which he still had to be disciplined.

But every time my father would think about punishing him,

my uncle would say, 'Brother, by your life, grant me his guilt, and don't forget that spear-thrust.'

Then my father would pardon him because of what his brother said.

§ A Reminiscence about that Aged Retainer

That Hamadat, mentioned earlier, was delightful to talk with. My father (may God have mercy upon him) told me, 'I once said to Hamadat one morning while we were on the road to Isfahan, "Commander Hamadat, have you eaten anything today?"

' "Yes, sir. I had a bit of crust soaked in broth," he replied.

'So I said, "But we've been riding all night, and we neither stopped nor did we light a fire. So how did you come by that broth-soaked crust?"

' "Well sir," he replied, "I made it in my mouth. I chewed up some bread in my mouth and drank water on top of it, which made it like a broth-soaked crust." '

§ Usama's Father: A Great Warrior who Died in his Bed

My father (may God have mercy upon him) was very experienced at warfare. His body bore some dreadful wounds, but he died in his bed. One day he took part in a battle in full armour, wearing an Islamic-style helmet with a nasal. Someone – in those days most of their battles were with Arab tribesmen – hurled a javelin at him and the spear-head struck the nasal of the helmet. It dented the nasal and caused his nose to bleed, but it didn't hurt him. But if God (glory be to Him) had decreed that the javelin should deviate from the nasal of the helmet, it would have killed him.

[52] On another occasion, he was struck in his lower leg by an arrow. He used to keep a dagger in his boot,[55] and the arrow struck the dagger without wounding him. This was due to the superior protection of God (may He be exalted).

He (may God have mercy upon him) once saw battle on Sunday, 29 Shawwal in the year 497 (25 July 1104) with Ibn Mula'ib,[56] the lord of Apamea, in the territory of Kafartab. He put on his cuirass but his servant in his haste forgot to fasten the buckles on one side of it. Someone hurled a javelin[57] at him and it hit him right on the spot that the servant had left uncovered, above his left breast, and the spear stuck out just above his right breast. His survival was a wonder of the divine will, just as the wound itself was a wonder that God (glory be to Him) had decreed.

On the same day, my father (may God have mercy upon him) struck a horseman with his spear and, turning his horse away, curled his hand around the spear and pulled it out of his opponent. He told me, 'I felt something burning my forearm, but I thought it was just from the heat of the metal lamellae of my cuirass. But then the spear fell from my hand and, pulling my hand back, I discovered that a spear-thrust had hit me in the hand, which became weak since the blow had cut some of my nerves.'

I was with him (may God have mercy upon him) when Zayd, the surgeon, was treating his wound, with a servant standing behind his head.

My father said, 'Zayd, take that pebble out of the wound.'

But the surgeon did not reply. So my father said again, 'Zayd, don't you see that pebble? Won't you remove it from my wound?'

Now that he had annoyed him, Zayd replied, 'What pebble? That's a nerve-ending that has been severed.' It really was as white as a pebble from the Euphrates.

On that same day he was also struck by another spear-thrust, but God kept him safe and sound until the day he died in his bed, may God [53] have mercy upon him, Monday 8 Ramadan of the year 531 (30 May 1137).

§§ Digression: Usama's Father, the Pious Calligrapher

My father wrote in an elegant hand and that spear-thrust did not affect his calligraphic style. But he never copied anything except the Qur'an.

One day I asked him, 'My lord, how many complete copies of the Qur'an have you written?'

'Soon you will know,' he replied.

When he was close to death, he said, 'In that chest there are some copy-books, and in each one I have written a complete text of the Qur'an. Put them (meaning the copy-books) under my cheek in the grave.' We counted the copy-books and there were forty-three of them.[58]

Among the complete Qur'ans that he copied there was one in a large format, written with gold ink. In it he included in black, red and blue ink the Qur'anic sciences – analysis of its variant readings, its obscure terms, its grammar and style, its abrogating and abrogated passages, its commentary, the causes for the revelation of its verses and its legal applications, calling it *The Great Commentary*.[59] He produced another complete copy in gold letters without the commentary. The rest of the complete copies were done in black ink with the opening words of the tenth and fifth parts[60] of the book, the verse-markers, chapter-headings and section-headings in gold.

My book does not require mention of this. I did so only to encourage my readers to pray for God's mercy upon my father. Now, to return to the previous subject.

§ *The Model of a Loyal Servant*

On that same day,[61] a servant that used to belong to my uncle 'Izz al-Dawla Nasr (may God have mercy upon him), called Sham'un, was struck by a wicked spear-thrust that he took protecting my other uncle Sultan (may God have mercy upon him). It happened that my uncle Sultan later sent him as a messenger to the king Ridwan,[62] son of Tutush, in Aleppo.

When Sham'un had come before him, the king said to his own servants, 'All servants and subjects[63] should be as loyal as this man was to his master.'

And he then said to Sham'un, 'Tell them your story about what you did with your master back in the days of my father.'[64]

Instead, Sham'un told him,[65] 'My lord, the other day I went into battle alongside my master, and a horseman attacked him [54] with his spear. So I jumped between him and my master to redeem my master with my own life, and the horseman speared me instead. He cut two of my ribs, and these two ribs – by your grace – I keep with me in a little box.'

At this, King Ridwan said to him, 'By God, I will not respond until you send someone to bring this box and the ribs.' So Sham'un rose and sent for someone to bring forth the box, and there were indeed two rib-bones inside it.

Ridwan was astonished by this and said to his companions, 'This is how you should be acting in my service.'

As for the story that the king had asked Sham'un about from the days of his father Tutush, it happened like this: my grandfather, Sadid al-Mulk 'Ali[66] (may God have mercy upon him), sent his son, my uncle 'Izz al-Dawla Nasr (may God have mercy upon him), into the service of Tutush, who was then encamped in the outskirts of Aleppo. But Tutush arrested Nasr and confined him, entrusting him to a special guard. No one could enter to see him except for his *mamluk* – this same Sham'un – and even then the special guard stood around the tent.

So my uncle wrote to my father (may God have mercy upon them both), 'Send a group of my companions (whom he named) with a horse for me to ride to such-and-such a place on the night of such-and-such (which he specified).'

And when that night came, Sham'un entered the tent and took off his clothes. Then his master put them on and went out into the night, right in front of the special guards: they did not even suspect him. He continued on to meet his companions, mounted up and rode off. Meanwhile, Sham'un slept in his master's bed.

Now, Sham'un's normal routine was to bring my uncle water early each morning so that he could perform the ablutions, for my uncle was (may God have mercy upon him) one of those ascetics who spent their nights reciting the Book of God (may He be exalted). But when the guards woke the next morning and did not see Sham'un go in to his master as usual, they went into the tent and found Sham'un, my uncle having escaped. They reported this to Tutush, who ordered Sham'un to be brought into his presence. When Sham'un was brought before him, the king asked him, 'So how did you do it?'

'I gave my master my clothes,' he replied. 'He put them on and fled, while I slept in his bed.'

'But weren't you afraid I would cut off your head?' the king asked.

'My lord,' he responded, 'if you had cut off my head and my lord escaped to return to his home, then I would have been happy. For he only bought me and raised me so that I might redeem him with my own life.'

So Tutush (may God have mercy upon him) said to his chamberlain, 'Give to this servant the horse of his master, as well as his [55] beasts of burden, tents and all his baggage, then let him go to follow his master.' And he did not blame Sham'un or harbour any ill-will for what he did in the service of his master. That is what the king Ridwan was referring to when he told him, 'Tell my companions what you did with your master back in the days of my father.'

§ A Spear in the Eye

I return now to the account of that war with Ibn Mula'ib mentioned earlier. On that same day, my uncle 'Izz al-Dawla[67] (may God have mercy upon him) received a number of wounds. One of them was a spear-thrust in his lower eyelid, near the inside corner of his eye. The spear-tip stuck into the inner corner of his eye, just on the rim, so the entire eyelid fell and hung there from a flap of skin at the rim of his eye. The eye itself kept moving around without resting, for it is the eyelids that hold the eye in place. But the surgeon sewed up the eye and treated it, and it returned to its original position so that you wouldn't even be able to tell the wounded eye apart from the other one.

§ Tales of Bravery: Usama's Uncle and Father

My father and my uncle (may God have mercy upon them) were two of the most courageous men of their kin. I was with them one day when the two of them had gone out hunting with goshawks in the direction of Tall Milh[68] (for there are abundant waterfowl there). Suddenly, before we realized it, the army of Tripoli made an attack on the town and arrayed themselves against it. So we went back, though my father was recovering from an illness at the time. As for my uncle, he sped off with those soldiers that were with him and went to cross the ford in the direction of the Franks, who watched him all the while. As for my father, he also went on, while I, just a youth,[69] went with him. As his horse trotted beneath him, he would suck from a quince that he held in his hand.

As we approached the Franks, he said to me, 'You go ahead and get inside by way of the dyke.'[70] But he crossed the river from the area where the Franks were.

[56] I observed his courage another time, when the horsemen of Mahmud ibn Qaraja made an attack on us while we were some distance from the town. The horsemen of Mahmud were closer to the town than we were. But I had already seen battle and experienced warfare, so I put on my *kazaghand*-armour, mounted my horse and took hold of my spear, but my father (may God have mercy upon him) rode upon a mule.

So I said to him, 'My lord, shouldn't you ride your horse?'

'Oh, no doubt,' he replied.

But he continued on just as he was, unflappable and unhurried, while I, because of my fear for him, insisted that he ride his horse. He continued on his mule until we arrived back at the town.

When the enemy went back and everything was safe and secure, I said, 'My lord, you saw that the enemy had stopped between us and our town, and you refused to ride even one of the spare horses. I pleaded with you to ride, but you didn't even listen!'

'Son,' he replied, 'it is written in my horoscope that I shall feel no fear.' For he was (may God have mercy upon him) quite a devotee of the stars, even with all his pious scrupulosity, religious conviction, daily fasting and reciting of the Qur'an. He used to push me to learn about astrology, but I was unwilling and would refuse. So he then urged me, 'At least learn the names of the stars, the ones that rise and set.'[71] And so it was that he would show me the stars and teach me their names.

§ *Jum'a al-Numayri Rescues his Son from the Franks*

I saw something of the bravery of men and their courage in time of war on another occasion. We woke up one morning at the time of the dawn prayer and noticed a detachment of Franks, about ten horsemen, who had come to the gate of the town before it had been opened.[72]

They asked the gatekeeper, 'What's the name of this here town?'[73] The gate was made of wood, with beam-bolts running across the doors, and the gatekeeper was on the inside of the gate.

'Shayzar,' he said. At that, they shot an arrow through a gap in the door, turned their horses around and trotted off.

So we mounted up. My [57] uncle (may God have mercy upon him) was the first to mount his horse and I went with him while the Franks rode ahead completely unworried. A few of our troops joined up with us.

'At your command,' I said to my uncle, 'I'll take our comrades and go follow them and unhorse them, seeing as they are not so far away.'

'No,' he replied (for he was more experienced than I in matters of war). 'Is there a Frank left in Syria who does not know Shayzar? This is a trick.'

He then called two of our horsemen riding swift mounts and said, 'Go and reconnoitre Tall Milh.' For that was where the Franks used to lie in ambush.

As soon as they were in position overlooking Tall Milh, the entire army of Antioch rushed out against them. So we went to confront their vanguard, hoping to seize our advantage over them before the battle finished. With us was Jum'a al-Numayri and his son Mahmud. Jum'a was our cavalier, our teacher.

His son Mahmud somehow fell into the midst of the enemy, so Jum'a shouted, 'Fellow horsemen! My son!'

And we turned back with him with sixteen horsemen, thrusting our spears at sixteen Frankish knights and took our comrade from their midst. But we became so mixed up with them in the melee that one of them put Jum'a in a choke-hold. A few more of our spear-thrusts were able to save him, though.[74]

§ A Lesson in Humility

Nevertheless, one should not trust one's bravery too much nor make too much of one's courage. By God, I once went out with

my uncle (may God have mercy upon him) to make a raid on
Apamea. It happened that the Franks had gone to escort a
caravan. Having done so, they returned and we met them in
battle and killed nearly twenty of their men. I saw Jum'a al-
Numayri (may God have mercy upon him) with half of a
quntariya-spear sticking in him. The spear had been thrust
through his saddle-pad, went through the saddle-lining into his
thigh until it stuck out behind him. Thus, the spear broke still
inside him.

This horrified me, but he said, 'Not to worry, I'm fine,' and
taking hold of the tip of the spear, he pulled it out of him and
he and his horse were safe and sound.

I then said to him, 'Abu Mahmud, I'd really prefer to get
closer to the citadel so that we can see it clearly.'

'Let's go,' he said.

And so he and I trotted off on our horses. When we got to a
spot looking onto the citadel, what should we find but eight
Frankish knights positioned on the road, which overlooks the
plaza there [58] from a height; and there was no coming down
from that height except by that road.[75]

So Jum'a said to me, 'Stay here and I'll show you what I can
do with them.'

'But that's not fair,' I protested. 'It's better if you and I attack
them together.'

'Let's go,' he replied.

And so we attacked them, routed them and withdrew, the
two of us thinking we had done something no one else had
done – two warriors routing eight Frankish knights.

We stopped on that elevation to have a look at the citadel,
but we were surprised to see that a tiny footman had climbed
all the way up that difficult ascent after us, wielding a bow and
arrows. He started shooting at us, but we had no way to get to
him, so we fled. By God, we really didn't think we would get
away from him with our horses safe and sound! We withdrew
and came into the meadows of Apamea, from which we drove
before us great herds of buffalo, cows and sheep. And so we
left, my heart full of regret at that man who made us flee
without there being any way for us to get to him, and at how

one man was able to rout us, when we had just routed eight Frankish knights.

§ *The Body Cured by Illness*

I was present one day when the cavalry of Kafartab – just a few of them – made a raid against us. Wanting to take advantage of their small numbers, we rushed out against them, but a group of their men had prepared an ambush for us. The attacking horsemen made to take flight, so we pursued them until we were some distance from the town. There the men lying in ambush came out against us and the horsemen we were pursuing turned around towards us. We realized that if we routed, they would unhorse all of us, so we confronted them, seeking death, and God granted us victory over them. We unhorsed eighteen of their horsemen including those who were struck with spears and died, those who merely fell and were safe and those whose horses were speared and so became footmen. Those who were safe on the ground then drew their swords, stopped everyone who passed [59] and struck at them.

Jum'a al-Numayri (may God have mercy upon him) passed one of them, so the man stepped towards him and struck him in his head. Jum'a was wearing a cap on his head,[76] but the blow cut through the cap and sliced open his forehead, from which blood poured until he was almost drained of it, leaving the wound open like a fish's mouth. I came upon him while we were still in the midst of our fight with the Franks and said to him, 'Jum'a, why don't you bandage up your wound?'

'This is no time for bandaging and dressing wounds!' he replied.

Now, Jum'a used always to have a black rag around his face since he had ophthalmia, with red veins in his eye. But when he was wounded and all that blood poured out of him, his eye complaints ended and he was never again troubled by any ophthalmia or pain. 'Mayhap the body is cured by illness.'[77]

As for the Franks, after we had killed those men of theirs, they assembled opposite us. My cousin Dhakhirat al-Dawla Hittan[78] (may God have mercy upon him) came to me and said,

'Cousin, you have two mounts being led alongside you, and here I am on this old nag!'

So I said to a servant, 'Bring him the chestnut horse.' And he brought it for him.

The moment Hittan was settled in his saddle, he made an attack on the Franks, single-handedly. So the Franks made room for him in order to surround him, and attacked him with spears, throwing him down and spearing his horse. They then turned their spears around and began hacking at him. But Hittan was wearing a strong mail hauberk upon which their spears had no effect. And so we began shouting, 'Your comrade! Your comrade!' and attacked them and forced them to flee. We delivered him from their midst and he was fine. As for the horse, it died that same day. Glory be to the Rescuer, the One who determines all fates!

Mind you, that battle did produce happiness for Jum'a, what with the curing of his eye. Glory be to Him who said, 'You may dislike something though it is good for you.'[79]

§ *Another Wound Heals a Servant*

Something like that happened to me, too. I was in Upper Mesopotamia[80] in the army of the atabeg, and [60] a friend of mine invited me to his home. One of my grooms, named Ghunaym, accompanied me. He suffered from dropsy, so his neck had become thin and his abdomen was enlarged. He had come with me into exile[81] and I used to treat him with special care on account of that. Ghunaym led his mule into the stables of that friend of mine with the servants of the other invited guests. Among us was a Turkish youth who got so drunk that he lost control of himself. He went out to the stables, drew his knife and rushed at the servants. They all fled and got out of there. But Ghunaym, because of his weakness and his illness, had thrown the saddle down under his head and gone to sleep, with the result that he did not even get up until everyone else had fled from the stables. So that drunkard stabbed him with his knife under his navel, slicing open his abdomen with a wound about four finger-widths wide. Ghunaym dropped on the spot.

Our host, who was the lord of Basahra' Castle,[82] had him

transported to my house, as was the man who hurt him, with
his hands tied behind his back. But I set him free. The surgeon
visited Ghunaym frequently and he recovered and was able to
walk about and carry on as before, except his wound would
not close. For two months it continued to ooze bits of scab and
yellow liquid. But then it closed up and his abdomen shrunk
back and he returned to his normal state of health. Thus it was
that that wound was the cause of his recovery.

One other day, I saw the austringer standing before my father
(may God have mercy upon him) saying, 'My lord, this goshawk
has caught the French Moult[83] and is dying. One of its eyes is
already lost. So go hunting with this one, since it is a clever
hawk, but it is as good as dead anyway.' So we went out on the
hunt and my father brought with him (may God have mercy
upon him) a number of hawks. He flew that particular hawk
at a francolin.[84] The hawk would dash into the coverts, so the
francolin took cover inside a thicket of brambles, but the hawk
followed her. Now, that hawk had something like a large spot
on its eye, and a thorn [61] from the thicket struck that spot
and popped it open. The austringer took the hawk with him,
its eye flowing even though closed, and said to my father, 'My
lord, the goshawk's eye is gone.'

'The whole bird is lost,' my father replied.

But then the next morning its eye opened and it was healthy.
That hawk lived in good health with us, moulting its feathers
twice. It was one of the cleverest hawks. I was reminded of him
by what had happened to Jum'a and Ghunaym, even if this is
not the place for bird-tales.

I have seen someone afflicted with dropsy who was treated
with blood-letting in his abdomen, but he died; whereas with
Ghunaym, that drunkard sliced open his abdomen, and he recovered and was healed. Glory be to He who determines fates!

§ More than Meets the Eye: A Frank
Miraculously Recovers

The army of Antioch once made an attack on us. Our comrades
encountered the enemy vanguard, but retreated before them.

For my part, I stationed myself in their path waiting for them to arrive, hoping that I might get a chance to attack the enemy. Meanwhile, our comrades crossed over towards me in flight. Mahmud, the son of Jum'a, was one of those who crossed over towards me. So I said, 'Mahmud, stop!' He paused for a moment, but then spurred his horse on and left me.

Then the vanguard of the enemy cavalry arrived, so I pushed away ahead of them, twisting my spear towards them and turning around so that I could watch them, in case one of their horsemen should catch up with me and try to thrust his spear at me. In front of me was a group of our comrades and we were surrounded by gardens enclosed by walls as high as a seated man. My horse bumped its chest into one of our comrades and knocked him down, so I turned its head to my left, prodded it with my spurs and it leapt over the wall. I then arranged my position so that I was even with the Franks, with the wall between us. One of their horsemen sped towards me, wearing a silk tunic emblazoned in green and yellow, without, it seemed to me, any armour underneath. So I let him pass by. I then prodded my horse with my spurs and it jumped back over the wall. Then, I thrust my spear at the Frank. He fell over sideways so far that his head was level with his stirrups, his shield and spear fell out of his hands and his helmet slipped off his head. By then we had reached [62] our infantrymen. The Frank then sat up again, upright in his saddle: he had a mail hauberk under his tunic and my spear-thrust had not even harmed him! His comrades caught up with him and they retreated. Our infantrymen took his shield, spear and helmet.

§ Jum'a Flees from Battle

When the battle was over and the Franks withdrew, Jum'a (may God have mercy upon him) came to me and apologized for his son Mahmud, saying, 'That dog fled from your side!'

'And what of it?' I replied.

'He flees from you and you say, "What of it?"' he said.

'By your life, Jum'a,' I swore, 'one day you too will flee from my side.'

'It shames me to think it!' he replied. 'By God, my death would be easier for me to bear than fleeing from you.'

Only a few days had passed when the cavalry of Hama made a raid on us. They took a herd of cattle from us and penned it in on the island below Jalali Mill, and their archers climbed up on the mill[85] in order to protect the herd. So I went over to them, with Jum'a and Shuja' al-Dawla Madi, one of our adopted men, a man of courage.[86]

I said to the two of them, 'Let's cross the river and go and get our animals.' So we crossed over.

As for Madi, his horse was struck by an arrow, which eventually killed it. But first the horse struggled on and carried Madi back to his comrades. As for me, my horse was struck by an arrow at the nape of its neck, the arrow penetrating a span's-depth. But, by God, it neither shied nor was disturbed, nor even showed that it felt the wound. As for Jum'a, he turned back in fear for his horse.

When we returned I said, 'Jum'a, didn't I tell you that you would flee from my side, when you were heaping blame on your son Mahmud?'

'By God,' he replied, 'I was afraid of nothing except for my horse. She is precious to me.' And he apologized.

§ Usama Gratefully Fails to Kill two Foes

On that same day, we encountered the horsemen of Hama in battle while some of them went ahead with the herd onto the island. We fought one another, and among the enemy were the leading cavaliers of the army of Hama: Sarhank, Ghazi al-Talli, Mahmud ibn Baldaji, Hadr al-Tut and the isbasalar [63] Khut-lukh.[87] They outnumbered us but we attacked them and routed them. I made directly for one of their horsemen intending to run my spear through him, but who should it turn out to be but Hadr al-Tut, who shouted, 'Mercy!' I then turned away from him towards another horseman and speared him, the spear hitting him just below his armpit. If he had just let it be, he would not have fallen, but he pressed his arm on it, trying to take away the spear, while my horse sped up with me. So he flew out of his saddle onto the neck of the horse and fell to the ground. He then stood up, finding himself on the side of the canyon leading down to al-Jalali.[88] So he struck his horse and, leading it before him, went down.[89] I thanked God (glory be to Him), who let no harm befall him from my spear-thrust: for that horseman was Ghazi al-Talli, and he was (may God have mercy on him) an excellent man.

§ Jum'a Accused of Cowardice

One day, the army of Antioch came and encamped against us at the spot where they usually made camp, while we stood on horseback facing them, the river between us. Not a single one of them came towards us. They pitched their tents and settled down in them, and so we withdrew and we too settled down in our homes, while we watched them from the citadel. Then about twenty horsemen from our army went out to Bandar-Qanin,[90] a village near town, to graze their horses, leaving their spears at home. Two Frankish horsemen went out in the vicinity of these troops who were grazing their horses, and on the way they fell upon a man leading an animal, capturing him and his beast while we watched from the castle. Those [64] troops of ours mounted up but then stopped, not having any spears.

At that my uncle exclaimed, 'Those twenty men cannot even save one captive from two horsemen! If Jum'a were with them, then you would see what he can do!'

Even as he was saying this, Jum'a galloped off towards them, fully armoured. 'Watch now and see what he does!' my uncle said.

But when he approached the two Frankish horsemen at full gallop, Jum'a turned the head of his horse and remained behind them, under cover. My uncle was watching all of this from a projecting window[91] that he had in the castle. When he saw that Jum'a had stopped his pursuit of the two Franks, he turned inside from the window in anger and exclaimed, 'This is mutiny!' In fact, Jum'a stopped because he was afraid there might be an ambush set up in a ditch which lay in front of the Franks. Once he arrived at the ditch and saw that there was no one in it, he attacked the two horsemen and rescued the man and his animal, chasing the horsemen back to their tents.

Bohemond's son,[92] the lord of Antioch, was watching what was happening. When the two horsemen arrived, he sent someone to take their shields, which he converted into food-troughs for the animals. Then he pulled down their tents and expelled them, saying, 'One Muslim horseman chases away two Frankish knights! You aren't men – you're women!'

As for Jum'a, my uncle reprimanded him, angry that he stopped pursuing the two knights once he got to them.

And so Jum'a said, 'My lord, I was afraid they might have an ambush set up in the ditch at Rabiyat al-Qaramita[93] and come out against me. Once I had a look at it and saw that there was no one in it, I rescued the man and his beast and chased the two Franks until they went back into their camp.'

But, by God, my uncle would not accept his excuse, nor was he pleased by his conduct.

§ The Status of the Knight among the Franks

The Franks (may God confound them) have none of the human virtues except for courage. They have neither precedence nor high rank except that of the knights, and have no men worthy of the name except the knights – it is they who are the masters of legal reasoning, judgment and sentencing. I once brought a case [65] before them concerning some flocks of sheep that the lord of Banias had seized from the woods while there existed a truce between us. At the time, I was based in Damascus.[94]

I said to the king, Fulk, son of Fulk,[95] 'This man has encroached upon our rights and seized our flocks right at the time of lambing. But they gave birth and the lambs died, so he returned them to us after so many lambs were lost.'

Then the king turned to six or seven knights: 'Arise and render a judgment for him.'

So they left his audience-chamber, sequestering themselves and deliberating until their minds were all agreed upon one decision, and then they returned to the king's audience-chamber.

'We have passed judgment', they said, 'to the effect that the lord of Banias should pay compensation equal to the value of the lambs that were lost from their flock of sheep.'

And so the king ordered him to pay compensation. He entreated me and begged and pleaded with me until I accepted from him four hundred dinars. That judgment, having been passed by the knights, cannot be changed or rescinded by the king or any Frankish leader. So the knight is someone of greatness in their view.

The king said to yours truly, 'By the truth of my religion, I was made very happy indeed yesterday!'

'May God keep the king ever joyful!' I said. 'What was it that led to your happiness?'

'They told me you were a great knight,' he replied, 'but I hadn't really believed it.'

'My lord,' I assured him, 'I am a knight of my race and people.' You see, if the knight is tall and thin, they find him more impressive.

§ An Encounter with Tancred of Antioch

Prior to this, Tancred,[96] who was the first lord of Antioch after Bohemond, had encamped against us. So we fought one another and then arranged a truce. Tancred sent a messenger requesting a horse that belonged to a servant of my uncle, [66] Sultan (may God have mercy upon him). It was a noble steed. So my uncle sent the horse to Tancred, mounted by one of our companions, a Kurd called Hasanun. He was one of our most courageous horsemen, even though he was but a youngster. A good-looking man, thin. He was supposed to race the horse against some others for Tancred, so he raced it and it beat all the other horses that were in play. He was brought before Tancred, and the knights began to inspect his gear and were amazed at his thin physique and his youthfulness, since they had heard he was a courageous horseman.

Tancred bestowed robes of honour on him, but Hasanun said, 'My lord, I ask that you grant me your guarantee of safe-conduct, so that if you overcome me in battle, you would have mercy upon me and release me.'

And so Tancred granted him his guarantee of safe-conduct, or so Hasanun assumed, for they only speak Frankish and we do not understand what they say.

After that, a year or more passed and the truce expired. Tancred came at us with the army of Antioch, and we fought one another before the walls of the city. Our cavalry had met their vanguard and one of our men, a Kurd called Kamil the Scarred, thrust his spear at them with gusto. He and Hasanun were peers in bravery. Hasanun had halted on his mare with my father (may God have mercy upon him), awaiting his charger which a servant of his was bringing out from the veterinary, along with his *kazaghand*-armour. But the servant was slow to return and Hasanun, seeing the spear-work that Kamil the Scarred was doing, was getting anxious.

So he said to my father, 'My lord, let me use some light equipment instead.'

'These are the mules with the equipment, standing right here,' my father indicated. 'Wear whatever suits you.'

At the time, I was standing behind my father, a mere youth, for this was the first day I had ever participated in battle. Hasanun had a look at the *kazaghand*-armour in their cases on the backs of the mules, but he couldn't make up his mind on any. He was boiling in his desire to ride out and do what Kamil the Scarred was doing. So he sped away on his mare, completely unarmoured. A Frankish horseman intercepted him and thrust his spear at the mare's croup. As a result, the mare took the bit in its teeth and bolted ahead with Hasanun until it threw him to the ground in the midst of a band of Franks.

They took him prisoner and tortured him in a variety of ways. They had wanted to gouge out his left eye, but Tancred (may God curse him) said to them, 'Take out his right eye; that way, when he carries his shield, his left eye will be covered and he will no longer be able to see anything.'

So they gouged out [67] his right eye, just as Tancred ordered. For his ransom, they demanded one thousand dinars and a black charger that belonged to my father, a noble horse of the Khafaja,[97] one of the finest. And so my father (may God have mercy upon him) ransomed him back with that horse.

On that day, many infantrymen marched out from Shayzar, too. The Franks attacked them but were unable to make them budge from their position. So Tancred flew into a rage and said,

'You are my knights! Each one of you earns a stipend worth a hundred stipends of these Muslims. These are but *serjents*[98] (which means infantrymen), and you cannot even dislodge them from their place!'

They replied, 'But we were only afraid for our horses; otherwise we would have run them down and put our spears through them.'

At this, Tancred said, 'The horses are mine. Whoever loses his charger in battle, let me replace it.' They then made a number of charges against our men, in which seventy of their horses were killed, but they still were unable to shake our men from their positions.

§ One Frankish Knight Routs Four Muslim Horsemen

At Apamea, there was one of the greatest Frankish knights, called Badrahu.[99] He was always asking, 'I wonder, will I never get to meet Jum'a in battle?' And Jum'a was always asking, 'I wonder, will I never get to meet Badrahu in battle?'

The army of Antioch now camped against us and pitched their tents at the spot where they used to do so, with the water[100] between us. We had a detachment posted at an elevated spot across from them. One of their knights rode out from their tents and stopped below our detachment, with the river between them, and shouted at them, 'Is Jum'a with you?'

'No,' they replied.

And, by God, he was not present among them. That knight was Badrahu. Looking around, he spotted four of our horsemen on his side of the river: Yahya ibn Safi Left-Hand,[101] Sahl ibn Abi Ghanim the Kurd and Haritha al-Numayri, along with another horseman. [68] Badrahu attacked them, put them to flight and caught up with one of them, at whom he thrust his spear. But it was a useless blow as his horse had not caught up enough to allow him a decent thrust. So he returned to camp.

That group of our horsemen went back into town, where their shame was made public. The people hurled abuse at them and cast aspersions on them and disparaged them, saying, 'Four horsemen routed by one knight! You should have split up in

front of him, so that, with him attacking one of you with his
spear, the other three could have killed him and you would not
have been put to such shame.' Their severest critic was Jum'a
al-Numayri.

But it was as if that defeat had granted to these men hearts
other than their own and a sense of bravery to which they
had never before aspired. For after that defeat, they grew in
self-worth – fighting and distinguishing themselves in warfare,
becoming some of our most noteworthy horsemen.

As for Badrahu, after that encounter he went off on some
errand from Apamea, headed for Antioch. But on his way there,
a lion came out at him from a thicket in al-Ruj,[102] tore him
from his mule and brought him back to the thicket and ate
him (may God *not* have mercy upon him).

§ A Lone Knight Thwarts the Army of Mawdud

Here is an example of a lone man's advance against a large
group. On Thursday, 9 Rabi' al-Awwal of the year 505
(15 September 1111), the isbasalar Mawdud[103] (may God have
mercy upon him) encamped in the hinterland of Shayzar after
Tancred, the lord of Antioch, had marched against him at the
head of a large force. So my uncle and father (may God have
mercy upon them both) went out to Mawdud and said to him,
'The right thing would be for you to break camp (for he was
encamped to the east of town along the river) and encamp
instead in town. The army can set up its tents in the various
open areas in the city and we can then go and encounter [69]
the Franks after securing our tents and baggage.'[104]

So Mawdud decamped just as they suggested. The next
morning, they went out to join him along with five thousand
well-armed infantrymen from Shayzar. Mawdud was overjoyed
at this and his spirits rose. He too (may God have mercy upon
him) had some excellent men with him.

They positioned their ranks along the southern side of the
water, while the Franks were encamped on its northern side.
All throughout the day, they prevented the Franks from drawing water or even approaching the river. So when night fell, the
Franks broke camp and withdrew to their territory, with our

men surrounding them. They encamped at Tall al-Turmusi, but our men prevented them from approaching the river, just as they had done the day before. So they broke camp again during the night and made for Tall al-Tulul,[105] where our army closed in on them and prevented them from moving, surrounding the water and thwarting their approach. Faced with this situation, they decamped during the night and made for Apamea. Our army rushed at them and surrounded them even as they marched. Suddenly, a lone Frankish horseman came forth and charged our men until he got right into their midst, so they killed his charger and wounded him mercilessly, but he continued to fight on foot until he made it back to his comrades. Mawdud (may God have mercy upon him) then withdrew to Damascus.

After a few months, a letter from Tancred, lord of Antioch, was delivered to us with a knight accompanied by servants and companions. The letter said, 'This is a much-revered knight of the Franks who came on pilgrimage but who now wishes to return to his own country. He has asked me to send him to you so that he might observe your own knights. And so I have sent him and ask that you treat him well.'

He was a good-looking, well-dressed youth, only he bore the marks of multiple wounds and his face bore the mark of a sword-blow that cut him from the top of his head to the middle of his face. I asked about him and they told me, 'This is the knight who charged the army of the isbasalar Mawdud. They killed his horse, but he fought them until he was able to get back to his comrades.'

Exalted thus is God, who accomplishes His will how He wills it! Fate is not slowed by being faint of heart, any more than it speeds for those who do their part.

§ One Man Defeats Many: Two Examples

[70] A similar example was related to me by al-'Uqab the Poet, one of our Bedouin troops.[106] He said, 'My father left Palmyra[107] headed for the market of Damascus, accompanied by four horsemen and four men on foot, leading eight camels for sale. My father said:

We were on our way when what should we see coming from the very heart of the desert but a horseman, who kept on coming until he was quite close to us. He said, 'Leave the camels!' We shouted at him and cursed him, so he charged his horse at us and speared one of our horsemen, unhorsing and wounding him. We chased after him but he kept on ahead. Then he turned back and said, 'Leave the camels!' We shouted and cursed him again, so he charged at us and speared one of our infantrymen, badly wounding him. We followed and he kept ahead, but then he turned back and charged, with us having lost two of our men. So one of our men confronted him. Our comrade thrust his spear at him, but the blow fell on his foe's saddlebow and broke our comrade's spear. The horseman now thrust his spear at our man and wounded him, then charged at us again and speared one of our men, felling him. He then said, 'Leave the camels! If not, I will wipe you out!' And so we said, 'Come here and take half of them instead.' 'No,' he replied, 'set aside four of them and leave them standing there; then take your four and be off with you!' And so we did, not trusting that we would escape with what he had let us keep. He led away those four camels as we watched, without being able to do anything about it. And so he went away with his plunder, and he was but a lone man while we were eight.

Another similar case occurred when Tancred, the lord of Antioch, made a raid on Shayzar, rustling a large quantity of our cattle and killing and taking prisoner some of our people. He encamped at a village called Zalin, in which there is an inaccessible cave hanging there in the middle of the mountain with no way to get to it climbing down from above or climbing up from below. Those seeking refuge there can only get down to it using ropes.

On that day, Thursday, 20 Rabi' al-Akhir, the year [71] 502 (27 November 1108), some devil of a Frankish horseman went to Tancred and said, 'Make me a box out of wood which I can sit in. Then lower me from the mountaintop down to them by chains fastened to the box. That way, they won't be able to cut them with their swords and send me falling.'

So they made him a box and lowered him on the suspended chains down to the cave and he captured it, bringing down everyone in it to Tancred. That was because the cave was one large room, containing no place where the people could secrete themselves. So that Frank just shot arrows at them; not an arrow fell that did not strike someone, thanks to the narrowness of the place and the large number of people in it.

§§ Digression: A Bridal Surprise

Among those who were taken captive that day was a woman of noble Arab stock. Prior to this, she had been described to my uncle Sultan (may God have mercy upon him) while she was still living at the home of her father. So my uncle sent an old woman, one of our followers, to have a look at her. Whether because they had switched women on her or whether she had seen some other woman, our old woman came back describing her, her beauty and her intelligence. So my uncle engaged her and married her. But when she was then introduced to him, he saw something that had not been described to him,[108] not to mention the fact that she was a mute. So he paid her dowry and sent her back to her people. It was this woman who was taken prisoner by the Franks on that day, taken from the home of her people. But my uncle said, 'I will not let a woman whom I have married and who has uncovered herself before me become a prisoner of the Franks!' and he ransomed her back (may God have mercy upon him) for five hundred dinars and delivered her to her family.

§ A Woman's Ruse Saves the Day

Another example was related to me in Mosul by the poet al-Mu'ayyad al-Baghdadi in the year 565[109] (1169–70). He said:

> The caliph had granted as fief to my father a village which he used to frequent. A gang of young toughs[110] lived there who engaged in highway robbery, and my father used to let them do it out of fear, and to benefit from a piece of

what they took in. One day, we were sitting in the village
when a Turkish attendant approached on his horse, accompanied by a saddle-mule bearing a saddle-bag, with a
serving-girl riding atop the bag.[111] He dismounted, helped
the girl to dismount and said, 'Hey boys, help me get this
saddle-baggage down.' So we came [72] and lifted it down
with him, and what do you know but it was *filled* with
gold dinars and jewellery! He sat down with the girl and
they ate something. Then he said, 'Help me get this saddle-
bag up,' and so with him we lifted it up. Then he asked us,
'Which way to al-Anbar?'[112] My father told him, 'The road
is over here (and he pointed to the road). But there are
sixty young toughs on that road and they've made me
afraid for you.' The Turk just scoffed at my father and
said, 'Pfft![113] Me, afraid of some tough-guys!'

So my father let him be and went off to the gang to tell
them about the Turk and what he was carrying with him.
They then all went out to intercept him on the road. When
the Turk saw them, he took out his bow, nocked an arrow
and bent his bow intending to shoot at them. But the
bowstring snapped, the gang rushed at him and he fled.
They seized the mule, the girl and the saddle-bag. But the
girl said to them, 'Now, boys, don't dishonour me, by
God! Instead, ransom me and the mule too for a jewelled
necklace that the Turk has with him, worth five hundred
dinars, and you can take the saddle-bag and its contents
too.' 'Let's do it,' they said. 'Send me', she said, 'with one
of you accompanying me to speak with the Turk and get
the necklace from him.' So they sent her with someone to
guard her until she came near the Turk and said to him, 'I
have ransomed myself and the mule for the necklace that
is in the leg of your left boot, your shoe. Give it to me.'
'Will do,' he replied and went to one side away from them
and took off his boot and – guess what? – there was a
bowstring in it which he strung on his bow! He then
returned to them. The gang kept on fighting him while he
picked them off one by one until he had killed forty-three
men. And while looking around, who should he see but

my father in the group of toughs still remaining. 'You! Among them!' he cried. 'So you want me to give you your share of my arrows!' 'No!' my father cried. 'Then take these seventeen men who are left', he said, 'and bring them to the governor of the region so he can hang them.' In the meantime, those men had thrown down their arms and were standing bug-eyed in fear. The Turk led his mule before him with everything that [73] was on it and marched away. Thus, through him, did God (may He be exalted) send a calamity and His great wrath upon that gang of toughs.

§ *Single-Handed Feats at the Battle of Kafartab*

A similar case that I witnessed took place in the year 509 (1115). My father (may God have mercy upon him) had gone out at the head of the army to join the isbasalar Bursuq ibn Bursuq (may God have mercy upon him), who had arrived to lead an expedition by order of the sultan.[114] He came at the head of an immense force, with a group of prominent amirs,[115] including: Commander of the Armies Uzbeh, lord of Mosul; Sunqur Diraz, lord of al-Rahba; the amir Kundughadi; the grand chamberlain Baktimur; Zangi ibn Bursuq, a real warrior-hero; Tamirak; Isma'il al-Bakji, and other amirs. They encamped against Kafartab, where the two brothers of Theophilos[116] and the Franks were, and attacked it. The troops from Khurasan entered the fosse and began digging a tunnel.[117] The Franks were convinced of their own destruction, so they set fire to the citadel and burned the roof, which fell upon the horses, beasts of burden, sheep, pigs and captives, burning them all up. But some of the Franks remained on the top of the citadel, clinging to its walls.

It then occurred to me to enter the sapping-tunnel and have a look at it. So I descended into the fosse, with arrows and stones falling on us like rain, and entered the tunnel. I saw there a very clever thing: they had tunnelled from the fosse to the barbican, and on either side of the tunnel they had set up posts, over which stretched a plank to prevent the earth above it from falling in. They extended the tunnel along in this way using timbers right up to the base of the barbican. Then they tunnelled under the walls of the barbican, keeping it supported, and reached as far as the foundations of the tower.[118] The tunnel here was narrow, as it was only intended as a way to get to the tower. As soon as they reached the tower, [74] they widened the tunnel along the wall of the tower, supported it on timbers, and, a little bit at a time, they started carrying out the pieces of chipped away stone. The floor of the tunnel, on account of the stone chipping, became like mud. Having inspected the tunnel, I left without the Khurasani troops recognizing me. If they had, they would not have let me leave without paying them a heavy fine.

They then set about cutting up dry wood and stuffing the tunnel with it. Early the next morning, they set it ablaze. We had put on our armour and marched to the fosse, under a great shower of stones and arrows, to launch an assault on the citadel once the tower collapsed. As soon as the fire began to do its work, the layers of mortar between the stones of the wall began to fall out, then the wall cracked, the crack widened and the tower fell. We had thought that, once the tower fell, we would be able to advance on the enemy. But only the outer face of the tower fell; the inner wall remained as it was.[119] So we stood there until the sun became too hot for us, and then went back to our tents having suffered a lot of damage from all the stones.

We rested until noon, when what should happen but an infantryman from our army went out all alone, armed with his sword and shield. He marched up to the wall of the tower that had fallen, whose sides had become like the steps of a stairway, and climbed up until he reached its highest point.[120] When the other infantrymen of our army saw him, about ten of them rushed to follow him, fully armed, climbing up one behind the other until they were all on top of the tower, while the Franks were completely unaware of them. As for us, we suited up in our tents and marched out. Many more of the infantrymen had climbed the tower before the rest of the army had arrived.

The Franks now turned upon our men and shot them with arrows, wounding the one who was the first to climb up. So he went back down. But the other men continued to climb until they were facing the Franks on the parapet between the two tower walls.[121] In front of them rose a tower with a doorway, in which stood an armoured horseman with shield and spear preventing entrance to the tower. On top of the tower was a group of Franks attacking our men [75] with arrows and stones. One of the Turks climbed up while we were watching and, abandoning himself to fortune, walked forwards until he approached the tower and hurled a bottle of naphtha[122] on those who were on top of it. I saw it blaze like a shooting star on the stones, while those Franks threw themselves to the ground out of fear of getting burned. The Turk then came back.

Another Turk climbed up and walked along the parapet with a sword and shield. From the tower that had the horseman in its doorway, there came against him one of their men wearing a doubled hauberk,[123] spear in hand, but no shield. The Turk met him, sword in hand, and the Frank thrust his spear at him. But the Turk pushed the spearhead away from him with his shield and stepped forward to his enemy, putting himself in where the Frank's spear had been.[124] So the Frank spun away from him, turning and bending his back like a man at prayer,[125] out of fear for his head. The Turk struck him with a number of blows, none of which had any effect. He then walked on until he entered the tower, where our men outnumbered and over-powered him and his comrades. The Franks then delivered the citadel and the captives came down to the tents of Bursuq.

The captives gathered together in the large tent of Bursuq to set for themselves the ransom by which they would be freed. I saw among them that one who had come out with his spear against the Turk. He stood up – he was a *serjent* – and said, 'How much do you want from me?'

'We want six hundred dinars,' they said.

But he just scoffed at them and said, 'Pfft! I'm just a *serjent*; my stipend is two dinars a month! Where am I going to get six hundred dinars?' and then returned and sat down among his comrades. He was of very large build.

The amir al-Sayyid al-Sharif,[126] who was one of the greatest amirs, said to my father (may God have mercy upon them both), 'Brother, can you believe these people? I seek refuge in God from them!'

And God (glory be to Him) decreed that our army should move from Kafartab to Danith;[127] we were surprised early Tuesday morning, 23 Rabi' al-Akhir (15 September 1115) by the army of Antioch. [76] The surrender of Kafartab had occurred on Friday, 13 Rabi' al-Akhir (5 September). The amir al-Sayyid (may God have mercy upon him) and a large host of Muslims were killed.

My father (may God have mercy upon him) returned after he had parted from me at Kafartab, his army having been crushed. We were still at Kafartab keeping watch on it, intending to rebuild it, since the isbasalar Bursuq had granted it to us. We were removing the prisoners in pairs, each pair chained to a soldier from Shayzar. One of them was half-burned, though his thigh was unharmed; another died in the fire: I saw in them a weighty example worthy of contemplation. We then left Kafartab and returned to Shayzar with my father (may God have mercy upon him), he having had all his tents, camels, mules, baggage and furniture taken from him, and the entire army having dispersed.

What had happened to the army at Danith was the result of a ruse foisted on them by Lu'lu' the Eunuch,[128] who was lord of Aleppo at the time. He made a plan with the lord of Antioch[129] to deceive them and divide them, at which point the latter would set out from Antioch at the head of his army to destroy them. So Lu'lu' sent a messenger to the isbasalar Bursuq (may God have mercy upon him) saying, 'Send one of the amirs to me with a detachment of troops and I will deliver Aleppo to him. I am truly afraid that the populace of the city will not agree to let me deliver the city to someone else, so I want a body of troops to accompany the amir and thereby overawe the Aleppines.'

So Bursuq sent him the Commander of the Armies[130] Uzbeh with three thousand horsemen. But Roger (may God curse him) surprised them one morning and, through the execution of the divine will, destroyed them. The Franks (may God curse them) returned to Kafartab, rebuilt it and settled in it.

[77] God (may He be exalted) decreed that the Frankish captives whom we had taken at Kafartab be released, since the amirs divided them among themselves and kept them until they could ransom themselves off. The exception to this was the case of the Commander of the Armies. For, before leaving for Aleppo, he ordered all those who fell to his share to be executed. And so the armies dispersed – those who survived Danith, that is – and they headed back to their homelands.

At any rate, it was that man who climbed all alone onto the tower of Kafartab who was the cause of its capture.

§ A Soldier from Shayzar Attacks a Frankish Caravan

Another example: there was a man in my service called Numayr al-'Allaruzi, an infantryman, courageous and strong. With a band of infantrymen from Shayzar, he set out for al-Ruj to attack the Franks. While in the region of the town, they stumbled across a Frankish caravan encamped in a cavern. So each one said to the other, 'Who's going to go in against them?' Numayr said, 'I will,' and handed his comrades his sword and shield. Drawing forth his dagger, he went in to the enemy. One of them came to confront him, but he struck him with his dagger, threw him down and knelt on him to kill him. Behind him stood another Frank with a sword, and he struck at Numayr, but Numayr was wearing a rucksack on his back with bread in it, and this cushioned the blow. Once he had killed the man that was pinned underneath him, he turned towards the Frank with the sword and made for him. The Frank struck him with his sword on the side of his face, cutting through his brow, eyelid, cheek, nose and upper lip, causing the whole side of his face to hang down onto his chest. So Numayr left the cavern and returned to his comrades, who bound his wounds and returned with him through a cold and rainy night, arriving at Shayzar while he was still in that condition. His face was stitched back up and his wounds were treated, so he recovered and returned to how he had been, except that his eye was gone. He was one of the three men whom the Isma'ilis threw from Shayzar Citadel that we mentioned earlier.[131]

§ *A Group of Soldiers is Forced by one Man to Flee*

[78] The following example was told to me by Chief Sahri,[132] who was in service to the amir Shams al-Khawwas Altuntash, lord of Rafaniya; between the latter and 'Alam al-Din 'Ali-Kurd, the lord of Hama, there was a standing enmity and dispute:

> Shams al-Khawwas ordered me to appraise the hinterland of Rafaniya and inspect its crops. I went accompanied by a band of troops and I appraised the land. One evening, I encamped at one of the villages of Rafaniya which had a tower, so we climbed up to the roof of the tower and had our dinner and relaxed while our horses were down at the tower door. Before we knew it, a man emerged from the tower battlements and screamed at us, then hurled himself at us with a knife in his hand. We fled from him, descending the first flight of steps with him in pursuit, then the second flight, with him still in pursuit, until we reached the door. We rushed out and what do you know, but he had stationed some men at the door! They grabbed every one of us and tied us up with cords and brought us in to Hama to 'Ali-Kurd. We only escaped execution because of a special dispensation of Fate. Instead, he imprisoned us and set a heavy ransom on us. And the one who caused all of this was that one man from the tower.

§ *One Man Captures a Fort by Treachery*

A similar occurrence took place at Hisn al-Khurayba.[133] This used to belong to al-Yaghisiyani (may God have mercy upon him); his chamberlain 'Isa was stationed there to govern it. It is an impregnable fortress built on a rock, steep on all sides. One climbed to it by means of a wooden ladder, then the ladder would be pulled up and there would be no other way to get to it. There was no one with the governor in the fort except his son, his servant and the gatekeeper. This last man had a companion called Ibn al-Marji who used to come up to see him from time to time on business. This companion had been talking with the Isma'ilis and he hatched [79] a plot with them, in which he was assured a satisfactory amount of money and a fief in return for handing over to them Hisn al-Khurayba. So he went to the fort and, asking permission to enter, climbed up. He began with the gatekeeper, killing him. The servant then confronted him, so he killed him too. Then he went in to the governor and killed him. He then returned to the governor's son and killed him, and handed the fort over to the Isma'ilis, who stood by their part of the bargain with him.

§ *The Value of one Good Man: The Case of Yunan of Tripoli*

Thus, when men embolden their spirits to do something, they do it. Moreover, men compare differently with respect to their sense of resolve and their dignity. As my father (may God have mercy upon him) once said to me:

> Every good member of a given species can always find its equivalent value in bad members of the same species. For example, a good horse is worth one hundred dinars, but five bad horses are also worth one hundred dinars. The same goes for camels, and the same for different kinds of clothing. The only exception is the son of Adam, for, truly, one thousand bad men will never be worth the same as one good man.

And he was right, may God have mercy upon him.

I once sent a *mamluk* of mine on an important errand to Damascus, but it happened that the atabeg Zangi (may God have mercy upon him) had captured Hama and was encamped against Homs, thereby blocking the route home for my man. So he made instead for Baalbek and from there to Tripoli, where he hired a mule from a Christian man called Yunan.[134] The latter transported my *mamluk* to the place where he hired out animals, saw him off on his journey and then returned. My man travelled out as part of a caravan, intending to get to Shayzar via the mountain forts.

But a man intercepted them and told the owners of the caravan-animals, 'Don't go on. On your route at such-and-such a place there is a band of robbers – sixty, seventy men – who will take you all captive.' And so, my man told me:

We stopped, not knowing what to do. We neither relished
the idea of turning back nor dared, out of fear, to proceed.
And that's the state we were in when who should appear
but Chief Yunan, approaching in a hurry. 'What brings
you here, Chief?' we asked. 'I heard,' he replied, 'that there
are robbers on your route, so I came to travel with you.
Let's go.' We went with him to that location where – sure
enough – a large band of [80] robbers came down the
mountain intending to capture us. But Yunan intercepted
them saying, 'Boys, keep your ground! I am Yunan, and
these people are under my protection. By God, there's not
a man among you could even get close to them.' In this
way, he turned them back – all of them, by God – without
them so much as eating a loaf of our bread. Yunan continued on with us until we were safe, then saw us off and
withdrew.

§ Relief after Misfortune: Escape from a Frankish Prison

This same man of mine, who went up to Egypt with me in the
year 538 (1144), told me a story about the son of the lord of
Mount Sinai[135] (Mount Sinai is a distant province belonging to
Egypt; when al-Hafiz – may God have mercy upon him – wanted
to banish one of the amirs, he would make him governor of
Mount Sinai. It's close to Frankish territory).

'The son of the governor of Mount Sinai,' my man said, 'told
me the following story:[136]

My father was made governor of Mount Sinai, and I went
with him to the province, being rather fond of hunting. So
I went out one day to go hunting and a band of Franks fell
on me, took me captive and carried me back to Bayt Jibril,
where they shut me up in a pit all by myself. The lord of
Bayt Jibril set a ransom of two thousand dinars for me. I
remained in that pit for a year, without anyone ever asking
about me. But one day as I was in the pit, what should
happen but the cover was lifted and a Bedouin man was
lowered down towards me. 'Where'd they get you?' I

asked. 'Right from the road,' he replied. He stayed with me for a few days and they set for him a ransom of fifty dinars. One day he said to me, 'You want to know something? I'm the only one who can rescue you from this pit. Rescue me, and I'll rescue you.' I said to myself, 'This is a man who, having fallen into misfortune, desperately wants to escape,' and I did not answer him. Then, after a few days more, he repeated what he said to me. I said to myself, 'By God, I damn well *will* try to rescue him, and perhaps God will rescue me in recompense.' So I shouted for the jailer and said, 'Tell the lord that I wish to speak with him.' He then came back and pulled me out of the pit and brought me before the lord. I said to him, 'I have been in your prison for a year now and no one has asked for me and no one even knows whether [81] I am living or dead. But you have imprisoned this Bedouin with me and set for him a ransom of fifty dinars. Add that amount to my own ransom and let me send him to my father to get him to free me.' 'You may do so,' he said. So I returned and informed the Bedouin who, saying goodbye, went away.

I waited for two months for him to do something, but I saw no trace of him and heard no news, so I despaired of him. But one night, to my astonishment, he emerged before me from a tunnel dug through the side of the pit. 'Get up!' he said. 'By God, it's been five months that I've been digging this burrow from a ruined village to get to you.' So I stood up with him and we went out through that burrow. He then broke my chain and brought me to my home. I don't know what should surprise me more – his integrity, or his sense of direction being so good that his burrow ended right at the side of the pit!

When God (glory be to Him) decrees that relief should come, then what an easy thing it is to bring it about!

§ Usama Ransoms Muslim Captives at Acre

I used to travel frequently to visit the king of the Franks during the truce that existed between him and Jamal al-Din

Muhammad (may God have mercy upon him) on account of an act of generosity that my father (may God have mercy upon him) had done for King Baldwin, the father of the queen, the wife of King Fulk, son of Fulk.[137] The Franks used to bring their captives before me so that I might buy their freedom, and so I bought those whose deliverance God facilitated.

Once a real devil of a Frank called William Jiba[138] went out in a boat of his on a raid and he captured a ship carrying Muslim pilgrims from the Maghrib, around four hundred souls, men and women. Groups of these captives would be brought to me by their owners and I would buy those of them I could afford to buy. There was a young man among them who would offer a greeting but then sit and refuse to speak. I asked about him and I was told [82] that he was an ascetic and his master was a tanner.

So I asked his master, 'For how much will you sell this one to me?'

'By the truth of my religion,' he replied, 'I won't sell him except as a pair with this old man, and for the same price I paid when I bought them, forty-three dinars.'

So I bought both of them. I also bought a few more for me and another few for the amir Mu'in al-Din (may God have mercy upon him), all for 120 dinars. I paid out all the money I had with me and offered a guarantee for the remainder.

I then went to Damascus and told the amir Mu'in al-Din (may God have mercy upon him), 'I bought back some captives for you, putting them specifically under your charge, but I didn't have the full amount with which to pay for them. And now I've arrived back at my home. If you want them, you can pay the remainder of their price; if not, I will.'

'No, I'll pay for them,' he said. 'By God, there's no one who desires the spiritual rewards of such a good deed more than I.'

He was (may God have mercy upon him) the most eager person when it came to performing good works and meriting the spiritual rewards that came from them, so he paid for them. After a few days, I returned to Acre.[139]

There remained thirty-eight captives still with William Jiba, including the wife of a man that God (may He be exalted) had already delivered by my hand. So I bought her without paying her price just then. I then rode to Jiba's home (may God curse him) and asked him, 'Will you sell me ten of them?'

'By the truth of my religion,' he replied, 'I'll only sell all of them together.'

'I don't have enough on me to buy all of them together,' I said. 'I'll buy some of them now. At the next opportunity, I'll buy the rest.'

He merely replied, 'I'll only sell all of them together!'

So I left. But God (glory be to Him) decreed that the captives should run away that very night, all of them. Now, the inhabitants of the villages of Acre are all Muslims, so whenever a captive came to them, they would hide him and bring him to the lands of Islam. That damned Frank searched after his captives but never got hold of any of them, for God (glory be to Him) saw their deliverance to be good.

The next morning, the Frank demanded from me the price of that woman whom I had bought but whose price I had not yet paid, and who had been among those who had run away.

I said, 'Bring her to me, and you can take her price.'

He replied, 'Her price has rightfully been mine since yesterday before she ran away.'

And he obliged me to pay her price. So I paid it to him, considering it an easy thing given the joy I took at the deliverance of those poor people.

§ An Amazing Escape: Conspiracy at Amid

[83] Another example of an amazing escape due to the intervention of Fate and the pre-ordination of the divine will was the following:

The amir Qara Arslan (may God have mercy upon him) made a number of attempts against the city of Amid[140] while I was in his service, but without achieving his goal. During the last attempt he made on the city, a Kurdish amir on the pay-roll at Amid, along with a group of his comrades, sent a message to Qara Arslan. They arranged that, on a certain night which they agreed upon, Qara Arslan's army would arrive at his position and he would help them up by means of ropes, so that they could take possession of Amid. Qara Arslan made this important task the responsibility of a Frankish servant of his called Yaruq,[141] whom the whole army loathed and despised because of his bad character. Yaruq rode forward at the head of some troops and the rest of the amirs followed behind him. Then he began to slow down during the journey, so the amirs got to Amid before him.

That Kurdish amir and his comrades appeared on a tower before them, and dangled down ropes to them, urging them, 'Climb up!' Not a single one of them did.

So the men on the tower came down and broke the locks of the city gate saying, 'Come in here!' But no one went in.

All of this happened because Qara Arslan depended upon an ignorant youth to carry out this most important of tasks, instead of relying upon the great amirs.

The amir Kamal al-Din 'Ali ibn Nisan[142] was aware of the plot, as was the local militia and the army. So they fell on the traitors, killing some, capturing others, while still others threw themselves off the wall. One of those who had thrown himself from the wall extended his hand in mid-air, as if he wanted something to grab on to. It happened that his hand fell upon one of those ropes that were hung down from the wall earlier in the evening and which no one had climbed. So he hung on to it and out of all his comrades he alone escaped, though he did strip the skin off his palms on the rope. All this took place in my presence.

[84] The next morning the lord of Amid chased down those who had moved against him and killed them. Only that one man escaped. Glory be to He who decrees one's escape, He delivers men even from the maw of a lion! This is a true statement of fact, not a mere example.

§ Saved from the Jaws of a Lion

At the Bridge Fortress was one of our comrades known as Ibn al-Ahmar from the Banu Kinana tribe.[143] One day he rode his horse out from Bridge Fortress making for Kafartab on an errand of his and passed through Kafarnabudha[144] just as a

caravan was crossing the road. The people in the caravan saw
a lion there.

Ibn al-Ahmar had a spear that shone in the sun, so the people
in the caravan shouted to him, 'You, with the flashing wood!
Beware of that lion!'

His sense of honour at hearing their cries pushed him to
attack the lion, but his horse shied away and he fell. The lion
came and crouched on him. But, since God wished that he
would be saved, the lion was already satiated and it merely
mouthed his face and forehead. Having wounded his face, the
lion then began to lick the blood, while he crouched on him
without injuring him. Ibn al-Ahmar said:

> I opened my eyes and I saw the maw of the lion. I dragged
> myself out from under him, lifting his thigh off me. I then
> slipped out, clung to a nearby tree and climbed up. The
> lion saw me and came after me, but I was well ahead of
> him and climbed the tree. So the lion then went to sleep
> underneath the tree, while a whole bunch of ants began
> clambering all over my wound (for ants seek out people
> wounded by lions just as mice seek out those wounded by
> leopards[145]). I then saw the lion sit up, pricking up its ears
> as if listening to something. Then it stood up and rushed
> off, for what should I see but a caravan, which had
> approached from the road; it was as if the lion had heard
> its sound.

The people of that caravan recognized Ibn al-Ahmar and transported him back to his home. The marks of that lion's fangs on
his forehead and cheeks were like a brand of fire. Glory be to
the Deliverer!

§§ On Reason and Warfare

[85] A digression:[146] We were chatting about warfare one day
in the hearing of my tutor, the learned sheikh known as Ibn
al-Munira[147] (may God have mercy upon him).

So I said to him, 'Say, master! If you would mount a charger,
put on a *kazaghand* and helmet, belt on a sword, carry a spear
and shield and position yourself at the Judge's Mosque[148] (a

narrow place where the Franks – God curse them – used to pass by), not a single one of them would be able to get by you!'

'Oh no,' he replied. 'By God, they'd all get by.'

I said, 'But they'd be terrified of you, and they wouldn't know who you were!'

'Glory be to God!' he replied. 'Don't I know myself?'

Then he said to yours truly, 'A man of reason does not fight.'

So I said, 'But master! Are you judging so-and-so and so-and-so (and I listed some of our comrades who were courageous horsemen) to be witless?'

'That is not what I meant,' he replied. 'I merely meant that all reason is absent at the time of battle. If it were present, then men would not confront swords with their faces, nor spears and arrows with their chests. This is not the sort of thing that reason calls for.'

He was (may God have mercy upon him), however, more experienced with scholarship than he was with combat. For it is precisely reason that fills one with resolve in the face of swords, spears and arrows out of disdain towards being cast as a coward and smeared with bad reputation. The proof of that is that a man of courage, before going in to battle, will be stricken with shakes, he shivers and changes in colour due to all the dangers he thinks upon and talks to himself about, dangers stemming from what he plans to do and the risks he is about to encounter. A man's soul will always shudder at such dangers and loathe them. But once that man of courage enters the fray of battle and wades among its throngs, all that shaking, shuddering and changing of colour disappears.

§ Examples of Ignorance: Playing with Fire

Indeed, every act in which reason is absent results in error and failure. Here is an example. Once, the Franks encamped against Hama in its fields, [86] in which there was a fat harvest of corn; they pitched their tents right in the midst of that harvest. Now, a group of robbers came out from Shayzar to reconnoitre the Frankish army and rob them, and they noticed their tents were pitched in the corn.

So the next morning, one of them went before the lord of

Hama and said, 'Tonight I will burn up the entire Frankish army.'

'If you do that,' replied the lord, 'I will cover you with honours.'

Once evening fell, the robber went out with a group of like-minded companions, and they started the fire in the corn west of the tents, so that the breeze would drive the flames towards the tents of the enemy. Thanks to the light of the fire, the night became like day, so the Franks caught sight of them, rushed towards them and killed most of them. Only those who threw themselves in to the river and swam over to the other side managed to escape. And so here we see the impact of ignorance and its consequences.

I happened to witness a similar case, though it did not take place during combat. The Franks had amassed their troops in great numbers against Banias, and they were accompanied by their patriarch.[149] The patriarch had pitched a large tent to use as a church in which they could pray. An old deacon was responsible for maintaining the church and he had covered the floor using rushes and grass, which infested the place with fleas. It then occurred to that deacon to burn the rushes and grass so as to burn up the fleas. So he set the rushes and grass – which had all dried out – on fire. The flames rose higher and higher and caught on the tent, leaving it a pile of ashes. Reason was surely not present in this man.

§ An Example of Reason: A Soldier Fends off a Lion

A contrasting example.[150] One day we rode out from Shayzar on the hunt. My uncle (may God have mercy upon him) and a body of troops accompanied us. As we went into a cane-brake in pursuit of a francolin, a lion emerged to attack us. A man from the group of Kurdish troops called Zahr al-Dawla Bakhti-yar the Cypriot, so named because of his elegant frame,[151] charged at the lion. He was (may God have mercy upon him) one of the real cavaliers of the Muslims. The lion confronted him, but the man's horse shied away from it and threw its rider. The lion came at him while he was lying flat on the ground. So,

Zahr al-Dawla raised his lower leg and the lion began chewing
it. We rushed the lion and killed it, [87] delivering our comrade
safe and sound.

We asked him, 'Zahr al-Dawla, why did you lift your leg
right up to the mouth of the lion?'

He replied, 'As you can see, my body is lean and lanky, and
I'm only wearing a cloth garment and a tunic. There is nothing
on me better covered than my lower leg, with its gaiter, boots
and leggings. So I said to myself, "I'll use my leg to distract him
from my ribs or my hand or my head until God (may He be
exalted) brings me relief."'

And so, reason was surely present in this man, in a situation
where minds are often lost. But with those other examples,
reason was not present. Humanity, therefore, requires reason
above all things. It is praised by the rational and the ignorant
alike.

§ On Reason and Governance: The Cases of Shayzar and Diyar Bakr

Here is an example of that. Roger, the lord of Antioch, sent a
messenger to my uncle saying, 'I have dispatched one of my
knights on an important errand in Jerusalem. I ask you to send
your cavalry to escort him from Apamea to Rafaniya.'

The knight in question then rode out and sent a message on
to my uncle. When he finally met him, the knight said to my
uncle, 'My lord has sent me on an errand of his, which is a
secret matter. But I can see that you are a rational man, so I'll
tell you about it.'

'But how do you know I'm so rational if you've never seen
me before?' asked my uncle.

'Because', the knight replied, 'I noted that the lands I passed
through are in ruins, while your lands are prosperous. I knew
that you could not have caused them to prosper except through
your reason and good governance.' He then told him the
purpose of his journey.[152]

Another case was reported to me by the amir Fadl ibn Abi
al-Hayja', the lord of Irbil: 'Abu al-Hayja'[153] related a story to
me, saying:

The sultan Malikshah, when he arrived in Syria, sent me
on a mission to the amir Ibn Marwan,[154] the lord of Diyar
Bakr. I was to tell him, 'I need thirty thousand dinars.' So
I met [88] with Ibn Marwan and repeated my message to
him. He replied, 'Take a rest, and then we'll talk.' The
next morning, he ordered his servants to admit me into his
bath-house, sending me the various bath-house accessories,
all of them of silver, as well as a change of clothes. They
told my valet, 'These accessories are your property.' But
when I left the bath, I put on my own clothes and returned
all the bath-things to Ibn Marwan. He let me alone for a
few days, then ordered me again to be admitted into the
bath, with no ill-will that I had returned his things. They
now brought to me in the bath a set of accessories even
finer than the first set, and a change of clothes even finer
than the first suit, and Ibn Marwan's valet told my valet
the same thing he told him before. But when I left the
bath-house, I put on my own clothes and returned the
bath-things and the clothes. So Ibn Marwan let me alone
for three or four days, then admitted me once again into
his bath, his servants bringing to me accessories and a
change of clothes that were even finer than before. But
when I came out, I just put on my own clothes and returned
the lot.

When I presented myself before the amir, he asked me,
'Tell me, son, I sent you clothes which you would not
wear, bath accessories which you would not accept, and
you returned them. What's behind all this?' I said, 'My
lord, I have come with a message from the sultan on an
errand that has not yet been completed. Am I to accept all
those things that you were kind enough to give and return
home without having accomplished the sultan's errand, as
if I only came here for my own needs?' 'Son,' he replied,
'didn't you notice the prosperity of my lands, their many
beauties and gardens, their numerous peasant-farmers and
prosperous villages? Do you really think I would risk the
ruin of all that for the sake of thirty thousand dinars? By
God, I had that gold packaged up for you the day you

arrived. I was only waiting for the sultan to pass out of my lands, after which you would rejoin him with the money; for I was afraid that if I gave him then what he demanded, he would demand even more from me when he approached my lands. So don't you trouble your heart about it: your business is done.' Then he had the three changes of clothes sent to me – the ones he had already sent to me but which I had returned – with all of the bath accessories that he had sent to me over those three bath visits, and I accepted it all. Once the sultan had moved on from Diyar Bakr, he gave me the money and I carried it off and, bearing it with me, I rejoined the sultan.

§ Good Governance Offers Rich Rewards: The Cases of Bitlis and Qal'at Ja'bar

In good governance will be found great gains, stemming from the prosperity of the land. Here is an example:

The atabeg Zangi (may God have mercy upon him) became engaged to the daughter of the lord of Khilat.[155] Her father [89] having died, it was her mother who governed the region. But Husam al-Dawla ibn Dilmaj, lord of Bitlis,[156] now sent a messenger requesting that the girl be engaged to his son. So the atabeg marched at the head of a good-sized army to Khilat, using a road other than the one that goes through the Bitlis pass. By this route, we passed through the mountains. We camped without tents, all of us stopping on the road, in formation, until we arrived at Khilat. The atabeg set up camp outside the city and we entered its citadel and drew up the terms of the marriage-contract and dowry.

Once business was concluded, the atabeg ordered al-Yaghisiyani to take the larger part of the army and march to Bitlis and attack it. So we rode out in the early part of the evening and greeted the next morning at Bitlis itself. Its ruler, Husam al-Dawla, came out and met us on an open space just outside the city and had al-Yaghisiyani set up camp in the training-grounds.[157] He offered al-Yaghisiyani generous hospitality, waiting upon him and drinking with him there in the training-grounds.

He asked his guest, 'My lord, what are you planning? You have put yourself through trials and tired yourself out just to get here.'

Al-Yaghisiyani replied, 'The atabeg was angered by your seeking the hand of the girl to whom he was already engaged. You offered to give ten thousand dinars as dowry and we demand it from you now.'

'Hearing is obeying,' Husam al-Dawla replied, and he had a portion of the money brought to him right then, and then asked permission for a few days' grace, the precise period which he fixed, for the payment of the remaining sum. We then turned back, and thanks to his wise governance his district remained prosperous and did not suffer the slightest damage.

That was similar to what befell Malik ibn Salim[158] [90] (may God have mercy upon his soul). What had happened was that Joscelin[159] had made a raid on al-Raqqa and al-Qal'a, seizing everything in its vicinity, taking prisoners and rustling many animals, finally encamping directly across from al-Qal'a, with the Euphrates between them. Malik ibn Salim set out in a skiff with three or four of his men and crossed the Euphrates to Joscelin. There were old bonds of acquaintance between these two and Joscelin actually owed Malik a favour. Joscelin was under the impression that the skiff merely carried a messenger from Malik, but one of the Franks came and told him, 'That's Malik in the skiff.'

'That's not true!' replied Joscelin.

But another man came and said, 'Malik just disembarked and here he comes!'

So Joscelin rose and, intercepting Malik, received him generously and returned to him all the prisoners and animals that he had seized. Thus, had it not been for Malik ibn Salim's governing skills, his lands would have been ruined.

§ Neither Courage nor Strength is Proof against Fate

When one's time has come, neither courage nor strength is of any use. I once witnessed a battle in which the Frankish army had advanced against Shayzar to attack us. A group of them proceeded with the atabeg Tughdakin to the Bridge Fortress to attack it. The atabeg, along with Il-Ghazi ibn Artuq and the Franks, had assembled in Apamea[160] to make war on the army of the sultan, which had arrived in Syria under the command of the isbasalar Bursuq. The isbasalar had encamped at Hama on Sunday, 19 Muharram of the year [91] 509 (13 June 1115). As for us, we fought against them close to the very walls of the city. But we prevailed against them and repulsed them, giving them a warm welcome indeed. I saw one of our comrades called Muhammad ibn Saraya, a young man, strong and powerful. A Frankish horseman (may God curse him) had rushed on him and thrust his spear into his thigh, sending his *quntariya* into it. But Muhammad grabbed on to the spear while it was in his thigh. Meanwhile, the Frank was trying to pull the spear out to take it just as Muhammad was trying to pull it out to keep it, dragging it back and forth through his thigh until it hollowed his thigh out. But the Frank was deprived of his *quntariya* after ruining our man's thigh. Muhammad died two days later, may God have mercy upon him.

On that same day, while I was with one part of the army locked in battle, I saw a cavalryman charge one of our own horsemen and thrust his spear in our comrade's horse, killing it. Our man was now fighting on foot on the ground, but I could not make out who he was due to the distance between us. So I spurred my horse on towards him, fearing for his safety once that Frank had speared him. The Frank's *quntariya* was still stuck in the man's horse as it lay there dead with its intestines spilling out. The Frank withdrew from him a short distance and, drawing his sword, took his position facing him. As I approached our man, I discovered that he was my cousin Nasir al-Dawla Kamil (may God have mercy upon him). So I stopped by him and, removing my own foot from my stirrup, told him, 'Mount!' Once he had mounted, I turned the head of my horse to the west, with the city lying to the east.

My cousin then asked me, 'Where are you going?'

I said, 'Over to that one who put his spear through your horse: now's our chance!'

But he just stretched his hand out and grabbed the reins of

my horse and said, 'Never exchange spear-thrusts while there are two men in armour on your horse. If you get me out of here you can come back and cross spears with him!' So I rode off and got him out of there and went back in search of that dog, but by then he had returned to his comrades.

§ Examples of God's Benevolence: An Ascetic is Concealed from the Franks

I myself have witnessed[161] a case of God's benevolence (may He be exalted) and His good protection. The Franks (may God curse them) [92] encamped against us with their cavalry and infantry, with the Orontes between us. The river was at full spate to such a degree that they could neither cross over to us nor we to them. So they encamped on the mountain in their tents. A band of them then came down towards the orchards on their side and, letting their horses graze freely on the green fodder, they went to sleep. Now, a group of youths from the infantry of Shayzar stripped down, flinging off their clothes, picked up their swords and swam over to those men sleeping there. They killed a few of them, but the Franks outnumbered our comrades so our men threw themselves into the water and crossed back over. Meanwhile, the Frankish army had streamed down from the mountain like a flash-flood. On their side stood a mosque known as the Mosque of Abu al-Majd ibn Sumayya, in which lived a man known as Hasan the Ascetic. He was standing on the roof of some rooms in the mosque praying, wearing a black woollen garment. We stood watching him without any way to get over to him.

The Franks had come and were now stopped at the door to the mosque. They climbed up towards him while we thought to ourselves, 'There is no power or strength save in God! They're going to kill him now!'

But he, by God, never interrupted his prayers and remained in his place. The Franks turned around and went down, mounted their horses and rode away, while Hasan remained standing where he was, praying. There is no doubt in my mind that God (glory be to Him) blinded them to him and concealed him from their gaze. Glory be to the Almighty, the Merciful!

§ God's Benevolence: A Prisoner of the Byzantines is Freed

Another example of the benevolence of God (may He be exalted): when the king of the Romans encamped against Shayzar in the year 532 (1138), a group of infantrymen left Shayzar to join the battle. But the Romans intercepted them, killed some and took some others prisoner. Among the group of those whom they captured was an ascetic from the Banu Kurdus of the Salihiyya cohort, that is, one of the men born into the household of Mahmud ibn [93] Salih,[162] the lord of Aleppo. When the Romans returned home, he went with them as a prisoner and arrived in Constantinople.[163]

He was there for a few days when what should happen but he met a man who asked him, 'Are you Ibn Kurdus?'

'Yes,' he replied.

'Come with me', the other man said, 'and show me to your master.'

So he went on with him and pointed out his master to him. The man haggled with his master about his price until the man and the Roman settled upon a satisfactory amount.

The man paid out the price and gave Ibn Kurdus some money for expenses, saying, 'Use this to go back to your family. Go, may God the Exalted keep you!'

And so he left Constantinople and travelled until he returned to Shayzar. All that was due to the granting by God (may He be exalted) of relief and His inscrutable benevolence. He never learned who it was that bought him and freed him.

§ An Angel Rescues Usama

A similar thing happened to me when the Franks attacked us on the road from Egypt[164] and killed 'Abbas and his son Nasr. We were able to flee to a nearby mountain. Our men climbed up on foot leading the horses behind them, while I was mounted on an old nag, unable to walk.[165] I climbed up, riding, but the slopes of that mountain were all loose stones and pebbles, which at every step slipped beneath the feet of the horses. I beat the old hack to get it to climb, but it could not, so it fell down, bringing stones and pebbles with it. I dismounted and stood there, utterly incapable of walking. Just then a man came down the mountain and grabbed me by the hand to help me climb, my pack-horse led in my other hand. And no, by God, I don't know who he was and I never saw him again.

During those dire days, anyone who performed the slightest act of kindness would put you under obligation and demand recompense for it. I once took a drink of water from a Turk and gave him two dinars for it. But even after we arrived in Damascus he continued to ask me to see to his needs and come to me with [94] his selfish requests – just because of that drink he poured for me. But that other man who helped me, he was nothing but an angel whom God (may He be exalted), in His mercy to me, sent to rescue me.

§ A Vision of the Prophet Rescues a Prisoner

Another example of the benevolence of God (may He be exalted) was related to me by the chief intendant 'Abdallah, who said:

> I was put in prison in Hayzan,[166] chained and treated harshly. While there, with the jailer at the door, I saw the Prophet (God's blessing and peace be upon him) in a dream. He said, 'Remove your chains and go forth.' I then woke up and pulled at my chains, which slipped off my foot, and went to the door to open it, but I found it already open. I then tip-toed past the guard to a small opening in the outer wall, which I couldn't imagine my hand would go through. But I went through it and fell on top of a dung-hill, in which I left footprints and traces of my fall. I then descended into a valley outside the town walls and went into a cave in the slope of the mountain that was on the side where I happened to be. I said to myself, 'Now they'll come out, see my footprints and get me again.' But God (may He be exalted) sent a snowfall that covered up those prints. They came out and looked around for me all day long while I watched them. When evening came and I felt safe from being caught, I left that cave and went to a secure place I knew.

This man was the chief intendant over the kitchens of al-Yaghisiyani (may God have mercy upon him).

§ Motives for Fighting: Two Muslim Martyrs during the Second Crusade

Among men there are those that go to battle just as the Companions of the Prophet[167] (may God be pleased with them) used to go to battle: to obtain entrance to Paradise, and not to pursue some selfish desire or to gain a reputation. Here is an example:

The Frankish king of the Germans (may God curse him), when he arrived in Syria, [95] assembled all the Franks that were in Syria to his side and marched on Damascus.[168] So the army of Damascus and its populace came out to do battle with the Franks. Among them were the jurist al-Findalawi and the sheikh and ascetic 'Abd al-Rahman al-Halhuli (may God have mercy upon them both). The two of them were among the most virtuous of all Muslims.[169]

As they approached the enemy, the jurist said to 'Abd al-Rahman, 'Aren't these the Romans?'

'Yes, indeed,' he replied.

'Then how long are we going to stand here?' the jurist asked.

'Go, in the name of God – may He be exalted!' replied 'Abd al-Rahman.

And so the two men advanced and did battle until they were killed in the same place. May God have mercy upon them both.

§ Fighting from a Sense of Commitment: Faris the Kurd

Some men fight out of integrity. An example of that is a Kurdish man called Faris who was like his name, a cavalier[170] – and what a cavalier! My father and uncle (may God have mercy upon them both) fought a battle with Ibn Mula'ib, who plotted against them and deceived them, for he had mustered and assembled troops while they were completely unprepared for what happened. The reason for this was that Ibn Mula'ib had sent a message to them, saying, 'Let's go over to Asfuna,[171] where there are some Franks, and capture it.' Our comrades got to Asfuna before him and, dismounting, attacked the fortress and began sapping the walls. As they were engaged in battle, Ibn Mula'ib arrived and seized the horses belonging to our companions who had dismounted. And so fighting broke out between them, after it had been directed at the Franks, and the fighting grew fiercer still.

Our Faris the Kurd fought furiously and was injured numerous times. But he continued fighting even though he ended up getting covered with wounds. Then the fighting ceased. My father and uncle (may God have mercy upon them both) passed by Faris as he was being carried away amidst our men. They stopped and congratulated him for surviving the melee.

To this, Faris replied, 'By God, I did not fight out of desire for well-being, but because I am under obligation to you for your many kindnesses and favours [96] and because I had never seen you in such unfortunate straits as you were during this battle. So I thought I should go into battle with you and be killed before you to reward you for your kindness.'

God (glory be to Him) determined that Faris should recover from those wounds. He then travelled on to Jabala, where Fakhr al-Mulk ibn 'Ammar[172] was based while the Franks held Latakia. It happened that a group of cavalry went from Jabala to make a raid on Latakia, while a group of cavalry went from Latakia to make a raid on Jabala. So the two sides encamped en route, with a hill standing between them. A Frankish horseman climbed the hill from their side to reconnoitre from the hill, while Faris the Kurd climbed up from the other side to reconnoitre for his comrades. The two horsemen encountered one another on the top of the hill, each one charging on his opponent. They exchanged spear-thrusts and both fell dead. The horses remained on the hill attacking one another while the two horsemen lay there dead.

That Faris left with us a son whose name was 'Allan. He was in the garrison and owned lovely horses and a splendid outfit, but he was not like his father. One day Tancred, lord of Antioch, encamped against us, fighting us before pitching his tents. This 'Allan, the son of Faris, was stationed on a small elevation, riding a lovely, sprightly steed, one of the nicest horses around. As he stood there utterly heedless, a Frankish horseman charged

him and thrust a spear into his horse's neck. The spear stuck
into the horse, so the horse reared and threw 'Allan. The Frank
then turned back, leading 'Allan's horse alongside him with the
spear still in its neck as if he were leading it like a saddle-horse,
swaggering off with his splendid bit of plunder.

§ *Speaking of Horses: Stout-Hearted Steeds*

Speaking of horses, it must be said that there are among them,
as among humans, both stout-hearted and faint-hearted speci-
mens. Here is an example of the former:

There was a Kurdish soldier in our garrison called Kamil the
Scarred, a man of courage, [97] piety and virtue (may God have
mercy upon him). He had a black charger, tough like a camel.
He once met a Frankish horseman in battle, and the Frank
thrust his spear into the horse around the collar-area. The force
of the blow caused the horse's neck to bend to one side so that
the spear came out through the base of the neck of the horse,
piercing the thigh of Kamil the Scarred and emerging from the
other side. Neither horse nor horseman was shaken by that
blow. I often saw that wound in his thigh after it had closed up
and healed, and it was the biggest scar. The horse recovered
and Kamil again rode him into battle, where he encountered
another Frankish horseman who thrust his spear into the forehead of the horse, making an indentation. But the horse was
not shaken and survived that second blow. After the wound
had closed up, if a person balled up his hand, there was enough
room for him to stick it into the forehead of the horse where
the indentation was.

Here's an amusing thing that happened with regard to that
horse. My brother 'Izz al-Dawla 'Ali (may God have mercy
upon him) bought the horse from Kamil the Scarred. After it
had started to slow down, he gave it away as part of the
rent for a village that we leased from a Frankish knight from
Kafartab. The horse remained with the knight for a year, and
then died. So the knight sent a messenger to us demanding we
pay its price.

We said, 'You bought it, you rode it and it died in your care.
What right do you have to demand its price?'

He replied, 'You must have given it something to drink so that it would die after a year!'

We were stunned by his ignorance and his weak-mindedness.

Once, a horse I was riding was wounded while attacking Homs. A spear-thrust split open its heart and a number of arrows struck him. But it carried me out of battle, its two nostrils gushing blood like the mouths of open water-skins, and I sensed nothing wrong with it. After I arrived in the midst of my comrades, it died.

Another horse I was riding in the district of Shayzar during a war with Mahmud ibn Qaraja was wounded three times. And by God, there I was, fighting mounted on it, without even knowing that it had been wounded, because I sensed nothing wrong with it at all.

§ Faint-Hearted Horses

As for faint-hearted horses and their weakness when wounded, here is an example.

The army of Damascus, which belonged to Shihab al-Din Mahmud ibn Buri, was encamped against [98] Hama, which belonged to al-Yaghisiyani, and I was there too. The Damascenes marched on us in large numbers. The governor of Hama at the time was al-Yaghisiyani's son Ahmad, who was on Tall Mujahid.[173]

The chamberlain Ghazi al-Talli[174] came to him and said, 'Our infantry is spread out all over the place – you can see their helmets shining among all the enemy tents. Any moment now the enemy will charge our men and annihilate them!'

'Then go and pull them back,' Ahmad replied.

'By God, the only ones who can pull them back are you and him,' the chamberlain said (referring to me).

So Ahmad said to me, 'You go and pull them back.'

So I pulled a hauberk off one of my attendants who was wearing it and put it on, rode out and, using my mace, I pulled our men back. I was riding a chestnut charger, one of the noblest-bred long-necked horses you ever saw. As I was pulling the men back, the enemy marched on us while there was not a single horseman outside the walls of Hama besides me. Some of our men fled into the city, thinking they would most certainly be captured; others marched beside my stirrup. Because of the narrowness of the place and the press of the crowd, when the enemy attacked us I had to rein in my horse while facing them, but when they turned around I would follow behind them cautiously. My horse was struck by an arrow in its leg, the arrow merely scratching it. But my horse fell to the ground with me astride it, then rose and fell again, with me beating it all the while.

One of the men in my escort said to me, 'Go into the barbican and mount another horse.'

I said, 'By God, I will not dismount!'

And thus it was that I observed a weakness in this horse that I never observed in any other.

§ *Another Stout-Hearted Horse*

Here is a good example of stout-heartedness in horses:

Tirad ibn Wahib al-Numayri took part in a battle of the [99] Banu Numayr. They had killed 'Ali ibn Salim ibn Malik, the governor of Raqqa, and had taken possession of the city. The battle was between them and this 'Ali's brother, Malik ibn Salim.[175] Tirad ibn Wahib was riding a horse belonging to a noble breed, a horse of great value. It was struck by a spear in its side and its entrails were hanging out of it, but it continued to fight until the battle subsided. The horse returned to Raqqa with Tirad and then died.

§ *Usama Receives a Gift-Horse*

This discussion of horses has reminded me of something that happened to me with al-Yaghisiyani (may God have mercy upon him). It took place like this: the King of Amirs, the atabeg Zangi (may God have mercy upon him), encamped against Damascus in the year 530 (1135), in the territory of Darayya.[176] The lord of Baalbek, Jamal al-Din Muhammad (may God have mercy upon him), had sent a message to Zangi notifying him that he would join him, and so he left Baalbek intending to enter the service of the atabeg.[177] The atabeg was informed that the army of Damascus was marching out to capture Jamal al-Din, so he told al-Yaghisiyani that we were to ride out to meet up with Jamal al-Din and keep the Damascenes at bay. Al-Yaghisiyani's messenger came to me during the night to say, 'Saddle up!' My tent was next to his, and he had already mounted and was positioned in front of his tent.

I mounted up that very instant, and he asked me, 'Did you know already that I had saddled up?'

'No, by God,' I said.

At which he said, 'But I just now sent the order to you and yet you were mounted and ready this very instant.'

'My lord,' I replied, 'my horse always eats his barley and then my groom bridles him and sits at the door of my tent with the reins in his hand. Meanwhile, I put on my gear and strap on my sword and sleep. When your messenger came to me there was nothing to delay me.'

Al-Yaghisiyani remained in his place until a part of the army had assembled before him. He then said, 'Put on your armour.' Most of the men present did so while I stood by his side.

He then said, 'How many times do I have to say "Put on your [100] armour"?'

'My lord,' I said, 'you don't mean me?'

'Yes!' he replied.

'But, by God,' I objected, 'I can't put on anything more! It is still the early part of the night, and my *kazaghand* has two layers of mail. When I see the enemy, I'll put it on.'

Al-Yaghisiyani fell silent and we started out.

When morning broke, we were at Dumayr.[178]

So al-Yaghisiyani said to me, 'Why don't we dismount here and eat something? This staying up all night has made me hungry.'

'It's up to you,' I replied. So we dismounted.

But no sooner had we set foot on the ground than he said, 'Where's your *kazaghand*-armour?'

At my order, my attendant brought it. I took it out of its leather bag and, pulling out my knife, I ripped open a bit at its chest and revealed the side with the two coats of mail. It had a Frankish coat of mail extending to its hem, with another above it extending as far as the middle. Both had all the linings, felt pads, rough silk and rabbit fur. Al-Yaghisiyani then turned to one of his attendants and said something to him in Turkish – I didn't understand what he was saying. The servant presently brought before al-Yaghisiyani a horse that the atabeg had given him once upon a time, a dark chestnut charger looking like a block of granite quarried from the summit of some mountain. 'This horse', he said to his attendant, 'befits that *kazaghand*. Deliver it to the attendant of this man.' And so he delivered it to the attendant of yours truly.

§§ *Digression: Testing Usama's Presence of Mind*

My uncle Sultan (may God have mercy upon him) used to make sure that I kept my presence of mind during battle and would put me to the test with questions. One day we were engaged in some war or another that had broken out between us and the lord of Hama, who had mustered and assembled troops, stationing them in one of the villages of Shayzar, burning and looting. So my uncle selected about sixty or seventy horsemen from the army and told me, 'Take these men and set out against the enemy.' We headed out at full gallop and soon encountered the vanguard of their cavalry. But we broke them, thrust our spears at them and dislodged them from the position that they had occupied.

I then dispatched [101] one of the horsemen in my company with a message for my uncle and father (may God have mercy upon them both), who had taken up position with the rest of the army, including numerous infantrymen. 'Move out with the infantry,' I said in my message to the two of them, 'for I've broken the enemy.' And so they marched out to me, and when they came near we charged together on the enemy and destroyed them. The enemy launched their horses into the Sharuf,[179] which was in full spate, and swam across it. They went off and we returned home victorious. My uncle then asked me, 'What was that message you sent to me?'

'I sent a messenger to tell you, "Advance with the infantry, for I have broken the enemy",' I answered.

'And whom did you send?' he asked.

'Rajab al-'Abd,' I replied.

'Correct,' he said. 'I see that you kept your presence of mind and didn't get flustered by battle.'

On another occasion, we and the army of Hama were fighting one another, and Mahmud ibn Qaraja had secured the assistance of the army of his brother Khir-Khan ibn Qaraja,[180] lord of Homs, against us. At the time, people had just started using compound spears,[181] in which one spear was attached to part of another, thereby increasing its length to eighteen or twenty cubits. In position facing me was a detachment of their cavalry, while I was at the head of a band of about fifteen horsemen. Presently, 'Alwan the Iraqi charged at us – he was one of their true cavaliers and braves. But when he got close to us and saw that we weren't budging, he turned back, pointing his spear behind him. I noticed that it was like a rope dragging on the ground and that he wouldn't be able to lift it back up. So I launched my charger upon him and thrust my spear into him, even though he had arrived back among his comrades. I turned around, the enemy banners fluttering above my head. But my comrades, among them my brother Baha' al-Dawla Munqidh (may God have mercy upon him), confronted the enemy and repulsed them. When I struck that blow, half of my weapon snapped off in 'Alwan's *kazaghand*.

We happened to be alongside my uncle, who was observing me. So when the battle ceased, my uncle asked me, 'Where did you strike 'Alwan the Iraqi with your spear?'

[102] 'I meant to hit him in the back,' I replied, 'but the wind pulled at my spear's streamer and it landed on his side instead.'

'Correct,' he said. 'I see that you kept your presence of mind that time.'

§§ *Digression: Usama's Father Encourages him*

[103] I never knew my father (may God have mercy upon him) to forbid me from fighting or riding out into danger despite all the concern and preference he showed me. I observed this in him on one particular day. At the time, there were some hostages – some Frankish and Armenian knights – with us at Shayzar that Baldwin, king of the Franks, had offered as security for the terms of his own release that he had set with Timurtash[182] (may

God have mercy upon him). They paid the amount they owed, but while they were making ready to return to their territory, Khir-Khan, the lord of Homs, sent a body of cavalry to lie in ambush for them outside Shayzar. When the hostages set out, the cavalry fell on them, capturing them. The alarm was sounded, so my uncle and father (may God have mercy upon them both) rode out and took their position, sending off everyone who came to them to pursue the hostages. I myself arrived and my father said to me, 'Follow them with whatever men you have with you – launch yourselves upon them and rescue your hostages!'

So I set off in pursuit and caught sight of them after galloping for the better part of the day. I rescued the hostages they had with them and even captured some of the cavalry of Homs. I was struck by my father's words, 'Launch yourselves upon them!'

One time I was with him (may God have mercy upon him) while he was standing in the courtyard of his home. A gigantic snake had stuck its head out on the frieze atop the arched portico that was in the courtyard, and my father was standing there looking at it. I went and carried over a ladder that was on one side of the courtyard, leaned it up just below the snake and climbed up to it – all the while my father watched me and never forbade me. I took out a little knife from my waist and poked it into the neck of the snake while it slept – with less than a cubit between it and [104] my face. I started cutting into its head but the snake slid out and wrapped itself around my wrist until I cut its head off and threw its body down to the courtyard, dead.

However, one time I did see my father (may God have mercy upon him) act differently. We had gone out one day to kill a lion that had appeared near the Bridge.[183] When we arrived, the lion attacked us from the thicket it was in. It menaced the horses, then stopped while my brother Baha' al-Dawla Munqidh (may God have mercy upon him) and I stood between the lion and the detachment of men that my father and uncle were in (may God have mercy upon them both), which also included a body of troops. The lion had by then gone and crouched along the edge of the river and was beating the ground with its chest and roaring. So I attacked it. My father (may God have mercy upon him) shouted at me, 'You lunatic! Don't go any-where near it! It'll get you!' But I thrust my spear at it and no, by God, it didn't budge from its place and it died on the spot. My father never forbade me to fight other than on that one day.

§ *The Varieties of Creation: A Soldier Dies from a Trifling Wound*

God, the Mighty and Majestic, made His creatures of various sorts,[184] differing in temperament and nature: the white and the black, the beautiful and the ugly, the tall and the short, the strong and the weak, the valorous and the craven – all in accordance with His wisdom and the universality of His power.

I saw a son of one of the Turkoman amirs who was in the service of the atabeg Zangi (may God have mercy upon him) when an arrow struck him, though it did not penetrate his skin deeper than a grain of barley. He went all loose, his limbs buckled, his ability to speak left him and he lost consciousness. And yet he was a man like a lion, as massive of body as ever a man could be. They brought the physician and the surgeon over to him. The physician said, 'Don't worry about him for now. But if he gets wounded again, he'll die.' So the man calmed down and began riding and conducting himself just as he used to. But after a short time another arrow struck him, even feebler and less harmful than the first, and he died.

§ *A Man Foretells his own Death by a Hornet-Sting*

[105] I once saw something else like that. At Shayzar there were two brothers, called the Banu Majaju. One was named Abu al-Majd, the other Muhasin, and they were renting Bridge Mill for eight hundred dinars. Near the mill, there was a slaughtering-place where the butchers of the town used to kill sheep and where hornets would swarm because of the blood. One day, when Muhasin passed by the mill, a hornet stung him. He suddenly went stiff, his ability to speak left him and

he seemed on the brink of death. He remained that way for a bit, but then he regained consciousness and for a while afterwards stopped going to the mill. So his brother Abu al-Majd chided him, saying, 'Brother, we've got this mill for eight hundred dinars and you won't even look over it or check it out! Someday we'll be short on our rent and we'll both die in prison!'

At this, Muhasin exclaimed, 'You just want another hornet to sting and kill me!'

And the next morning he went to the mill, where a hornet stung him, and he died.

Thus may the most harmless things kill if your allotted time is up, and an omen may employ speech as its agent.[185]

§ Another Predicts a Lion will Seek him Out

Here is another example of this. It came to our attention that a lion had appeared in the territory of Shayzar. We rode out to it and we found an attendant belonging to the amir Sabiq ibn Waththab,[186] named Shammas, pasturing his horse in the same place.

My uncle asked him, 'Where's the lion?'

'In those grasslands,'[187] he replied.

'Get in front of me and let's go over to it,' my uncle ordered.

'You just want the lion to jump out and take me!' he responded, but walked in front of him. The lion then came out as if he was sent on purpose to Shammas, and it took him and killed him out of all the other people there. But the lion, too, was killed.

§ Lions have their Braves and Cowards too: Three Stalwart Specimens

[106] I have seen lions do things I never thought they could do. Yet I would never have believed that lions, like men, have among them the brave and the cowardly. Here is an example:

One day our horse-herdsman[188] came to us at full gallop and said, 'There are three lions in the thickets at Tall al-Tulul!' So we mounted up and rode over there and what should we find but a lioness, with two lions behind it. As we reconnoitred that thicket, the lioness came out and attacked the men but then stopped. My brother Baha' al-Dawla Munqidh (may God have mercy upon him) thrust at the lioness with his spear and killed her, snapping his spear in her body.

We returned to the thicket and one of the two lions came out at us and chased away the horses. My brother Baha' al-Dawla and I stopped in its path as it returned from chasing off the horses. For whenever a lion leaves a place, it is sure to return to it, no doubt about it. We turned the rumps of our horses towards the lion and pointed our spears backwards in its direction, since we expected that it would make straight for us and we would then stick our spears in it and kill it. But all of a sudden it passed by us like the wind and made for one of our comrades called Sa'dallah al-Shaybani. The lion struck his horse and brought it down. I struck at it, thrusting my spear right in its middle, and it died on the spot.

We then turned back to the other lion, accompanied by about twenty men from our Armenian troops, the finest archers. Out came the other lion walking, the biggest of the lot. The Armenians kept it at bay with arrows, while I was positioned to one side of the Armenians expecting the lion to attack them and grab one of them, at which I would thrust my spear at it. But it kept walking forward. Every time an arrow would fall on it, it would roar and thrash its tail and I would say, 'Now it's going to attack!' But then it would walk forward again. It carried on like this until it fell down dead.

So I observed in that lion something I would never have expected.

§ A Cowardly Lion

I later witnessed something even more marvellous than that in another lion. In the city of Damascus, there was a lion cub that a lion-keeper raised until it became full-grown and began chasing [107] horses and thereby caused damage to some people. The amir Mu'in al-Din (may God have mercy upon him) was told while I was in his presence, 'This lion has caused damage to people. The horses bolt away from it when it is in the road.'

The lion used to spend day and night on a bench near the

residence of Mu'in al-Din. So Mu'in al-Din said, 'Tell the lion-keeper to bring it here.'

He then said to the table-master,[189] 'Bring out a sheep from the animals to be slaughtered for the kitchen and leave it in the inner courtyard so we can see how the lion destroys it.'

And so he brought a sheep out to the courtyard. Then the lion-keeper entered with the lion accompanying him. The moment the sheep saw the lion – the lion-keeper having released it from the chain that was around its neck – it charged the lion and butted at it. The lion fled and took to circling the pool,[190] while the sheep was behind it chasing it and butting at it. We were overcome with laughter. The amir Mu'in al-Din said, 'This is an ill-omened lion! Take it away, slaughter it, flay it and bring me its hide.'

And so they slew the lion and flayed it. As for the sheep, it was granted a full pardon[191] from being slaughtered.

§ A Dog Attacks a Lion

Here is another example of something marvellous about lions. A lion appeared in our territory of Shayzar, so we went out against it. We were accompanied by some infantrymen from the troops of Shayzar, among them an attendant of the senile old fool[192] to whom the mountain folk give allegiance and practically worship. The attendant had a dog of his with him. The lion rushed out at the horses, which moved off from it, startled. The lion then fell upon the infantrymen. It grabbed that attendant and crouched on top of him. So the dog pounced on the back of the lion, which bolted away from the man and turned back to the thicket. The man then came up before my father (may God have mercy upon him) laughing, and assured him, 'By your life, my lord, it didn't injure me or cause me any harm.'

So they killed the lion. As for the man, he went back to his home and died that very night, not from any wound he received, but from his heart having stopped.

§ Lions Induce Fear in other Beasts

[108] I used to marvel at the intrepid spirit of that dog attacking the lion, for every animal shies away from lions and avoids

them. I have seen the head of a lion carried to one of our houses, at which cats were seen fleeing from the house in question and throwing themselves from the rooftops, without ever having seen a lion before. And when we skinned lions, we used to throw the body from the citadel down to the foot of the barbican and no dog or any kind of bird would come near it. And if ravens saw the carcass they would descend upon it, but as they got nearer they would caw and fly off. The fear that the lion induces in other animals is very similar to the fear that the eagle induces in other birds. For an eagle, if a chicken that has never seen an eagle before should catch sight of it, will cause the chicken to scream and flee. Such is the fear that God (may He be exalted) visits upon the hearts of animals for these two creatures.

§ A Lion-Slayer Killed by a Scorpion

On the subject of lions, among our companions we had two brothers called the Banu al-Ru'am, who were infantrymen and used to go back and forth from Shayzar to Latakia (Latakia once belonged to my uncle[193] 'Izz al-Dawla Nasr, and my uncle Sultan was stationed in it – may God have mercy upon them both) carrying the messages that passed between my two uncles. They told me:

> We left Latakia and looked down from al-Manda Pass, which is a high mountain-pass overlooking all the lowlands below it, and we saw a lion crouched along the river beneath the pass. So we stopped in our tracks, not daring to go down for fear of the lion. But then we saw a man approaching. We shouted at him and waved [109] our clothes at him to warn him about the lion, but he didn't hear us. He merely strung his bow, nocked an arrow in it and walked on. The lion saw him and pounced on him, but the man shot at him and didn't miss his heart – he killed it. He walked up to the lion and finished it off. Taking his arrow, he went to the river and pulled off his shoes, took his clothes off and climbed in to bathe. He climbed out to put on his clothes, as we watched, and he began shaking the water out of his hair to dry it. Then

he put on one of his shoes and leaned over on his side. He was leaning there for a long time, so we said, 'By God, he didn't do too badly. But who's he showing off to?'

We went down to him while he remained in the same position, and we found that he was dead. We couldn't tell what had got him. So we took off the one shoe from his foot and – guess what? – there was a tiny scorpion inside that had stung him on his big toe, and he had died instantly. We marvelled at this giant who killed a lion yet was himself killed by a scorpion as small as his finger. Glory be to God the Almighty, whose will is ever executed among His creatures!

§ *Observations on the Behaviour of Lions*

As I was saying: I have fought with lions on countless occasions. I killed a number of them without anyone accompanying me, just as I killed a number accompanied by other people, until I became an experienced lion-hunter and came to know things about fighting lions that others don't know. For example, I know that the lion, like all wild beasts, fears humans and flees from them. The lion is stupid and witless, as long as it is not wounded. But when it is wounded, it becomes a *real* lion; at that time, one should be very afraid. Whenever it sets out from a forest or thicket to attack horses, it is sure to return to the thicket it came out of, even if there are fires in its path. I came to know this through direct experience, and so whenever a lion would come out to attack the horses, I would position myself on the route of its return before it got wounded. And so, as it returned, I would leave it alone until it passed by me; only then would I thrust my spear at it and kill it.

§ *Usama Helps Kill a Leopard*

[110] As for leopards, fighting them is more difficult than fighting lions, thanks to their light-footedness and the long distances they can leap. In addition, leopards will go into caves and burrows like hyenas do, whereas lions will only go into forests and thickets. A leopard once appeared in our lands in a village in the district of Shayzar called Ma'arzaf.[194] So my uncle Sultan

(may God have mercy upon him) rode out there and sent a horseman to me while I was out riding on an errand of mine with a message: 'Meet me at Ma'arzaf.' So I met up with him and we went to the spot where they claimed the leopard was, but we didn't see it. There was a pit there, so I dismounted from my charger and, taking my *quntariya*-spear with me, I sat at the edge of the pit. It was shallow, about the height of a man, and in its side there was a hole which looked like a burrow. So I poked my spear in that hole that was in the pit, and the leopard stuck its head out of that hole to take hold of the spear. Once we had determined that the leopard was there, a few of my comrades climbed down with me. Some of us began poking our spears into that spot, so that when the leopard came out the other man would stab it with his spear. Every time the leopard tried to climb out of the pit, we would stick it with our spears until we killed it. It was a massive creature. It's just that it had eaten so many of the animals of the village that it was unable to defend itself.

§ *The Holy-Warrior Leopard*

Of all the animals, the leopard alone can jump more than forty cubits. In the church at Hunak,[195] there was a window forty cubits in height above the floor. A leopard used to go there during the hottest part of the day, jump up to the window and sleep there until the end of the day, then jump down and go away. At the time, the landlord[196] of Hunak was a Frankish knight called Sir Adam, a real devil of a Frank. He was told the story of the leopard, and he said, 'When you see the leopard, inform me of it.'

The leopard came as usual and jumped up to that window, so one of the peasants went and informed Sir Adam. Sir Adam put on his hauberk, mounted his charger, took up his shield and spear and went off to the church, which was in ruins except for one standing wall where the window was located. When [111] the leopard saw Sir Adam, it pounced down from the window on top of him while Sir Adam was still on his charger and broke his back, killing him. It then went away. The peasants of Hunak used to call that leopard 'the holy-warrior leopard'.[197]

One of the special qualities of the leopard is that if it wounds a man, and a mouse urinates on the wound, the man will die. A mouse never gives up trying to reach a man wounded by a leopard: one person, out of fear of the mice, even had a bed made for himself sitting in the water, with cats tied all around it.

§ Cheetahs versus Leopards: Let the Buyer Beware

It is practically impossible to tame a leopard or to get it to be friendly with people. One time, I was passing through the city of Haifa on the coast, while it was held by the Franks. One of the Franks asked me, 'You want to buy a nice cheetah?'

'Yes,' I replied. So he brought me a leopard that he had raised until it had grown to the size of a dog.

'No,' I said, 'this doesn't suit me. This is a leopard, not a cheetah.' But I marvelled at that leopard's tameness and demeanour with the Frank.

The difference between the leopard and the cheetah is that the face of the leopard is long like the face of a dog and its eyes are pale, whereas the face of the cheetah is round, and its eyes are black.

§ A Leopard Runs Amok at a Drinking-Party

A man from Aleppo captured a leopard and brought it in a sack to the lord of Qadmus, which belonged to one of the Banu Muhriz.[198] The latter was engaged in a drinking party at the time. So the man opened the sack and the leopard came out and attacked the people in the sitting-room. As for the lord, he was near an opening in the tower, so he went in through it and closed the door. The leopard roamed through the house, killing some and wounding others until they killed it.

§ An Encounter with a 'Tiger'

[112] I have heard, though I have not seen it, that there is a variety of wild beast called a tiger. I didn't really believe in them, but the sheikh and imam Hujjat al-Din Abu Hashim Muhammad ibn Muhammad ibn Zafar[199] (may God have mercy upon him) told me:

I once went to the Maghrib accompanied by an elderly attendant who used to belong to my father and who had travelled and experienced things. Our supply of water ran out and we were struck with thirst. There was no third person with us, just the two of us, him and me, riding two well-bred camels. We made directly for a well on our route, but we found that there was a tiger by it, sleeping, so we withdrew. My companion dismounted from his camel, handed me its reins and took up his sword and shield and a water-skin we had. He said to me, 'Hold tight to the head of the camel,' and he walked towards the well. When the tiger saw him it stood up and jumped, facing him so that it could pass by him. Then it let out a growl and some cubs rushed out at full speed to join it. It neither blocked our way nor caused us any harm. So we drank, replenished our water supply and then went on our way.

This is what he told me (may God have mercy upon him), and he was one of the most religious and learned Muslims.

§ *A Marvel of Destiny: The Byzantine Siege of Shayzar*

[113] One of the marvels of destiny occurred when the Romans came down against Shayzar in the year 532 (1138). They positioned against it some terrifying mangonels that they had brought with them from their country for hurling heavy payloads. Their stones, weighing twenty or twenty-five *ratls*,[200] could be launched a distance greater than any arrow could fly. One time they hurled a piece of a millstone at the house of a companion of mine called Yusuf ibn Abi al-Gharib (may God have mercy upon him), levelling the house from top to bottom with one stone.

On top of the tower in the amir's residence, there was a spear with a banner attached to it. The path within the citadel that the people took ran right under it. It happened that a stone from a mangonel hit the spear and snapped it in two, and the broken half with the spear-head flipped over, spun around and fell into the path just as one of our comrades was crossing it.

The spear-head, attached to the spear fragment, fell from a great height right through his clavicle and into the ground and killed him.

Khutlukh, a *mamluk* belonging to my father (may God have mercy upon him), related the following account to me:

> During the Roman siege, we were sitting in the hallway of the citadel with our gear and swords when suddenly an old man came [114] running up to us, saying, 'Muslims! Your women! The Romans have come in right on our heels!' So we grabbed our swords and went out. We discovered that they had climbed up through a hole that the mangonels had punched into the wall. We beat them with our swords until we expelled them, and then went out in pursuit and delivered them to their comrades. Then we came back and dispersed.
>
> I remained with the old man who had sounded the alarm. He stood there, and then turned about to face the wall to relieve himself, so I turned away from him. Next, I heard a loud crash, turned around and, lo and behold, the old man had been struck on the head by a mangonel-stone, which crushed his skull and pinned him so that his brains ran down the wall. So I carried him away and we prayed over him and buried him on the spot, may God have mercy upon him.

A mangonel-stone also struck one of our comrades and broke his leg. So we carried him to my uncle as he was sitting in the hallway of the citadel. He said, 'Go get the bone-setter.'

At Shayzar there used to be an artisan called Yahya, who was skilled at bone-setting. He presented himself, sat down and began setting that man's leg-bones, in a recess just outside the gate of the citadel. But another stone struck that injured man on the head, smashing it to pieces. The bone-setter returned to the hallway, so my uncle said, 'You've really set his bones quickly!'

'My lord,' he replied, 'a second stone came and absolved him of the need for any bone-setting.'

§ The Franks March on Damascus[201]

Here is an example of the execution of the divine will in the fates and lifespans of humankind. The Franks (may God confound them) unanimously agreed to march on Damascus and capture it.[202] So they assembled a large host and the lord of Edessa and Tell Bashir joined them, as did the lord of Antioch.[203] The lord of Antioch encamped at Shayzar on his way to Damascus. The Franks had already haggled between themselves for the houses in Damascus, [115] its baths and its bazaars, and the burgesses[204] had in turn purchased all this from them and paid out their prices – so little did they doubt that they would conquer the city and possess it. At that time, Kafartab belonged to the lord of Antioch, who now selected and removed one hundred horsemen from his army and ordered them to stay in Kafartab to ward off any attacks from us or from Hama. When the lord of Antioch left for Damascus, all the Muslims of Syria assembled to march on Kafartab. They sent one of our comrades called Qunayb ibn Malik to spy on Kafartab for them during the night. He went to the town, had a look around and returned, telling us, 'Rejoice! We can collect our plunder in complete safety.'

So the Muslims marched against the enemy there and met in battle at Mudhkin.[205] God (glory be to Him) granted victory to Islam and they killed all the Franks. Qunayb, who had spied on Kafartab for them, had spotted a large number of animals in the town's fosse. When they defeated the Franks and killed them, he wanted to capture those animals, hoping to obtain the plunder all for himself. So he set off at full gallop to the fosse. But a Frankish soldier hurled a stone at him from the citadel and killed him.

He left with us his mother, an old woman, who was a public wailer at our funerals[206] and who now wailed for her own son. When she would keen over her son Qunayb, her breasts would flow with milk, wetting her clothes. But when she stopped her keening, and her broken heart was quiet, her breasts became again like two pieces of skin without a drop of milk in them.

Glory be to He who permeates our hearts with tenderness for our children!

When the lord of Antioch, who was just then attacking Damascus, was told 'The Muslims have killed your comrades', he said, 'That's not true. I left a hundred horsemen behind at Kafartab who can handle all the Muslims put together.'

But God (glory be to Him) decreed that the Muslims at Damascus would be victorious over the Franks and would inflict upon them [116] a great slaughter, capturing all their animals. And so the Franks left Damascus on a most miserable and contemptible journey – praise be to God, the Lord of the Worlds!

§ A Kurd Takes his Brother's Head as a Trophy

One of the marvels that occurred during that battle with the Franks was the following. In the army of Hama, there were two Kurdish brothers, one of them named Badr and the other named 'Annaz. Now, this 'Annaz had bad eyesight. And when the Franks were defeated and killed, some of the men cut off their heads and hung them off their saddle-straps. So 'Annaz cut off a head and hung it from his saddle-strap.

A group of men from the army of Hama saw him and said to him, 'Hey, 'Annaz, what's with that head you have with you?'

'Glory be to God,' he replied, 'for what happened between this man and me – I killed him.'

'Oh, man,' they told him, 'that's the head of your brother Badr!'

So he looked at the head, examining it. Sure enough, it was the head of his brother. And so in his shame before the men, he left Hama. We never knew where he set off for, nor did we ever hear any further news of him. But it was the Franks who killed his brother Badr during that battle, may God the Exalted confound them.

§ Tales of Sharp Swords: Isma'ilis Attack Shayzar

The blow of the mangonel-stone upon that old man's head[207] (may God have mercy upon him) has reminded me of the blows of sharp swords. Here is an example. When the Isma'ilis made an attempt on the citadel of Shayzar,[208] one of our comrades called Hammam the Pilgrim encountered one of the Isma'ilis in a portico in the residence of my uncle (may God have mercy upon him). The Isma'ili had a knife in his hand and Hammam had a sword. The Batini[209] charged at him with his knife, but Hammam struck him with his sword above the eyes. He cut through the top of his skull and his brains fell out, spattering and spreading out on the ground. Hammam then threw the sword from his hand and vomited up everything in his stomach, stricken with nausea at seeing those brains.

[117] On the same day, one of them came at me with a long knife in his hand, while I had one of my swords. He charged at me with his knife, but I struck him in the middle of his forearm as he grasped the handle of the knife, its blade held back close to his raised arm. A length of four finger-widths was cut from the blade of the knife and his forearm was cut in half, clear off. The traces of that knife-blade remained ever afterwards on the edge of my sword. An artisan in our town saw it and said, 'I can get rid of that dent there.'

But I said, 'Leave it as it is. It's the best thing about the sword.' Even today, when someone looks at that sword they know it is the mark of that knife.

§ *How the Sword al-Jami'i got its Name*

That same sword has another tale that I will tell. My father (may God have mercy upon him) had a groom called Jami'. Once, the Franks made a raid on us, so my father put on his *kazaghand*-armour and left his house to mount up. But he could not find his horse, so he stood there for a while, waiting. Eventually Jami' the groom, who had been delayed, arrived with the horse. My father struck him with this same sword while it was still hanging from his waist in its scabbard. The blade cut through the scabbard-trappings, the silver scabbard-tip and the thick garment and woollen mantle that the groom was wearing, and then through the bone of his elbow. His forearm fell to the ground. As a result, my father (may God have mercy upon him) supported this groom and his children after him on account of this wound. That sword was named al-Jami'i after that groom.

§ Another Noteworthy Sword-Blow: The Lord of Abu Qubays

Among other noteworthy sword-blows is the following:

Four brothers related to the amir Iftikhar al-Dawla Abi al-Futuh ibn 'Amrun, the lord of Abu Qubays Castle,[210] went up to see him in the castle as he slept and covered him with wounds. There was no one else with him in the castle except his son. They then went out, thinking they had killed him, and went looking for his son. Now, God had granted this Iftikhar al-Dawla amazing physical strength. So he rose up from his bed [118] all undressed, took his sword, which was hanging there in his house, and went out to get the four brothers. One of them, the most intrepid and courageous of the bunch, came and confronted him. So Iftikhar al-Dawla struck him with his sword and then jumped to one side, fearing that his opponent might get him with the knife that he held. When he turned around, he saw that his foe was flat on the ground, the sword-blow having killed him. He then went on to the second man and, striking a blow on him, killed him. The two remaining men fled, throwing themselves from the castle. One of them died as a result, but the other escaped.

Once we heard the news about this in Shayzar, we sent a messenger to congratulate Iftikhar al-Dawla on his safety. Three days later, we went up to Abu Qubays Castle to visit him, since his sister lived with my uncle Sultan and he had children by her. He related his story to us and how the whole thing happened. Then he said, 'The back of my shoulder is itching, but I can't get at it.' So he called an attendant of his to have a look at the spot to see what sort of thing had bitten him. The attendant examined it, and what do you know, but it was a cut in which was stuck the head of a dagger that had broken off in his back. He hadn't even known it was there nor did he feel it until it started generating pus and began to itch.

Such was the physical strength of this man that he could grab a mule by its ankle and beat it without its being able to free its foot from his grasp. He could take a horseshoe nail between his fingers and drive it into a board of oak wood, too. His appetite was like his strength – no, even greater!

§ A Brief Exposition on the Franks of Antioch

So far, I have mentioned something of the deeds of men, so I will now mention something of the deeds of women after a brief exposition by way of introduction.[211]

§ Roger of Antioch and the Field of Blood

Antioch belonged to a real devil of the Franks called Roger.[212] This Roger went on pilgrimage to Jerusalem, whose lord was Baldwin [119] the Prince.[213] Baldwin was then an old man, while Roger was still a youth. Roger said to Baldwin, 'Let's make a contract between us. If I die before you, Antioch will be yours, but if you die before me, Jerusalem will be mine.' So they agreed upon this and bound themselves to it.

Now God (may He be exalted) decreed that Il-Ghazi (may God have mercy upon him) should meet Roger in battle at Danith on Thursday, 5 Jumada al-Ula in the year 513 (14 August 1119),[214] and kill him, as well as all of his army. Fewer than twenty of their men made it back to Antioch. So Baldwin travelled to Antioch and took control of it.

Forty days later, Baldwin stationed his battle-lines against Il-Ghazi. Now, when Il-Ghazi used to drink wine, he would be drunk for twenty days. And he took to drink after destroying the Franks and killing them, going on a drunken spree from which he never recovered until the day King Baldwin the Prince arrived in Antioch at the head of his army.

§ Tughdakin Beheads Robert FitzFulk after the Second Battle of Danith

The second battle between these two was a draw. Some Franks defeated some Muslims, and some Muslims defeated some Franks. A number of men from both sides were killed. The Muslims took captive Robert, the lord of Sahyun, Balatunus[215] and that area. He was a friend of the atabeg Tughdakin, the lord [120] of Damascus at that time, and had been with Il-Ghazi when he joined with the Franks at Apamea when the army of the East arrived under Bursuq.[216] This Robert the Leper had said to the atabeg Tughdakin, 'I don't know how best to offer you my hospitality. However, I give you permission to use my lands. You may let your horsemen pass through them and they may take whatever they find, as long as you do not kill anyone or take them captive. But animals, money, crops: those they have full permission to take.'

Now, when Robert was taken prisoner – and the atabeg Tughdakin had been present at the battle assisting Il-Ghazi – he set for himself a ransom of ten thousand dinars. So Il-Ghazi said, 'Take him to the atabeg. Maybe he can frighten him into raising his ransom for us.'

So they took Robert to the atabeg, who was in his tent drinking. When Tughdakin saw Robert approaching, he stood up, tucked the hem of his robe up under his belt, grabbed his sword, ran out and struck off his head. Il-Ghazi sent a messenger to the atabeg to reproach him, saying, 'We need every single dinar to pay our Turkoman troops. And this man, who had set his ransom at ten thousand dinars, we sent him to you so you could scare him and he might raise his ransom. And you killed him!'

Tughdakin replied, 'I can't think of a better way to scare someone.'

§ Baldwin II Becomes Regent of Antioch

And so Baldwin the Prince took possession of Antioch. My uncle and father (may God have mercy upon them both) had him under a great obligation to them dating from the time when he was the prisoner of Nur al-Dawla Balak (may God have mercy upon him). After Balak was killed, Baldwin came into the possession of Timurtash,[217] who brought him to us in Shayzar so that my uncle and my father (may God have mercy upon them both) might act as middlemen in ransoming him. They both treated him [121] kindly. Now, when Baldwin took control, we owed the lord of Antioch an indemnity, but Baldwin exempted us from paying it.[218] Moreover, we gained a certain influence in Antioch.

§ Bohemond II Arrives and Becomes
Lord of Antioch

And so Baldwin was occupying himself with his own affairs –
and one of our messengers was there with him – when a ship
arrived at al-Suwaydiya,[219] carrying a youth dressed in shabby
clothes. He came into the presence of Baldwin and made him
know that he was the son of Bohemond.[220] Baldwin therefore
ceded Antioch to him and went out of the city, pitching his
tents outside the town. That messenger of ours who was there
with him swore to us that he (that is, King Baldwin) bought the
fodder for his horses that very night in the marketplace, while
the official granaries of Antioch were full of grain. Baldwin
then returned to Jerusalem.

§ Bohemond II Misses an Opportunity

That devil, the son of Bohemond, turned out to be a great
affliction for our people. One day, he encamped against us at
the head of his army and pitched his tents. We had already
ridden out to face them, but not a single one of them attacked
us. They just remained in their tents, while we remained in the
saddle on an elevated spot from which we could observe them,
with the Orontes between us. So my cousin Layth al-Dawla
Yahya (may God have mercy upon him) left our group and
went down to the Orontes – we assumed he was going to water
his horse. But he waded into the water, crossed over and headed
for a band of Franks standing near their tents. As he approached
them, a single knight came down towards him. The two now
charged at each other, but they both swerved away from the
spear-thrust of the other. I immediately sped towards them with
some of my young peers. The rest of the band now came down
and the son of Bohemond and his army also took to their horses
and poured down on us like a torrent. In the meantime, my
cousin's horse had been wounded by a spear-blow.

The vanguard of our cavalry soon met [122] theirs. Now, in
our troops there was a Kurdish man named Mika'il, who came
fleeing before the vanguard of the enemy cavalry, and behind
him was a Frankish knight who was sticking close to him in

pursuit. The Kurd was running right in front of him, howling and screaming at the top of his lungs. So I intercepted the Frank, who turned away from that Kurdish horseman and darted off my path, heading for some horsemen in a group of our men positioned beyond us along the river. I went in hot pursuit, struggling to make my charger catch up with him so I might thrust my spear into him. But I could not catch up. That Frank did not look back at me until he reached our horsemen, although I pursued him, his only desire being those assembled horsemen. My companions now attacked his charger and pinned him down with their spear-thrusts, but his comrades followed after him and they outnumbered us. So now the Frankish knight turned back, his charger on its last legs, and met his comrades and ordered them all to withdraw. And so he went back, accompanied by his comrades. That knight was none other than the son of Bohemond, the lord of Antioch. Being still a boy, his heart had become filled with terror. If he had just left his comrades behind, they would have routed us and chased us all the way back to town.

§ Deeds of Women: Burayka, the Witch of Shayzar

As all this was transpiring, an old female servant called Burayka, owned by one of our Kurdish comrades called 'Ali ibn Mahbub, was standing there in the midst of our horsemen on the bank of the river with a jar in her hand, filling it with water and giving it to our men to drink. Most of our comrades who were on that elevated spot, once they saw the Franks advancing in such numbers, rushed back towards the city. But that she-devil just stood there, unafraid of the fearsome events taking place.

I will now mention something concerning this Burayka, even though it's not the place for it, but conversation drifts from one topic to another. [123] Her master, 'Ali, was a pious man and never drank wine. One day he said to my father, 'By God, amir, I do not consider it licit to subsist on an official stipend. I will not subsist on anything other than what Burayka brings in.'

So this idiot thinks that that illicit profit was more lawful than the stipend by which he was employed![221]

This servant-woman had a son named Nasr, an older man, and he, along with another man called Baqiya ibn al-Usayfir, used to act as the supervisor of some lands that belonged to my father (may God have mercy upon him). This Baqiya related the following to me:

One night, I went into town on my way to my house on some errand I had to do. As I approached the town, I could see between the tombstones some sort of shape by the light of the moon, a shape neither human nor beast. So I stopped and stood a way off, in fright. But then I said to myself, 'I'm Baqiya, am I not? Should I be afraid of some solitary thing?' So I put down my sword,[222] leather shield and javelin and crept ahead, inch by inch. As I did so, I could hear a voice coming from that shape and some vulgar singing. Once I had got close to it, I pounced on top of it, holding my dagger in my hand. I grabbed on to it and what should it be but Burayka, head uncovered, hair all wild, sitting astride a reed, neighing and traipsing about the tombs. 'Shame on you!' I said. 'What are you getting up to at this hour in such a place?' 'I am practising black magic,' she replied. And so I said to her, 'May God abominate you and your magic, and out of all the crafts, may He abominate this craft of yours!'

§ The Bravery of Usama's Aunt

The strength of that bitch's spirit reminds me of the events that happened in connection with our women during the battle between us and the Isma'ilis, even though Burayka and our women were hardly of the same sort.

[124] On that day, the leader of the group of Isma'ilis, 'Alwan ibn Harrar, and my cousin Shabib (may God have mercy upon him) encountered one another in the citadel. Shabib was the same age as me and we were born on the very same day, Sunday, 27 Jumada al-Akhira in the year 488 (4 July 1095), though he had not seen battle prior to that day, whereas I had become a master of it.

'Alwan wanted to put Shabib under his obligation, so he said to him, 'Go back to your home, carry off whatever you can and get out of here. You won't be killed. We've already taken the castle.'

So Shabib returned to his house and said, 'If anyone has any valuable things, give them to me.' He said this to his aunt and his uncle's women. Every one of them gave him something.

As he was doing this, a figure suddenly entered the house wearing a mail hauberk and a helmet, with a sword and shield. When Shabib saw this figure, he felt certain of death. The figure threw off its helmet and behold! It was his aunt, the mother of his cousin Layth al-Dawla Yahya (may God have mercy upon him).

'What is it you are intending to do?' she asked him.

'I'm taking whatever I can carry and then I'll climb down from the castle on a rope and go and make my way in the world,' he replied.

'What a wicked thing you are doing! You would leave the daughters of your uncle and the rest of your household in the hands of these cotton-carders[223] and just take off? What sort of life would you be living, brought to shame in the eyes of your family and fleeing from them? Get out there and fight for your family until you are killed in their midst! And may God do something with you, and do it again!'[224]

And so she (may God have mercy upon her) prevented him from fleeing. After that, Shabib became one of our most noted horsemen.

§ *Women's Courage for the Sake of Honour:*
Usama's Mother

On that same day, my mother (may God have mercy upon her) distributed my swords and *kazaghand*-armour. She came to a sister of mine, an older woman, and said, 'Put on your shoes and covering.'

And so she got dressed and my mother took her to a balcony in my house that looked out over the river valley to the east, and made her sit [125] there while she took a seat at the entrance to the balcony.

God – glory be to Him – granted us victory over the enemy.

But when I came to my house in search of some of my weapons, I found nothing except the scabbards of the swords and the sacks for the *kazaghands*. So I asked, 'Mother, where are my weapons?'

'My son,' she replied, 'I gave the weapons to whoever would use them to fight for us. I didn't know if you were safe or not.'

I replied, 'And my sister? What is she doing here?'

'My son,' my mother replied, 'I made her sit here on the balcony while I took my seat just outside. That way, if I should see that the Batinis had reached us, I could push her off, throwing her down to the valley. For I would rather see her dead than see her a prisoner of peasants and wool-carders.'

I thanked her for that, and so did my sister, who prayed that God would reward my mother on her behalf. Their courage for the sake of honour is more intense than such courage among men.

§ Women's Disdain for Danger

On the same day, an old woman named Funun, who had been a servant-girl of my grandfather Sadid al-Mulk 'Ali (may God have mercy upon him), covered herself with her veil, took up a sword and went out into battle. And she kept at it until we were able to climb up and overpower the enemy. So no one can deny that noble women possess disdain for danger, courage for the sake of honour and sound judgment.

§ The Wisdom of Women: Usama's Grandmother and the Lion

At some other time, I went out on the hunt with my father (may God have mercy upon him). Now, my father was really passionate about hunting, and he had a collection of goshawks, peregrines, sakers, cheetahs and *zaghariya*-hounds[225] unlike anything anyone else had. He used to ride out at the head of forty horsemen who included his sons and his *mamluks*, each one of them experienced in the hunt, knowledgeable about the chase. He had at Shayzar two preferred hunting-grounds: one day he might ride to the marshes and streams to the west of town to hunt francolin, waterfowl, hare, gazelle, and to kill wild boar. On another day, he might ride to the hill south of town to hunt partridge and hare.

One day, when we were on the hill, the time came for the afternoon prayers. My father dismounted, so we all dismounted and prayed, each of us on our own. Suddenly, an attendant came galloping up and said, [126] 'There's a lion!' I therefore finished my prayers before my father (may God have mercy upon him), so that he couldn't prevent me from killing the lion. I mounted my horse with my spear by my side and charged at the lion. The lion faced me and let out a roar. My horse reared and my spear, because of its weight, fell out of my hand. The lion chased me for a good stretch, then turned back to the foot of the hill and stood there. It was one of the biggest lions I had ever seen, like the arch of a bridge, and ravenous. Every time we approached it, it would come down from the hill and chase after the horses, then return to its place. It never made a descent without leaving its mark on our comrades.

I saw it leap onto the haunches of the horse belonging to an attendant of my uncle called Bastakin Gharza, tearing the man's clothing and leggings with its claws. Then it returned to the hill. There was thus no way of getting at the lion until I climbed above it on the slope of the hill and then rushed my horse down upon it and thrust my spear at it, piercing it. I left the spear sticking in its side. The lion then rolled over onto the slope of the hill with the spear still in it. The lion died and the spear was broken. My father (may God have mercy upon him) was just standing there watching us; with him were the sons of his brother Sultan, who were keeping an eye on what happened, and they were just boys.

We carried off the lion and entered the town as night approached. In the dark of night, my grandmother on my father's side (may God have mercy upon them both) came to me, carrying a candle before her. She was a prodigiously old woman, nearly one hundred years of age. I had no doubt that she had come to congratulate me on my safety and to inform me of her joy at what I had done.

And so I met her and kissed her hand, but she said to me with annoyance and anger, 'My boy, what in the world brings you to face these trials where you risk your life and your horse, you break your weapons and you simply add to the bad feelings and ill-will towards you in your uncle's heart?'

'My lady,' I replied, 'I have only endangered myself today and on similar occasions to bring me closer to my uncle's heart.'

'No!' she said. 'By God, this does not bring you closer to him, but rather increases his estrangement from you and encourages his bad feelings and ill-will towards you.'

I learned then that she (may God have mercy upon her) was giving me wise counsel with these words and speaking the truth. By my life, these are indeed the mothers of men!

And, moreover, this old woman (may God have mercy upon her) was one of the most upright Muslims in her immaculate approach to religion, her piety, fasting and prayer. Once, I was present on the night of [127] Nisf Sha'ban[226] while she prayed in the home of my father. My father (may God have mercy upon him) was one of the finest chanters of the Book of God (may He be exalted), and he led his mother in prayer. My father was concerned for her and said, 'Mother, if you take a seat, you can still pray from a seated position.'

'My son,' she replied, 'are there enough days left in my life for me to live to see another night like this one? No, by God, I will not sit.' By then my father had reached seventy years of age while she had approached one hundred (may God have mercy upon her).

§ A Courageous Woman Kills her Bandit Husband

I was a witness to one marvellous example of the courage that women have for the sake of honour. There was a man among the companions of Ibn Mula'ib called 'Ali 'Abd ibn Abi al-Rayda', whom God (may He be exalted) had endowed with eyesight like that of Zarqa' al-Yamama.[227] He used to go on raids with Ibn Mula'ib and could spot a caravan coming a full day's distance away.

A fellow member of his gang, called Salim al-'Ijazi, passed into the service of my father after Ibn Mula'ib was killed.[228] He told me:

One day we went out on a raid and sent out 'Ali 'Abd ibn
Abi al-Rayda' early in the morning to act as a lookout for
us. He came back to us and said, 'Cheer up, everyone, for
soon we'll have some plunder! There's a long caravan
headed this way.' We looked, but we couldn't see a thing.
So we said, 'We don't see a caravan or anything else.' 'By
God,' he replied, 'I'm telling you I see a caravan! At the
front there are two horses with black spots on their foreheads, shaking their manes.' We stayed hidden in our
ambush until late afternoon. Then a caravan appeared
with two horses at the front, with black spots on their
foreheads. So we rushed out and captured the caravan.

Salim al-'Ijazi also told me the following tale:

One day we went out on a raid and 'Ali 'Abd ibn Abi
al-Rayda' went up to act as a lookout for us. But he fell
asleep, and before he knew it, a Turk from a detachment
[128] of Turks took him captive. They asked him, 'What's
your business?' 'I am a poor beggar,' he said, 'and I have
rented my camel to a merchant in a caravan. Give me your
hand in promise that you will return my camel to me and
I will lead you to the caravan.' So the leader of the Turks
gave him his hand. 'Ali walked along in front of them and
led them to where we were, lying in ambush. So we rushed
out at them and took them captive. As for 'Ali, he latched
on to the Turk that was in front of him and took his horse
and his gear. We carried off some nice plunder from them.

When Ibn Mula'ib was killed, that 'Ali 'Abd ibn Abi al-Rayda'
passed into the service of Theophilos the Frank, lord of Kafartab. He used to go out on raids with the Franks against the
Muslims and plunder them. He did as much harm to the
Muslims as he could, seizing their wealth and shedding their
blood, to the point of making the roads unsafe for travellers.

He had a wife at Kafartab, in the hands of the Franks, who
objected to what he did and tried to forbid him from doing so,
but he didn't stop. In the end, she sent for a relative of hers
from some village – her brother, I think – to come to her and

she hid him in the house until nightfall. Then they ganged up on her husband 'Ali and killed him and ran off with all his belongings. In the morning, she was with us at Shayzar. She said, 'On behalf of the Muslims, I was angry because of what this infidel was doing to them.' Thus, she gave the people a respite from that devil. We took special consideration for her, given what she did. She stayed with us and was treated with great generosity and respect.

§ *A Frankish Woman Fights Back*

There was an amir in Egypt named Nada al-Sulayhi,[229] who had two scars on his face. One went from his right eyebrow up to his hairline, the other from his left eyebrow up to his hairline. I asked him about them and he told me:

> When I was young, I used to go out on raids from Ascalon on foot. One day, I was on a raid on the road to Jerusalem hoping maybe to knock off some Frankish pilgrims. We came across a group of them. I encountered one of them, a man carrying a spear, with his woman behind him holding a small rough-ware jar with water in it. The man gave me this first spear-wound, at which point I hit him [129] and killed him. Then his wife advanced on me and struck me with that rough-ware jar in my face and made this other scar. Both of them left their mark on my face.

§ *Intrepid Women: A Shayzari Woman Captures Frankish Pilgrims*

Here is an example of the intrepid spirit of women. A group of Frankish pilgrims went on pilgrimage and, on their return, they passed through Rafaniya, which belonged to them at the time.[230] They then left it, making for Apamea. But during the night they got lost and wound up at Shayzar, which at that time did not have any town-walls. So they entered the town, and they were about seven, maybe eight hundred people including men, women and children. But the army of Shayzar had already left town in the company of my uncles Sultan and Fakhr al-Din Shafi' (may God have mercy upon them both) to meet

two brides whom my uncles had married. They were sisters of
the Banu Sufi family, originally of Aleppo. However, my father
(may God have mercy upon him) was in the citadel. It happened
that a man went outside the city on an errand during the night
and came across a Frank there. So he came back, grabbed his
sword and went out and killed him. Then he raised the alarm
throughout the town. The populace rushed out and attacked
the Franks, seizing what they could of their women, children,
silver and beasts of burden.

In Shayzar, there was a woman called Nadra bint Buzurmat,
the wife of one of our comrades. She went out with the rest of
the populace and took a Frank captive and brought him back
to her house. Then she went out and captured another one and
brought him back to her house, then went and captured
another. So three Frankish captives were collected at her house.
After taking what suited her from their possessions, she went
out and called for a group of her neighbours, who came and
killed them.

During the night, my two uncles and the troops arrived.
Now, some of the Franks had taken flight and so some of the
men from Shayzar had pursued and killed them in the hinterland of the town. The horses of my uncles' army, [130] in the
dark of the night, started stumbling over the dead bodies without knowing what they were stumbling over, until one of them
dismounted and noticed the corpses in the darkness. That terrified our men, who thought that the town had been taken by
surprise.

§ Franks do not Mix: From Queen-Mother to Shoemaker's Wife

That was a source of plunder that God (the Glorious, the
Almighty) bestowed upon our people. A number of serving-girls
were taken from the ranks of these prisoners and passed on to
the house of my father (may God have mercy upon him). But
the Franks (God curse them) are an accursed race that will not
become accustomed to anyone not of their own race. My father
spotted among them a lovely young serving-girl, so he said to
the manager of his household,[231] 'Bring this one into the baths,

repair her clothes and get her ready for a journey.' And so she was prepared. My father then handed her over to a servant of his and packed her off to the amir Malik ibn Salim, the lord of Qal'at Ja'bar, who was a friend of his.

My father wrote a message to him, explaining, 'We have captured some plunder from the Franks. I send you a share of it herewith.' Malik found the girl very agreeable, and he was pleased with her, and took her for his very own. In time she bore him a son, named Badran. Malik made him his heir apparent, and then he came of age and his father died. Badran then took control of the town and its populace, though his mother was the real power. She hatched a plot with a group of people and let herself down from the castle by a rope. The group of people took her to Saruj,[232] which belonged at that time to the Franks. So: she married a Frankish shoemaker, while her son was the lord of Qal'at Ja'bar!

§ A Frank Converts to Islam, Temporarily

Among those Frankish captives who passed into my father's household was an old woman accompanied by her daughter – a young woman, beautifully formed – and a son who had come of age. The son converted to Islam and was quite a good Muslim, judging from what one saw of his praying and fasting. He learned the craft of working with marble from a stonecutter who used to [131] cut stone for my father's house. After staying for a long time in my father's household, my father gave him as wife a woman from a pious family and paid all the expenses required for his wedding and home. His wife bore him two sons and they grew well and their father was pleased with them.

When the boys were six or seven years old, their father, the attendant Ra'ul, took them and their mother and everything he had in his house and, the next day, joined the Franks at Apamea. There, he and his sons became Christian again after having been Muslim, despite all their praying and fasting. May God (may He be exalted) purify the world of these people!

§ *The 'Wonders' of the Frankish Race*[233]

[132] Glory be to the Creator, the Maker! Indeed, when a person
relates matters concerning the Franks, he *should* give glory to
God and sanctify Him! For he will see them to be mere beasts
possessing no other virtues but courage and fighting, just as
beasts have only the virtues of strength and the ability to carry
loads. I shall now relate something of their ways and the
wonders of their intelligence.

§ *The Franks' Lack of Intelligence:*
An Invitation to Visit Europe

In the army of King Fulk, son of Fulk, there was a respected
Frankish knight who had come from their country just to go
on pilgrimage and then return home. He grew to like my company and he became my constant companion, calling me 'my
brother'. Between us there were ties of amity and sociability.
When he resolved to take to the sea back to his country, he said
to me:

'My brother, I am leaving for my country. I want you to send
your son (my son, who was with me, was fourteen years old)
with me to my country, where he can observe the knights and
acquire reason and chivalry. When he returns, he will be like a
truly rational man.'

And so there fell upon my ears words that would never come
from a truly rational head! For even if my son were taken
captive, his captivity would not be as long as any voyage he
might take to the land of the Franks.

So I said, 'By your life, I was hoping for this very thing. But
the only thing that has prevented me from doing so is the fact
that his grandmother adores him and almost did not allow him
to come here with me until she had exacted an oath from me
that I would return him to her.'

'Your mother,' he asked, 'she is still alive?'

'Yes,' I replied.

'Then do not disobey her,' he said.

§ The Marvels of Frankish Medicine

Here is an example of the marvellous nature of their medicine. The lord of al-Munaytira[234] wrote to my uncle to request that he send him a physician to treat some of his companions who were ill. So my uncle sent him a native Christian physician called [133] Thabit. He was barely gone ten days when he returned to Shayzar. So we said to him, 'My, you healed your patients so quickly!' He explained:

They brought before me a knight in whose leg an abscess had formed and a woman who was stricken with a dryness of humours.[235] So I made a small poultice for the knight and the abscess opened up and he was healed. For the woman, I prescribed a special diet and increased the wetness of her humours. Then a Frankish physician came to them and said, 'This fellow don't know how to treat them.' He then said to the knight, 'Which would you like better: living with one leg or dying with both?' 'Living with one leg,' replied the knight. The physician then said, 'Bring me a strong knight and a sharp axe.' A knight appeared with an axe – indeed, I was just there – and the physician laid the leg of the patient on a block of wood and said to the knight with the axe, 'Strike his leg with the axe and cut it off with one blow.' So he struck him – I'm telling you I watched him do it – with one blow, but it didn't chop the leg all the way off. So he struck him a second time, but the marrow flowed out of the leg and he died instantly.

He then examined the woman and said, 'This woman, there is a demon inside her head that has possessed her. Shave off her hair.' So they shaved her head. The woman then returned to eating their usual diet – garlic and mustard. As a result, her dryness of humours increased. So the physician said, 'That demon has entered further into her head.' So he took a razor and made a cut in her head in the shape of a cross. He then peeled back the skin so that the skull was exposed and rubbed it with salt. The woman died instantaneously. So I asked them, 'Do you need anything else from me?' 'No,' they said. And so I left, having

learned about their medicine things I had never known
before.

Now, I have observed in their medicine a case exactly the
opposite of this. Their king[236] named as treasurer one of their
knights, called Bernard (may God curse him), one of the most
accursed and filthy Franks around. A horse kicked him in his
leg and his lower leg started to fester and open up in fourteen
different places. Every time these wounds [134] would close in
one place, another would open somewhere else. I prayed that
he would just perish. But then a Frankish physician came and
removed all the ointments that were on him and had him
washed with strong vinegar. The wounds closed up and he was
well and up again, like the very devil.

Here is another wondrous example of their medicine. We
had at Shayzar an artisan called Abu al-Fath, who had a son
on whose neck scrofula sores had formed. Every time one would
close in one place, another would open up in another place.
Once Abu al-Fath went to Antioch on an errand and his son
accompanied him. A Frankish man noticed him and asked him
about the boy. 'He is my son,' Abu al-Fath said.

The Frank said to him, 'Do you swear to me by your religion
that, if I prescribe for you some medicine that will cure your
boy, you will not charge money from anyone else whom you
yourself treat with it?'

Our man swore to that effect. The Frank then said, 'Take
him some uncrushed leaves of glasswort, burn them, then soak
the ashes in olive oil and strong vinegar. Treat him with this
until it eats up the pustules in the affected area. Then take some
fire-softened lead and soak it in butter. Then treat the boy with
this and he will get well.'

So our man treated the boy as he was told and the boy got
well. The wounds closed up and he returned to his previous
state of health. I have myself treated people afflicted by this
ailment with this remedy, and it was beneficial and removed all
of their complaints.

§ Newly Arrived Franks are the Roughest

Anyone who is recently arrived from the Frankish lands is rougher in character than those who have become acclimated and have frequented the company of Muslims. Here is an instance of their rough character (may God abominate them!):

Whenever I went to visit the holy sites in Jerusalem, I would go in and make my way up to the al-Aqsa Mosque,[237] beside which stood a small mosque that the Franks had converted into a church. When I went into the al-Aqsa Mosque – where the Templars, who are my friends, were – [135] they would clear out that little mosque so that I could pray in it. One day, I went into the little mosque, recited the opening formula 'God is great!' and stood up in prayer. At this, one of the Franks rushed at me and grabbed me and turned my face towards the east, saying, 'Pray like *this*!'

A group of Templars hurried towards him, took hold of the Frank and took him away from me. I then returned to my prayers. The Frank, that very same one, took advantage of their inattention and returned, rushing upon me and turning my face to the east, saying, 'Pray like *this*!'

So the Templars came in again, grabbed him and threw him out. They apologized to me, saying, 'This man is a stranger, just arrived from the Frankish lands sometime in the past few days. He has never before seen anyone who did not pray towards the east.'

'I think I've prayed quite enough,' I said and left. I used to marvel at that devil, the change of his expression, the way he trembled and what he must have made of seeing someone praying towards Mecca.[238]

§ When God was Young

I saw one of the Franks come up to the amir Mu'in al-Din (may God have mercy upon him) while he was in the Dome of the Rock,[239] and say, 'Would you like to see God when He was young?'

'Why yes,' Mu'in al-Din replied.

So this Frank walked in front of us until he brought us to an icon of Mary and the Messiah (Peace be upon him) when he was a child, sitting in her lap. 'This is God when He was young,' he said.

May God be exalted far beyond what the infidels say![240]

§ *Franks have no Honour or Propriety*

The Franks possess nothing in the way of regard for honour or propriety.[241] One of them might be walking along with his wife and run into another man. This other man might then take his wife to one side and chat with her, while the husband just stands there waiting for her to finish her conversation. And if she takes too long, he'll just leave her alone with her conversation partner and walk away!

[136] Here is an example that I myself witnessed. Whenever I went to Nablus, I used to stay at the home of a man called Mu'izz, whose home was the lodging-house for Muslims. The house had windows that opened onto the road and, across from it on the other side of the road, there was a house belonging to a Frankish man who sold wine for the merchants. He would take some wine in a bottle and go around advertising it, saying, 'So-and-So the merchant has just opened a cask of this wine. Whoever wishes to buy some can find it at such-and-such a place.' And the fee he charged for making that announcement was the wine in the bottle. So one day, he came back home and discovered a man in bed with his wife. The Frank said to the man, 'What business brings you here to my wife?'

'I got tired,' the man replied, 'so I came in to rest.'

'But how did you get into my bed?' asked the Frank.

'I found a bed that was all made up, so I went to sleep in it,' he replied.

'While my wife was sleeping there with you?' the Frank pursued.

'Well, it's her bed,' the man offered. 'Who am I to keep her out of it?'

'By the truth of my religion,' the Frank said, 'if you do this again, we'll have an argument, you and I!'

And that was all the disapproval he would muster and the extent of his sense of propriety![242]

Here is another example. We had with us a bath-keeper called Salim, who was originally an inhabitant of Ma'arra,[243] and who served in the bath-house of my father (may God have mercy upon him). He told me:

> I once opened a bath-house in Ma'arra to earn my living. Once, one of their knights came in. Now, they don't take to people wearing a towel about their waist in the bath, so this knight stretched out his hand, pulled off my towel from my waist and threw it down. He looked at me – I had recently shaved my pubic hair – and said, 'Salim!' Then he moved in closer to me. He then stretched his hand over my groin, saying, 'Salim! Good! By the truth of my religion, do that to me too!'
>
> He then lay down on his back: he had it thick as a beard down in that place! So I shaved him and he passed his hand over it and, finding it smooth to the touch, said, 'Salim, by the truth of your religion, do it to Madame!' – *madame* in their language means 'the lady',[244] meaning his wife. He then told one of his attendants, 'Tell Madame to come here.'
>
> The attendant went and brought her and showed her in. She lay down on her back and the knight said, 'Do her like you did me!' So I shaved her [137] hair there as her husband stood watching me. He then thanked me and paid me my due for the service.

Now, consider this great contradiction! They have no sense of propriety or honour, yet they have immense courage. Yet what is courage but a product of honour and disdain for ill repute?

Here is an example close to that one. I once went to the baths in the city of Tyre[245] and took a seat in a secluded room there. While I was there, one of my attendants in the bath said to me, 'There are women here with us!' When I went outside, I sat down on the benches and, sure enough, the woman who was in the bath had come out and was standing with her father directly across from me, having put her garments on again. But I couldn't be sure if she was a woman. So I said to one of my companions, 'By God, go have a look at this one – is she a

woman?' What I meant was for him to go and ask about her.
But instead he went – as I watched – and lifted her hem and
pulled it up. At this, her father turned to me and explained,
'This is my daughter. Her mother died, and so she has no one
who will wash her hair. I brought her into the bath with me so
that I might wash her hair.'

'That's a kind thing you're doing,' I assured him. 'This will
bring you heavenly reward.'

§ *Another Example of their Medicine*

Another example of their wondrous medicine was related to us
by William de Bures,[246] lord of Tiberias and a man with some
standing among the Franks. It happened that he travelled with
the amir Mu'in al-Din (may God have mercy upon him) from
Acre to Tiberias, and I accompanied him. On the way, he
related to us the following story:

> In our land there was a highly esteemed knight who took
> ill and was on the point of death. We went to one of our
> notable priests and asked him, 'Will you come with us and
> have a look at Sir So-and-So?' 'Yes,' he replied and walked
> back with us. We were certain now that if only he would
> lay his hands upon him, he would recover. When the priest
> saw the knight he said, 'Bring me some wax.' So we
> brought him a bit of wax, which he softened and shaped
> like a knuckle-bone. Then he inserted one in each nostril
> and the knight died. [138] 'He's dead!' we remarked. 'Yes,'
> the priest replied. 'He was in great pain, so I closed up his
> nose so that he could die and find relief.'

§ *Two Old Women Race*

Let this go and bring the conversation back to Harim.[247]

And let us stop discussing their medical practices and move
on to something else.[248]

I was present in Tiberias during one of their feast-days. The
knights had gone out to practise fighting with spears, and two
decrepit old women went out with them. They positioned the
two women at one end of the practice-field and at the other

end they left a pig, which they had roasted and laid on a rock. They then made the two old women race one another, each one accompanied by a detachment of horsemen who cheered her on. At every step, the old women would fall down but then get up again as the audience laughed, until one of them overtook the other and took away the pig as her prize.

§ Examples of Frankish Jurisprudence

I was an eyewitness one day in Nablus when two men came forward to fight a duel. The reason behind it was that some Muslim bandits took one of the villages of Nablus by surprise, and one of the peasants there was accused of complicity. They said, 'He guided the bandits to the village!' So he fled.

But the king sent men to arrest the peasant's sons, so the man came back before the king and said, 'Grant me justice. I challenge to a duel the man who said that I guided the bandits to the village.'

The king said to the lord of the village, its fief-holder, 'Bring before me the man whom he has challenged.'

So the lord went off to his village, where a blacksmith lived, and took him, telling him, 'You will fight in a duel.' This was the fief-holder's way of making sure that none of his peasants [139] would be killed and his farming ruined as a result.

I saw that blacksmith. He was a strong young man, but lacking resolve: he would walk a bit, then sit down and order something to drink. Whereas the other man, who had demanded the duel, was an old man but strong-willed: he would shout taunts as if he had no fears about the duel. Then the *vicomte*[249] came – he is the governor of the town – and gave each one of the duellists a staff and a shield and arranged the people around them in a circle.

The two men met. The old man would press the blacksmith back until he pushed him away as far as the circle of people, then he would return to the centre. They continued exchanging blows until the two of them stood there looking like pillars spattered with blood. The whole affair was going on too long and the *vicomte* began to urge them to hurry, saying, 'Be quick about it!'

The blacksmith benefited from the fact that he was used to swinging a hammer, but the old man was worn out. The blacksmith hit him and he collapsed, his staff falling underneath his back. The blacksmith then crouched on top of him and tried to stick his fingers in the old man's eyes, but couldn't do it because of all the blood. So he stood up and beat the man's head in with his staff until he had killed him. In a flash, they tied a rope round the old man's neck, dragged him off and strung him up. The blacksmith's lord now came and bestowed his own mantle upon him, let him mount behind him on his horse and rode away with him.

And that was but a taste of their jurisprudence and their legal procedure, may God curse them!

On one occasion, I went with the amir Mu'in al-Din (may God have mercy upon him) to Jerusalem, and we stopped at Nablus. While there, a blind man – a young man wearing fine clothes, a Muslim – came out to the amir with some fruit and asked him for permission to be admitted into his service in Damascus. The amir did so. I asked about him and I was told that his mother had been married to a Frank, whom she had killed. Her son used to attempt various ruses on their pilgrims, and he and his mother used to work together to kill them. They finally brought charges against him for that and made him subject to the legal procedure of the Franks, to wit:

They set up a huge cask and filled it with water and stretched a plank of wood across it. Then they bound the arms of the accused, tied a rope around his shoulders and threw him into the cask. If he were innocent, then he would sink in the water and they would then pull him up by that rope so he wouldn't die in the water; if he were guilty, then he would not sink in the water. That man tried [140] eagerly to sink into the water when they threw him in, but he couldn't do it. So he had to submit to their judgment – may God curse them – and they did some work on his eyes.[250]

The man later arrived in Damascus, so the amir Mu'in al-Din (may God have mercy upon him) assigned him a stipend to meet all his needs and said to one of his attendants, 'Take him to Burhan al-Din ibn al-Balkhi[251] (may God have mercy upon him) and tell him to order someone to teach the Qur'an and some jurisprudence to this man.'

At this the blind man said, 'Victory and mastery be yours! This wasn't what I was thinking!'

'Then what were you thinking I would do?' asked the amir.

'That you would give me a horse, a mule and weapons, and make a horseman out of me!' the man answered.

The amir then said, 'I never thought that a blind man would join the ranks of our cavalry.'

§ Franks that are Acclimatized are Better

Among the Franks there are some who have become acclimatized and frequent the company of Muslims. They are much better than those recently arrived from their lands, but they are the exception and should not be considered representative.

Here is an example. I sent one of my men to Antioch on an errand. At the time, Chief Tadrus ibn al-Saffi[252] was there, and his word had great influence in Antioch; there was a mutual bond of friendship between us. One day he said to my man, 'A Frankish friend of mine has invited me to his home. You should come along so you can observe their ways.' My man told me:

I went along with him and we came to the home of one of the old knights who came out in one of the first expeditions of the Franks. He was since removed from the stipend-registry and dismissed from service, but he had some property in Antioch off which he lived. He presented a very fine table, with food that was extremely clean and delicious. But seeing me holding back from eating, he said, 'Eat and be of good cheer! For I don't eat Frankish food: I have Egyptian cooking-women and never eat anything except what they cook. And pork never enters my house.' So I ate, though guardedly, and we left.

After passing through the market, a Frankish woman suddenly hung onto me while babbling at me in their language – I didn't understand what she was saying. Then a group of Franks began to gather around me and I was certain that I was going to perish. But suddenly, who should turn up but that knight, who saw me and approached. He came and said to that woman, [141] 'What's the matter with you and this Muslim?'

'This man killed my brother 'Urs.'[253] This 'Urs was a knight in Apamea whom someone from the army of Hama had killed.

The knight shouted at her and said, 'This man is a *bourgeois*[254] (i.e., a merchant), who neither fights nor attends battle.' And he yelled at the assembled crowd and they dispersed. He then took me by the hand and went away. Thus, the effect of that meal was my deliverance from death.

§ *Brave Men may Hold Unusual Fears*

[142] One of the wonders of the human heart is that a man may face certain death and embark upon every danger without his heart quailing from it, and yet he may take fright from something that even boys and women do not fear.

I have seen my uncle, Sultan (may God have mercy upon him) – who was one of the most courageous members of his household, having taken famous stands in battle and struck renowned spear-thrusts – suddenly, upon seeing a mouse, change the expression on his face, become overcome by shudders at the mere sight of it, and take himself away from the place where he saw it.

Among his attendants was a courageous fellow whose name was Sunduq, known for his bravery and audacity. He was so afraid of snakes that he would practically lose his mind. My father (may God have mercy upon him) said to him as he was standing before my uncle, 'Sunduq, you're a good man, known for your bravery. Aren't you ashamed to be so afraid of snakes?'

'My lord,' he replied, 'what's so surprising about that? In Homs there is a brave man, a hero's hero, who is scared to death of mice,' meaning his master.[255]

And so my uncle (may God have mercy upon him) cursed at him, 'May God abominate you, you dirty so-and-so!'

I also knew a *mamluk* belonging to my father (may God have mercy upon him), called Lu'lu'.[256] A good man, stalwart fellow.

One night I went out from Shayzar, taking with me a large number of mules and other beasts, which I hoped to use to carry some wood that I had cut up in the mountains for a water-wheel that belonged to me. We left the lands surrounding Shayzar, thinking that daybreak was approaching, but we arrived at a village called Dubays before even passing half the night.

So I said, 'Let's set up camp. We shouldn't go into the mountains at night.'

[143] Once we had dismounted and settled in, we heard the neighing of horses.

'The Franks!' we said. So we mounted up in the dark, and I told myself that I would put my spear through one of them and take his horse while they were trying to rustle the animals and capture the men who were tending them.

I said to Lu'lu' and three of the attendants, 'Go ahead and find out what all that neighing is about.'

They went on ahead at full gallop and met some others, lots of people in quite a crowd. Lu'lu' was the first to reach them and said, 'Let's hear it! Or else I'll kill you one and all' – he being an excellent archer.

But they recognized his voice and said, 'Chamberlain Lu'lu'?'

'Yes,' he replied. And what do you know, but they were the army of Hama! They were under the command of the amir Sayf al-Din Sawar[257] (may God have mercy upon him), and had made a raid on the lands of the Franks and were on their way back home. Such was this man's audacity against that crowd. Yet if he should see a snake in his house, he would run out fleeing, saying to his wife, 'The snake's all yours!' And she would have to get up and kill it.

§ The Devil is in the Details

The warrior, even if he is lion-hearted, can be ruined and reduced to impotence by the most trifling impediment, as happened to me before Homs. I rode out, but my horse was killed and I was struck by fifty swords – all through the execution of the divine will and, on top of it, through the sloppiness of my groom in arranging the reins of my bridle. He attached the reins to the rings without sliding them all the way through. So when I pulled on the reins, hoping to escape from the enemy, the reins came undone from the rings and there happened to me what happened.

One day, the alarm was sounded at Shayzar, from the south. We suited up and prepared ourselves. But it [144] was a false alarm. My father and uncle (may God have mercy upon the two of them) went away but I stayed behind. The alarm was then sounded from the north, from the direction of the Franks. I galloped on my horse towards the sound of the alarm and saw our men crossing the ford,[258] some riding on the shoulders of the others, shouting, 'The Franks!'

I crossed the ford and told the men, 'Don't worry, I stand between you and the enemy!' I then galloped up to Rabiyat al-Qaramita and there were the enemy cavalry, advancing in a large body, preceded by a horseman wearing a mail hauberk and a helmet. He was already close to me. So I made straight for him, taking the opportunity to attack some of his comrades after him. He stood ready to receive me. But the moment I spurred my horse on towards him, my stirrup snapped. And there was no way for me to avoid meeting him. So I confronted him without a stirrup. When we got so close to one another that there was nothing to do but thrust our spears about, the horseman greeted me and offered his services to me, for it was none other than Commander[259] 'Umar, the uncle of Commander Zayn al-Din Isma'il. He had gone out with the army of Hama to the territory of Kafartab, where the Franks made a sortie against them. So they returned to Shayzar in flight, led by the amir Sawar (may God have mercy upon him).

Thus, the best course for the warrior to follow is to inspect the tack on his horse frequently. For even the smallest and most insignificant of things can lead to injury and destruction – all that dependent upon the course of fate and destiny.

§ A Lion-Slayer Wounded by a Hyena

I have witnessed the killing of lions on occasions beyond reckoning. A certain number of these I have killed without anyone joining me in the kill and without any sort of injury befalling me.

Yet, one day, I went out on the chase with my father (may God have mercy upon him) on a mountain close to town, hunting partridges with goshawks. My father – and we with him – and the austringers were on top of the mountain, while some attendants and other austringers were at the foot of the mountain for when the hawks released their prey and to locate the birds' coverts. Suddenly, a female hyena appeared before us and went into a cave. In the cave there was its den, which it entered. So I shouted to an attendant of mine, a groom named Yusuf. He stripped off [145] his clothes, took up his knife and went into that den, while I had a *quntariya*-spear in my hands pointed at that spot so that if the hyena came out I could strike it.

Suddenly, my attendant shouted, 'It's headed out your way!' So I thrust my spear at it, but missed, as the hyena has a slight body.

Then my attendant shouted, 'I've got another hyena here!' And it rushed out on the heels of the first.

I stood up and took position at the door of the cave – which was narrow, but about the height of two men – and looked out to see what our companions in the plain were doing about the hyenas that had come down their way. As I was busy looking at the first two, yet a third hyena came rushing out, knocked me over and threw me down from the door of the cave to the surface of the ground, almost breaking me in two. Thus was I injured by a female hyena, yet never hurt by lions. Glory be to He who determines destinies, who sets all things in motion!

§ *Faint-Hearted Men*

I have witnessed weakness and faint-heartedness in men that I never thought to see even in women. Here is an example:

One day, I was at the door of the house of my father (may God have mercy upon him). I was just a young boy, not being more than ten years old. An attendant belonging to my father named Muhammad al-'Ajami slapped one of the young servants of the house. The latter ran away from him and came and clung to my clothes. The attendant Muhammad caught up with him and slapped him again, even as he clutched at my clothes. So I struck back at him with a rod I happened to have in my hand and he pushed back at me. I then pulled out a knife from my waist and stabbed him with it. It struck his left breast and he fell down. An older attendant belonging to my father called Commander Asad came, examined him and saw the wound – whenever he breathed, blood spurted out of it like bubbles of water. Asad turned pale, shuddered and fell in a faint. In that state he was carried away to his house – he used to live with us in the citadel. He did not regain consciousness until the last part of the day. But by then the injured attendant was dead and buried.

Here is something similar to that example. A man from Aleppo used to visit us in Shayzar, a man possessing virtue and refinement. He played chess continuously, even when he was away. He was called Abu al-Murajja Salim ibn Thabit (may God have mercy upon him). He used to stay with us for a year, maybe more, maybe less. If by chance [146] he became ill, the physician would prescribe blood-letting for him. And when the blood-letter would appear before him, Abu al-Murajja would turn pale and start to shudder. And when the blood-letter actually bled him, Abu al-Murajja would faint and remain unconscious until the incisions were bandaged up. Only then did he recover.

§ Stout-Hearted Men

Here is an example that contrasts with the above. Among our comrades of the Banu Kinana, there was a black man called 'Ali ibn Faraj, in whose foot there developed a pustule, which just became worse. His toes fell off and the rest of his leg began to rot. The surgeon said to him, 'There is no treatment for your leg except amputation. If you don't have it done, you will die.'

So the surgeon went and got a saw and started to saw his leg until 'Ali fainted from the loss of blood. Once he regained consciousness, the surgeon would start sawing away again until finally he cut his leg off at the middle. They treated it and it was healed.

This 'Ali (may God have mercy upon him) was one of the most enduring and powerful men. He used to ride in the saddle with one foot in a stirrup and, on the other side, he would put his knee in a strap. In this state he would attend battle and exchange spear-thrusts with the Franks. I used to see him with my own eyes (may God have mercy upon him): no man could match him at arm-wrestling or keep a hold on him.

Yet with all his strength and courage, he was a light-hearted fellow. Early one morning, while he and the Banu Kinana were living in our fortress at the Bridge, he sent a message to some of the leaders of the Banu Kinana, saying, 'It's a rainy day today and I haven't got any flour, bread or wine in the house. Yet all of you have in your homes everything you need for the day. I propose that you send to your homes and have your food and wine brought out – I'll provide the house. Let's get together today to drink and shoot the breeze.'

To this they all replied, 'Fine! Great idea, [147] 'Ali!'

They then sent for and brought out all the food and drink from their homes and passed their day at his place. He was quite a respected man. Exalted is He who created His creatures in various sorts![260] How can the endurance and stout-heartedness of this man be compared to the weakness and faint-heartedness of those others?

The following is an example similar to that case. A man from the Banu Kinana told me at the Bridge Fortress that there was a man there who had been afflicted with dropsy. But he sliced open his stomach and recovered, returning to health as he was before. I said, 'I would like to examine this man and get some information out of him.'

The one who told me about this man was someone from the Banu Kinana called Ahmad ibn Ma'bad ibn Ahmad. He brought the man before me and I got information from him about his condition and how he did what he did to himself. He said:

I am just a poor beggar, all on my own. My abdomen became afflicted with dropsy and I got so big that I was unable to move, and I grew weary of life. So I took a razor and cut myself with it above my navel, across my abdomen, and sliced myself open. About two cooking-pots-worth of

water (meaning two measures) came out of it. The water
continued to seep out until my abdomen shrank back. I
then stitched it up, treated the wound and it was healed.
In this way my ailment passed.

He then showed me the scar where he had sliced himself open
on his abdomen, which was more than a span in length. There
is no doubt that this man still had a livelihood on earth that
was yet due to him.

In other cases, I have seen people afflicted with dropsy who
had their physician bleed their abdomen and extract water from
it – just as the water came out of this man who punctured
himself – yet who nevertheless died from the blood-letting. Fate
is indeed an impregnable citadel.

§ Only God can Bring Victory in Battle

Victory in war is from God alone (may He be blessed and
exalted), not from organization or skilled conduct, and not
from strength of numbers of troops or allies.

Whenever my uncle (may God have mercy upon him) used
to send me to fight Turks or Franks, I would ask him, 'My lord,
tell me how I should conduct myself when I finally meet the
enemy.'

'War conducts itself, my boy,' he would say. And he was
right.

[148] He once asked me to take his wife, Khatun[261] bint Taj
al-Dawla Tutush, and his sons with the army and proceed to
Masyaf Castle, which belonged to him at the time, hoping to
spare them the heat of Shayzar.[262] I rode out, and my father
and uncle (may God have mercy upon them both) rode with us
for part of the way, and then returned, accompanied only by
the young *mamluks* to lead the pack horses and carry the
weapons. The entire army remained with me. When my father
and uncle approached the town, they heard the beating of
war-drums coming from the Bridge.[263] They said, 'Something is
happening down at the Bridge,' and spurred their horses
towards it. At the time, there was a truce between us and the
Franks (may God curse them!). Nevertheless, the Franks had

sent some men to scout a ford for them by which they might cross over to the part of town by the Bridge. This was on a peninsula to which no one could cross except by an arched bridge of stone and lime mortar, and which the Franks could not reach. But a scout showed them a place to ford. So they all rode from Apamea and, the next morning, found themselves at that spot that the scout had indicated. They then crossed the water, took possession of the town, pillaged it, took away prisoners and killed some people. They dispatched some of the plunder and captives back to Apamea. They also took possession of the houses, every one of them affixing a cross-symbol to a house and raising his banner over it.

When my father and uncle (may God have mercy upon them both) approached the citadel, the inhabitants shouted, 'God is great!' and gave forth a cry. In this way God, glory be to Him, struck terror and despair into the Franks and so they forgot the spot by which they had crossed. Dressed in their mail hauberks, they urged their horses into the river where there was no ford. As a result, a large number of them were drowned. A rider would plunge into the water, fall from his saddle and sink in the water, only the horse coming out of it. Those of them that survived ran away in flight, [149] without anyone paying heed to anyone else. And although they were a numerous force, my father and uncle had with them only ten young *mamluks*.

My uncle took position at the Bridge, while my father returned to Shayzar. As for me, I delivered the sons of my uncle to Masyaf and returned home on the same day, arriving in the evening. I was informed about what had happened, so I presented myself before my father (may God have mercy upon him) and sought his counsel over whether I should go and join my uncle at the Bridge Fortress.

'You will arrive at night,' he said, 'while they are sleeping. Go to them instead early in the morning.'

And so the next morning I went out and presented myself before my uncle. We went riding and stopped at that spot where the Franks had drowned. A group of swimmers had come down to the place and were pulling out some of their dead horsemen.

'My lord,' I said to my uncle, 'why don't we cut off their heads and dispatch them to Shayzar?'

'Make it so,' he replied. We cut off about twenty heads and the blood flowed from the dead bodies as if they had been killed that very moment, yet they had been there a day and a night. I believe the water preserved the blood inside them. The local people took many weapons from them as plunder, including mail, swords, *quntariya*-spears, helmets and mail chausses.[264]

Indeed, I saw one of the peasants of the Bridge present himself before my uncle with his hand beneath his clothes.

My uncle said to him, playfully, 'And what is it you've set aside for me as plunder, then?'

He replied, 'I have set aside for you a charger with its tack and horse armour,[265] a shield and a sword.' And he went and brought this all before him.

My uncle accepted the horse's tack, but granted the charger to him, and asked, 'But what's that in your hand?'

'My lord,' the peasant replied, 'me and a Frank got to grappling and I didn't have any gear or sword. So I threw him down and punched him in the face, even though he was covered with an aventail, until I knocked him out. Then I took his sword and killed him with it. But the skin on my knuckles was all torn to shreds and my hand swelled up and was of no use to me.'

He then showed us his hand, which was just as he had said – even the bones of his fingers were exposed.

In the garrison of the Bridge was a Kurdish man called Abu al-Jaysh, who had a daughter named Raful, who had been carried off by the Franks. Abu al-Jaysh became pathologically obsessed with her, saying to everyone [150] he met, 'Raful has been taken captive!'

The next morning we went out to walk along the river and we saw a form by the bank of the river. We told one of the attendants, 'Swim over there and find out what that thing is.'

He made his way over to it, and what should the form be but Raful, dressed in a blue garment. She had thrown herself from the horse of the Frank who had captured her and drowned. Her dress was caught in a willow-tree. In this way were the pangs of despair of her father silenced.

Thus, the cry that frightened the Franks, their flight and their destruction were all due to the benevolence of God, the Mighty and Majestic, not due to any power or army. Blessed indeed is God, who is capable of whatever He wills.

§ *Overawing the Enemy in War*

That said, overawing the enemy can sometimes be effective in warfare. Here is an example:

In the year 529 (spring 1135), the atabeg arrived in Syria, and I with him, and he continued onward intending for Damascus.[266] When we encamped at al-Qutayyifa, al-Yaghisiyani (may God have mercy upon him) said to me, 'Saddle up and go ahead of us to al-Fustuqa.[267] Take up a position along the road so that none of the troops can flee towards Damascus.'

So I went on ahead and took up my position for a while, when al-Yaghisiyani arrived at the head of a small detachment of his comrades. We could see smoke coming from 'Adhra', so we sent some cavalry to go and find out what all the smoke was. It turned out it was a detachment from the army of Damascus burning the hay in 'Adhra', and they took flight. Al-Yaghisiyani pursued them, with us accompanying him, amounting to maybe thirty or forty horsemen, and we arrived at al-Qusayr, where what should we find, but the army of Damascus in its entirety, cutting us off from the bridge. We were by then at the khan itself.[268] So we halted, taking cover behind the khan. [151] Five or six of our horsemen would then go out so that the army of Damascus could catch sight of them, and then they would go back behind the khan, fooling them into thinking we had set up an ambush there.

In the meantime, al-Yaghisiyani sent a horseman to the atabeg to inform him of what we were up against. Soon we saw about ten horsemen approaching us at top speed, our army marshalled behind them. The horsemen arrived at our position and we saw that it was the atabeg leading the vanguard, with the army in tow.

The atabeg rebuked al-Yaghisiyani for what he had done, saying, 'You ran ahead to the very gate of Damascus with only thirty horsemen just to ruin my reputation!'[269] And he cast blame on him. They were both speaking in Turkish, so I did not understand what they were saying.

When the vanguard of the army arrived, I said to al-Yaghisiyani, 'By your leave, I will take these men who have just arrived, cross over to the Damascene cavalry stationed opposite us and dislodge them.'

'No,' he replied. 'Whoever loyally works in the service of this man is a dirty little so-and-so![270] Didn't you just hear what he said to me?'

Had it not been for the benevolence of God (may He be exalted), and that attempt to overawe and play with the imagination of the enemy, they would have removed us.

A similar thing happened to me. I had set out with my uncle (may God have mercy upon him) from Shayzar, making for Kafartab. We were accompanied by a crowd of peasants and beggars who were to plunder the crops and cotton in the environs of Kafartab. The people all spread out in plunder, while the cavalry of Kafartab had taken to their mounts and were positioned outside town. But we stood between them and the people spreading out through the fields and cotton. Suddenly, one of our comrades, a horseman, came galloping from the scouts and said, 'The cavalry of Apamea has come!'

At this, my uncle said, 'You take up your position opposite the cavalry of Kafartab, while I go at the head of the troops to intercept the cavalry of Apamea.'

I took up my position with ten horsemen, hidden in the midst of some olive trees. Of these, three or four would leave us to worry the imaginations of the Franks, and then return to the olive trees. The Franks, thinking that we were a large group, would assemble, cry out and urge their horses [152] closer to us. But we remained unfazed and they retreated. We remained in that position until my uncle returned, having routed the Franks who had come from Apamea.

One of his attendants said to him, 'My lord, did you see what he (meaning me) has done? He stayed behind and didn't go with you to intercept the cavalry of Apamea.'

My uncle responded, 'If it were not for the fact that he took his position with ten horsemen opposite the cavalry and infantry of Kafartab, the Franks would have taken the whole crowd captive.'

Thus, overawing and playing upon the imagination of the Franks was, on that occasion, more effective than fighting them, since we were but a small detachment and they a large group.

I was involved in a similar case at Damascus. One day, I was accompanying the amir Mu'in al-Din (may God have mercy upon him) when a horseman came to him and said, 'Bandits have captured a caravan carrying a load of raw cloth up in the pass!'

'Let's ride after them,' he said to me.

'As you command,' I replied. 'But order the officers of the guard[271] to have the troops ride out with you.'

'What do we need the troops for?' he asked.

'Would it hurt to have them ride with us?' I responded.

'We don't need them,' he retorted. He was one of the bravest of horsemen, but in certain circumstances, such stout-heartedness can be a fatal flaw and a real liability.

We rode out with about twenty horsemen. Shortly before noon, we sent two horsemen out this way, two that way, two yet another way and one horseman some other way in order to reconnoitre the roads. We continued on our way in a small band and then the time for mid-afternoon prayer came. Mu'in al-Din said to an attendant of mine, 'Sawinj, go up and keep watch to the west until we are done praying.' We had barely finished the last of our prayers when that attendant came galloping towards us.

'There are men on foot', he said, 'bearing bolts of raw cloth on their head, down in the valley!'

'Let's ride!' said Mu'in al-Din (may God have mercy upon him).

'Give us a second to put on our *kazaghands*. Then when we find the bandits, we can charge at them with our horses and run them through with our spears, and they won't even be able to tell whether we are many or few.'

The amir replied, 'We can put our armour on when we get there!' [153] and rode off as we headed towards them.

We encountered them in the Valley of Halbun,[272] which is a narrow valley where the distance between the two mountains alongside is perhaps five cubits. The mountains on either side are rough and steep and the path is so narrow that horsemen can only pass through one after the other. Yet the bandits were about seventy men, wielding bows and arrows.

When we reached the bandits, our attendants were still behind us with our weapons and unable to get to us. And those bandits: there was a group of them in the valley and a group of them on the slope of the mountain. But I thought that the people in the valley were our men, some peasants from the village who had come out in pursuit of the bandits, and that the men on the slope of the mountain were the real bandits. So I drew my sword and charged those who were on the slope. My horse climbed up that rough slope but nearly breathed its last breath. When I got to them, with my horse stopped still, unable to advance further, one of the bandits nocked an arrow in his bow to shoot me. But I shouted at him and threatened him and he held back. I then made my horse climb down again, hardly believing that I had escaped from them.

The amir Mu'in al-Din climbed to the top of the mountain, thinking he could find some peasants there that he could get to chase the bandits. He shouted at me from the top of the mountain, 'Don't leave them before I get back!' and then disappeared from sight.

So I returned to that group in the valley, having learned in the meantime that they were part of the bandit-party. I charged at them on my own, due to the narrowness of the place, and they fled, throwing down the raw cloth they had with them. I also liberated two animals that were likewise bearing loads of raw cloth. The bandits climbed up to a cave on the slope of the mountain as we watched them, without us having any way to get to them.

The amir Mu'in al-Din (may God have mercy upon him) came back at the end of the day without finding anyone to get to chase the bandits. If we had only had the army with us, we would have struck off all the heads of those bandits and recovered everything that they had with them.

Something like this happened to me on another occasion, too. It was a result of the execution of the divine will and also a lack of experience in warfare. It happened like this:

We set out with the amir Khusraw ibn [154] Talil, making for Damascus to enter the service of Nur al-Din[273] (may God have mercy upon him), eventually arriving at Homs. When Khusraw decided to continue via the Baalbek road, I said to him, 'I'll go on ahead of you so I can have a look at the Church of Baal,[274] until you arrive.'

'Make it so,' he replied.

I mounted up and set out. When I was inside the church, a horseman arrived from Khusraw, with his message: 'Some bandits on foot have attacked a caravan and captured it. Saddle up and meet me in the mountains.'

So I mounted my horse and met up with him. We climbed into the mountains and spotted the bandits in a valley below us, the mountain that we were on being surrounded by the valley in question. One of Khusraw's companions said to him, 'You should go down and get them.'

But I said, 'You shouldn't do that. Let's instead make our way around the mountain until we get right above their heads and we can interpose ourselves between them and their path off to the west and then capture them.' For the bandits had come from the territory of the Franks.

Another person said, 'In the time it will take us to go around the mountain, we could go down and capture them.' So we went down. But once the bandits caught sight of us, they climbed up into the mountains.

So Khusraw said to me, 'Climb up after them!' I tried my hardest to climb up, but I could not do it.

Now, there remained six or seven of our horsemen on the mountain. They went on foot, leading their horses with them, towards the bandits, who formed a large group. The bandits attacked our comrades and killed two of our horsemen. They took their two horses as well as another horse, whose owner survived safely. The bandits then climbed down the opposite side of the mountain with their plunder.

And so we went back, two of our horsemen dead, and three

horses and a caravan captured. This heedless risk-taking was
the result of a lack of experience in matters of war.

§ Risk-Taking: A Warrior's Duty

As for taking risks in acts of valour, it does not happen because
one has renounced life. Indeed, it comes about when a man
[155] becomes known for his audacity and is given the label of
courage. When he then takes part in battle, his ambition
demands that he perform noteworthy deeds that his peers cannot accomplish. His spirit so quails at death and riding into
danger that it almost overwhelms him, stopping him from what
he wants to do, until he forces his spirit and makes it undertake
that which it hates to do. As a result, shudders spread throughout his body and his colour changes. But when he enters into
battle, his terror disappears and his cravenness subsides.

I was present at the siege of the citadel of al-Sawr with the
King of Amirs, the atabeg Zangi (may God have mercy upon
him), someone I have already touched on. The citadel belonged
to the amir Qara Arslan (may God have mercy upon him), and
was fully manned with crossbowmen. This was after Zangi's
defeat at Amid.[275] As soon as his tents were set up, Zangi
dispatched one of his comrades, who shouted up underneath
the citadel, 'Enemy crossbowmen! The atabeg says to you, "By
the grace of the sultan, if but one of my comrades is killed by
your arrows, I will absolutely cut off your hands."'

Zangi then set up the mangonels against the citadel, which
took down one side of it. But not enough of it was brought
down for the men to use the breach to get up into the citadel.
However, one of the atabeg's bodyguards, a man from Aleppo
called Ibn al-'Ariq, climbed up through the breach and set to
striking the enemy with his sword. But they injured him with a
number of wounds and threw him down from the tower into
the moat. By then, our men had overwhelmed them at that
breach and we took possession of the citadel. The representatives of the atabeg climbed up to the citadel and took possession
of its keys, sending them to Timurtash, and granting Zangi the
citadel.

[156] Now, it happened that a crossbow-bolt struck a man

from the Khurasanian troops in his knee, cutting through the cap that is on top of the joint, and he died. The moment the atabeg took possession of the citadel, therefore, he summoned the crossbowmen, who were nine in number. They came with their bows slung from their shoulders. Zangi ordered that their thumbs be sliced from their wrists so their hands became limp and useless.

As for Ibn al-'Ariq, he treated his wounds and recovered after being at death's door. He was a brave man who pushed himself to face all manner of dangers.

I saw something like that on yet another occasion. The atabeg had encamped before the citadel of al-Bari'a,[276] which is surrounded by solid rock upon which tents cannot be pitched. The atabeg therefore encamped in the plain and delegated his amirs to conduct the siege in turns. One day, the atabeg rode over to the siege; it was the turn of the amir Abu Bakr al-Dubaysi,[277] but he did not have sufficient materiel for battle. The atabeg stopped there and said to Abu Bakr, 'Advance and fight them!' So Abu Bakr marched at the head of his comrades even though they were practically unarmed, and the infantrymen from the citadel came out to attack them. At this, one of Abu Bakr's comrades, called Mazyad, who was not then known for his prowess in battle or his courage, came forward and fought furiously, striking at them with his sword and dispersing their crowds. He was wounded many times. I saw him as they carried him back to camp and he was about to breathe his last breath. But then later he got well. Abu Bakr al-Dubaysi presented him and Zangi promoted him and invested him with a robe of honour and made him a member of his own bodyguard.

§ The Brutality of al-Yaghisiyani

The atabeg used to say to me, 'I have three retainers:[278] one of them fears God (may He be exalted) but does not fear me [157] (meaning Zayn al-Din 'Ali Kujak, may God have mercy upon him); the second fears me, but does not fear God (may He be exalted) (meaning Nasir al-Din Sunqur, may God have mercy upon him); and the third fears neither God nor me (meaning Salah al-Din al-Yaghisiyani, may God have mercy upon him).'

I witnessed something of al-Yaghisiyani (may God overlook his excesses) that confirms what the atabeg said. One day we marched against Homs. But the night before, such a great rain had fallen on the ground that the horses were unable to manage with the thick layer of mud there, while our infantry were already engaged. Al-Yaghisiyani had halted and I was by his side, and we could see the infantry before us. Just then, one of our infantrymen ran over to the infantry of Homs and hid among them while al-Yaghisiyani watched him. So he said to one of his comrades, 'Go and fetch the man who was next to the one who deserted.' And he went and got him.

Al-Yaghisiyani asked him, 'Who was that who fled from his post by your side and entered Homs?'

'By God, my lord,' the soldier replied, 'I don't know him.'

'Cut this man in half!' ordered al-Yaghisiyani.

At this, I said, 'My lord, you should imprison this man and investigate further the case of that man who deserted. If it turns out that he does know him or is related to him, then you can execute him. If not, then you can deal with him as you see fit.'

He looked as if he was inclined to my suggestion, but a retainer of his standing behind him said, 'If a soldier flees, the man that was next to him is taken and either has his head struck off or is cut in half.'

The retainer's words revived al-Yaghisiyani's rancour and so he ordered him to be cut in half. They trussed the soldier up following the usual procedure and chopped him in two. But no fault can be brought to al-Yaghisiyani except for his obstinacy and his lack of fear of the punishment of God, may He be exalted.

I was in his presence on another occasion after our return from the battle at Baghdad.[279] The atabeg was going to great lengths to give an appearance of endurance and strength and had ordered al-Yaghisiyani to march against the amir Qafjaq and [158] take him by surprise. We set out from Mosul for a journey of six days, although we were extremely weak. When we arrived at Qafjaq's location, we found that he had perched himself up in the mountains of Kuhistan.[280] So we went down to a fortress called Masurra and encamped against it at sunrise.

Just then, a woman came up to us from the fortress, saying, 'Have you got some raw cloth with you?'

We replied, 'Is this really the time for buying and selling?'

'We need the cloth', she said, 'to use as your winding-sheets. In five days, you'll all be dead.' By this, she was telling us that the place was stricken with disease.

Al-Yaghisiyani set up camp and planned out an attack on the fortress for the early morning. He ordered the sappers to go in under the walls of one of the towers, since the fortress was built entirely of mud-brick, and the soldiers manning it were just peasants. Meanwhile, we marched on the fortress and climbed up towards its hill. The Khurasanian troops undermined one tower, which collapsed with two men on it. One of these men was killed, but the other was taken captive by our comrades, who brought him to al-Yaghisiyani

'Cut him in half!' he said.

'My lord,' I said, 'this is the month of Ramadan, and this man is a Muslim. We cannot bear such a sin.'

Al-Yaghisiyani replied, 'Cut him in half so they'll surrender the fortress!'

'My lord,' I said, 'you will be taking possession of the fortress in but a moment.'

'Cut him in half,' he repeated. And they trussed the man up and chopped him in two.

We took the fortress that very moment.

Al-Yaghisiyani then went to the gate, intending to descend from the fortress, a crowd and the victors accompanying him.

He delegated control of the fortress to a group of his comrades and went on down to his tent just for a moment, but long enough for the army that was with him to disperse. Then he took to his horse and said to me, 'Mount up!'

We rode out and climbed up to the fortress, where he seated himself and ordered the intendant of the fortress to be brought before him so that he might find out from him what was in it. He likewise had the women and children brought before him, Christians and Jews.

An old Kurdish woman came and presented herself before

him. She asked the intendant of the fortress, 'Have you seen my son?' and gave his name.

'Killed,' he replied. 'An arrow got him.'

'And my other son?' she asked, giving his name.

'The amir cut him in half,' he replied.

The woman screamed and uncovered her head, her hair looking like carded cotton.

[159]'Quiet! The amir!' said the intendant of the fortress to her.

'And what more could he possibly do to me?' she asked. 'I had two sons and he has killed them both!'

But they just pushed her away.

The intendant then went and brought forward a very old man, with lovely white hair, who was walking on two canes. He greeted al-Yaghisiyani.

'And who is this old man?' asked the amir.

'The imam of the fortress,' replied the keeper.

'Come forward, old man,' the amir beckoned, saying, 'Come, come,' until the old man sat before him. The amir then reached out and grabbed the old man's beard and, pulling out a knife that was hanging from the belt of his robe, cut off his beard right close to his chin and dangled it from his hand like a *parcham*-ornament.[281]

So the old man said to him, 'My lord, what have I done to make you do such a thing to me?'

'You have rebelled against the sultan!' he replied.

'By God,' the old man responded, 'I didn't even know you had arrived until just now when the intendant came and told me when he summoned me.'

We then departed and encamped against another fortress belonging to the amir Qafjaq, called al-Karkhini.[282] We captured it and found there a treasury full of raw cloth that had been woven as alms for the poor of Mecca. Al-Yaghisiyani also took captive all the Jews and Christians in that fortress, people of the covenant, and plundered both fortresses as if he were plundering Romans![283] Glory be to God, and may He overlook his excesses.

I will stop in this section at this point, following the example of my own verses:

Stop now from the mention of those whom passion has
    slain,
    Their tale would turn the hair of our newborns white.

§ Bravery Saves the Day

I will return now to an account of something that happened to us while the Isma'ilis were in the citadel of Shayzar.

On that day, a cousin of mine called Abu 'Abdallah ibn Hashim (may God have mercy upon him) was walking along [160] when he saw a Batini man in a tower of my father's home, wielding a sword and shield. The door was open and a great crowd of our comrades stood outside it, but no one dared to go in.

So my cousin said to one of those men standing there, 'Get in there after him!' and he did.

But the Batini did not waste any time and struck the man, injuring him, and the man came back out, wounded. Now my cousin said to another man, 'Go in after him!'

The man did so, but the Batini struck him, too, and wounded him and he came back out, just as his comrade had done. So then my cousin said to Chief Jawad, 'Chief Jawad, you go in there after him.'

At this, the Batini shouted down to my cousin, 'Hey, hang-behind! How come *you* don't come in here? You send every-body else in, but you just stand there. Get in here so's you can get a look!'

Chief Jawad now went in and killed the Batini. This Jawad was a master of combat, a man of courage and an expert fighter.

§ Night-Wanderings: Reflections on Old Age

Only a few years had passed[284] when I saw Jawad again in Damascus, in the year 534 (1139). He had become a feed-merchant, selling barley and hay. He had grown so old that he looked like a squeezed-out water-bag, one who could barely defend his stores from the mice, much less from any man. I paused in wonder at his earlier condition, at how his present condition had affected him, and what his own longevity had produced in his current state.

I did not then realize that the disease of age is vast, afflicting all over whom Death has passed. Now that I have ascended to my ninetieth year, to its very peak, I find that the passage of years has left me weak. I have become like Jawad, the seller of feed, not like the generous host,[285] profligate indeed. Bent with weakness to the ground I nearly touch, my limbs twist into each [161] other, I have aged so much. My present self I do not recognize, my past I smother with dismal sighs. I composed the following in description of my current state:

> When I finally reached the stage in life of which I
>   dreamed,
>   I found I yearned now only for death.
> Longevity has not left me with any force
>   With which to fight off the hostile onslaught of Time.
> My strength has become weakness, betrayed by my best
>   advisers,
>   My eyes and my ears, now that I have ascended to this
>   height.
> When I rise, I feel upon me the burden
>   Of a mountain-range; when I walk, I walk as one in
>   fetters.
> I creep about, a cane clutched in my hand
>   Whose custom in war was to wield a spear or an Indian
>   blade.
> I spend my nights on downy pillows, sleepless,
>   As wide awake as if I had made my bed on sharpened
>   stones.
> Man, in life, repeats his cycle:
>   The moment he finishes, he becomes as he was when he
>   began.

I also composed the following verse in Egypt, in condemnation of a life of rest and retreat, for how quickly it passes, how fleet:

Just look at how the vicissitudes of Fate have taught me,
   Now that my hair has turned grey, new habits unlike the
      old.
In the changes wrought by Fate there is an example for
     contemplation.
   For is there any condition that the passage of days does
     not alter?
I was always the firebrand in war: whenever it sputtered
     out
   I fanned the flames with the striking of swords on our
     enemies' heads.
My concern has ever been personal combat with my rivals,
     whom I considered
   But simple prey, such that they shook in terror of me.
More encompassing in fear than black of night, more
     reckless in battle
   Than a flood, more dauntless on the battlefield than
     Destiny.
But now I have become like some soft young girl
     languishing in her bed
   Of stuffed cushions, behind screens, behind curtains.
I have almost rotted through from all this rest just as
   An Indian blade rusts as it abides in its sheath.
Having once dressed in the mail of war, I wrap myself now
     in robes
   Of fine Dabiqi cloth – shame on me, shame on this cloth!
A life *de luxe* has never been my dream or my goal;
   Comfort is not my concern or my business.
I could never be satisfied with a glory gained through ease,
   Nor with the highest rank granted without shattering
     swords and spears.

I used to think that the novelty of Time would never wear thin
and that its strength would never become weak again. Indeed,
when I returned to Syria, I hoped my days would be as they
were when I left – that after me Time forgot them, of changes
bereft. When I did return, the promises of my desires proved
pure badinage, my hopes and dreams but a shining mirage.

O God! Forgive me for including this parenthetical digression: it was but a sigh of anguish that fends off depression. To important matters let me now turn back, and leave off my wanderings into night so black.

§ *Fate can neither be Hastened nor Slowed*

[162] If only the heart could be made clean of sin's filthy sheen and entrusted to the Knower of the unseen, for riding forth into war's perils – you will have reckoned – will not shorten your term by even a second.

On the day when we encountered the Isma'ilis in the citadel of Shayzar, I saw in those events, indeed, an example from which to derive a lesson that clarifies, for intelligent brave just as for ignorant knave, that the duration of life has been already appointed and made, and one's fate can neither be hastened nor delayed.

It happened that day, that after being done with the war, someone at the edge of the citadel cried, 'Wait, here's some more!' I had with me a group of my comrades bearing their weapons, so we rushed over to the man who had cried out.

'What's all this about?' we asked.

'There are sounds of the enemy coming from over there,' he replied.

We all crossed over to an empty, darkened stable and went inside. We discovered that there were two armed men there and killed them both. We also found one of our own comrades who had been killed, but he was lying on top of something. Lifting him up, we discovered another Batini, who had wrapped himself up in a cloth like a shroud and covered himself with the dead body of our comrade. So we lifted off the body of our comrade and killed the man hiding underneath him and placed the body of our comrade, covered in terrible wounds, inside the nearby mosque, never doubting that he was dead, since he neither stirred nor breathed. I swear by God that I even nudged his head with my foot as he lay there on the floor of the mosque, and we never doubted that he was dead. The poor fellow had been passing that stable and had heard something, so he stuck his head in to investigate. But one of the enemy pulled him in and they stabbed him with their knives until they thought he was dead. But God, may He be exalted, decreed that, once those wounds on his neck and body were all stitched up, he would recover and return to the state of health that he had previously enjoyed. Blessed be God who determines all fates and fixes our destiny and our life's term!

I witnessed something similar. It happened when the Franks (God curse them) made a raid against us during the last third of the night. We mounted up, intending to go in pursuit of them, but my uncle Sultan (may God have mercy upon him) [163] prevented us from doing so, saying, 'A raid conducted at night? It's a trick!'[286] But some of our infantry left the town in pursuit of them anyway, without our knowing. On their way back, the Franks fell upon them to kill them, but a few escaped.

The next morning, as I was standing in Bandar Qanin, a village near town, I caught sight of three people approaching: two of them looked human enough, but the middle one, his face was not like the face of a man. As they got closer to us, it became clear that the one in the middle had been hit by a Frankish sword in the middle of his nose and his face was cut through clear to his ears. Half of his face was so loose that it hung down to his chest. Between the two halves of his face was a cut almost as wide as a hand's span, and so he walked between the other two men. He entered town and the surgeon stitched up his face and treated his wound. The wound eventually closed up and he recovered, returning to his previous state of health until he died of natural causes in his own bed. He used to sell work-animals and was named Ibn Ghazi the Scarred, but he only got that name after he received that blow.

Thus, let no one assume that death is hastened by facing straits that are dire, nor is it delayed if you choose to retire; indeed the example of my long life provides lessons for you to acquire. For how many terrors have I faced, how many dangers and fears have I out-raced? Horsemen I have battled, lions I have grappled, struck have I been by blades, run through have I been by spears, pelted have I been with arrows and with stones, all while I from Fate was like a stout fortress without fear, that is, until I completed my ninetieth year. For then

I came to see health and lingering ease like the Prophet (upon him be peace): 'Health suffices as its own disease.' Indeed, the result of my escape from those frights is something more daunting than all those earlier battles and fights. Far easier is death at an army's head than the taxations of a lingering life of pain and dread. For the passage of time has removed, from my life's long measure, all objects of joy and gentle pleasure. Now this does misery's dust-storm obscure: an ample life, once so pure. I am as I once described in verse:

> After eighty years, Time begins to work its mischief on my
>   constitution:
>   The weakness of my foot, the trembling of my hand,
>   they grieve me.
> Even as I write, my lines seem troubled
>   Like the writing of one with hands terror-stricken,
>   palsied.
> I wonder at this feebleness in my hands as they lift up a pen
>   When previously they had shattered spears in the hearts
>   of lions.
> If I walk, it is with cane in hand, bemired
>   Are my legs as if I waded through a mud-soaked plain.
> [164] So say to him who hopes his life will be a long one:
>   'These are the consequences of long life and age.'

For weakness and feebleness have replaced my power, all sweetness in life has ended and reached its hour. This long sojourn among men has me bent like an infant, just as the flame that dispels darkness is itself made dark in an instant. I have become just as I describe in the following poem:

> Destiny has forsaken me, leaving me like
>   An exhausted pack-camel abandoned in the wastes.
> My eighty years have sapped all my strength
>   So that when I try to stand, I am broken.
> I perform my prayers seated, for bowing
>   If I tried it, would be, for me, impossible.
> This condition has warned me
>   That a journey is coming, and its time is nigh.

The weakness that old age brings keeps me now from serving kings. I no longer darken their door and rely upon them no more. I have resigned from their service and have returned what they sent of their favour. For I realize that the weakness of one so worn has never the duties of service lightly borne. What an old man can offer, it's clear, will never be bought by an amir. I have thus taken to my residence, letting only my obscurity give me precedence.

§ In Praise of Saladin

I used to take such relief at isolation in lands abroad, and sweet separation from the native sward, hoping that through mere wanderlust, I could settle my homeland's bitter dust. I persevered with the patience of a prisoner whose chains he'd see burst, the control of a man held back from water, dying of thirst.[287]

Called me to him,[288] the message did, an invitation from our lord the Victorious King, Salah al-Dunya wa'l-Din, Sultan of Islam and the Muslimin! Unifier of the creed of faith by his light, subjugator of the worshippers of the Cross by his might, raiser of the banner of justice and right. The reviver of the dynasty of the Commander of the Faithful, Abu al-Muzaffar Yusuf ibn Ayyub. May God embellish Islam and the Muslims with his continued fruition, and grant them victory by the sharpness of his sword and his vision. May He enclose them all in his shadow's protective embrace, just as He has purified of filth the sources of his grace, and extend across the globe his every commanding and forbidding, lodging his swords in the necks of his foes to do his bidding.

In his mercy [165] he sought me out across the land – a place beyond mountains, beyond plains I was in, a forsaken corner of the world, having no kith, no kin. By his good-will, from misfortune's fangs was I snatched, bearing me up to his exalted gateway in his grace overflowing, unmatched. The parts of me Time had broken, he put them in splints to hold, and in his generosity he found a market for that which others had deemed unsaleable, too old. He surrounded me with the most wondrous favour, sending me, in his beneficence, gifts of the sweetest

flavour, so much that he recompensed me with his generosity's
flow for such services as I gave even to others ages ago. Yet still
these he considers and takes into account, as if he had seen and
enjoyed them in equal amount. His gifts, as I sleep, bang on my
door, making their way to me though I am retired, in service
no more. Every day I gain something more from the kindness
he gave; he treats me like family though I am his lowliest slave.
His good-will has allowed me from all calamities to survive,
and his munificence has paid back to me what the disasters of
Time did deprive. After granting me all that his duty and
example deem fair, his additional trifles are more than my back
can bear. His ampleness left me with no desire to sate, so in
prayer for him do I spend my days, from early to late.

As the mercy by which God brought relief to His servants he
stands; as the one who revived by its blessings our lands. The
sultan who restored the example of the Rightly-Guided (as
the first caliphs were called); a new pillar of religion and state
he installed. A source whose waters never dry from all the
drinkers, he is a lake; a bountiful giver who never stops giving,
no matter how much they take. In an impregnable defence are
the faithful, thanks to the safety his swords always bring;
by his liberality we flourish as in the green season of spring.
The light of his justice dispels the darkness of the oppressor,
and holds back the grasping arm of the warring transgressor.
Through his triumphant governance may we rest in his protective shade, in a state of continuing joy that follows the path of
a joy already laid – as long as night follows upon day, and the
heavenly spheres spin as they may!

> [166] I prayed and the two angels said 'Amen',
>   For the Enthroned One sits close to His caller.
>   For He has said, may He be exalted, to His servants:
>   'Invoke me, for I listen as I do answer.'[289]

Praise be to God, Lord of Worlds, and may His blessing be
upon our lord Muhammad and all the members of his family.
God is enough for us, He is the best protector.[290]

PART III
CURIOUS TALES: HOLY MEN AND HEALERS

[169] Section[1]

'Whatever good things you possess come from God.'[2]

§ Introduction

Usama ibn Murshid ibn 'Ali ibn Muqallad ibn Nasr ibn Mun-qidh (may God forgive him, his parents and all the Muslims for their sins) said:

Here are some curious tales, in some of which I figure myself, though some others were told to me by people I trust. I add them here as an appendix to my book, since they are not really concerned with the subjects I focused upon in the preceding pages. I will begin with some tales about holy men, may God be pleased with them all.

§ The Miracle of the Sweet-Wrapper

[170] The sheikh and imam Siraj al-Din Ibrahim, the preacher of the city of Is'ird,[3] related to me the following in Dhu al-Qa'da in the year 562 (August–September 1167) on the authority of Abu al-Faraj al-Baghdadi, who said:

I was in attendance at a meeting led by the sheikh and imam Abu 'Abdallah Muhammad al-Basri[4] in Baghdad, when a woman presented herself. She said, 'Master, you were among those who served as a witness when my dowry was fixed, but I have since lost the dowry-certificate. I ask you, then, to show me your favour by confirming your testimony before the court tribunal.' 'I won't do this', he replied, 'until you bring me some sweets.' The woman just

stood there, thinking he was joking, given what he said.
'Don't waste time,' he said. 'I won't go anywhere with you
until you bring me some sweets.'

So, she went away and later returned and took out a
paper cornet filled with dry sweets from a pocket under
her wrap. The sheikh's companions were amazed at his
request for sweets, given his ascetic outlook and abstin-
ence. He took the cornet and opened it up, tossing aside
the sweets one by one until it was empty. He then examined
the paper and what should it be but the very dowry-
certificate that the woman had lost! 'Take your dowry,' he
said. 'Here it is!'

Those who were present with him thought this was an
extraordinary occurrence, but he just said, 'Eat what is
lawful,[5] and you will do this, and even more.'

§ A Holy Man's Last Request

The sheikh Abu al-Qasam al-Khidr ibn Muslim ibn Qasim
al-Hamawi told me the following in Hama [171] on Monday,
the last day of Dhu al-Hijja, in the year 570 (21 July 1175). He
said, 'A man from al-Kufa once came to me, a descendant of
the Prophet,[6] and related to us on the authority of his father,
saying:

I used to visit the Chief Judge al-Shami al-Hamawi,[7] who
would receive me with great generosity and honour. One
day he said to me, 'I love the people of al-Kufa because of
one man among them. I was in Hama as a young man when
'Abdallah ibn Maymun al-Hamawi passed away there (may
God have mercy upon him). They had asked him to draw
up his last will, and he said, "When I am dead and you are
preparing my body for burial, take me out to the desert
and have someone climb up the hill that overlooks the
cemetery and call out, ' 'Abdallah ibn al-Qubays! 'Abdallah
ibn Maymun is dead! Present yourself and pray over
him!' " When the man died, they did what he had told
them to do, and a man approached, wearing a robe of raw
cloth and a mantle of wool, coming from the direction

towards which the announcement had been made. He came
and prayed over the body while everyone stood in shock,
speechless. When he finished his prayers, he left, returning
whence he came. The people then began complaining to
one another for not having got hold of the man to question
him. They ran after him, but he lost them without ever
speaking a word to anyone.'

§ A Similar Tale

I witnessed a similar occurrence in Hisn Kayfa. In the Mosque
of al-Khidr there, there was a man known as Muhammad
al-Samma'.[8] He had his own prayer-room adjacent to the
mosque and would come out to pray at the time of communal
prayer but then return to his own room. He was one of the
saints.[9] I once presented myself before him when he was close
to the hour of his death.

He said, 'I have always wished that God (may He be exalted)
would bring before me my master, Muhammad al-Busti.'[10]

No sooner had they made the preparations for the washing
of his body and the funeral procession when his master Muhammad al-Busti arrived at his side. He oversaw the washing of the
body and went out behind the body to lead the way for the
procession, and prayed over it.

Later, al-Busti repaired to his pupil's prayer-room, where he
resided for a short time, during which time he visited me and I
him. He was [172] (may God have mercy upon him) an ascetic
of great learning, the likes of whom I have never seen nor heard.
He would practise daily fasting,[11] neither drinking any water
nor eating any bread or grains. He would merely break his fast
with a couple of pomegranates or apples or a bunch of grapes.
Once or twice a month, he would take a few small bites of fried
meat.

I said to him one day, 'Sheikh Abu 'Abdallah, how is it that
you neither eat bread nor drink water and are always fasting?'

'At first', he said, 'I fasted and suffered from the hunger-
pangs, but then I found that I could put up with it. I suffered
for three days and said to myself, "I'll practise it according
to the rules about eating dead animals,[12] which are lawful if

absolutely necessary after three days of going without food."
And I found that I could put up with that too, so I gave up
eating and drinking altogether. Now my spirit is used to it and
does not complain, so I keep doing what I have been doing.'

One of the great men of Hisn Kayfa had a prayer-room built
for the sheikh in a garden, which he also granted to the sheikh.
The sheikh came to me on the first day of Ramadan and said,
'I have come to say farewell.'

I said, 'But what about the prayer-room that has been prepared for you, and the garden?'

'My brother,' he replied, 'I have no need for either of them.
I am not staying.' And he bade me farewell and set off, may
God have mercy upon him. That was in the year 570 (1175).

§ *A Miraculous Messenger*

The sheikh Abu al-Qasam al-Khidr ibn Muslim ibn Qasim
al-Hamawi related to me in Hama in the year just mentioned
that a man who used to work in a garden belonging to Muhammad ibn Mis'ar (may God have mercy upon him) went up to
the latter's family as they sat at the doors of their homes in
Ma'arra[13] and said, 'I have just now heard an amazing thing!'
'What is it?' they asked and he replied:

> A stranger passed by me carrying a water-skin and asked
> me to fill it up with water. So I gave him his water and he
> did his ablutions. I offered him two cucumbers, too, but
> he refused to take them. I said, 'Half of this garden is mine
> by the right of my labour in it. The other half belongs to
> Muhammad ibn Mis'ar by right of ownership.' At this he
> asked, 'Did Muhammad go on pilgrimage to Mecca this
> year?' 'Yes,' I replied. 'Yesterday,' the stranger said, [173]
> 'after we departed from making the station,[14] he died, and
> we prayed over his body.'

Muhammad's family then went out looking for this man to
ask him more about it, but they saw him at such a distance
away that they could not catch up with him. So they returned
and made a note of the man's account – dates included – and
the affair turned out just as the man had said.

§ Cured by 'Ali in a Dream

The most glorious Shihab al-Din Abu al-Fath al-Muzaffar ibn As'ad ibn Mas'ud ibn Bakhtakin ibn Sabuktakin,[15] the freedman of Mu'izz al-Dawla ibn Buwayh, related to me in Mosul, on 18 Ramadan of the year 565 (5 June 1170), the following account:

The Commander of the Faithful al-Muqtafi (may God have mercy upon him) made a visit to the mosque of Sandudiya, in the vicinity of al-Anbar[16] on the western Euphrates, accompanied by his vizier. I was also in attendance. The caliph entered the mosque, which was known as the Mosque of the Commander of the Faithful 'Ali[17] (may God be pleased with him), wearing a Dimyati robe and girded with a sword with an iron hilt.[18] No one, except those who knew him personally, could have known he was the Commander of the Faithful. Indeed, the caretaker of the mosque began invoking God's blessings upon the caliph's vizier. At this, the vizier said, 'For shame! You should be invoking blessings on the Commander of the Faithful!' At that, al-Muqtafi (may God have mercy upon him) said, 'Ask him something useful. Ask him what happened to the disease that afflicted his face. For I saw him back in the days of our lord al-Mustazhir[19] (may God have mercy upon him), and he had some ailment in his face. He had a tumour that covered most of his face, so that when he wanted to eat he would tie it back with a kerchief so that he could get food into his mouth.'[20]

To this the caretaker replied, 'It was just as you say. I frequently used to come to this mosque from al-Anbar. I then met someone who said to me, "If you would just visit so-and-so (meaning the governor of al-Anbar) as frequently as you visit this mosque, then he would surely have called a physician for you to remove that malady from your face." Something in what he had said impressed itself upon my soul, something that hardened my heart. I went to sleep that night [174] and saw the Commander of the Faithful 'Ali ibn Abi Talib (may God be pleased with him) in a dream. He was in the mosque. "What sort of sojourn is this?" he said, meaning a sojourn here on earth. So I complained to him about what was wrong with me and he turned away from me. But I tried to gain his good-will and complained again, telling him about what that man had said to me. He replied, "You are one of those who desire only the fleeting life."[21] Then I woke up, and the tumour had been tossed to one side and my ailment was gone.'

Hearing this, al-Muqtafi (may God have mercy upon him) remarked, 'He speaks the truth.' Then the caliph said to me,[22] 'Talk with him and look into what he needs. Then draw up a document to that effect and give it to me to sign.'

So I spoke with the caretaker, who said, 'I am the head of a family and responsible for my daughters. I desire three dinars every month.' I drew up a statement to this effect, on the top of which my servant wrote:

CARETAKER OF THE MOSQUE OF 'ALI.

The caliph put his seal on it, acknowledging the request, and said to me, 'Go and register this in the appropriate bureau.' So I went without reading the document except for the imprimatur, 'Let this be executed.'

Official procedure was to write a copy of the document for the beneficiary of the statement, and to take from him the original with the signature of the caliph on it. But when the scribe opened the original document to copy it, he found underneath the words 'CARETAKER OF THE MOSQUE OF 'ALI . . .' only the words '. . . Signed by al-Muqtafi, Commander of the Faithful' – God's blessings be upon him. So if the caretaker had demanded more, it would have been authorized for him.[23]

§ *The Prophet Appears in a Poor Man's Dreams*

In the vicinity of Hisn Kayfa on Thursday, 22 Rabi' al-Awwal of the year 566 (3 December 1170), the qadi and imam Majd al-Din Abu Sulayman Dawud ibn Muhammad ibn al-Hasan ibn Khalid al-Khalidi (may God have mercy upon him) related to me on the authority of someone he trusts the following:

An old man once requested an audience with the Khawaja Buzurk[24] (may God have mercy upon him). When he was admitted, [175] Khawaja Buzurk saw that he was a fine and imposing old man, and asked him, 'Where are you from, old man?' 'From a foreign land,'[25] the old man replied. Khawaja Buzurk asked, 'Is there something you need?' He replied, 'I am the messenger of the Messenger of God, may God bless him and grant him peace, to Malikshah.'[26] To this, Khawaja Buzurk responded, 'Old man! What sort of talk is this?' 'If you take me to him,' the old man replied, 'then I shall deliver the message to him. If not, then I shall remain here until I meet with him and deliver what I have with me.'

So Khawaja Buzurk went in to the sultan and informed him of what the old man had said. 'Bring him to me,' the sultan said. Once the old man was brought in, he presented a toothpick and a comb to the sultan, saying, 'I am a man with daughters of my own. But I am a poor man, unable to provide for their trousseaus or to marry them off. Every night I would pray to God (may He be exalted) that He would grant me with enough to provide their trousseaus. On Friday night of a certain month, I prayed to God, glory be to Him, to assist me with their needs, and went to sleep. I then saw the Messenger of God, may God bless him and grant him peace, in the way sleeping people see things. He said to me, "Is it you who prays to God (may He be exalted) to grant what you need to provide your daughters' trousseaus?" "Yes, Messenger of God," I replied. The Messenger of God then said, "Go to so-and-so (and he named Malikshah, meaning the sultan), and say to him: 'The Messenger of God, may God bless him and grant him peace, tells you to provide the trousseaus for my daughters.'" So I said, "Messenger of God, what if he asks me for a sign as proof, what should I tell him?" He replied, "Tell him that the sign is that every night before going to sleep he recites the sura of *tabaraka*."'[27]

When the sultan heard this, he said, 'This sign is true. None but God, may He be blessed and exalted, could have

perceived this. For my tutor ordered me to recite it every
night before going to sleep, and I still do it.' The sultan
then ordered that the old man receive everything he
requested for providing the trousseaus of his daughters,
and granted him the finest gifts before sending him on his
way.

§ *The Prophet Appears in another Dream*

That story is similar to one I heard from Abu 'Abdallah Muhammad ibn Fatik the Qur'an-master.[28] He said:

One day I was reciting the Qur'an under the tutelage of
Ibn Mujahid[29] the Qur'an-master, in Baghdad, when an
old man came towards him wearing a beat-up turban, a
head-cloth and robe that was also worn out. Ibn Mujahid
knew the old man and said to him, 'What's the story with
the little girl?'

The [176] old man replied, 'Ibn Mujahid, yesterday a
third daughter was born to me. My womenfolk asked me
for a *daniq* to buy some butter and honey with which to
rub her palate,[30] but I didn't have it. As a result, I went to
sleep full of anxiety. But I saw in my dream the Prophet,
may God bless him and grant him peace. He said, "Don't
be distressed or sad. When you wake up tomorrow, go in
to 'Ali ibn 'Isa,[31] the caliph's vizier. Send him my greetings,
and tell him, 'By the sign that you have prayed for the
Prophet at his tomb four thousand times, pay me one
hundred gold dinars.'"'

At this, Ibn Mujahid said, 'Abu 'Abdallah! This is a
precious thing!' and he interrupted the recital and took the
old man by the hand and, rising, brought him in to 'Ali ibn
'Isa. Seeing Ibn Mujahid with an old man he did not know,
'Ali ibn 'Isa asked, 'Where, Ibn Mujahid, did you get him?'
He replied, 'Let the vizier call him to approach and listen
to his words.' So 'Ali invited him to approach him and
asked, 'What is your trouble, old man?'

The old man began, 'As Ibn Mujahid knows, I have
two daughters. Yesterday, a third was born to me. My

womenfolk asked me for a *daniq* with which to buy some honey and butter to rub the child's palate, but I didn't have it. So I went to sleep last night full of worries. But I saw the Prophet, God's blessing and peace be upon him, in a dream, and he said, "Don't be distressed or sad. When you wake up tomorrow, go in to 'Ali ibn 'Isa. Send him my greetings, and tell him, 'By the sign that you have prayed for the Prophet at his tomb four thousand times, pay me one hundred gold dinars.'"'

At this, Ibn Mujahid said to me, 'Abu 'Abdallah, Tears flowed and poured from the eyes of 'Ali ibn 'Isa. Then the latter said, "God and His Messenger have spoken the truth, and so have you spoken, my good man. This is a thing that no one besides God (may He be exalted) and His Messenger (may God bless him and grant him peace) could know. Attendant! Bring the money-bag." The attendant went and brought the bag before him. 'Ali thrust his hand in and pulled out one hundred dinars, saying, "Here are the hundred dinars, which the [177] Messenger of God (may God bless him and grant him peace) spoke of to you. And here are another hundred for the good tidings you bring. And here are another hundred just as a gift from us to you." And so the old man departed, with three hundred dinars in his sleeve.'

§ *Another Cure by 'Ali in a Dream*

The Commander al-Hajj Abu 'Ali related to me in Ramadan of the year 568 (April–May 1173) at Hisn Kayfa the following:

I was in Mosul sitting in the shop of Muhammad ibn 'Ali ibn Muhammad ibn Mama when a *fuqqa'*-vendor[32] with a stocky body and thick legs passed by. So Muhammad called to him, 'By God, 'Abd 'Ali, tell him your story,' indicating yours truly.

The man said, 'As you can see,[33] I am a *fuqqa'*-vendor. One Tuesday night, I went to sleep healthy, but when I woke up it was as if I had become unhitched at the middle. I was unable to move and my legs dried up and became so thin that they were all skin and bones. I had to drag my feet behind me because my legs wouldn't follow along with me, and I couldn't get any movement out of them at all. So I sat down in the path of Zayn al-Din 'Ali Kujak[34] (may God have mercy upon him). He ordered that I be carried to his residence, and so I was.

'Zayn al-Din summoned some physicians and told them, "I would like you to heal this person." "We shall certainly heal him, God willing," they said. They then took a nail and heated it red hot and cauterized my leg with it, but I didn't feel a thing. "We're not able to heal this man," they told Zayn al-Din. "There's nothing we can do about it." So Zayn al-Din gave me two dinars and a donkey. The donkey remained with me for about a month, but then died. So I went back and sat down in the path of Zayn al-Din again, and he gave me another donkey, which also died. He gave me yet a third donkey, and it died, too.

'So I asked him for help yet again, but he just said to one of his companions, "Remove this man and throw him in the ditch." And so I begged his companion, "By God, throw me in on my hip so that I don't feel anything when it happens!" To this he replied, [178] "The only way I'll throw you is on your head!" But after this a messenger of Zayn al-Din's (may God have mercy upon him) came to me and brought me back to him, for what he had said about throwing me into the ditch was just a joke. Once I was presented before him, he granted me four dinars and a donkey.

'My condition remained as it was until one night when I saw in a dream a man standing by me. "Arise!" he said. "Who are you?" I asked him. "I am 'Ali ibn Abi Talib," he replied. And so I awoke and stood up. I woke my wife and said, "You won't believe it! I've just had a vision," and described it. "Hey! You're standing up!" she exclaimed.

'So I walked on my feet, my trouble gone, and returned to the condition that you see me in now. I went before Zayn al-Din, the amir 'Ali Kujak (may God have mercy upon him) and told him the story of my dream and he could see that the ailment that he had seen me with had now gone, so he granted me ten dinars.'

Glory be to the Healer, the Restorer of Health!

§ A Good Deed is Amply Rewarded

The sheikh and hafiz Abu al-Khattab al-'Ulaymi[35] related to me in Damascus early in the year 572 (summer 1176) the following on the authority of a man, who told it to him in Baghdad on the authority of al-Qadi Abu Bakr Muhammad ibn 'Abd al-Baqi ibn Muhammad al-Ansari al-Furdi, also known as Qadi al-Maristan,[36] who said:

> During my pilgrimage, as I was circumambulating the Ka'ba, I spotted a necklace of pearls, so I tied it to the edge of my pilgrim-garment.[37] After a while, I heard someone in the Sacred Precinct[38] seeking after it and offering twenty dinars to whomever would return it to him. I asked him to name some feature by which he could identify the lost object, and he provided it, so I handed the necklace over to him.
>
> 'Come with me to my home,' he said, 'so that I can give you the reward I promised you.' But I said, 'I don't need any of that. I didn't return it to you just for the sake of the reward. God has provided me with ample good fortune.' 'So you returned it to me only for the sake of God, the Mighty and Majestic?' he asked. 'Yes,' I said. 'Then let us turn and face the Ka'ba so that you can say "amen" to my prayer.' So we turned to face the Ka'ba and he prayed, 'O God, pardon the sins of this man, and grant me the means by which I might repay him!' Then he said farewell to me and left.
>
> It happened later that I travelled from Mecca to the land of Egypt, from where I took ship on the sea [179] heading for the Maghrib. But the Romans captured the ship, and I, with others, was taken captive. As plunder, my lot fell to one of the priests, whom I continued to serve until his own death approached, upon which he arranged in his will for me to be set free.

I therefore set out from the land of the Romans and headed for a certain part of the Maghrib, where I found myself a spot as a scribe in a baker's shop. Now, that baker used to offer his trade to one of the great landowners of that city. When the first of the month came, an attendant of the landowner came to the baker and said, 'My master summons you to settle the accounts with him.' The baker asked me to accompany him, and so the two of us went to the landowner and the baker settled his account according to his bills. When the landowner saw that I wrote in a fine hand and that I was knowledgeable about accounting, he demanded me from the baker. He then changed my clothes and submitted all the revenues of his property to me, which was a considerable fortune. He also reserved a house for me next to his own residence.

After a small stretch of time passed, my new master said to me, 'Abu Bakr, what do you think about getting married?' 'My lord,' I replied, 'I can barely manage to provide for myself; how will I manage to provide for a wife?' At this, he said, 'I will provide for you the dowry, your new home, your clothing and everything else you might need.' 'The decision is yours,' I said. Then he said, 'My boy, this wife has quite a few defects,' and he didn't leave out any of her physical flaws from her head down to her toes. 'I am satisfied,' I said. And, indeed, my internal thoughts were in accord with my external expressions. Finally, he concluded, 'And this wife is my daughter.' He then got a group of people together and we settled the contract.

A few days later, he said to me, 'Prepare to enter your home.' He then ordered some fancy clothes for me and I went into a house that had inside it luxurious furniture and other accoutrements. I was seated upon a cushioned platform and my bride came out, covered by her coloured wrap. I rose to meet her, and when I raised her covering I beheld a vision more beautiful than anything I have seen in this world. I immediately fled from the house. But the old man intercepted me and asked me what was the cause of my flight.

I told him, 'This wife is not the one you described to me
with all the defects!' The man smiled and said, 'My boy,
[180] she is your wife! I have no other child but her. I only
described her the way I did so that you wouldn't think less
of her when you saw her.' I went back, and the bride was
exhibited before me.[39]

The next morning, I started to admire the jewellery and
precious gems she wore. Among the mass of things she
wore, I noticed the necklace that I had found back in
Mecca! I was astounded and lost myself in thought about
it. When I was leaving the building, my father-in-law called
to me and asked how I was doing, saying, 'Lawful enjoyment has bent the nose of jealousy.'[40] I thanked him for
what he had done for me, but was then seized with the
thought of that necklace and how it could have come to
him. He asked me, 'What are you thinking about?'

'About a certain necklace,' I said. 'For I was on pilgrimage to Mecca in a certain year when I found that necklace
in the Sacred Precinct, or one very like it.' The man cried,
'You're the one who returned the necklace to me!' 'That
I am,' I replied. 'Take joy at this news!' he said, 'for God
has forgiven me and you! For I had prayed to God – glory
be to Him! – when it happened to forgive me and you and
to provide me with the means to repay you. And now I
have turned over to you my property and my child, and
I have no doubt that my time draws near.' He later made
me the beneficiary of his will and died after a short period
not long after that, may God have mercy upon him!

§ Raw Egg Cures a Boil

[181] The amir Sayf al-Dawla Zanki ibn Qaraja (may God have
mercy upon him) related to me the following incident. He said:

So, Shahanshah (he's the husband of Zanki's sister) invited
us to come to Aleppo. Once we gathered together at his
place, we sent word to a companion of ours whom we like
to spend time with and have drinking-sessions. He was a
real sweetheart and made good company, so we invited

him to come along. When he showed up, we offered him
a drink, but he said, 'I'm under strict orders not to drink.
My physician has ordered me to fast for a few days until
this boil splits open.' He had this huge boil on the back of
his neck. But we just told him, 'Come on and join us today,
and you can start fasting tomorrow.' So he did, and he
drank with us all day. Eventually, we asked Shahanshah
for something to eat. 'I haven't got anything,' he said. So
we harassed him until he finally agreed to bring us some
eggs to fry up on the brazier. He had the eggs brought out
along with a plate, and we cracked the eggs and poured
them out onto the plate and put the frying-pan on the
brazier to get all hot. But I gestured to our man with the
boil on his neck, and he lifted the plate up to his mouth to
drink a bit of it and he totally poured the whole plate-load
down his throat! So then we said to the master of the
house, 'Let's have some compensation for those eggs!' But
he replied, 'By God, I won't do it.' So we just drank some
more and went our separate ways.

I was actually still in bed at dawn when somebody
knocked on my door. A serving-girl went out to see who
was there, and – guess what? – there was that friend of
ours. 'Let him in,' I said. So he came over to me while
I was still in my bed and said, 'My lord, that boil that was
on my neck has disappeared without a trace!' I checked
the spot, and, sure enough, it looked just like
any other part of his neck. 'What got rid of it?' I asked. 'It
was God, glory be to Him!' he replied. 'As far as I know,
I didn't use anything I didn't [182] use before, unless it was
drinking those raw eggs.'

Glory be to the Almighty, the Afflicter, the Healer!

§ Raven-Flesh Cures a Hernia

We had with us at Shayzar two brothers from Kafartab, the
oldest named Muzaffar, the other Malik ibn 'Ayyad. As merchants, they both travelled to Baghdad and other lands. Muzaffar was afflicted with a terrible hernia, which tired him out.

Once, while he was part of a caravan crossing the Syrian Desert to Baghdad, the caravan encamped with one of the nomadic Arab tribes, who treated them with hospitality and cooked some fowl for them. They had their supper and then went to sleep. But then Muzaffar woke up and awakened his travelling companion, who was next to him, saying, 'Am I asleep or awake?'

'Awake,' he reasoned. 'If you were asleep, you wouldn't be talking.'

Muzaffar said, 'My hernia has disappeared without leaving any trace.' His companion examined him and, sure enough, he had returned to a state of health such as anyone else enjoys.

When they woke up the next morning, they asked the Arab tribesmen who had received them as guests what it was that they had fed them.

They said, 'You encamped among us while our animals were out to pasture, so we just went out and captured some young ravens and cooked them up for you.'

When the caravan reached Baghdad, they went to the hospital and told Muzaffar's story to the director of the hospital. The director sent word and obtained some young ravens and fed them to whomever was afflicted with this same malady, but it was of no benefit and had no effect whatsoever.

'This raven that he ate,' the director surmised, 'its father must have bill-fed it some vipers, and for that reason it did the man some good.'

§ Some Cures from Ibn Butlan

[183] There was a case similar to that one. A man once went to Yuhanna ibn Butlan the physician, who was famed for his knowledge, wisdom and prominence in the field of medicine. This was when Ibn Butlan had his clinic in Aleppo.[41] The man complained to Ibn Butlan about his ailment and the physician could see that he was stricken by dropsy – his stomach was enlarged, his neck emaciated and his whole appearance changed. So he said to the man, 'By God, my boy, I haven't got anything to help you, and medicine will no longer be of any use.' So the man left.

After a while, the man passed by again while Ibn Butlan was in his clinic, and his ailment had entirely left him, his abdomen had shrunk back and his condition was improved. So Ibn Butlan called to him and said, 'Aren't you the one who came to see me a while ago with a case of dropsy, with an enlarged stomach and emaciated neck, and I told you, "I haven't got anything to help you"?'

'I am indeed,' he replied.

'With what have you been treated such that your ailment has left you?' the physician asked.

'By God,' he responded, 'I haven't been treated with anything. I'm but a poor beggar, without any possessions or anyone to look after me other than my mother, an old and feeble woman. She had two casks full of vinegar which she used to feed to me every day with bread.'

Ibn Butlan asked him, 'Is there anything left of this vinegar?'

'Yes,' the man said.

'Then take me and show me the cask that has the vinegar in it,' the physician said.

The man led him to his house and showed him the cask of vinegar. Ibn Butlan emptied out the vinegar that was inside, and discovered two vipers at the bottom that had decomposed. So he said to the man, 'My boy, no one could have treated you with vinegar containing two vipers to the point that you would have recovered – except for God, the Mighty, the Majestic.'

[184] This Ibn Butlan had an amazing propensity for accurate diagnosis. Here is an example. A man once came to him while he was in his clinic in Aleppo. The man had lost his ability to speak and was barely intelligible when he spoke.

'What is your trade?' Ibn Butlan asked the man.

'I am a sifter,' he replied.

'Bring me half a *ratl* of sharp vinegar,' the physician said, and it was brought to him. 'Drink!' he said to the man.

So the man drank it and sat down for a moment until he was overcome with nausea. He then started vomiting large amounts of clay mixed in with all that vinegar. As a result, his throat opened up and his speech became unimpaired.

Ibn Butlan thereupon said to his son and his pupils, 'Don't

treat just anyone with this remedy, as it will kill him. In this case, a layer of dirt from the sifting-dust had been deposited along the oesophagus, and nothing could clear it out except vinegar.'

Ibn Butlan used to be attached to the service of my great-grandfather, Abu al-Mutawwaj Muqallad. It happened that my grandfather, Sadid al-Mulk 'Ali (may God have mercy upon him), developed a white patch of skin when he was just a little boy. His father became anxious about it, fearing it might be leprosy. So he summoned Ibn Butlan and said to him, 'Have a look at what has appeared on 'Ali's body.'

So Ibn Butlan examined him and said, 'I'll need five hundred dinars to treat him and make this malady leave him.'

'If you had treated 'Ali, I would not have considered it fair to you to pay only five hundred dinars,' replied my great-grandfather.

When he saw that my great-grandfather was angry, Ibn Butlan said, 'My lord, I am your servant and slave, existing by your bounty. What I said, I said only by way of a jest. The ailment afflicting 'Ali is just a skin-irritation that affects the young. When he reaches adolescence, it will pass. So don't be worried about it and don't let anyone tell you "I'll treat him if you pay me money". For all this will clear up when he matures.'

And it turned out just as he had said.

There was in Aleppo a woman, one of the notable women of Aleppo, called Barra. She caught a bad head-cold. She used to fashion for her head some old cotton, a tall pointed cap, some velvet and some pieces of cloth [185] so that she looked like she had a gigantic turban on her head, and she would still beg for relief from her cold. So she summoned Ibn Butlan and complained to him of her malady.

He said to her, 'Tomorrow, obtain for me fifty *mithqals* of strong-smelling camphor, either purchased or rented from one of the perfumers, with the understanding that it will be returned intact.'

And so she obtained the camphor for him. The next morning, Ibn Butlan pulled off everything she had on her head, laced her hair with the camphor and returned all the wraps she had had on her head. All the while she was begging for relief from her cold. She then went to sleep for a short while and woke up complaining of the heat and the weight on her head. So Ibn Butlan began removing one piece after another from her head until only one veil was left. Then he shook that camphor from her hair and her cold left her. Afterwards, she would go about covered in one veil only.

§ Usama's Cure for the Common Cold

Something close to that happened to me at Shayzar. I was stricken with a terrible cold and I had chills without any fever, even though I wore furs and many layers of clothing. Whenever I moved while sitting, I would shiver and my body-hair would stand on end and my muscles seize up. I summoned sheikh Abu al-Wafa' Tamim, the physician, and complained to him about how I was feeling.

'Bring me an Indian melon,' he said. So I had one brought.

He split it open and said to me, 'Eat as much of it as you can.'

'But doctor,' I said, 'I am dying of cold, and this pomegranate thing is cold. How can I eat this with all its coldness?'[42]

'Eat like I told you,' he said to me. So I ate. No sooner had I finished eating it than I started to sweat and the cold that I had been feeling passed.

The physician said to me, 'What was afflicting you was caused by an over-abundance of bile, not by actual cold.'

§ Another Cure from a Dream

I have already mentioned above something about curious dreams, and in my book entitled [186] On Sleep and Dreams[43] I have also presented some accounts of sleep and dreams and what others have said concerning them, the timing of visions and what scholars have pronounced on the subject. I have quoted statements that have appeared in Arabic poetry, expanding my commentary and giving a full explanation of everything. As a result, there is no need to mention anything more about the subject here. However, I did include the following account and enjoyed it so much I wanted to repeat it here:

My grandfather, Sadid al-Mulk 'Ali (may God have mercy upon him), had a serving-girl called Lu'lu'a, who raised my father, Majd al-Din Murshid (may God have mercy upon him). And when he grew up, he moved out of the house of his father and she moved with him. Then I was brought into the world and that same servant, now an old woman, raised me until I grew up, got married and moved from the house of my father (may God have mercy upon him), and she moved out with me. Then I was blessed with children, whom she in turn raised. She was (may God have mercy upon her) one of the most pious women, constantly fasting and praying. But she was time and again laid low with the colic. One day, it struck her and became so bad that she lost consciousness and they despaired for her. But she remained in that state for two days and two nights. Then she came out of it, exclaiming, 'There is no God but God! What a marvellous experience I have just had! I met with all our dearly departed ones and they spoke with me about wondrous things. Among the things they said to me was, "This colic will never come back to you again."'

And she lived for a long time afterwards and was never again stricken by colic. She lived until she was almost a hundred years old and never missed her prayers, may God have mercy upon her!

I once went in to see her in the rooms I had set aside for her in my residence. In front of her was a wash-basin and she was washing a headscarf for use in prayer.

'What's that, mother?' I asked.

'My son,' she replied, 'this headscarf has been handled by someone with cheese on their hands. For no matter how much I wash it, it still gives off an odour of cheese.'

'Show me the block of soap that you're washing it with,' I said.

So she took the soap out from the headscarf and, sure enough, it was a piece of cheese which she had thought was soap. Every time she rubbed that headscarf with cheese, it gave off its odour.

'Mother,' I said, 'that's a piece of cheese, not a piece of soap!'

She looked at it and said, 'You're right, my son. I didn't [187] think it was anything except soap.'

Blessed thus is God the most truthful of all speakers: 'If We extend anyone's life, We reverse his development.'[44]

Prolongation will just lead to frustration, since there are accidents and misfortunes too numerous to be reckoned. I beseech God, the Mighty and Majestic, for His protection and for my health in what remains to my last breath, and for His mercy and favour at the moment of my death. For He, glory be to Him, is the most generous granter of requests, the one in whom every hope rests.

Praise be to God alone, and may His blessings and peace fall upon our lord Muhammad and his family.

PART IV

EPISODES OF HUNTING

[191] I put my trust in God, may He be exalted![1]

§ Introduction

To God belongs one side of my life, I never forget it;
But the other side belongs to play and idleness.[2]

I have mentioned something of the varieties of warfare, and
some examples of the battles, confrontations and dangerous
feats that I have witnessed – at least those whose memory I
could trace that Time and its passage did not efface. For my
life presses on without conclusion and I have taken up a life of
isolation and seclusion. After all, oblivion is a legacy passed
down without cease from our father Adam (upon him be peace).

I shall now present a section devoted to episodes of hunting,
the chase and the use of birds of prey that I witnessed or personally attended. Some of these are experiences I had at Shayzar
in my formative years; others I had with the King of Amirs, the
atabeg Zangi ibn Aq-Sunqur (may God have mercy upon him);
others I had in Damascus with Shihab al-Din Mahmud ibn Buri
(may God have mercy upon him); others I had in Egypt; still
others I had with Nur al-Din, the son of the atabeg Zangi (may
God have mercy upon him), or in Diyar Bakr with the amir
Qara Arslan (may God have mercy upon him).

§ Usama's Father

[192] As for my hunting at Shayzar, it was done with my father
(may God have mercy upon him), who had a great passion for
the hunt and all varieties of birds of prey, always talking about
it, and, on account of his delight in it, he never considered what
he spent on it to be too much. It was his favoured pastime, for,
once he had finished attending to the needs of his companions,

he had no other thing to occupy him besides warfare, jihad against the Franks and copying the Book of God (the Mighty, the Majestic). He (may God have mercy upon him) fasted every day and kept up his practice of reciting the Qur'an. For him, the hunt was as it is described in the old saying, 'Air out your heart, and it will better retain the remembrance of God.' I have truly never seen anything like his hunting and his ability to organize it.

§ *Hunting with Zangi*

I have observed the hunt with the King of Amirs, the atabeg Zangi (may God have mercy upon him), who had a large number of birds of prey. I would see him, as we proceeded along the river-banks, preceded by the austringers, who would cast off[3] the goshawks at the waterfowl. The drums would be beaten following the usual custom and the hawks would hunt down what they could hunt, and miss what they missed. Behind them were the 'mountain' peregrines on the falconers' fists. Once the goshawks had done their hunting (successful or not), they slipped the peregrines on those birds which had managed to fly far away, making a 'desert run',[4] and they would take them and make a kill. They are also slipped on partridge, taking them and making their kill as the birds take off at the base of the mountain. For peregrines are characterized by a truly marvellous swiftness of flight.[5]

One day I observed Zangi while we were in the water-gorged plain in the environs of Mosul. We were crossing through eggplant fields. In front of the atabeg was an austringer with a female sparrow-hawk[6] on his fist. A male francolin took to the air, so the austringer slipped the sparrow-hawk on it, [193] and it took the francolin and came down to earth. Once it reached the ground, the francolin escaped from its grasp and once again took to the air. When the francolin had got high up in the air, the hawk took off again and seized it and came back down to earth, clasping its quarry firmly.

I have also seen the atabeg many times engaged in hunting wild game. Once the hunting-party had drawn up in a circle, with the beasts corralled inside the circle, then no one could enter it. As soon as any of the beasts tried to leave the circle, we shot arrows at it. The atabeg was himself one of the best archers there. Whenever a gazelle would draw near, he would shoot it, but it looked to us as if it had merely stumbled. Then it would fall to the ground and be slaughtered. When I was with him, on every hunting expedition I attended, he would send the first gazelle he killed to me with one of his attendants.

I was present once when the circle had been formed while we were in the region of Nisibis[7] on the banks of the Hirmas. They had already pitched our tents and the beasts came right up to our tents. The attendants came out with staves and poles and struck down quite a few of them. A wolf, corralled inside the circle, pounced upon a gazelle in the middle of the circle and, having caught it, crouched down upon it. It was killed while it sat upon its prey.

I was also with the atabeg one day while we were in Sinjar.[8] One of his companions, a horseman, came and told him, 'There's a hyena bitch over here, sleeping!' So the atabeg started off, and we with him, to a valley there where the hyena was asleep on a rock on one side of the valley. The atabeg dismounted and walked up to the hyena until he stood facing it. He then shot it with an arrow, which knocked the hyena down to the floor of the valley. His followers climbed down and brought it before him, dead.

I also saw the atabeg in the environs of Sinjar when his party had roused a hare from its form. He gave orders and the cavalry made a circuit around the hare. He then called for an attendant, who carried a caracal[9] along behind him in the way one carries a cheetah. The attendant came forward and slipped the caracal on to the hare, which jumped in among the legs of the horses and so was unable to be caught. Before that, I had never seen a caracal used in a hunt.

§ *Hunting in the Principality of Damascus*

I had experience of hunting birds, gazelle, onager and roe-deer in Damascus in the days of Shihab al-Din Mahmud ibn Buri. I observed him one day as we went out [194] into the woods that surround Banias, where there was a thick carpet of grass. We hunted a large number of roe-deer and then pitched our tents in a circle and made camp. From the middle of the circle, a roe-deer that had been sleeping in the grass now stood up and it was taken there in the midst of the tents.

As we were returning, I observed a man who, spying a squirrel in the trees, informed Shihab al-Din about it. So Shihab al-Din came and stood under the squirrel and shot two or three arrows at it, without hitting it. He left and continued onward, somewhat annoyed at not having bagged the squirrel. Then I saw one of the Turks come up and shoot the squirrel. The arrow cut it in two; its forepaws just dangled there, but it remained hanging by its hind legs, the arrow having pinned it – they had to shake the tree before it fell off. If that arrow had struck a human being, he would have died on the spot. Glory be to the Creator of all creatures!

§ *Hunting in Egypt*

I have also seen hunting in Egypt. Al-Hafiz (may God have mercy upon him) had many birds of prey: goshawks, sakers and 'overseas' peregrines.[10] These were all cared for by a master-falconer, who would take them out two days a week, most of them just on the fists of the falconers, who walked on foot. On the day they went out to hunt, I used to ride out to enjoy the sight of them hunting.

As a result, the master-falconer went to al-Hafiz and told him, 'Your guest (calling me by name) goes out when we do,' saying this to seek his opinion about it.

Al-Hafiz replied, 'Go out with him and let him enjoy the sight of the birds.'

[195] So we went out one day and one of the austringers was carrying an intermewed goshawk with red irises.[11] We saw some crane, so the master-falconer said to the austringer, 'Go up ahead and cast off on them the goshawk with the red irises.'

So he went forward and cast off the hawk on the crane, which took to flight. The goshawk intercepted one of them in mid-air some distance away from us and brought it down. I said to one of my attendants who was riding a thoroughbred mount, 'Push forward to the goshawk, dismount and shove the crane's bill into the ground. Hold it down that way and keep its legs under yours until we can get to you.'

So he went and did as I had told him. The austringer then arrived and slaughtered the crane and then gorged[12] the goshawk.

When the master-falconer returned, he told al-Hafiz what had happened and what I had said to my attendant, adding, 'My lord, he talks the talk of a true huntsman.'

At this, al-Hafiz remarked, 'What business does this fellow have besides fighting and hunting?'

They also had some sakers that they would slip against grey heron,[13] while the latter were in flight. When the heron sees the saker, it climbs up in a spiral. The saker then does the same, a little apart, until it climbs up higher than the heron. Then it stoops[14] on the heron and takes it.

In that land there are birds which they call *al-bujj*, similar to the flamingo,[15] which they also hunt. The waterfowl are easy to hunt in the canals cut from the Nile. They have very few gazelles but there is in that land the 'cow of the Children of Israel'.[16] These are yellow cows with horns like the horns of normal cows. However, they are smaller than normal cows and can run at an incredible pace.

They also have an animal that comes from the Nile that they call the 'river-horse', which is like a small cow and has little eyes. [196] It is hairless, like a water-buffalo. In its lower jaw, it has long fangs, while in its upper jaw it has holes through which the points of its fangs can issue just below its eyes. It makes noises like the noises of a pig and is always to be found in a pool of water. It eats bread, grass and barley.[17]

§ Hunting in Frankish Acre

I had gone with the amir Mu'in al-Din (may God have mercy upon him) to Acre to visit the king of the Franks, Fulk, son of Fulk. We saw there a Genoese man who had just arrived from the land of the Franks and who brought with him a large intermewed goshawk that hunted crane. He also had a small bitch with him, which, when he cast off the goshawk at crane, would run below.

When the hawk made its kill and came down to earth, the bitch took the crane in her mouth and it was unable to escape from her. The Genoese man said to us, 'In our country, if the goshawk has thirteen feathers in its tail, then it can hunt crane.'

We counted the tail-feathers[18] of that goshawk, and it was just so.

The amir Mu'in al-Din (may God have mercy upon him) asked the king to give him that hawk, so he took it from the Genoese, along with the bitch, and gave it to the amir, and it came back with us. On our way, I saw the hawk pounce on gazelle as if it were pouncing on pieces of meat. We arrived with it in Damascus, but its life there was not long, and it did not hunt anything before it died.

§ Hunting at Hisn Kayfa

I have also seen hunting at Hisn Kayfa with the amir Qara Arslan [197] (may God have mercy upon him). In that region, there are many partridges and see-sees[19] as well as francolins. As for the waterfowl, they inhabit the river-bank, which is a wide open space, and so goshawks are unable to catch them. Most of their quarry are mountain goats, male or female. They make nets for them that they spread in the valleys. They then drive the mountain goats into them so that they are trapped. These mountain goats abound in their region and are very convenient to hunt. The hares are like that too.

§ Hunting with Nur al-Din

I also saw some hunting with Nur al-Din (may God have mercy upon him). I was in his company while we were in the territory of Hama, when the men roused a hare. Nur al-Din shot a chisel-headed arrow at it, but the hare just leapt up and beat us to its burrow and went in. We all galloped after it, and Nur al-Din stood waiting for it. Meanwhile, the Sharif al-Sayyid Baha' al-Din (may God have mercy upon him) passed the hare's leg to me, which the arrow had cut off above the tendon. The point of the arrowhead had sliced through its abdomen, causing the hare's uterus to slip out. Yet after all that, it beat us all and went into its burrow. Nur al-Din gave the order to one of his bodyguards, who went down, took off his sandals and went in after the hare, but he could not get to it. I said to the man who had the hare's uterus – which still had two leverets in it – 'Cut it open and cover the leverets in soil.' And so he did, and the animals kept moving and lived.

I was in Nur al-Din's presence another day, when he had slipped a bitch on a fox while we were in the environs of Qara Hisar, in the territory of Aleppo. He and I both galloped along behind the bitch, which caught up with the fox and grabbed the fox's tail. The fox then turned its head backwards and clamped down on the bitch's snout. The bitch began yelping while Nur al-Din (may God have mercy upon him) just laughed. Then the fox let go and slid into its earth and we were unable to catch it.

[198] One day, as we were riding beneath the citadel of Aleppo to the north of the city, Nur al-Din was presented with a goshawk. So he said to the amir Najm al-Din[20] (may God have mercy upon him), 'Go tell so-and-so (meaning me) to take this hawk and amuse himself with it.'

So Najm al-Din told me, and I replied, 'I don't know how.'

At this, Nur al-Din said, 'You, who are always engaged in hunting, don't know how to train a goshawk?!'

'My lord,' I responded, 'we don't do our training ourselves. We have austringers and attendants who do that and who go ahead of us with them to hunt.' I did not take the hawk.

§ Usama's Father as a Huntsman

[199] I have experienced so much hunting with these great men that time does not permit me to mention everything in detail. They were all quite capable hands at the hunting-expeditions they ventured upon and with hunting-gear and all that. But I have never seen anything like the hunting done by my father (may God have mercy upon him). Yet I don't know whether I am viewing him through the eyes of one who loves him – 'Everything the beloved does is beloved,' as the poet said – or if my view of him is based on reality. But I will mention something of his experience at hunting, and those who come upon the work may judge for themselves.

My father (may God have mercy upon him) filled all his time with reciting the Qur'an, fasting, hunting during the day and copying the Book of God (may He be exalted) during the night. He had written out forty-six complete copies of the Qur'an in his own hand (may God have mercy upon him), two of which had the entire text of the Qur'an in gold ink. He would go hunting one day, then rest the next. And he fasted every day.

We had two hunting-grounds at Shayzar: one was for partridge and hare, in the hills south of town; the other was for waterfowl, francolin, hare and gazelle, in the cane-brakes along the river to the west of town.

My father used to spare no expense when he sent a group of his followers to other lands to purchase hawks, even dispatching men to Constantinople to bring hawks back for him. His attendants brought with them what they thought would be enough pigeons to feed the hawks that they brought back. But the sea changed on them and their voyage dragged on, with the result that they used up what food they had brought for the hawks. So they were forced to start feeding the hawks fish, which had a bad effect on their wings. It made their feathers brittle and prone to breaking. Shayzar certainly had some exceptional hawks once they returned! But there was [200] in the service of my father an austringer, called Ghana'im, with great experience in training and healing hawks. He imped the wings[21] of the hawks and went hunting with them, and some of them moulted under his care.

On most occasions, my father would order hawks and buy them from the Valley of Ibn al-Ahmar[22] at high prices. So he summoned a group of people from the mountains near Shayzar, folk from Bashila, Yasmalikh and Hillat 'Ara, and talked with them about setting up traps for hawks in their own localities. He bestowed gifts and clothing upon them, so they went off and built trapping hides where they caught many hawks, including passagers, haggards and tiercels.[23]

They brought them to my father, saying, 'My lord, we have given up our livelihood and our farming to serve you. We therefore request that you take all the birds we catch and decide upon a price for us which we will all know and which will not be the result of any individual bargaining.'

So my father fixed the price of a passager goshawk at fifteen dinars, the passager tiercel at half that, the haggard goshawk at ten dinars and the haggard tiercel at half of that.

Thus, a new way of making money was opened up for the mountain-folk that did not involve tiring them out. The trapper only has to provide a stone house for himself which is built according to his own height. He covers it with branches concealed under hay and grass, with an opening in it. He takes a pigeon, securing its feet to a perch, and displays it through the opening. He then wiggles the perch and the pigeon flaps its wings. The wild hawk sees the pigeon and swoops down to take it. When the trapper feels the hawk, he pulls the perch back through the opening, stretches out his hand and seizes the hawk's legs, while it is still clutching the pigeon. He then brings it down and seels its eyes.[24] The next morning, he brings the hawk to us and receives the fixed price for it, returning home two days later.

[201] As a result, the number of trappers increased, as did the number of hawks, to the point that at Shayzar hawks were as common as chickens. Some of them one could hunt with, others died on the perch because there were so many of them.

My father had in his service austringers, falconers and houndsmen. He also taught a group of his *mamluks* to train hawks, and they became experts at it. He used to go out on the hunt with us, his four male children, accompanying him. We were further accompanied by our attendants, our extra mounts and our weapons, since we never really felt safe given the proximity of the Franks to us. Many hawks would come out with us, around ten or more. And my father would also bring two falconers, two cheetah-trainers and two houndsmen, one of them leading the saluki-hounds, the other leading *zagharis*.[25]

On the day when he went forth to the mountain to hunt partridge, while he was on the way there yet still distant from it, he would tell us, 'Go, split up. Any of you who still hasn't done his recitation should now go and do it.' For we, his children, had memorized the Qur'an. And so we would then disperse and recite the Qur'an until he arrived at the hunting spot and ordered someone to summon us. He would then ask each of us how much we had recited. Once we had informed him, he would say, 'Me, I've recited one hundred verses,' or something close. My father (may God have mercy upon him) could recite the Qur'an just like it was when it was first revealed.

Once we arrived at the hunting-grounds, he would order the attendants to disperse, some of them accompanying the austringers. In whichever direction the partridge took flight, there would be a goshawk ready to be slipped on it. My father was accompanied also by forty horsemen from his *mamluk*s and companions, quite experienced at the chase. No bird could take to the air, no hare or gazelle could be roused, that they could not bag. We would end up hunting on the mountain until the late afternoon, then we would return having gorged the hawks and set them loose to drink and bathe in the little pools on the mountain. We would generally return to town after nightfall.

But when we rode out in pursuit of waterfowl and francolin, *that* was a day of real amusement. We would start off [202] for the hunt from the town gate. Then we would reach the cane-brakes. The cheetahs and sakers would stay outside the cane-brakes, while we would go in with the goshawks. If a francolin flies up, the hawk will take it. If a hare is roused, we slip one of the hawks on it. If she takes it, splendid. If not, then the hare will just run out towards the cheetahs, which will be slipped after it. Likewise, if a gazelle is roused, it leaves the cane-brakes in the direction of the cheetahs, which are slipped after it. If a cheetah takes it, splendid. If not, they would slip the sakers after it. Thus, hardly any game escaped us, except by some twist of fate.

In the cane-brakes there were large numbers of wild boar that would come out. We would gallop after them and kill them, and our joy in killing these beasts would be greater than our joy at hunting other game.[26]

My father had a certain way of organizing the hunt as though he were faced with organizing a military campaign or some grave affair. No one was to busy themselves with chatting with his companion – they were to have no concern other than scanning the ground to spot any hares or birds that might be in their nests.

§ Al-Yahshur: A Very Special Hawk

A special relationship of friendship and letter-exchanging existed between my father and the sons of Rupen – Thoros and Leon – who were the Armenian lords of al-Massisa, Tarsus, Adana and the Passes,[27] largely because of his desire to acquire hawks. Every year, they would send to my father ten or so hawks in the care of Armenian austringers, as well as *zaghari*-hounds. In return, my father would send them horses, perfumes and Egyptian garments. In this way, we used to get the finest hawks of rare quality from them. In a certain year, we had acquired numerous hawks from the Passes, including a passager as big as an eagle, and other smaller hawks.

[203] From the mountains came a number of other hawks, including a young hawk that was so broad in the chest it looked like a falcon, though it could not keep up with the other hawks in flight. Yet the austringer Ghana'im used to say, 'Out of all our hawks, there is not a single one like this goshawk, al-Yahshur. There is nothing it will pass up to hunt.'

We did not believe him. But later he trained that hawk, and it turned out just as he had thought it would – one of the strongest, quickest and most cunning of hawks. It moulted while in our care and emerged from the moulting even finer than it was before. That hawk lived a long time with us and moulted over a period of thirteen years. Al-Yahshur became like a member of our household: hunting to fulfil its service to us, unlike the habit of other birds, who hunt only for their own sake.

Al-Yahshur's roost was with my father (may God have mercy upon him), who would not leave it in the care of the austringer because the latter would always carry the hawk around at night and starve it to get better hunting out of it. But al-Yahshur would see to its own needs and still do whatever was asked of it. We would often go out hunting partridge, bringing a number of hawks with us, but my father would hand al-Yahshur to one of the austringers, saying, 'Take him away, and don't slip him with the other birds. Go hide somewhere on the mountain.'

As soon as they had removed themselves, if a partridge was seen perched up in a tree and if it was reported to my father, he would say, 'Give me al-Yahshur!'

The moment my father would raise his arm, al-Yahshur would fly from the wrist of the austringer and perch on my father's wrist, without any other call. Then it would stretch its neck and head proudly. Upon nearing the sleeping partridge, my father would throw a stick that he was holding, flushing it. Al-Yahshur would now be slipped on the partridge, which it could seize anywhere within a range of ten cubits. The austringer would then come down, slay the quarry that the hawk held in its claws and take al-Yahshur up on his wrist. My father would then again say, 'Take him away.'

Whenever they saw another partridge perched in a tree, he would do the same thing again, until five or six partridges had been caught, al-Yahshur taking them all within a range of ten cubits.

My father would then say to the austringer, 'Gorge the hawk.'

'But, my lord,' the austringer would reply, 'why don't you let it be, so that we can get better hunting out of it?'

'My boy,' my father would respond, 'we have ten other hawks which can still give us some good hunting. This one has done his part. If he kept going like this, it would shorten his life.' And so the austringer would gorge the hawk, and take it away.

[204] When we were done hunting, we would gorge the hawks, and put them on the water to drink and bathe, while al-Yahshur rested on the wrist of the austringer. As we approached town on our return from the mountains, my father would say, 'Give me al-Yahshur!'

He would then carry the hawk on his wrist and continue home. If a partridge should be flushed out before him, then he would slip al-Yahshur on it to catch it, the hawk flying ten or more courses along the way, depending upon how many partridges took to flight. And, having earlier been gorged, it would never touch its beak to a partridge's throat or taste its blood.

When we entered the house, my father would say, 'Go and get me a bowl of water.'

After they brought him a bowl with water in it, my father (may God have mercy upon him) would present it to al-Yahshur as it sat on his wrist and the hawk would drink from it. If it wanted to bathe, the hawk would stir its beak in the water, making it known that it wished to bathe. My father would then command that a large basin with water in it be brought out and he would bring the hawk to it. So the hawk would fly up and descend into the middle of the basin and flap its wings about in the water until it was satisfied with its bathing. Then it would climb out. My father would then put it on a large perch of wood that he had had built for the hawk and place a brazier of hot coals up close to it. After the hawk was combed and rubbed with oil until it was dry, my father would put a folded scrap of fur by it and it would hop down and go to sleep. The hawk would remain with us on that scrap of fur sleeping until quite late in the night, when my father would want to retire to his private apartments, at which he would say to one of us, 'Carry him.' And so the hawk would be carried as it slept on its bit of fur until it was put down alongside the bed of my father (may God have mercy upon him).

Of the wondrous qualities of the hawk – and it had many such qualities – I shall only relate those that my memory can bring forth, for a long time has passed and my years have made me forget many of its ways. In my father's house there were pigeons, green waterfowl and their hens, and 'white-birds'[28] of the kind that live among the cattle and keep flies from the house. My father would go into the courtyard with al-Yahshur on his wrist and sit down on a bench there, the hawk on its perch alongside him. But the hawk would not seek after any of those other birds there, nor would it pounce on them, as if it was simply not its custom to hunt such birds.

In winter, water would flood the lands around Shayzar such that swamps would form outside its walls, [205] like pools of water, in which birds would congregate. My father would then

order the austringer and an attendant to go out and approach
those birds. He himself would take al-Yahshur on his wrist
and, standing with it on the citadel, he would indicate the birds
to the hawk. He would be standing to the east of the town and
the birds would be to its west. As soon as the hawk saw the
birds, my father would cast it off on them and it would descend
and leave the town behind it, heading out until it reached the
birds. The austringer would then beat the drum to flush out the
birds, and al-Yahshur would catch some of them, even though
the distance between there and the place where it was cast off
was significant.

We used to go out to hunt waterfowl and francolin, returning
after dusk. If we heard the sounds of birds in any of the big
streams near town, my father would say, 'Give me al-Yahshur.'
He would then take the hawk, which had already been gorged,
and advance on the birds, the drum beating until the birds took
to flight. Then he would slip al-Yahshur on them. If it caught
anything, it would come to ground in our midst; the austringer
would then go down and slay the quarry still caught in the
hawk's talons, and then lift it back up on his wrist. If it did not
catch anything, it would come to ground on some flank of the
river such that we could not see it or guess where it had come
down. So we would just leave it alone and go back into town.
The following morning, the austringer would go back out at
dawn to find al-Yahshur and return it to my father (may God
have mercy upon him) in the citadel. On one such instance, the
austringer said, 'My lord, this hoar-frost has so burnished the
back of the hawk's head it'd turn a razor! So let's go out and
see what it'll get up to today!'

No variety of game could escape this hawk, from quail to
'salamander goose'[29] and hare. The austringer was always keen
to use it to hunt crane and argala,[30] but my father would not
let him, saying, 'Argala and crane [206] should be hunted with
sakers.'

However, one year, this hawk seemed to have fallen short of
its usual abilities in the hunt, such that whenever it was slipped
on its quarry and missed it, it would not respond to the lure. It
became frail and would not bathe, and we did not know what

was wrong with it. But then it finally recovered from its weakness and went hunting again. One day, after it had bathed, the austringer lifted it from the water, and its feathers on one side were parted because of being so wet. As a result, the austringer spied there on its side a boil the size of an almond.

The austringer accordingly brought the hawk before my father and said, 'My lord, this is what caused the hawk to weaken and nearly killed it.' He then held the hawk firmly and squeezed the boil, which popped off like a dry almond. The spot where the boil had been closed up and al-Yahshur returned to executing birds with sword and mat.[31]

Mahmud ibn Qaraja, the lord of Hama in those days, used to send someone every year to request that the hawk al-Yahshur be sent to him with an austringer, to stay with him for twenty days so that he could use it in his hunting. The austringer would take the hawk there and return with it. Eventually the hawk died in Shayzar.

Now, it happened that I was paying a visit to Mahmud in Hama just then. One morning, while I was there in Hama, I woke up to find that the Qur'an-reciters and the men who chant 'God is great!' and a great crowd of townspeople had assembled. So I asked, 'Who has died?'

'A daughter of Mahmud ibn Qaraja,' they told me.

Naturally, I wanted to go out and walk in the funeral procession, but Mahmud argued with me and dissuaded me from doing so. The procession continued outside the town and interred the dead body in Tall Saqrun.[32]

When they returned, Mahmud said to me, 'Do you know whose that dead body was?'

'They told me it was one of your children's,' I replied.

'No, by God,' he said, 'it was al-Yahshur's! I heard that it had died, so I sent a man to get it, and I fashioned a coffin for it, arranged a funeral procession and interred it. For surely it deserved that much.'

§ An Exceptional Cheetah

My father also had a female cheetah that was to other cheetahs like al-Yahshur was to other hawks. [207] They captured this cheetah when it was still wild, one of the largest cheetahs ever. The cheetah-keeper took it, put a ring in its nose and trained it. It was content to ride out,[33] but would not hunt. It would also have fits just like a madman would be taken by fits, frothing at the mouth. When a young deer was presented to it, it would not seek the game out nor show any interest except to sniff at it and mouth it. It went on like this for a long time, close to a year.

But one day we went out to the cane-brakes. The horsemen went in while I stood at the mouth of the cane-brakes, with the cheetah-keeper and the cheetah near me. A gazelle sprang up and came out towards me. I urged on the horse I was riding, a real thoroughbred, wishing to drive the gazelle back in the direction of the cheetah. But the horse was too quick for the gazelle and struck it in the chest, throwing it to the ground. The cheetah suddenly sprang upon it and caught it, as if it had been sleeping, had woken up and said, 'Take what game you wish!' It caught any gazelle that showed itself. Its keeper was unable to control it and it would drag him along, throwing him down. It did not stop as cheetahs usually do when hunting. On the contrary, every time the keeper said, 'It's stopped!' it would run off again and take a gazelle.

We used to hunt *idmi*[34] gazelle in Shayzar, which is a large variety of gazelle. Whenever we took this cheetah out to al-'Ala and the lands to the east where there are white gazelles,[35] we would not let the cheetah-keeper run with it, so that it was not able to drag him along and throw him down. It would attack gazelles as if they appeared to be young ones because of the small size of the white gazelle.

This cheetah alone of all the other cheetahs was allowed in the home of my father (may God have mercy upon him). He had a special serving-girl who tended it. On one side of the courtyard, the cheetah had a folded-up blanket with dry grass underneath, and in the wall a metal spike had been driven. The cheetah-keeper would come in with it from the hunt and put it down at the entrance of the courtyard where it took its rest. The cheetah would then walk into the courtyard to the spot all made up for it, and it would go to sleep there. Then the serving-girl would come and chain it to the spike in the wall. Yet, by God, in that same house there were some twenty *idmi* and white gazelles, rams, goats and fawns [208] that had been born there. Yet the cheetah would neither seek them out nor frighten them. It would never stir from its place. Left by itself, it would just enter the courtyard without even turning to look at the gazelles.

I observed the serving-girl currying the cheetah's coat with a comb, and the cheetah never resisted or tried to get away. One day after the cheetah had urinated on that blanket that was made up for it, I saw the serving-girl shake the cheetah and strike it for urinating on the blanket, and the cheetah never growled or struck back.

On another day, I saw the cheetah when two hares were started right before the cheetah-keeper. It caught up with one and grabbed it, biting it with its fangs. It then pursued the other one and, having caught up with it, began to maul it with its front paws, while its mouth was busy with the first hare. After giving it a few blows with its paws, the cheetah dropped it and the hare leapt away.

One of those who joined us on the hunt was the learned sheikh Abu 'Abdallah al-Tulaytuli,[36] the grammarian (may God have mercy upon him). In the field of grammar he was the Sibawayh of his age.[37] I studied grammar under him for close on ten years. Prior to that, he was director of the House of Learning in Tripoli.[38] When the Franks captured Tripoli, my father and uncle (may God have mercy upon them both) sent a messenger and redeemed this sheikh Abu 'Abdallah, and Yanis, the copyist.[39] The latter was a member of that generation of calligraphers that was not too far removed from those of the school of Ibn al-Bawwab.[40] He stayed with us in Shayzar for a period of time and copied for my father (may God have mercy upon him) two complete texts of the Qur'an. Then he moved to Egypt and died there.

I witnessed a wonderful thing with regard to the sheikh Abu 'Abdallah. One day I entered his room in order to study with him [209] and I found piled before him many books of grammar: *The Book of Sibawayh*, *The Peculiarities of Speech* by Ibn Jinni, *The Explanation* by Abu 'Ali al-Farisi, the *Salient Features* and the *Sentences*.[41] So I said to him, 'Master Abu 'Abdallah, have you read *all* of these books?'

'Read them?' he replied. 'Not just that! By God, I have written them all out on tablets and memorized them by heart. Do you want me to prove it to you? Take a volume, open it up and read out the first line from the top of the page.'

So I took up a volume, opened it and read out a line. He then recited the entire page from memory, and he could do the same with all those volumes. And so I saw in him a great phenomenon, beyond all human capacity.

This was just a parenthetical statement that has no real place in the course of this particular narrative.

The sheikh had joined us on the hunt with that cheetah, he on horseback with his feet covered in sores,[42] for the ground had many thistles, which had pricked at his feet and made them bleed. But he was absorbed watching the cheetah hunt and so he never felt the pain in his legs – preoccupied by watching the cheetah creep slowly towards the gazelles, jump after them and catch them.

§ *Other Remarkable Birds of Prey*

My father (may God have mercy upon him) was fortunate enough to have some rare and clever birds of prey. This was because he had so many of them that he could choose from them the most sharp-set[43] and clever. One year, he had an intermewed goshawk with red eyes, which was one of the smartest hawks. Now, a letter arrived from Egypt from my uncle Taj al-Umara' Muqallad (may God have mercy upon him) – he had gone to live there in the service of al-Amir.[44] It said, 'In the audience-chamber of al-Afdal[45] [210] I heard someone mention the red-eyed hawk, and al-Afdal questioned the speaker about it and how it hunts.'

So my father (may God have mercy upon him) sent the

hawk with an austringer to al-Afdal. When the austringer was admitted into al-Afdal's presence, the latter asked him, 'Is this the hawk with the red eyes?'

'Yes, my lord,' he replied.

'And what does it hunt?' asked al-Afdal.

'It hunts quail, argala and other kinds of game in between,' the austringer informed him.

And so that hawk remained in Egypt for a while, then it escaped and disappeared, staying for a year in the desert among the sycamore trees, where it moulted. Then they went back and captured it. A letter later came from my uncle (may God have mercy upon him) saying, 'The red-eyed hawk got lost and moulted amidst the sycamores, but they went back and captured it and use it for hunting. A great calamity is once again loosed upon the birds!'

One day we were with my father (may God have mercy upon him) after one of the peasants of Ma'arrat al-Nu'man had come to him, bringing with him an intermewed goshawk, the size of a large eagle, whose wing- and tail-feathers were damaged. I had never seen such a hawk before.

The peasant said, 'My lord, I was setting up a snare for wood-pigeons[46] when this goshawk struck at a pigeon that was caught in the snare. I captured the hawk and have brought it to you.'

My father took it and gave generously to the man who had presented it. The austringer imped its feathers, brought it to the hunt and tried to train it. But the hawk was already an accustomed hunter that had moulted in the mews and had escaped from the Franks. It moulted again on the mountain of al-Ma'arra. It proved to be the most sharp-set and cleverest of my father's birds of prey.

One day I witnessed the chase with my father (may God have mercy upon him) when a man came up to us from a distance, carrying something that we could not at first recognize. When he came close, it turned out to be a passager peregrine, of the largest and best kind. The bird had clawed his hand as he carried it, so he had let it hang, holding it by the jesses[47] and feet. The peregrine was thus hanging upside-down with wings outstretched.

When we arrived, he said, 'My lord, I caught this bird and have brought it for you.'

My father handed it over to the falconer, who treated it and imped all its broken feathers. But its bark proved to be worse than [211] its bite – the trapper had damaged it by what he had done to it. For the peregrine is a balance, which even the least thing will spoil or destroy.

This falconer had great skill in the handling of peregrines.[48] We used to go out on the chase, leaving from the city-gates, taking with us all manner of hunting-gear, even nets, hatchets, shovels and hooks for whatever game went to earth. We would also take hunting-animals – hawks, sakers, peregrines, cheetahs and hounds. Once we had left the town, the falconer would let two peregrines circle around, and they would continue to circle above the hunting-party. If one of them should strike out on its own, the falconer would merely cough and point with his hand in the direction in which he wanted the falcon to go. And, by God, the peregrine would instantly turn back in that direction.

I once saw that falconer get a peregrine to wait on[49] over a flock of pigeons that had come down in a meadow. When it had found its pitch, the drum was beaten to flush the pigeons. Out they flew and the peregrine stooped on them. It struck the head of one, cutting it off. It bound to the pigeon and descended to the ground. By God, we really turned the place over looking for that head, but we never found it. All indications were that it fell at some distance into the water, for we were close to the river.

One day, an attendant called Ahmad ibn Mujir – and this attendant was not among those who rode out with us on the chase – said to my father, 'My lord, I am very eager to see a hunt.'

My father told someone, 'Offer Ahmad a horse that he can ride out hunting with us.'

And so out we went to hunt francolin. A male francolin took to the air, fluttering its wings as is its habit. My father (may God have mercy upon him) had al-Yahshur on his wrist, so he cast it off on the francolin. Al-Yahshur flew close along the ground, the earth and grass striking its chest as it flew. Meanwhile, the francolin had risen to a great height. At this, Ahmad said to my father, 'By your life, my lord, he is just toying with the francolin in order to catch him!'

§ Hunting-Dogs

[212] Zaghari-dogs would also be sent to my father from the lands of the Romans, good thoroughbreds, both hounds and bitches. They bred while in our possession, and the hunting of birds was instinctive to them. I saw a small bitch pup that went out following the hounds under the control of the houndsman. He slipped a goshawk after a francolin, which took cover in some long grass on the bank of the river. They loosed the hounds into the long grass to flush the francolin while this pup stood on the bank. When the francolin took to the air, the puppy leapt after it from the bank and fell into the river, despite the fact that she had no experience of hunting and had never hunted at all.

I once saw one of these zagharis when a partridge had taken cover in the mountains in an impenetrable thicket. That hound went right in but then seemed to be taking some time to come out. Then we heard a commotion from deep inside the thicket.

My father (may God have mercy upon him) said, 'There's a wild animal inside that thicket that's killed the hound!'

But then, after a while, the hound came out, pulling a jackal by the leg. The jackal had been in the thicket too, but the hound had killed it and was dragging it out to us.

My father (may God have mercy upon him) once travelled to Isfahan,[50] to the palace of the sultan Malikshah (may God have mercy upon him). He told me the following about it:

When I had finished my business [213] with the sultan and wished to travel, I wanted to take with me some hunting-bird with which I might entertain myself while on the road. So they brought me some hawks and a weasel[51] that was trained to flush birds out of thickets. However, I chose a saker that hunts hare and bustard,[52] for I thought it would be difficult to handle goshawks on that long and difficult route.

My father (may God have mercy upon him) had salukis – hounds of the finest breeding. One day he slipped his sakers on a gazelle while the ground, swamped by rain, was heavy with mud. I, still a youngster, was with him on one of my nags. The horses of the rest of the hunting-party could not run in the mud, while my nag managed to overcome it because of my light weight. The sakers and the hounds had got the gazelle down, so my father said to me, 'Usama, get over to the gazelle, dismount and hold on to its hind legs until we get there.' I did this and my father arrived on the scene and slaughtered the gazelle. He had standing with him a fawn bitch of good breeding called Hamawiya, which had brought down the gazelle. All of a sudden, the herd of gazelles that we had already been hunting returned, passing by us. My father seized Hamawiya's collar and set off running with her until she sighted the gazelles. He then slipped her at them and she took another gazelle.

Despite his heavy body and his old age and the fact that he was always fasting, my father (may God have mercy upon him) rode at a gallop all day long. He would never go on the hunt except upon a thoroughbred or a fine pack-horse. We, his four sons, would accompany him and get all worn out and tired, while he would never weaken or get tired and worn out. Nor could any servant, equerry or weapons-bearer fall behind in the chase after game.

I had an attendant named Yusuf who carried my spear and my shield and led my extra horse, but who did not join the chase or follow along. So my father upbraided him for it, time and again.

Eventually, the attendant said to him, 'My lord, not one of the men present with you is as much help to you as this your son (and I seek refuge in God if it is not so). Let me then remain behind with his other horse and weapons. If you should ever need him, you will find him. Do not consider me part of the hunting-party at all.'

My father never once blamed him again or disapproved of his not chasing after the game.

§ *The Hunt Must Go On*

[214] The lord of Antioch once camped against us and we went to battle. But then he left without negotiating any truce. Even though the Frankish rearguard had not yet gone very far from the town, my father (may God have mercy upon him) had already ridden out to go hunting. When he had gone some way from town, the Franks turned back upon our own horsemen who had gone in their pursuit. The Franks eventually arrived outside the town. In the meantime, my father climbed up Tall Sikkin[53] to observe them as they stood between him and the town. He remained in his position on top of that hill until they withdrew from the town. He then returned to the hunt.

§ *Arab Horses versus Common Hackneys*

My father (may God have mercy upon him) used to pursue roe-deer in the land around the Bridge Fortress. On one particular day, he must have bagged five or six of them while on a black horse of his called 'Khurji's horse'[54] after the name of its owner, who sold it to my father. He bought it from him for 320 dinars. Anyway, as he was chasing the last of the roes, the front leg of the horse went into a pit that had been dug to catch wild boar and so the horse tumbled on top of him and broke my father's collar-bone. Then the horse stood back up and galloped along for another twenty cubits or so, while my father was still flat on the ground. But then the horse returned and stood by his head neighing and whickering until he stood up and his attendants came and helped him to remount. This is how an Arab horse behaves.

Now, I went out with my father (may God have mercy upon him) towards the mountain to hunt partridge. An attendant of his, named Lu'lu' (may God have mercy upon him), was riding a common hackney. This attendant started dismounting in order to attend to some errand of his own while it was still early in the morning and we were close to town. But when his hackney saw the shadow of his quiver, it became startled and threw him down, and ran off loose. So I, by God, galloped after it, along with an attendant of mine; we tried to catch it from early that morning until late in the afternoon until finally [215] we drove it to take refuge with a herd of animals pasturing in one of the cane-brakes. The herdsmen went and stretched out a rope for the hackney and captured it just like one captures a wild beast. So then I took it and returned. In the meantime, my father (may God have mercy upon him) was standing outside town waiting for me – he neither went hunting nor went to rest in his house. Thus, hackneys are more like wild beasts than horses.

§ A Scholar Tries to Save a Partridge

My father (may God have mercy upon him) told me the following story:

I used to go out hunting accompanied by chief Abu Turab Haydara ibn Qatramir – may God have mercy upon him (he was his sheikh, under whom he memorized the Qur'an and studied Arabic[55]). When we arrived at the hunting-grounds, Abu Turab would dismount and sit on a rock and recite the Qur'an while we did our hunting around him. Once we finished with the hunt, he would mount up and ride with us. One day he told me the following:

'Sir, as I was sitting on a rock a partridge suddenly came trotting up, exhausted, towards the very rock upon which I was sitting. It slipped under cover of the rock just as a goshawk came in hot pursuit, though it was still a way off. The hawk now descended across from me while Lu'lu' was shouting, "Your eyes, your eyes,[56] master!" He then came galloping up, while I was saying, "O God, protect the partridge!" Lu'lu' then said to me, "Master, where is the partridge?" I replied, "I didn't see a thing. It didn't come through here." But then he dismounted from his horse and walked around the rock and, looking under-neath it, he saw the partridge and said, "I say the partridge is here, yet you say it isn't!" Then he took the partridge and ... dear sir ... he broke its legs and threw it to the hawk even as my heart was breaking into pieces because of it.'

§ Lu'lu' and the Hares

This Lu'lu' (may God have mercy upon him) was one of the most experienced men when it came to hunting. I saw him one day [216] when a number of hares, having been roused, came towards us from the wilderness. We used to go out and hunt them in large numbers. They were small, reddish hares. I saw Lu'lu' one day, he having roused ten hares, hit and kill nine of them with his pike.[57] Then he made for the tenth. But my father (may God have mercy upon him) just said to him, 'Leave it alone. Let it run for the hounds and we'll have some fun watching it.' So they let it run and loosed the hounds on it. But the hare out-ran the hounds and escaped. At this Lu'lu' exclaimed, 'My lord, if you had just let me try to hit it, I would have got it!'

One day I saw a hare, which we had roused from its burrow and on which we had loosed our hounds. But it was driven into a hole in the bed of a *wadi*.[58] A black bitch that was chasing it went into the hole after it, but the bitch came immediately out again, yelping, then fell to the ground and died. We had not even left her before she broke out in sores and she lay there dead and rotting. This was because a viper had bitten her when she went into the hole.

§ Amazing Bird-Stories

Another amazing occurrence while hunting with goshawks was the following. I had gone out hunting with my father (may God have mercy upon him), right after a period of constant rain that had kept us from any riding for days. Once the rain stopped, we went out with the hawks, hoping to catch some waterfowl. We saw some birds in a meadow beneath a rise. My father went forward and slipped on them a goshawk that was intermewed. The hawk flew up with the flushed birds, footed[59] one of them and came to earth. But we could not see that it had any game. We dismounted where it had landed and – of all things – it had caught a starling,[60] closing its talons around it without injuring or hurting it. The austringer bent down and released the starling, which was safe and sound.

[217] I have seen fortitude and courage in the 'salamander-goose' like the fortitude and courage of men. Here is an example. We once slipped our sakers on a flock of salamander-geese and beat the drum. They flew off and the sakers came up on the geese and took one, which they brought down to the ground far away from us. The goose cried out and five or six others rushed to it, beating back the sakers with their wings. Had we not arrived quickly on the scene, they would have got away with the goose that had been taken and would have cut up the sakers' wings with their beaks.

This is in contrast to the courage of the bustard. When the saker gets near to the bustard, it descends to the ground. In whatever way the saker circles round it, the bustard keeps its tail facing the saker. When the saker closes in, the bustard mutes[61] on it, covering its feathers and filling its eyes. If the bustard misses, then the saker will take it.

One of the most unusual hunts that a hawk engaged in with my father (may God have mercy upon him) took place like this:

My father had on his wrist a young hawk, still downy.[62] On a stretch of water was an 'ayma,[63] which is a large bird the colour of a heron, but bigger than a crane, measuring fourteen spans from the tip of one wing to the other. The hawk began to seek out the 'ayma, so my father slipped it upon it and beat the drum for it. The 'ayma flew up, but the hawk struck at its middle and managed to take it. They both then fell into the water. As it was, this was the cause of the hawk's escape, for if it hadn't done so, the 'ayma would surely have killed it with its beak. But one of the attendants threw himself into the water, clothed and armoured, and grabbed the 'ayma and lifted it out. When it got to dry ground, the hawk just looked at it, [218] screeched and flew away from it, and didn't bother it again. I have never seen a hawk try to hunt an 'ayma, save that one. For the 'ayma is as Abu al-'Ala' ibn Sulayman[64] said regarding the phoenix:

'I consider the phoenix too great to be caught in the chase.'

My father (God have mercy upon him) used to head out for the Bridge Fortress, which was rich with game, and would stay there for a few days. We would accompany him, hunting partridge, francolin, waterfowl, roe-deer, gazelle and hare. One day he headed out there and we rode out to chase francolin. My father slipped at a francolin a certain goshawk that was carried and trained by a *mamluk* named Niqula. Niqula then set off at a gallop behind the hawk, but in the meantime the francolin had taken cover in a thicket of brambles. Suddenly, the cries of Niqula filled our ears and he returned at full gallop.

'What's wrong with you?' we asked.

'A lion came out of the thicket where the francolin came down,' he replied, 'so I left the hawk behind and fled.' But – guess what? – the lion was as cowardly as Niqula! When it heard the jingling bells[65] of the hawk in flight, it ran out of the thicket and fled towards the Ghab.[66]

§ *The Skill of Shayzar's Fishermen*

On our return from hunting-trips, we would often encamp on the Bushamir, a little river near the citadel, and send for the fishermen to present themselves so that we could observe the wonderful things they did. One of them had with him a shaft of cane, with a spear-head; the shaft had a recess in it for the spear-head, as with a javelin.[67] From the same recess, three iron hooks stuck out, each hook a cubit in length. On the other end of the cane-shaft was a long cord tied to the fisherman's hand. The fisherman would then stand on the bank of the river, which had a rather narrow course, and when he spotted a fish he would stab at it with that cane-spear with the iron head. He never missed. He would then pull it out by the cord, bringing the fish up with it.

Another fisherman had with him a pole as thick as a fist, with an iron [219] fork-head. On the other end was a cord tied to his hand. He would climb down and wade into the water and when he spotted a fish he would snatch it with that fork-head and leave it stuck in it. Then, climbing out, he would pull it up by the cord, landing both fork and fish.

Still another would climb down and wade into the water, passing his hand under the willow-trees that grow on the banks towards a fish until he was able to put his fingers into its gills, while it neither moved nor escaped. He would then take it and climb out. Thus we gained as much amusement with the fishermen as we did hunting with hawks.

§ Ghana'im the Austringer

Rain and wind prevailed over us for days once while we were at the Bridge Fortress. But then the rain stopped for a while, and so Ghana'im, our austringer, came and said to my father, 'The hawks are hungry and primed for the chase. It's a nice day and the rain has let up – don't you want to mount up?'

'Indeed I do,' replied my father.

So we rode out, but we had barely got as far as the desert when the very gates of heaven opened upon us, pouring rain. We complained to Ghana'im, 'You claimed it was a nice day and the rain had stopped just to bring us out into this deluge!'

'What, you don't have the eyes to see the clouds and other signs of rain yourself?' he replied. 'You could have said, "You're lying into your beard – it's not nice out or clear!"'

This Ghana'im was a master-craftsman in the art of training peregrines and goshawks, of great experience with regard to birds of prey, a pleasant conversationalist and delightful company. Of birds of prey, he had seen all that was known and unknown.

One day we went out hunting from the citadel of Shayzar and at al-Jalali Mill we saw something that turned out to be a crane lying on the ground. An attendant dismounted and turned it over and it was dead, still warm, not yet cold. Ghana'im saw it and said, 'This has been taken by a *luzzayq*; [220] have a look under its wing.' And there was the side of the crane that had been pierced and its heart eaten out. Ghana'im remarked, 'This *luzzayq* is a bird of prey, like the kestrel.[68] She binds to the crane, clings beneath its wing, piercing its ribs, and then eats out its heart.'

God (glory be to Him) later decreed that I should enter into the service of the atabeg Zangi (may God have mercy upon him). A bird of prey like a kestrel was brought to him, with a red bill, red legs and red eyelashes. It was one of the best birds of prey and they said, 'This is a *luzzayq*.' It remained with him only a few days, however, for it tore through the jesses with its beak and flew off.

§ Hunting Wild Asses

One day, my father (may God have mercy upon his soul) went out to hunt gazelle, and I – still but a lad – accompanied him. Arriving at Wadi al-Qanatir, he came upon some slaves – bandits[69] engaging in highway robbery. So he caught them, tied them up and handed them over to a group of his attendants to deliver them to the dungeon at Shayzar. As for me, I took a spear from one of them and we continued on to the hunt.

Suddenly, a herd of wild asses appeared. So I said to my father, 'My lord, I've never seen wild asses before. With your permission, I'd like to gallop ahead to get a look at them.'

'You may do so,' he replied.

Under me was a chestnut horse, a thoroughbred. I galloped ahead with that spear, the one I took from the bandit. I went directly into the midst of the herd, singled out one ass and began thrusting the spear at it, but it didn't do a thing to the animal, on account of the weakness of my arm and the dullness of the spear-point. So I drove back the ass until I had steered it back to my companions, who bagged it. My father and the men with him were amazed by the way that thoroughbred ran.

God (glory be to Him) decreed that I should go out one day to pass the time looking at the river of Shayzar, riding that horse. I was accompanied by a Qur'an-reciter who would recite poetry for a bit, then the Qur'an for a bit and then sing for a bit. I dismounted under [221] a tree and handed over my horse to my attendant, who made hobbles for it. He happened to be alongside the river and the horse took fright and fell into the river on its side. But every time it wanted to stand up, it would fall back down again in the water because of the hobbles. The attendant was a young boy and he was not able to save it. All the while we didn't even know what was going on. Finally, when the horse was nearing death, the attendant yelled for us, and we came over to the horse, but it was breathing its last. We

cut the hobbles and brought it out, but it died. The water in
which it drowned did not even reach to the upper part of its
leg – it was rather the hobbles that killed it.

§ Animals are also Subject to Fate

One day my father (may God have mercy upon him) went out
hunting, accompanied by an amir called al-Samsam, one of the
comrades (by way of service) of Fakhr al-Mulk ibn 'Ammar,[70]
the lord of Tripoli. He was a man with little experience of
hunting. My father slipped a goshawk on some waterfowl and
it footed one of them and fell into the middle of the river.

Al-Samsam then began slapping one hand against the other,
saying, 'There is no power or strength save in God![71] Why did
I have to go out today?'

So I said to him, 'Samsam, are you worried the hawk is
drowning?'

'Yes,' he replied, 'it's drowned. Is it a duck, that it should
fall into the water and not drown?'

I laughed and said, 'It'll be up in a moment.'

The hawk seized the head of the bird and swam with it
until it climbed out of the water with it. Al-Samsam remained
astounded by this, repeating 'Glory be to God!' and praising
Him for the safe escape of the hawk.

Myriad are the fates of animals. My father (may God have
mercy upon him) once slipped a white hawk[72] on a francolin.
The francolin fell in a thicket of brambles and the hawk went
in with it. [222] In the thicket was a jackal, which caught the
hawk and tore off its head. It was one of the finest and most
skilful birds of prey.

I also witnessed the fate that had befallen a bird of prey. One
day, I had ridden out with an attendant of mine before me,
who carried a sparrow-hawk with him. He threw him off on
some song-birds and it caught one, so he went and slaughtered
the bird still clutched in the claws of the hawk. The hawk then
shook its head, coughed up blood and fell to the ground dead,
the slaughtered bird still in it clutches. Glory be to He who
determines all fates!

One day in the citadel, I passed by a door we had opened for a building that was there; I was carrying a blowpipe. I noticed a song-bird on a wall, below which I was standing. So I shot a ball at it, but I missed the bird, which flew off. However, my eyes followed the ball, which went down the wall where, a bird having just poked its head out of a hole in the wall, it struck the bird on its head and stunned it. It fell right in front of me and I slaughtered it. And yet the shooting of that particular bird was never intended.

One day my father (may God have mercy upon him) slipped a goshawk on a hare which stood up before us in a cane-brake, full of thorns. The hawk captured the hare but it got loose from it. So the hawk sat on the ground and the hare ran away. I galloped off with a black thoroughbred beneath me to drive the hare back. But the horse's foreleg fell into a hole and it tumbled on top of me. My hands and face were now covered in those thorns, and the hind leg of the horse was dislocated. But then the hawk, after the hare had gone all this distance, flew from the ground, caught up with the hare and captured it, as though it had had no other goal but to ruin my horse and hurt me with that fall into the thorns.

§ Hunting Wild Boar

[223] Early one morning on the first of Rajab, while we were fasting,[73] I said to my father (may God have mercy upon him), 'I wish I could go out hunting to keep my mind off the fast.'

'Then go,' my father said.

So I went out with my brother Baha' al-Dawla Abu al-Mughith Munqidh (may God have mercy upon him) towards the cane-brakes, and we brought a few goshawks with us. As we went in among the liquorice-bushes[74] a wild boar emerged, and so my brother thrust his spear at it and wounded it, and it fled back into the liquorice-bushes.

My brother said, 'Pretty soon that wound will start hurting him and then he'll come out. I'll face him head-on, stick him with my spear and kill him.'

'You'd better not do that,' I advised. 'You might hit your horse and kill it.'

As we were talking, the boar came out, heading for another

cane-brake. My brother confronted it and thrust his spear in the hump on the boar's back, but the front of the spear he used snapped while still stuck in the boar. The boar ran under the chestnut mare my brother was riding. The horse was pregnant and had three white legs and a white tail. The boar collided with the horse and knocked it over and over again. As for the horse, its hip was dislocated and it was ruined. As for my brother, he dislocated his little finger and broke his ring!

I galloped off behind the boar, which went into an area thick with liquorice-bushes and asphodel.[75] There were some cattle sleeping there, but I did not see them due to that undergrowth. A bull rose up out of the herd and struck the chest of my horse, knocking it down. I fell to the ground, and the horse too, with its bridle snapped. I got up, took my spear, mounted up and caught up with the boar,[76] which had thrown itself into the river. I stood on the bank of the river and hurled my spear at it. The spear stuck in the boar, but snapped at a length of two cubits, leaving the spear-head imbedded. The boar swam on towards the other side of the river, so we shouted to a group of people on that side who were preparing mud-bricks to build some houses in a village belonging to my uncle. They came and stood over the boar while it was below the bank, unable to climb up. Then they started throwing large rocks at it, trying to kill it. I said to one of my grooms, 'Go down to it.' So he took off his gear and stripped naked. Taking up his sword, he swam over to the boar and finished it off. Then he dragged it by the leg and brought it to me, saying, 'May God acquaint you with the blessings of the Rajab fast! For we have inaugurated it with the impurity of swine.'

[224] If the boar had claws and fangs like a lion, it would be even more dangerous than the lion. I once saw a wild sow that we had roused from its litter of suckling piglets. One of the young began ramming with its snout the hoof of the horse of an attendant who was with me. It was the size of a cat. The attendant took an arrow from his quiver and, leaning down to it, skewered it on the arrow and lifted it up. I was amazed at how it had attacked, ramming a horse's hoof while, at the same time, it could be carried about on a mere arrow.

§ *The Stamina of Butrus*

One of the wonderful experiences I had hunting would take place when we went out to the mountains to hunt partridge, bringing ten goshawks with us to hunt with all day long. The austringers would be scattered all through the mountains, each one of them accompanied by two or three horsemen from our *mamluk* troops. We had with us two houndsmen: the name of one of them was Butrus and the other Zarzur Badiya. Every time one of the austringers would slip a bird onto a partridge and flush it out, he would shout, 'Hey, Butrus!' and Butrus would come running over to him like a racing-camel. He would keep that up all day long, running about from mountain to mountain, he and his colleague. Once, when he had gorged the hawks and turned back for home, Butrus took a stone and run after one of the *mamluk*s and hit him with it, and the *mamluk* in turn took a stone and hit Butrus. Butrus, who was on foot during all this, kept chasing the attendants, who were mounted, throwing stones at them all the way back from the mountains to the city-gates, just as if he hadn't spent the entire day running back and forth from one mountain to another.

§ Zaghariya-*Hounds and Sakers in Tandem*

One of the strange things about *zaghariya*-hounds is that they will not eat birds. They will not eat any part of them, except their heads and feet (which have no meat on them) and the bones from which the hawks have already eaten the meat.

My father (may God have mercy upon him) had a black *zaghariya*-bitch; our attendants used to rest [225] a lamp on her head during the night while they sat and played chess. She never made a movement, and she continued doing this until she became dim-sighted. My father (may God have mercy upon him) used to upbraid the attendants, telling them, 'You've gone and blinded this bitch!' but they never refrained from it.

The amir Malik ibn Salim, the lord of Qal'at Ja'bar, sent a beautifully trained bitch to my father as a gift, which could be loosed beneath the sakers on gazelles. We saw her do many wonderful things.

Now, hunting with sakers has a system to it. First, the leader is cast off and it strikes the gazelle, binding to its ear. The assistant is then slipped and strikes another gazelle. A second assistant is slipped and does likewise, and the fourth saker is slipped in this way too. Each saker strikes one separate gazelle. The leading saker, clutching the gazelle's ear, isolates it from the others and all the sakers join it and abandon the other gazelles previously struck. Meanwhile, this bitch is below the sakers, concentrating solely on the gazelle to which the sakers are binding. Sometimes it happens that an eagle might appear, so the sakers let go of the gazelle, which escapes, while the sakers circle. We noticed that the bitch would leave the gazelle at the same time as the sakers did and that she would go round in a circle on the ground beneath the sakers, just as they did in the air. She would continue doing this until the sakers were called down. Then she would stop and walk behind the horses.[77]

§ *The Strong Prey upon the Weak*

Between Malik ibn Salim and my father (may God have mercy upon them both) there was a formal bond of friendship, and they corresponded with letters and messengers. One day, Malik ibn Salim sent a message to my father saying, 'I went out hunting gazelle and we caught three thousand fawns in one day.'

But that was just because gazelles abound up around them [226] in the region of Qal'at Ja'bar. They just go out during the season when the gazelles are giving birth, on horse and on foot, and take up whatever young have been born that night, the previous night and two or three nights before. They just sweep them up, the way grass or twigs are swept up.

Francolins abound too in the cane-brakes along the Euphrates. If a francolin is cut open, cleaned out and stuffed with hair, then its odour will not turn for many days.

One day, I saw a francolin that had been cut open and its crop removed. Inside the crop there was a snake that the francolin had eaten, about a handspan in length. One time while we were hunting, we killed a snake and another snake came out of its stomach. The first snake had swallowed it whole and it was only a little smaller than the first.

It is thus in the nature of all beasts for the strong to prey upon the weak:

Injustice is a feature of every living soul. Should you find
 Someone of integrity, then he only refrains because of
  some defect.[78]

§ Concluding Reflections

To cover all the experiences of the hunt that I have witnessed over the past seventy years of my life is not possible, nor can I accomplish it. For to waste your time telling tales to amuse you is one of the worst calamities that could ever abuse you. As for me, I seek forgiveness from God the Exalted for wasting the dregs of my life that remain in activities other than obedience to Him and the pursuit of divine recompense and heavenly gain. For He – may He be blessed and exalted – all sins He forgives, and from His mercy rich bounties He gives. He is the Generous One – never disappointing those who in hope do persist, for those who entreat Him, He can never resist.

The End of the Book

[227] Praise be to God, the Lord of the Worlds, and the blessings of God and peace be upon our master Muhammad, His prophet and upon all his pure family. God is sufficient for us, and in Him we trust.[79]

At the end of the book are the following words that are reproduced here:

I have read this book from beginning to end over numerous sessions under my lord, my grandfather, the pre-eminent amir, the virtuous scholar, the perfect leader, 'Adud al-Din, companion of kings and sultans, most notable of Arabs, sincere counsellor to the Commander of the Faithful – may God perpetuate his good fortune! I asked him to provide me with a certificate to authorize me to transmit the contents of this book to others, and he agreed to do so, inscribing it in his noble hand. That was on Thursday, 13 Safar, in the year 610 (4 July 1213):

'I certify that this is true. Signed by his grandfather Murhaf ibn Usama ibn Munqidh, who praises God and begs His blessing.'

OTHER EXCERPTS

Guide to Contents

Lost Fragments from *The Book of Contemplation*

Fragments from the *Book of the Staff*

Fragments from *Kernels of Refinement*

LOST FRAGMENTS FROM *THE BOOK OF CONTEMPLATION*

§ *From the Introduction*[1]

I have faced combat and battles with perils most dire, warmed myself I have on their blazing fire. I came to war early, while I was but fifteen years of age until I passed into my nineties, when I became a home-body, one of those left behind, from all warfare resigned. For I am no longer reckoned of any import, no longer called to assemblies of any sort, after being the first to be named when considering my kind, the most worthy at any gathering of worthies, you'd find. I was the first, at my comrades' attack, to advance the banner royal, the last to be drawn from the field, for any ripostes I could foil.

> To how many battles have I borne witness? If only
>> Before I was laid low with age, in one of them, I had
>>> been slain.
> For it is a finer thing for a stripling to be killed in battle,
>> more welcome,
> Before Time can lay him waste or afflict him.
> By your father's name! I never held back from facing
>> perdition in war:
> My free-wheeling blade will testify to that much!
> [17] But God has determined that I will be detained
>> Until my appointed time. What, then, can I do?

§ *An Enumeration of Usama's Battles*

These battles include: the combat between us and the Isma'ilis
in Shayzar citadel, when they attacked the castle in the year
507 (1114); the combat between the army of Hama and the
army of Homs in the year 525 (1130–31); the battle at Tikrit
between the atabeg Zangi and Qaraja, the lord of Fars province,
in the year 526 (1132); the battle between al-Mustarshid and
the atabeg Zangi near Baghdad in the year 527 (1132); the
atabeg Zangi's battle near Amid against the Artuqids and the
lord of Amid, in the year 528 (1134); the battle at Rafaniya between the atabeg Zangi and the Franks in the year 531 (1137);
the battle at Qinnasrin between the atabeg Zangi and the
Franks, though there was no actual engagement, in the year
532 (1138); the combat between the Egyptians and al-Afdal
Ridwan in the year 542 (1147); the fighting among the black
troops in Egypt in the days of al-Hafiz in the year 544 (1149);
the combat between Ibn al-Sallar and Ibn Masal in the same
year; another battle between these two in the same year, at
Dalas; the strife during which Ibn al-Sallar was killed in the
year 548 (1153); the strife during which al-Zafir, his brothers
and his cousin were killed in the year 549 (1154); the strife
between the Egyptians and 'Abbas in the same year; the other
period of strife a month later when the army rose up against
him; and the combat between us and the Franks in the same
year.[2]

§ *A Summary History of Shayzar*[3]

In the year 468 (1076), my grandfather Sadid al-Mulk 'Ali ibn
Munqidh began building the Bridge Fortress[4] and thereby put
pressure upon the citadel of Shayzar.

At Shayzar, there was a governor for the Romans, whose
name was Demetrios.[5] When this aforementioned Demetrios
considered the blockade to have gone on too long, he (and
those Romans with him) sent a message to my grandfather
concerning handing over the citadel of Shayzar to him, adding
certain conditions that they imposed upon him, including: a
certain amount of money that he would give to the aforemen-

tioned Demetrios; maintaining the property of the bishop of the place, who lived there, for he continued to dwell there under the authority of my grandfather until he died at Shayzar; and that he would pay the *quntariya*[6] – that is, the Roman infantry-men – their salaries for three years.

[16] So my grandfather handed over to them what they stipulated, and the citadel of Shayzar surrendered on a Sunday in Rajab, in the year 474 (December 1081). The aforementioned Sadid al-Mulk 'Ali remained as its lord until he died there on 6 Muharram, in the year 479 (22 April 1086). His son, Abu al-Murhaf Nasr, ruled after him until he died in the year 491 (1097–8). Nasr's brother, Abu al-'Asakir Sultan, ruled until he died there and his son Muhammad ibn Sultan ruled until he died beneath its rubble, he and three of his own sons, in the earthquake[7] in this aforementioned year, that is, the year 552, on Monday 3 Rajab (11 August 1157).

§ *The Bravery of the Caliph al-Mustarshid*[8]

The imam al-Mustarshid matched the foremost of his predecessors in ascending to the very height of zeal, good governance and great bravery. When he and Zangi encountered one another in battle at 'Aqarquf[9] (and I participated in that battle), a black satin tent was pitched for him and a litter built for him in it. As he sat upon it, the cavalry pursued and broke the army of the atabeg. That was on Monday, 27 Rajab of the year 526 (13 June 1132). In this way, the caliph took charge of everything there and the atabeg Zangi fled all the way to Mosul. The caliph's great bravery was the cause of Zangi's destruction.

§ *Usama Gives Advice to a Friend in Peril*[10]

I met with Jamal al-Din al-Mawsili[11] in the year 555 (1160), while I was travelling on pilgrimage to Mecca. There existed between us an old bond of amity, familiarity and close companionship. He invited me to come into his home in Mosul, but I declined, and remained in my tent on the river-bank. Every day during my sojourn there, he would ride out and cross the bridge over to Nineveh, the atabeg having ridden out to the training-grounds.[12]

He would send a message to me saying, 'Come out and ride: I'm standing waiting for you.'

So I would mount up and come, and he and I would talk. One day, I ran into him while we were apart from my companions. I said to him, 'I've got something on my mind that I've wanted to tell you ever since we met, but it has never happened that there was a free moment. Now at the moment we are free.'

'So tell me,' he said.

I said, 'I'll tell you what al-Sharif al-Radi[13] said:

This counsel for you comes from the innermost heart of one
    Who does not just heap spite on you by way of blame.
For my affection for you denies me permission
    To see you involved with any sin you may claim.

You have given very freely in the spending of treasury-moneys for alms and for the leading men of piety and good works, but rulers cannot bear to see money given away, and their hearts become unsettled about it, even if people give it away out of their own inheritance – this is what happened to the Barmakids.[14] So think carefully about what you have given away of the funds you brought in.'

He remained silent for a moment, eyes downcast, and said, 'May God reward you with good fortune! But the matter [22] has already surpassed what you feared.'

So I left him, travelled to the Hijaz[15] and returned from Mecca by the Syrian Road. Jamal al-Din was ousted and he died later in prison.

§ *Isma'ilis Capture Apamea*[16]

A group of Isma'ilis from the populace of Apamea endeavoured to take possession of the place. They hatched a plot [23] whereby six of them, after having obtained a horse, a mule, some Frankish gear, a shield and a mail hauberk, went out from the region of Aleppo to Apamea with all that gear and those animals.

They said to Ibn Mula'ib (he was a generous and courageous man), 'We came intending to enter your service, and we encountered a Frankish knight and killed him. So we bring you his horse, his mule and his gear.'

And so Ibn Mulaʿib treated them with hospitality and bade them stay in the citadel of Apamea in a suite of rooms adjoining the city wall. The Ismaʿilis dug a hole in the wall and set with the Apameans an appointed time – Saturday night, 24 Jumada al-Ula in the year 499 (1 February 1106) – to strike. The Apameans climbed up through that hole, killed Ibn Mulaʿib and took possession of the citadel of Apamea.

FRAGMENTS FROM THE *BOOK OF THE STAFF*

§ *Introduction*

Verily, the soul is content when that which it desires is learned, and becomes importunate in its pursuit when it is spurned. My blessed father Majd al-Din Murshid (may God be pleased with him) related to me that when he went forth to serve the Sultan Malikshah[17] (may God have mercy upon him), while the latter was in Isfahan, he made for the home of the judge, the imam, the honourable and learned Abu Yusuf al-Qazwini[18] (may God have mercy upon him), to visit him and to offer his greetings, as they had known [2] one another of old, and as Abu Yusuf was bound by a bond of gratitude to my grandfather Sadid al-Mulk ʿAli (may God have mercy upon him).

That bond of gratitude came about because, in the days of al-Hakim,[19] the ruler of Egypt, the aforementioned judge travelled to Egypt. Al-Hakim treated him favourably, bestowed honours upon him and presented him with a splendid gift. But Abu Yusuf begged to be excused from this gift and asked if al-Hakim could instead make a gift to him of some books that he proposed to take from the caliphal library. Al-Hakim agreed to that and Abu Yusuf entered the library and selected from it what books he wanted. Later, he took ship, and those books with him, heading for the lands of Islam in the Levant. But the wind turned on him and hurled the ship to the city of Latakia,[20] which was controlled by the Romans. He grieved at his plight and feared for himself and the books he had with him, and so

he wrote a letter to my grandfather Sadid al-Mulk (may God
the Most High have mercy upon him), saying: 'I find myself
in Latakia in the midst of the Romans, and with me books
of Islam; I am to be got cheap; are you willing to make the
leap?'

[3] So that very day, Sadid al-Mulk dispatched to him his
son, my uncle 'Izz al-Dawla Nasr (may God have mercy upon
him), sending with him many horsemen from his attendants
and troops, and a mount to transport him and carry his belongings. Nasr came to him and carried him and his belongings
away. Abu Yusuf remained with my grandfather (may God
have mercy upon him) for a long period of time. During this
time there formed between him and my father (may God have
mercy upon him) bonds of solicitude and intimacy. And so
when my father travelled to Baghdad, he went to Abu Yusuf to
renew his acquaintance with him. My father (may God have
mercy upon him) gave me the following account of it:

I went in to him, and with me was the sheikh Ibn al-
Buwayn[21] the poet, for he had been a scribe for my grandfather (may God have mercy upon him). I found that Abu
Yusuf had reached such an age that those features with
which I once could recognize him had changed and he had
forgotten much of what he had once known. But, when he
saw me, he recognized me after some questioning, for he
had left me when I was but a youth and he now saw me as
a grown man.[22]

And so he inquired after my travels and I informed him
about my journey to the palace of the sultan. He said,
'Extend my greetings to Khawaja Buzurk Nizam al-Din,[23]
and inform him that the first part of the commentary that
I compiled, which part is the commentary on the Qur'anic
verse "In the Name of God the Compassionate, the Merciful!", has gone missing. Ask him to request that a copy be
made from the copy that is in [4] his library and have it
sent to me.' He had compiled a commentary on the Qur'an
in one hundred volumes.

As a result of his weakness and his advanced age, he

reclined on his bed in a position somewhere between sitting and lying down, his books surrounding him, and he writing. The sheikh Ibn al-Buwayn greeted him, but he didn't recognize him, and Abu Yusuf said, 'Who are you?' Ibn al-Buwayn replied, 'Your servant, Ibn al-Buwayn, scribe to the amir Sadid al-Mulk.' '*Al-Buwayn?*' Abu Yusuf retorted. 'What's that? God damn *al-Buwayn!*' Then he thought for a moment and asked, 'Are you the poet, grammarian and scribe?' Ibn al-Buwayn replied, 'Yes.' So Abu Yusuf recited:

> They said, 'It's al-Sulami!' So I said, 'Lady, cover yourself.
> 　That's a teat-squeezer, a seller of milk.'[24]

Then he returned to his conversation with me and noticed that the sheikh Ibn al-Buwayn had taken a book from those books that were surrounding his bed, and so Abu Yusuf snapped at him: 'The idiot comes to a person, takes his ease and reads whatever is around of books, as if to say "I am of the learned sort!". What you really need is for what is in your hand to be brought down upon it!' And he took it from him, and that book was the *Book of the Staff*.

Ever since I heard this nearly sixty years ago, I have sought out the *Book of the Staff* in Syria, Egypt, Iraq, the Hijaz, Upper Mesopotamia and Diyar Bakr, but I never found anyone who knew of it. Every time its existence was denied to me, my covetousness for it increased, until despair induced me to compile [5] this book and title it the *Book of the Staff*. I do not know whether that other book took the same form as mine or a different form. Nevertheless, I saw to it that my soul attained what had set it afire, just as when Jacob satisfied his soul's desire.[25] I have no doubt that the author of that book had a purpose and in its composition and adornment he excelled, while I, having missed out on something I desired, was to its mere execution and over-embellishment compelled. This book of mine, even if it is empty of the sort of learning with which

literary works are embellished or which those highest in virtue
pursue, is at least not devoid of narratives and verses that
comfort the soul in their expanse, and whose placement here
will improve the lot of those who upon them should chance.

I open the book with an account of the staff of Moses (upon
him be peace), then an account of the staff of Solomon, son of
David (upon him be peace), then I abandon myself to mentioning narratives and poems that make reference to staves. I
do not claim to have accomplished a definitive accounting about
staves in what I have collected; only those accounts that I have
memorized and heard myself have I selected.

In God (to whom belong glory and power) I seek refuge and
beg Him to protect, should my hand write anything that is
with sin or defect. From His mercy (may He be exalted) for
forbearance and forgiveness I look, for my preoccupation with
trifles instead of reciting His Holy Book. For He – may He be
praised! – is the closest of those you might call, in entreating
Him the most generous of all.

§ *A Catchy Tune*

At Hisn Kayfa in Shawwal of the year 567 (May–June 1172),
someone in whom I trust related to me the following. 'There
was in the service of the amir Malik ibn Salim, lord of Qal'at
Ja'bar, a lute-player called Abu al-Faraj. He told me:

> One day I was in the assembly-hall of the amir Malik
> ibn Salim while he was drinking to the point of [184]
> drunkenness. I withdrew to my own house, but no more
> than two hours of the night had elapsed when his messen-
> ger came before me and said, 'The amir calls for you.' I
> said, 'I waited until he got drunk before I went home!' The
> messenger replied, 'He has commanded me to take you
> into his presence.'
>
> And so I went with him and I saw the amir sitting down.
> The amir said, 'Abu al-Faraj! After you withdrew, I fell
> asleep and I saw in a dream a person singing to me a song,
> which I remembered but then forgot, and I would like you
> to remind me of it.' So I said, 'My lord, recite for me a

word from it.' He replied, 'I do not remember anything about it. But instead, recite for me what you have on hand.' So I recited for him many songs while he kept saying, 'This is not the song that I dreamt about!' He then said, 'Leave me! And think so that you might remember!'

So I withdrew and woke early in the morning to rise to his service. The amir said, 'Hey, Abu al-Faraj! Anything happen with that song?' I replied, 'My lord, only God (may He be praised and exalted) knows the unseen.' The amir then said, 'By God! If you do not remember it, I will expel you from the castle!' 'By God, my lord,' I said, 'I don't know! How can I recall a song I never heard and from which not one word was ever mentioned?' [185] 'Take him and expel him,' the amir ordered. And so, they took me out to al-Bulayl[26] and I remained there for a day, after which he had me returned and I entered again into his service just as I was before.

Then, one day, I was in the assembly-hall singing when one of the servants said to me, 'There is a man at the door asking for you.' So I went out to him and saw a man wearing a dark turban, like those of the Maghrib. He greeted me and said, 'I have come to you so that you might obtain access for me to be admitted into the hall of the amir, for I am a singer.' So I went in and informed the amir of this man and said, 'My lord, if he is a good poet, then listen to him and let him into your service, or, if not, then give him something and he will go away.' The amir then admitted him, and the man entered, greeted the amir, sat down, took out his lute and sang:

> The scout informed her that between her
>> And the villages of Najran and al-Darb there was no infidel.
> So she threw down her staff and took rest,
>> Just as a traveller's eyes take delight upon finding home.

The amir said, 'There is no God but God! This, by God, is the song that I dreamt about and of which I asked you!' I and all who were present were astounded at this coincidence.

§ Usama on Pilgrimage in Jerusalem

I went on pilgrimage to Jerusalem in the year 532 (1137–8), and accompanying me was one of its citizens who informed me about the places where one can pray and expect blessings. He led me into a structure next to the Dome of the Rock in which there were candles and curtains.

He said to me, 'This is the House of the Chain.'[27] I asked him to tell me about the chain and he said to me:

In this house in the time of the Israelites there was a chain. Whenever there was a dispute between two Israelites in which an oath bound one of them, they would enter this house and stand beneath the chain.[28] The defendant would swear his innocence to his accuser, then extend his hand. If he spoke the truth, he would be able to grasp the chain; if he lied, the chain would retract from his hand and he would not be able to grasp it.

A man from the Israelites once entrusted a gem to another man, then demanded it back from him. That other man said, 'I have given it to you already.' Then he added, 'Look, if you don't believe me, put me to the test at the chain.'

He – the one entrusted with the jewel – went and took a staff and split it and pressed the jewel into it and left it there. Then he stuck it together and painted it, and, taking it in his hand, he entered the House of the Chain with his adversary. The man entrusted with the jewel said to his adversary, 'Hold this staff for me.' So the first man took the staff from the man with the jewel and the man with the jewel swore that he had returned the jewel to him. He extended his hand and grasped the chain, then took [235] back his staff and the two men left. From that day on, the chain has been raised.

I did not see this account in writing, rather, I have merely related it as I heard it.

§ *A Staff of Invisibility*

There was with us at Shayzar an ascetic, an excellent Muslim named Jarrar (may God have mercy upon him), who was exclusively devoted to a mosque on Jabal Jurayjis. He would not leave that mosque except to perform the communal prayers on Fridays. I used to visit him there and obtain blessings from him. Someone who had dealings with him once related to me what Jarrar had told him:

> I once wanted to make a visit to the sheikh Yasin[29] (may God have mercy upon him) and I thought him to be at Mambij,[30] so I went out with a company of travellers. I hoped to ask for a staff from him. When we arrived in the vicinity of Mambij, we had with us some excess supplies and so we took apart a pile of stones and buried the supplies inside it and returned the stones on top. We then went to the sheikh (may God have mercy upon him) and we stayed there a while. Eventually, we said our farewells to him and made ready to depart, so he prepared some supplies for us, saying, 'Take this, for a fox has eaten up your supplies.' He then brought out a staff, took the skull-cap out from under his turban and said to me, 'Take this staff and this cap.'
>
> So we said our farewells again and departed, I being happy on account of the staff and the cap, and all of us in wonder over what he had said about the supplies. When we arrived at the spot where our supplies were, we looked for them but could not find them, for – guess what? – a wild beast had eaten them. We continued on and then we parted ways, [237] each one of us riding off to his own destination. I arrived in the territory of Shayzar, and what should be happening but the Franks were marauding the countryside, spreading out over the land between me and my destination. It then came upon me to take that skull-cap out from under my turban and place it on the tip of the staff while I walked along the road. The Franks were to the right and left of me while in my hands was that staff with the skull-cap on top of it. And no one – by God, not

anyone – espied me. They were (God be praised and exalted) blinded to my presence, and no harm befell me from them, so I was able to return to the security of my home.

§ *The Blind Men of Damascus*

I was present in Damascus when a dispute occurred between the blind men of the city and a man who used to administer their endowment, known as Ibn al-Ba'labakki. They had brought the matter before the lord of Damascus, Shihab al-Din Mahmud[31] (may God have mercy upon him), numerous times, and so he said to the amir Mujahid al-Din Buzan ibn Mamin, 'Mujahid al-Din, by God, take these people off my hands. Call them together in your residence and summon their supervisor[32] at the same time and settle this affair.'

'To hear is to obey,' he replied.

Mujahid al-Din then said to me, 'Please, [243] attend with us.'

And so we gathered in a great hall in a residence, and the supervisor Ibn al-Ba'labakki was present as was the former supervisor, who was called Ibn al-Farrash,[33] and also present were about three hundred blind men, carrying their leader. They entered the hall, each one of them with a staff in his hand at his side. Then the discussion began, some of them preferring to talk with the first supervisor, Ibn al-Farrash, some of them preferring Ibn al-Ba'labakki. They contended and strove with one another for a while without any progress, due to their noise and their great number. Then they turned violent, and close to three hundred staves were raised in the hall, all in the hands of blind men who did not know whom they were hitting. The uproar and the shouting became so loud that I regretted being there. But the two supervisors gave in on the matter, the dissent between them quietened down and we resolved the affair according to what the blind men wished. We could hardly believe it when the blind men finally left.

§ *On the Utility of Deception in Battle*[34]

Those who are practised in war and know its stratagems – who know well that men fear deception and are wary of tricks and ruses that might have bad results or prove to be weak – these people do not hold to be true the tales that historians and poets have told about those events. For resoluteness in war is more effective than audacity. I have battled the Franks (may God confound them) in places and countries so numerous that I cannot count them, and I never once saw them defeat us and then persist in pursuing us, nor do their horses do more than amble or trot, fearing that some stratagem will befall them. How could anyone with a brain in his head [260] convince himself to get into a sack tied up around him or into a chest? How can a man hide with a sack tied around him?

§ *At the Tomb of St John the Baptist near Nablus*[35]

I went on pilgrimage to the tomb of Yahya ibn Zakariya (peace be upon him) at a village called Sebaste[36] in one of the sub-districts of Nablus. When I had performed my prayers, I went out into an open space overlooking the tomb. There I saw a partially closed door; so I opened it and entered and saw there a church in which there were about ten old men. Their heads were bared and looked like carded cotton.[37] They were facing east and had at their breasts staves topped by curved cross-bars the width of their chests. They propped themselves upon them while in front of them an old man recited to them.[38]

I saw there a sight that moved my heart but also grieved me and made me lament that I had never seen exertions like theirs among the Muslims. A period of time passed and one day, when he and I were passing by al-Tawawis,[39] Mu'in al-Din Unur (may God have mercy upon him) said to me, 'I'd like to dismount and visit the sheikhs.' I said, 'Certainly,' so we dismounted and walked to a long building at the corner. We entered it and I did not think there was anyone there, but then I saw that there were around one hundred prayer-mats, on each one a Sufi exuding tranquillity, their humility apparent. What I saw of them there gladdened me and I praised God (may He be glorified and exalted) that I saw in the Muslims exertions greater than those of those priests. I had not before that time seen Sufis in their house, nor did I know anything of their practice.

FRAGMENTS FROM *KERNELS*
OF REFINEMENT

§ *The Coptic Patriarch in a Fatimid Prison*

The words of the philosopher, 'The king has power only over his subjects' bodies, not [73] their hearts', reminded me of an affair I witnessed in Cairo in the year 547 (1152–3), to wit:

The messenger of the King of Ethiopia came bearing a letter to Ibn al-Sallar[40] (may God be pleased with him). The king asked him to order the patriarch of Egypt to remove the patriarch of Ethiopia[41] (for that entire country answers to the opinion of the patriarch of Egypt). So Ibn al-Sallar ordered the patriarch to be brought before him, and he came while I was in his presence. He was an old, emaciated and starving man. He was brought forward to the door of the throne room, where he stopped. He then greeted Ibn al-Sallar, turned away and sat down on a low bench in the outer court.

So Ibn al-Sallar sent a message to him saying, 'The king of the Ethiopians complained about the patriarch who is currently appointed over his country, and he asked me to order you to remove him from his post.'

The patriarch replied, 'My lord, I did not appoint this man simply to try him out. I think he is quite suitable to carry out the Holy Law to which he himself is subject. There does not appear to me to be anything in his conduct which would necessitate his removal. Moreover, it is not permitted in my religion to do anything about this matter that is not absolutely necessary, and so it is not lawful for me to remove him.'

Ibn al-Sallar (may God have mercy upon him) was enraged at his reply and ordered him to be imprisoned. After two days, Ibn al-Sallar sent a message to him (and I was present), saying to him, 'You will eventually have to remove that patriarch, since it was the king of the Ethiopians who requested it.'

The patriarch answered, 'My lord, I have no reply other than the one that I have already given you. Your authority and your power lie only over the humble body you see before you. As for my religious beliefs, you cannot touch them. By God! I will not remove him, even should every loathsome thing befall me!'

And so Ibn al-Sallar (may God have mercy upon him) ordered him to be released, and he apologized to the king of the Ethiopians.

§ *The First Crusade and its Sequel in the North*[42]

Something happened in my own time that was similar to this tale of Alexander, and I shall relate it. When the Franks (may God confound them) came in the year 490 (1096-7) and conquered Antioch and were victorious over the armies of Syria, they were seized with greed and gave themselves up to fancies of possessing Baghdad and the lands of the East. So they mustered and collected themselves, and marched forth, making for those lands.

At that time, the lord of Mosul was Jikirmish,[43] and he assembled the Artuqid Turkoman amirs and those under their power and met the Franks in battle[44] on the Khabur River; he defeated them, capturing their leaders King Baldwin the Prince and Joscelin,[45] and conducted them to Qal'at Ja'bar, into the hands of the amir Malik ibn Salim, and entrusted them to him. The surviving Franks [133] returned to their lands. Their leader was Bohemond, lord of Antioch, who put to sea and returned to his land, where he sought the military assistance of the Franks; they mustered and collected troops. But he died before anything came of it, as did Jikirmish,[46] lord of Mosul.

So then the sultan gave Mosul as a fief to Jawali Saqawa,[47] who decided to go on campaign. He made for Syria and arrived at Qal'at Ja'bar. There, he asked for the Frankish prisoners who were in the hands of the lord of the place, Malik ibn Salim.

'They are in your custody,' replied the lord of the place.

'Set for them a price so that they may ransom themselves,' said Jawali Saqawa.

So Malik ibn Salim conferred with them and established the price of 100,000 dinars for them; he informed Jawali of that, who said, 'Bring Joscelin to me.'

When Joscelin was brought before him, Jawali said, 'You have set a price of 100,000 dinars for your ransom?'

'Yes,' Joscelin replied.

'Would you like me to give you 10,000 dinars?'

'For someone like you to give 10,000 dinars is no bad thing.'

'Would you like me to give you 20,000 dinars?'

'It does not become a king such as you to play around with one such as me.'

'By God! I am not playing around with you! If I had wanted to take that money from you, I wouldn't have to see you or speak to you. I will set you free and forgive you the entire sum, but I have one favour to request. Will you grant it?'

'What is it?'

'The lord of Antioch and the lord of Aleppo are my enemies. I would like you to assist me in [134] fighting against them.'

At that time, the lord of Antioch was Tancred and the lord of Aleppo was Ridwan ibn Tutush.[48]

Joscelin replied, 'We will go and assemble our cavalry and infantry and we will come to you to fight anyone who fights against you.'

So Jawali set them free, and they went and mustered and assembled troops, and came into his service. Then they all went together to meet the army of Aleppo and the army of Antioch in battle. Someone who participated in that battle told me:

The blows of the swords between them – that is, the Franks – were like the blows of axes on firewood, and so the lord of Antioch defeated them. As for the Muslims, those who surrendered fled. As for the Franks who assisted Jawali, a great number of their knights were taken prisoner.[49] On the second day of their imprisonment, they went to Tancred, the lord of Antioch, and asked of him, 'What do you want from us?'

'I want to take you off to Antioch and throw you in prison.'

'By God! There is not one among us who will follow you or go with you. We are destitute! We have neither clothes nor belongings, nor beds to sleep upon nor servants to wait upon us.'

'Then what are you going to do?'

'Let us go to our homes and attend to our affairs and then we will go to the prison.'

'Right. Well off you go, then,' said Tancred.

So they went and assembled their servants and belongings and their beds, and they went to Tancred in Antioch, where he threw them in prison until someone redeemed them.

§ *Isma'ilis and a Naked Tutor at Shayzar*

A battle took place between us and the Isma'ilis in the citadel of Shayzar in the year 507 (1114).[50] Thanks to a ruse they played on us, they gained possession of the fortress of Shayzar while our bravest fighting men were out riding beyond the town. The sheikh and scholar Abu 'Abdallah Ibn al-Munira[51] (may God have mercy upon him) was in my father's house instructing my brothers (may God have mercy upon them). When the alarm sounded in the fortress, we galloped back and used ropes to climb up.

The sheikh Ibn al-Munira had moved to his own home near [191] the mosque (for his home was in the mosque). My uncle Fakhr al-Din Shafi' (may God have mercy upon him) arrived just below the mosque, with the sheikh Ibn al-Munira looking from above. So a companion of my uncle shouted up to him: 'Hey, Sheikh Abu 'Abdallah! Dangle a rope down to us!'

Ibn al-Munira replied, 'But I don't have a rope!'

The other man then suggested, 'Well, dangle down your turban-cloth!'

But he took a long time over it, so the other man gave up on him and climbed up at another location. It was later asked of sheikh Ibn al-Munira: 'Were you actually *naked* while wearing a turban on your head?!'

He replied, 'No, I didn't even have on a turban!'

Then Ibn al-Munira thought for a bit and said, 'No, wait! By God, Wahb ibn al-Tanukhi, who was with the amir Fakhr al-Din Shafi', had said to me, "Dangle a rope down to us!" and I replied, "But I don't have a rope!" So he said, "Dangle down your turban-cloth!" And if he had not seen a turban on me, he would not have said such a thing!'

And so, he was naked (may God have mercy upon him), wearing only a turban, and he, whether through fear or weakness of heart, didn't even know what state he was in.

§ *An Unarmed Warrior Defeats two Bandits*

Something like that happened at Ascalon to one of the notables of the town, called Ibn al-Jullanar, who was infatuated with hunting with sparrow-hawks and famous for his strength. One day, he rode out from Ascalon with a sparrow-hawk on his wrist to hunt in a copse of sycamore trees, and a pair of Bedouin horsemen rode out against him.

They ordered, 'Dismount!'

So he dismounted from his horse and said to them, 'Do you want anything of this bird?'

'No,' they replied. So he perched the sparrow-hawk on the branch of a tree.

Then they disputed over the spurs[52] that bedecked his feet, so Ibn al-Jullanar said to them, 'There are two of you. Each one of you should take a single spur,' and he extended his legs to them.

So they sat down trying to detach the spurs from his feet, and Ibn al-Jullanar grabbed one by the neck and the other by the neck, and beat their two heads together. They were locked in his grip, so he killed them. Then Ibn al-Jullanar took their horses, their weapons and his sparrow-hawk and entered the city!

§ *A Lesson from a Bandit*

There was with us at Shayzar a man called Muhammad ibn al-Bushaybish who used to serve my grandfather Sadid al-Mulk 'Ali (may God have mercy upon him) [193] as the supervisor of a village in the area of Kafartab, called Araja. I knew him when he was a very old man. He was strong and courageous. He said:

I once went on a hot day to the well at Araja to drink, and I saw a man wearing a woman's get-up[53] and on his shoulders was a sack of clothes.

A desire for this sack came over me, and so I said to him, 'Hand over the sack,' and he appeared to be afraid of me.

He replied, 'Here it is, my lord,' and he lifted it off his shoulders and I reached out to take it.

But he extended his hand, grabbed me by the knees, lifted me off the ground and then beat the ground with me and knelt on me. He took out from his midriff a knife as bright as a flame to kill me, and I cried, 'Mercy!'

He then got up off me and let me go, saying, 'Don't be so contemptuous of your fellow-man.' He then opened the sack and took a shirt from it and gave it to me.

So I said to him, 'By God, where did you come from?'

He replied, 'From Ma'arrat.[54] Yesterday I knocked over a dyer's shop and took everything in it.'

Then he took his sack and walked away.

§ *Concluding Remarks*

Learning is not a peak that the searcher climbs to the top of; it has no end-point where the seeker can finally stop. So multifarious is it, that it is impossible to embrace; too vast it is to gather in one place. Alas, our lifetimes are dwindling and evermore restricted, and still the vicissitudes of Time can never be predicted.

If only the soul, when it rebelled, did not get scarred[55] in its spite, and, when it was chastised, did not quarrel or fight. For a man of ninety-one it is better to love piety and good deeds, than it is to compose books like these frivolous screeds. By Time was this man most convincingly persuaded – by its subtle effect on his senses, not some argument clearly related. In this way Time warned him to change his ways, as ever closer came the end of his days.

For though steadily through life has he sped, in fact he is most certainly dead, alive only metaphorically, it is said. Humbled in his captivity to the Lord of the Worlds does he now appear, he trusts in the promise, this son of his ninetieth year, a promise he heard from the Prophet Muhammad, sincere. May God grant His Messenger and his [468] family, who are pure without peer, and his pious Companions steadfast in God-fear, and his chaste wives the Mothers of the Faithful so dear, eternal blessings as the Day of Reckoning draws near.

Register of Proper Names

This Register of Proper Names is not a complete index to all the personal names that occur in the texts translated in this book. It is rather intended as a list of the complete forms of names of the most significant personages, corresponding with the name-form used in the translation, with a brief statement of identification. In general, if Usama has mentioned a person more than twice, he (there are no women that qualify) will be listed here.

'Abbas Rukn al-Din 'Abbas ibn Abi al-Futuh ibn Tamim ibn Badis. Murderous stepson of Ibn al-Sallar, who replaced him as vizier in the Fatimid court in Egypt.

al-Afdal Ridwan Al-Afdal Ridwan ibn al-Walakhshi. One-time vizier of Fatimid Egypt, he was exiled to Syria, where Usama tried to get him to ally with the Burids of Damascus against the atabeg Zangi. Instead, he returned to Egypt, where he was captured and imprisoned. After a daring escape, he raised a revolt, but was killed.

'Ali ibn Abi Talib Cousin of the Prophet Muhammad and fourth of the 'Rashidun' or Rightly-Guided caliphs recognized by all Muslims. He was also the first of the imams recognized by all Shi'ite Muslims, and thus a figure of significant veneration. He was murdered in 661.

Baha' al-Dawla Munqidh Baha' al-Dawla Abu al-Mughith Munqidh ibn Murshid. Usama's brother, he accompanied him to Damascus after his exile, and is known as an informant for some later historians of the era.

Baldwin Baldwin II of Le Bourcq. Participant in the First Crusade, count of Edessa (1100–1118) and later King of Jerusalem (r. 1118–31). Taken prisoner in 1123, he was billeted briefly at Shayzar while the terms of his ransom were negotiated.

Bohemond Bohemond I of Taranto. Leader of the Italian–Norman contingent of the First Crusade and prince of Antioch (r. 1099–1111). His son, known in the text simply as 'the son of Bohemond', reigned later as Bohemond II (1126–30).

Bursuq Bursuq ibn Bursuq was named governor of the Iranian province of Hamadhan and later made isbasalar or general over the Seljuk armies sent to counter the Franks in Syria in 1115 and was badly defeated at Danith. He died in 1116.

Dhakhirat al-Dawla Hittan Dhakhirat al-Dawla Abu al-Qana Hittan ibn Kamil ibn 'Ali ibn Munqidh. Usama's paternal cousin. In his later life, he became governor of Yemen for Saladin. He died in 1184. His name is sometimes read as 'Khitam'.

Fakhr al-Din Shafi' Fakhr al-Din Abu Kamil Shafi'. Usama's uncle.

Fulk Fulk V, count of Anjou, Touraine and Maine. Later King of Jerusalem (r. 1131–43) through his marriage to Queen Melisende, daughter of Baldwin II. As King of Jerusalem, he interacted with Usama on numerous occasions.

al-Hafiz Al-Hafiz li-Din Allah, Fatimid caliph (r. 1131–49). Usama entered his service in 1144.

Ibn Butlan Yuwanis ibn al-Hasan ibn 'Abdun ibn Butlan. Celebrated Baghdad-born, Christian physician (and theologian). He worked for Usama's grandfather in the late 1050s and died in 1066.

Ibn Masal Najm al-Din ibn Masal. Fatimid vizier deposed by Ibn al-Sallar. He died in 1150.

Ibn Mula'ib Sayf al-Dawla Khalaf ibn Mula'ib al-Ashhabi. Former governor of Homs, he was imprisoned by the Seljuks and, upon his release, was made governor of Apamea by the Fatimids. From there, he developed a taste for banditry and for harassing the Banu Munqidh at Shayzar. He was assassinated in 1106.

Ibn al-Munira Abu 'Abdallah Muhammad ibn Yusuf, known as Ibn al-Munira. Religious scholar born in Kafartab, but moved to Shayzar, where he worked as Usama's tutor.

Ibn Ruzzik Abu al-Gharat Faris al-Muslimin al-Malik al-Salih Tala'i' ibn Ruzzik al-Ghassani al-Armani. Fatimid vizier (1154–61).

Ibn al-Sallar Al-'Adil Abu al-Hasan 'Ali ibn al-Sallar (or al-Salar). Fatimid vizier (1150–53). Stepfather of 'Abbas, who had him murdered in 1153.

Il-Ghazi Najm al-Din Il-Ghazi ibn Artuq. Amir of the Artuqid dynasty, reluctant servant of the Seljuks and lord of Mardin and Nisibis. With Tughtakin, he joined in an alliance with the Franks against the Seljuk army, led by Bursuq in 1115. In 1118, he became lord of Aleppo and presided over the crushing defeat of the Franks at the Field of Blood in 1119. He died in 1122.

'Izz al-Dawla 'Ali 'Izz al-Dawla Abu al-Hasan 'Ali ibn Munqidh al-Kinani. Usama's older brother. He moved from Shayzar to Damascus and accompanied him upon his exile to Egypt, settling at Ascalon to wage jihad against the Franks. He died in battle there in 1152.

'Izz al-Dawla Nasr 'Izz al-Dawla Abu al-Murhaf Nasr ibn 'Ali ibn Munqidh al-Kinani. Usama's paternal uncle and former lord of Shayzar. He died in 1098.

Joscelin Joscelin I of Courtenay. Usama knew him as the lord of Tall Bashir, a fief in the county of Edessa, and he later became count of Edessa himself in 1119. He died in 1131.

Jum'a Abu Mahmud Jum'a al-Numayri. An Arab amir in the army of Shayzar, a famous local champion.

Kamil the Scarred Kamil al-Mashtub. A Kurdish amir in the army of Shayzar.

Khir-Khan ibn Qaraja Lord of Homs in Syria (r. 1118–29). Brother of Mahmud ibn Qaraja.

Layth al-Dawla Yahya Layth al-Dawla Yahya ibn Malik ibn Humayd ibn al-Mughith ibn Nasr ibn Munqidh al-Kinani. A cousin of Usama's whom the latter mentions as a warrior at Shayzar in his youth.

Mahmud Troubled son of the hero Jum'a.

Mahmud ibn Qaraja Shihab al-Din Mahmud ibn Qaraja, lord of Hama (r. 1118–23). A frequent foe and sometime ally of the Banu Munqidh of Shayzar.

Majd al-Din Murshid Majd al-Din Abu al-Salama Murshid ibn 'Ali ibn Muqallad ibn Nasr ibn Munqidh al-Kinani. Usama's father (1067–1137).

Malik ibn Salim Shihab al-Din Malik ibn Shams al-Dawla Salim ibn Malik al-'Uqayli, lord of Qal'at Ja'bar on the Euphrates. Not to be confused with his ancestor Najm al-Dawla Malik ibn Salim.

Malikshah Jalal al-Dawla Abu al-Fath Malikshah I ibn Alp-Arslan. Seljuk sultan (r. 1072–92). It was to him that Usama's father travelled on his journey to Isfahan.

Mawdud Sharaf al-Din Mawdud ibn Altuntakin. Seljuk governor of Mosul. The sultan appointed him his general or isbasalar over the army sent against the Franks of northern Syria in 1111.

Mu'in al-Din Mu'in al-Din Unur (or Anur, Anar). Vizier and atabeg for the Burid princes of Damascus and one of Usama's early patrons. He died in 1149.

Nasir al-Dawla Kamil Nasir al-Dawla Kamil ibn Muqallad ibn Munqidh. Usama's paternal cousin.

Nasr Nasir al-Din Nasr ibn al-'Abbas. Fatimid amir, son of the scheming vizier 'Abbas. Taken prisoner in 1154 while fleeing Egypt with his father and Usama. He was later executed in Egypt.

Nur al-Din Al-Malik al-'Adil Nur al-Din Mahmud ibn Zangi. Son of the atabeg Zangi and heir to his lands in Syria. He captured Damascus in 1154 and became Usama's patron when the latter returned to that city later that year. He died in 1174.

Qara Arslan Fakhr al-Din Qara Arslan ibn Da'ud. Artuqid lord of Hisn Kayfa and one of Usama's later patrons. He died in 1167.

Ridwan Fakhr al-Mulk Ridwan ibn Tutush ibn Alp-Arslan. Seljuk lord of Aleppo. He died in 1113.

Roger Roger of Salerno. Frankish regent of the principality of Antioch (r. 1112–19). He defeated the Seljuk army under Bursuq at Tall Danith in 1115 but was himself defeated and killed at the Field of Blood in 1119.

Sadid al-Mulk 'Ali 'Izz al-Dawla Abu al-Juyush Sadid al-Mulk 'Ali ibn Muqallad ibn Nasr ibn Munqidh al-Kinani. Usama's grandfather, the conqueror and first lord of Shayzar. He died in 1086.

Shihab al-Din Mahmud Shihab al-Din Mahmud ibn Taj al-Muluk Buri ibn Tughdakin. Burid lord of Damascus during Usama's first residence there (r. 1135–9).

Sultan 'Izz al-Din Taj al-Dawla Abu al-'Asakir Sultan ibn 'Ali ibn al-Muqallad ibn Nasr ibn Munqidh al-Kinani. Usama's uncle and lord of Shayzar during most of Usama's life. His name should not be confused with the title 'sultan' given to Seljuk rulers. He died in 1154.

Tancred Nephew of Bohemund, regent of Antioch and Edessa and frequent foe of Shayzar. He died in 1112.

Timurtash Husam al-Din Timurtash ibn Il-Ghazi. Artuqid lord of Mardin and (briefly) Aleppo, and son of Il-Ghazi. He died in 1154.

Tughdakin Sayf al-Islam Zir al-Din Abu Mansur Tughdakin (also Tughtakin, Tughtigin), atabeg in Damascus and founder of the Burid dynasty. He died in 1128.

Usama ibn Munqidh Majd al-Din Abu al-Muzaffar Usama (also Usamah) ibn Murshid ibn 'Ali ibn Munqidh al-Kinani. Author of the texts included in this book (1095–1188).

al-Yaghisiyani Salah al-Din Muhammad al-Yaghisiyani (also al-Ghisyani). Chamberlain, general and trusted amir of the atabeg Zangi, made governor of Hama. He was Usama's commanding officer while in Zangi's service.

al-Zafir Al-Zafir bi-A'da' Allah. Fatimid caliph (r. 1149–54), involved in various court intrigues during Usama's service in Egypt.

Zangi 'Imad al-Din Abu al-Muzaffar Zangi (also Zengi, Zanki, etc.)
ibn Qasim al-Dawla Aq-Sunqur. Turkoman commander, atabeg of
Mosul, later lord of Aleppo and northern Syria. Founder of the
Zangid dynasty and Usama's first patron. He died in 1146.

Glossary

amir A commander, generally any high-ranking soldier.

atabeg A Seljuk office combining the roles of tutor and regent. Atabegs (Turkish 'father-lord') were sent with young princes *in loco parentis* to instruct them in the ways of warfare and governance.

austringer A keeper and trainer of goshawks used in hunting.

barbican (Arabic *bashura*) a protruding tower or other fortification marking the approach to a town or fortress.

Batini See 'Isma'ilis'.

caliph (Arabic *khalifa*) literally, 'successor' or 'deputy', this title indicates a person considered to be supreme head of a religious community: for Sunnis in Usama's time this was the 'Abbasid caliph in Baghdad; for the mainstream Isma'ili Shi'ites of his day, it was the Fatimid caliph in Cairo.

daniq A minuscule unit of weight, said to be equal to the weight of two carob-seeds. By Usama's time it also was used, in certain contexts, to denote a fractional coin, i.e., not a full dinar, but perhaps a cut piece of a dinar-coin.

dinar (From Latin *denarius*) the standard gold coin of the Muslim world, ideally conceived to weigh equal to one *mithqal* (see below), or 4.25 grams.

farsakh A unit of length equal to about 6 km.

fuqqa' A frothy beer-like beverage made from fermented hops.

hafiz A Muslim who has committed the entire text of the Qur'an to memory.

imam In a generic sense, the man who leads prayer in a mosque; by extension, any renowned scholar and teacher, and a title also applied to the caliph.

isbasalar (From Persian *sipah-salari*) general. Used for commanders-in-chief of special armies formed for specific campaigns.

Isma'ilis A Shi'ite sect, sometimes called 'Seveners', also called Batinis, for their belief in an elite, esoteric knowledge (*batin*) to be gleaned from exoteric sources (*zahir*). The Fatimids were Isma'ilis; the Nizaris or 'Assassins' were a branch of the Isma'ilis.

jihad Striving for faith. Usama uses the term exclusively to refer to holy war conducted against non-Muslim enemies.

Ka'ba Islam's holiest place, the Ka'ba is the simple, black, cubical shrine in Mecca, around which pilgrims on the *hajj* circumambulate. It is said to have been built by Abraham.

kazaghand A multi-layered form of armour which included a layer of mail as well as internal padding and external (often decorative) fabric.

mamluk A slave or person of slave origin; the term was most often applied to men of servile origin (usually Turks) who served as soldiers.

maristan A hospital. Also *bimaristan*.

mithqal A unit of weight associated above all with gold and precious gems. It was held to be the ideal weight of one dinar, or 4.25 grams.

qadi An executive interpreter of Islamic law, often called a 'judge' or 'magistrate'.

quntariya A spear of Byzantine origin (cf. Greek *kontarion*), probably with a wooden haft, much in favour among Shayzar's warriors.

Qur'an Muslim scripture (also spelled Koran). The collected body of God's word as recited by the Prophet Muhammad. The Qur'an is divided into chapters (*suras*) and verses (*ayas*) and is used in prayer and in special rituals of recitation on, e.g., major feast-days. Copying the Qur'an was also considered a devotional act.

ra'is Literally, 'chief' or 'headman', 'boss' in the modern urban-political sense. The *ra'is* was the recognized leader of the local urban populaces and acted as intermediary between the populace and the local lord.

Ramadan Ninth and holiest month of the Muslim calendar. Fasting is enjoined upon all able Muslims from sunrise to sundown. Other devotional activities (such as Qur'an recital and additional prayers) were also common.

ratl A unit of weight roughly equal to a pound; when used as a unit of volume it is roughly equal to a pint.

saker (Arabic *saqr*) a long-winged falcon.

sheikh (Arabic *shaykh*) an elder. A title bestowed upon anyone of sufficient age and experience, more often than not a title denoting scholarly or pious renown.

vizier (Arabic *wazir*) the chief administrative officer of a Muslim kingdom, very often the second-most powerful official after the king or caliph.

zaghariya An imported hunting-dog.

MAPS

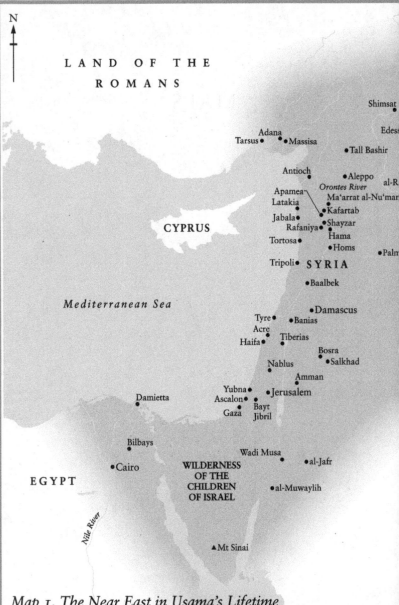

N

LAND OF THE
ROMANS

Shimsat

Adana
Tarsus ● ● Massisa

Edess

● Tall Bashir

Antioch ●
● Aleppo
al-R

Orontes River
Apamea ● Ma'arrat al-Nu'mar
Latakia ● ● Kafartab
Jabala ● ● Shayzar
Rafaniya ● Hama
Tortosa ● ● Homs
● Palm

Tripoli ● SYRIA

● Baalbek

Mediterranean Sea

● Damascus
Tyre ● ● Banias
Acre ● ● Tiberias
Haifa ●

Bosra ●
● Salkhad
Nablus ●
● Amman
Yubna ● ● Jerusalem
Ascalon ●
Gaza ● Bayt Jibril

Damietta ●

Bilbays ●
Wadi Musa ● ● al-Jafr
● Cairo WILDERNESS
OF THE
EGYPT CHILDREN
OF ISRAEL ● al-Muwaylih

Nile River

▲ Mt Sinai

CYPRUS

Map 1. The Near East in Usama's Lifetime

Khilat •
Bitlis •
YAR BAKR •
Amid •   • Is'ird
Hisn Kayfa •
• Mardin
• Nisibis
PER MESOPOTAMIA   KUHISTAN
Sinjar •   • Mosul
• Irbil

Tigris River

Euphrates River

al-Anbar •   • Baghdad

IRAQ

al-Kufa •

100 miles
100   200 kilometres

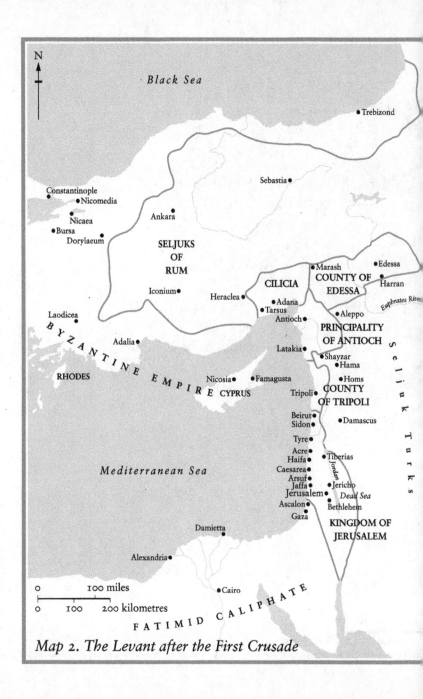

N

Black Sea

• Trebizond

Constantinople •
• Nicomedia
• Nicaea
• Bursa
Dorylaeum •

• Ankara

Sebastia •

**SELJUKS
OF
RUM**

Iconium •

Heraclea •

CILICIA

• Marash

• Edessa

**COUNTY OF
EDESSA**

• Harran

Euphrates River

Laodicea •

B Y Z A N T I N E

Adalia •

RHODES

E M P I R E

Nicosia • • Famagusta
CYPRUS

• Adana
• Tarsus
Antioch •

• Aleppo

**PRINCIPALITY
OF ANTIOCH**

Latakia •

• Shayzar
• Hama

• Homs

S
e
l
j
u
k

T
u
r
k
s

Tripoli •

**COUNTY
OF TRIPOLI**

Mediterranean Sea

Beirut •
Sidon •

• Damascus

Tyre •
Acre •
Haifa •
Caesarea •
Arsuf •
Jaffa •
Jerusalem •
Ascalon •
Gaza •

• Tiberias

Jordan

• Jericho

Dead Sea

• Bethlehem

**KINGDOM OF
JERUSALEM**

Damietta •

Alexandria •

0   100 miles
0   100   200 kilometres

• Cairo

F A T I M I D   C A L I P H A T E

Map 2. The Levant after the First Crusade

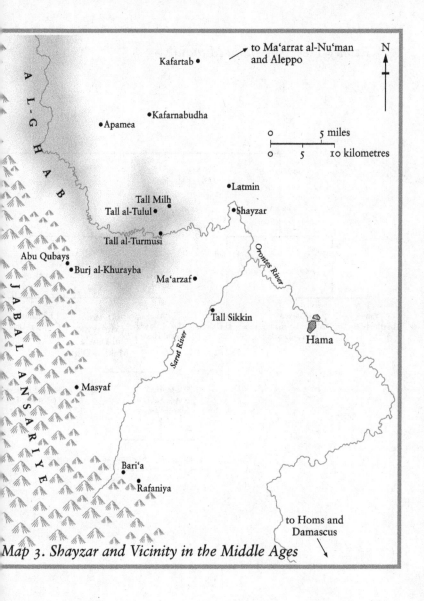

Map 3. *Shayzar and Vicinity in the Middle Ages*

Family Tree: The Banu Munqidh

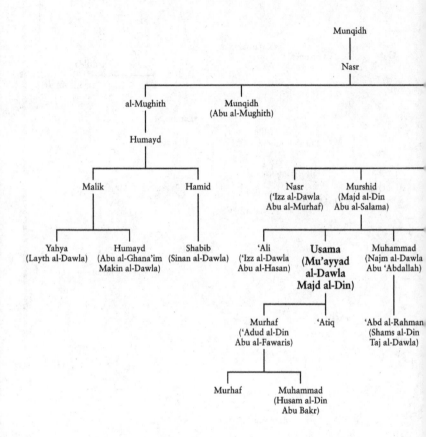

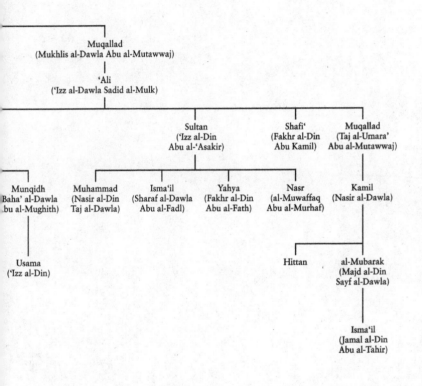

Muqallad
(Mukhlis al-Dawla Abu al-Mutawwaj)

'Ali
('Izz al-Dawla Sadid al-Mulk)

Sultan
('Izz al-Din
Abu al-'Asakir)

Shafi'
(Fakhr al-Din
Abu Kamil)

Muqallad
(Taj al-Umara'
Abu al-Mutawwaj)

Munqidh
(Baha' al-Dawla
Abu al-Mughith)

Muhammad
(Nasir al-Din
Taj al-Dawla)

Isma'il
(Sharaf al-Dawla
Abu al-Fadl)

Yahya
(Fakhr al-Din
Abu al-Fath)

Nasr
(al-Muwaffaq
Abu al-Murhaf)

Kamil
(Nasir al-Dawla)

Usama
('Izz al-Din)

Hittan

al-Mubarak
(Majd al-Din
Sayf al-Dawla)

Isma'il
(Jamal al-Din
Abu al-Tahir)

Notes

THE BOOK OF CONTEMPLATION

PART I

GREAT EVENTS AND CALAMITIES
DURING MY LIFE

1. *... there were not many Muslim casualties in that battle*: The first 21 folios of the manuscript are missing, so the text begins in the middle of the first surviving account. It is not certain what battle Usama refers to here. According to his own accounting (see 'An Enumeration of Usama's Battles' in the Lost Fragments from *The Book of Contemplation* in Other Excerpts, below), Usama was engaged in only two serious battles with the Franks under Zangi. Hitti (*Memoirs*, p. 25) favours the encounter near Qinnasrin of 532 (1138); Rotter (p. 238, n. 1) does not specify. But it is more likely the battle at Rafaniya of 531 (1137) that is intended here since Usama explicitly states of Qinnasrin that 'there was no actual engagement', which hardly fits this gory account. Moreover, Ibn al-Qalanisi (*Ta'rikh*, p. 259) describes a battle matching Usama's description, and locates it at the fortress of al-Bari'a, near Rafaniya.

2. *al-Rashid*: 'Abbasid caliph in Baghdad (r. 1135–6), succeeding his father al-Mustarshid, who took the throne in 1118.

3. *the atabeg*: By this title, Usama means his first patron, the atabeg Zangi ibn Aq-Sunqur, ruler of Mosul, Aleppo and much of northern Syria (r. 1127–46).

4. *gilded cuirass*: (Arabic *jawshan mudhahhab*) a lamellar cuirass of small (gilded) metal plates, not a 'gilden byrnie' as in Hitti (*Memoirs*, p. 25). Usama's point is one of irony, i.e., that this

ostentatious armour, intended to protect its wearer, instead attracted the attention of the enemy and so led to his death.

5.   *Ibn al-Daqiq*: This Arabic nickname 'Slender-son' or 'Flour-child', depending on your interpretation, is more likely an attempt to reproduce the sounds of a Frankish name or title. Miquel (p. 94, n. 6) suggests 'Benedict'. He is no doubt identical to the 'Philip ibn al-Daqiq' mentioned in Ibn al-Athir, *al-Bahir fi'l-dawla al-atabakiya*, ed. A. Tulaymat (Cairo: Dar al-Kutub al-Haditha, 1963), pp. 101–2.

6.   *king of the Romans*: (Arabic *malik al-Rum*) by 'Romans', Arabic writers usually meant the Byzantines, who indeed called them-selves *Rhomaioi*, Romans. I intentionally retain the inaccuracy. In this case, the Byzantine 'king' is the emperor John II Comnenus, who invaded Syria in the spring of 1138. The siege lasted from 28 April until 31 May.

7.   *Al-Yaghisiyani*: This is Usama's commanding officer, Salah al-Din Muhammad al-Yaghisiyani. He was Zangi's chamberlain and leading amir.

8.   *You'd better find ... your lands*: Zangi had made al-Yaghisiyani his governor over Hama. The latter's son Ahmad was named governor of Baalbek.

9.   *Mosul*: Headquarters of the atabeg Zangi and chief city of Upper Mesopotamia.

10.   *So I rode out and reached Shayzar*: The remainder of this passage is nearly illegible in the original and has vexed all editors and translators. My own translation is a compromise and mostly follows the readings of Samarrai (p. 27). Hitti (*Memoirs*, p. 27) reads this passage as describing Usama's woe at the destruction wrought by the Byzantine siege of Shayzar. But Gibb (p. 1006) was the first to point out that the treacherous al-Yaghisiyani is the most likely culprit. Cf. Miquel, p. 97. As Usama later describes, the siege of Shayzar was not, on the whole, so very destructive, and it does not feature in the list of prominent battles he witnessed (see 'An Enumeration of Usama's Battles' in the Lost Fragments from *The Book of Contemplation* in Other Excerpts, below).

What seems to be described is as follows: hearing in Hama of the approaching Byzantine troops, Usama's wish was to return to his family's nearby castle at Shayzar to help defend it. Al-Yaghisiyani, however, wished instead to retreat to Mosul, and so sought to force Usama's withdrawal by seizing his household in Hama while he was off in Shayzar. As we shall see, Usama remained in Shayzar for the siege and then deserted Zangi and sought service in Damascus.

11. *the lord of Damascus*: Shihab al-Din Mahmud ibn Buri, prince of the Burid dynasty (r. 1135–9), Usama's new lord. Not to be confused with Shihab al-Din Mahmud ibn Qaraja, lord of Hama.

12. *eight years ... numerous battles*: That is, 1138–44, eight years inclusive. Curiously, none of these 'numerous battles' is named in Usama's list accounting (see 'An Enumeration of Usama's Battles' in the Lost Fragments from *The Book of Contemplation* in Other Excerpts, below). Perhaps they were not major engagements.

13. *fiefs*: (Arabic *al-iqta‘*) these are not exactly the same as fiefs familiar in the medieval West, being more properly the granting of *rights* over tax-money rather than the land itself, and not involving homage. But as the practice developed, the two institutions were close enough by Usama's time to merit the translation here.

14. *the commander Mu‘in al-Din*: Mu‘in al-Din Unur (sometimes Anar, Anur), mighty atabeg of the Burid princes, d. 1149.

15. *certain things came to pass*: Usama was involved in court intrigues in Damascus against Mu‘in al-Din, involving the latter's rival, the local headman, Ibn al-Sufi. But the exact circumstances are very vague. See Cobb, pp. 30–31.

16. *Concerning this, I say*: With this poem, Usama tries to claim to Mu‘in al-Din that anything the latter may have heard against him (such as rumours of a plot) was just slander, and his flight from Damascus was not evidence of his guilt but rather a self-sacrificing gesture to remove the source of Mu‘in al-Din's troubles.

17. *al-Hafiz*: Al-Hafiz was caliph of the Fatimid dynasty (r. 1131–49).

18. *dinars*: The dinar was the standard gold coin of the Islamic world.

19. *al-Afdal ibn Amir al-Juyush*: Fatimid vizier, d. 1121.

20. *black troops*: (Arabic *al-sudan*) a special corps of black Africans purchased as slaves and trained as soldiers. The fighting began on 23 September 1149.

21. *Al-Hafiz was overwhelmed by all this*: Reading, with Miquel (p. 98, n. 3), *ghuliba minhum* for Hitti's *ghaba ‘anhum*.

22. *not even two goats locked horns over it all*: That is, the expected furore never occurred.

23. *Al-Zafir ... Ibn Masal*: Al-Zafir was Fatimid caliph (r. 1149–54).

Ibn Masal was effectively in control of Fatimid affairs even before being named vizier. On him, see *EI2*, s.v.

24. *the amir Ibn al-Sallar*: Also 'Ibn al-Salar' in some sources. On him, see *EI2*, s.v. 'al-'Adil ibn Salar'. He was governor of Alexandria at this time.

25. *Go out to al-Hawf*: That is, the eastern Delta region of Egypt, an area used by the rulers of Egypt to settle and recruit Arab tribesmen since early Islamic times.

26. *large host of Lawata*: A tribe of Berber origin, though Usama (and others) describe them as Arabs.

27. *'Abbas (a stepson of Ibn al-Sallar)*: As Usama states more specifically below, 'Abbas was the son of one of Ibn al-Sallar's wives and Tamim ibn Badis, a prince of the Zirid dynasty of Tunisia who died in exile in Alexandria.

28. *Dalas*: A town in Upper Egypt on the left bank of the Nile.

29. *'al-Malik al-'Adil'*: 'The Just Ruler'.

30. *that night*: 26 Ramadan 544 (27 January 1150).

31. *lote tree*: (Arabic *Nabq*) *Zizyphus spina Christii*, also known as the jujube tree.

32. *Nur al-Din*: Nur al-Din Mahmud (r. 1146–74) was son and successor of the atabeg Zangi and lord over Zangid possessions in northern Syria and, eventually, Damascus and central Syria as well. Like Ibn al-Sallar, he too bore the title al-Malik al-'Adil.

33. *Tiberias*: A large city in northern Palestine on the Sea of Galilee conquered by the Franks and held in fief by Raymond of Tripoli.

34. *Gaza*: A prominent town of southern Palestine, conquered by the Franks. As Usama notes, it was at that time being rebuilt, the citadel being granted to the Templars by Baldwin III of Jerusalem.

35. *Ascalon*: A coastal town in southern Palestine. It was the Fatimids' main bridgehead and military centre in Palestine, having held out against the Franks for over fifty years. As it was located just a few kilometres north of Frankish-held Gaza, it was largely isolated except by sea.

36. *a camel-load of clothes . . . and turbans*: It is worth noting that, correctly loaded, a camel can bear upwards of 200 kilos. Dabiq was a town (precise location unknown) of the Nile Delta noted for its gold brocades and colourful linens. Ciclatoun (Arabic *siqlatun*) is an undefined luxury cloth, perhaps of silk and gold; Chaucer mentions it in the Tale of Sir Thopas. Squirrel-fur was a luxury imported from the northern steppes and much prized in the south. Dimyat is better known as Damietta, a principal town

of the Delta that was, like Dabiq, renowned for its finely woven cloth.

37. *al-Jafr*: Located in modern Jordan, this is a desert outpost northeast of Maʿan, indicating that Usama was hoping to avoid crossing through the more densely settled Frankish lands west of the Jordan River by sticking to the less populous (and less firmly controlled) lands to the east. Al-Jafr is thus not an 'oasis in the desert between Egypt and Palestine' as claimed by Hitti (*Memoirs*, p. 35, n. 27).

38. *Mahri camels*: The region of Mahra in southern Arabia was famed for its noble and swift camels, prized in battle.

39. *mamluk-troops*: The term *mamluk* is used almost exclusively to denote soldiers of slave or servile origin, usually captured prisoners of war from peoples beyond the frontiers of the Islamic world, above all Turks.

40. *a garment, a brayer, a barker and a bead*: An odd locution; Usama is perhaps taking note, as many city-dwelling literati of his day did, of the quaint and curious vocabulary of the Bedouin. Or at least he is pretending to do so.

41. *sandarach resin*: (Arabic *sindarus*) the resin of the *Tetraclinis articulata* tree, used for incense and for medicinal purposes in the medieval Islamic world.

42. *who are you then?*: Usama condescends into the colloquial here (Arabic *aysh antum?*) to talk with the Bedouin.

43. *They only eat carrion*: A practice strictly forbidden in the Qur'an (5:4).

44. *Hisma*: The rocky highlands bordering the eastern edge of the Gulf of ʿAqaba in southern Jordan and northern Arabia.

45. *Since the feast of Ramadan*: Better known as ʿId al-Fitr, 'the Feast of Fast-Breaking', or al-ʿId al-Saghir, 'the Lesser Feast', marking the end of the Muslim holy month of Ramadan.

46. *orach leaves*: (Arabic *qataf*) orach or mountain spinach (*Atriplex hortensis*) may well be one of the oldest and most common of cultivated plants known, valued for its nutritious green leaves.

47. *Feast of Sacrifice*: (Arabic *ʿId al-Adha*) also known as the Great Feast, *al-ʿId al-Kabir*, celebrated on the tenth day of the month of Dhu'l-Hijja, meaning Usama's Bedouin hosts had been without food for nearly two months. As this trip took place in 544 (1150), we can place Usama's visit to al-Jafr at roughly 10 April 1150.

48. *abridged and combined ... camels ran off*: As Usama clarifies below, the point is that Usama and his men stopped to pray

while the camels with the guides continued ahead, leaving Usama without direction in the desert. In accordance with Islamic law, Muslims are allowed to shorten and combine prayers (normally said at intervals throughout the day) when travelling.

49. *bridle and some Maghribi dinars*: The original text is obscure. According to Hitti, it reads *sarfasar dananir maghribiyya*, which he says could also be *sarfasar dhahab wa-dananir maghribiyya*, 'a *gold* bridle and Maghribi dinars'. The bridle certainly seems out of place in this list of treasure unless it is precious. The reader should take note that a single gold dinar weighed, in the ideal, about 4.25 grams – Usama's bag of four thousand dinars, then, would have weighed 17 kilos, or a little under 40 pounds – no small parcel.

50. *Wilderness of the Children of Israel*: The Sinai Desert.

51. *Bosra*: An ancient city (Roman Bostra) of the Hawran region of central Syria, 140 km south of Damascus, the site of striking Roman ruins, including an amphitheatre that was used as a fortress in the Middle Ages.

52. *Asad al-Din Shirkuh*: Shirkuh ibn Shadi was one of the atabeg Zangi's Kurdish amirs. He went on to serve Zangi's son Nur al-Din, under whom he became one of the leading military men of the regime. He was also the uncle of the future sultan Saladin.

53. *Sunday night*: (Arabic *laylat al-ithnayn*) 'the night of Monday', but as the day was held to begin at nightfall by medieval Muslims, this corresponds to Sunday night.

54. *yours truly*: The Arabic actually reads *fa-qala li 'ya fulan . . .*, a common idiom used to avoid naming someone. Hitti translates this (as many do) as 'O so-and-so', which hardly makes sense to the uninitiated. In this case, Usama uses the idiom out of (a somewhat pretentious) humility to avoid mentioning his own name in his text.

55. *the very heart of Frankish territory*: And thus not 'by-passing the frontiers of the Latin Kingdom' as I claimed in Cobb, p. 36.

56. *'Ayn al-Dawla al-Yaruqi*: An amir once in the service of the Burids of Damascus and, as luck would have it, one of Usama's principal foes during his tenure there (see *Vie*, pp. 230–31). It is not clear that Nur al-Din sent him with Usama out of ill-will, as Miquel (p. 110, n. 85) suggests.

57. *the Cave of the Seven Sleepers*: (Arabic *al-Kahf wa'l-Raqim*) a location frequently designated by either of these two Arabic names or (as here) both of them at once. The names are first mentioned in the Qur'an in association with the legend of the

Cave of the Seven Sleepers (18:9–26). But the exact location is never specified, leaving the exegetes to assign various locales. The most popular was that accepted here by Usama, a place somewhere in the region of 'Amman, perhaps, as Hitti (*Memoirs*, p. 39) suggests, to be identified with the stunning (and cleft-ridden) ruins of the Nabatean city of Petra.

58. *pay us a little good-morning visit*: (Arabic *sabahuna*) to give the customary morning visit. Usama is indulging in bravado here.

59. *fools*: The word is illegible in the original, but the context clearly refers to the Muslim infantry – and not very kindly.

60. *My brother ... Ascalon*: Usama's brother 'Izz al-Dawla 'Ali had thus not been in Ascalon 'for the past few years', as stated in Cobb, p. 36, but had come with him.

61. *Bayt Jibril*: Better known as Bayt Jibrin, a small town about halfway between Gaza and Jerusalem, controlled by the Franks and, since 1134, a base for the Frankish military order of the Knights Hospitaller.

62. *Yubna*: Modern Yavne, on the coast about 30 km south of Tel Aviv, Frankish Ibelin. The castle there was built between 1140 and 1143.

63. *As for the unrest ... it happened like this*: On this confusing sequence of events, see *Vie* (pp. 236–54) and Cobb (pp. 37–42).

64. *Bilbays to defend the country from the Franks*: Once the principal city of the eastern Delta, Bilbays was an important Fatimid garrison on the invasion route into and out of Palestine. Ibn al-Sallar is here sending troops to garrison the city and guard Egypt's frontier, and so is certainly not sending them, as Hitti has it (*Memoirs*, p. 43), 'for the conquest' of the city.

65. *household managers*: Usama uses a Perso-Arabic title *ustadh-dar*, a director of the household affairs of the vizier or caliph; a major-domo.

66. *public chambers ... private quarters*: The 'private quarters' (Arabic *dar al-haram*) included, as the Arabic name suggests, what modern readers might call the 'harem', i.e., the women's quarters, but they also included much else besides that was not for the view or access of strangers. They are here contrasted with the public chambers (*dar al-salam*), where guests were received and lodged.

67. *came to loathe Nasr*: As other chroniclers hint, 'Abbas may have been angry that his son and the caliph had become lovers, an anger that Usama helped to fuel (see *Kamil*, 11:191–2).

68. *Then the caliph ignored him . . . ropes*: In this whole passage, the
    Arabic pronouns are indeterminate: it could well be Nasr, playing
    coy, who is ignoring the caliph.
69. *My lord . . . Day of Judgment*: Usama's little speech here is laced
    with Qur'anic vocabulary.
70. *son of al-Zafir*: This is the Fatimid caliph al-Fa'iz (r. 1154–60),
    having acceded at about the age of five.
71. *sons of al-Hafiz*: These are some of the brothers of the slain
    caliph al-Zafir alluded to above, and thus, despite their irenic
    statement to 'Abbas, they stood as possible rivals for the suc-
    cession.
72. *Then 'Abbas came out . . . blood was pouring out of him*: I have
    taken some liberties with the original Arabic syntax here. What
    is being described is 'Abbas dragging Yusuf out by the neck,
    using a wrestler's head-lock, not a decapitated head as in Miquel
    (p. 119), for reasons explained in the next note.
73. *brought the two of them . . . killed them there*: In Arabic *fa-
    adkhaluhima . . . wa-qataluhima*. The use of the dual in the
    Arabic indicates two victims, one Abu al-Baqa, the other clearly
    Yusuf, who thus cannot have been decapitated (see note above).
    This second victim therefore cannot be Abu al-Baqa's unnamed
    father as Miquel (p. 119) suggests.
74. *Ibn Ruzzik*: Governor in Upper Egypt who would become (as
    Usama chronicles here) the last of the truly powerful Fatimid
    viziers, holding the post from 1154 to 1161. A mosque that he
    built outside the walls of medieval Cairo still bears his name
    (al-Tala'i') and is one of the principal Fatimid monuments of the
    city. On him and the events being described by Usama, see *EI2*,
    s.v. ''al-Tala'i''.
75. *He then returned . . . command of things*: In Arabic '*ada ila
    darihi wa-amrihi wa-nahyihi*, literally, 'he returned to his palace
    and his commanding and forbidding'. 'Commanding and for-
    bidding' refers to the beloved Islamic ethical formula that all
    Muslims, especially statesmen, are encouraged to adopt, namely
    to command the good and forbid the wrong. Here it is used to
    suggest that 'Abbas was back to the business of running Egypt
    and, possibly, putting a bit of stick about, too.
76. *Barqiya*: In the eastern part of Cairo, named after Barqa, the
    north African region where many of the troops came from.
77. *Victory Gate*: (Arabic *Bab al-Nasr*) the principal north gate of
    the old city walls of Cairo, which still stands.
78. *From my fief . . . full of grain*: Here Usama is quite clear about

what an *iqta'* (see n. 13 above) of his day involved. Kum Afshin was about 15 km to the north of Cairo.

79. *the early morning hours of Friday*: One recalls here that the horoscope of 'Abbas had, after all, recommended a Saturday departure (see above).

80. *al-Muwaylih*: Usama is evidently taking more or less the same route he took on his first mission to Syria. Al-Muwaylih is a desert outpost about 50 km northeast of 'Aqaba, in modern Jordan – despite Hitti's claim (*Memoirs*, p. 53, n. 76).

81. *Wadi Musa*: 'The Valley of Moses', or Vaux Moyse to the Franks. This is the stunning canyon and area of badlands around Petra, in modern Jordan.

82. *stone-pelted devils*: An allusion to Qur'anic imagery of Satan and the practice of pelting places associated with him with stones.

83. *Rabi'a and Mudar*: Two of the principal genealogical groupings of Arab tribes. Usama's point is that there was plenty of water to go around.

84. *that battle with the Franks*: At al-Muwaylih, described above.

85. *130 mithqals*: A *mithqal* is an Arabic measure of weight ideally equal to the weight of a gold dinar coin, or about 4.25 grams, making this 'saddle' weigh 552.5 grams, just over one pound, thus absurdly light if the text is accurate. But the term *saraj*, usually translated as 'saddle', in fact refers not merely to the saddle itself, but to all its accoutrements, including straps and saddle-cloths, and it must be the latter that is drawing Usama's attention here. Saddle-cloths could indeed be richly sewn and decorated (for examples, see the medieval drawings of horsemen collected in Carole Hillenbrand, *The Crusades: Islamic Perspectives* (London: Routledge, 2000), pp. 446–55). Even so, an embroidered cloth of one pound in weight would be very thin (and unkind to its mount). Perhaps Usama refers solely to the weight of the gold used in the embroidery. Cf. Hitti, *Memoirs*, p. 54, n. 81.

86. *Husam al-Mulk*: This man, nephew of 'Abbas, is not to be confused with the Husam al-Mulk who was the son of 'Abbas, and who was killed by the Franks during this battle, as mentioned above.

87. *he apologized and kept silent*: That is, Husam al-Mulk is implying that Usama's men stole the saddle unfairly, while Usama hastens to point out that he, after all, is its proper owner.

88. *al-Afdal Ridwan*: This is al-Afdal Ridwan ibn al-Walakhshi, a Fatimid vizier who was ousted by a rising of the troops against

him on 14 June 1139. He fled to Syria, where Usama met him (see below). He is not to be confused with a Ridwan prominent in the early history of the Crusades, Ridwan ibn Tutush, Seljuk lord of Aleppo.

89. *Perhaps ... kindness*: Here Usama consciously echoes the 'injustice and ingratitude' he cited earlier.

90. *Salkhad*: A fortified city of the Hawran region of central Syria, some 120 km southeast of Damascus.

91. *Amin al-Dawla Gumushtagin al-Atabaki*: Gumushtagin was lord of Salkhad and then Bosra beginning in 1110 (despite Hitti, who misreads the name).

92. *Ridwan ... putting it to siege*: As Usama clarifies below, Ridwan has come to Baalbek seeking military aid from his fellow Fatimid officer in a bid to oust his enemies from Egypt. Zangi's siege of Baalbek took place from August to October 1139.

93. *Mu'in al-Din*: The atabeg of Damascus, where Usama was based at the time.

94. *ruler of Egypt*: (Arabic *'Aziz Misr*) an allusion to the title given to the iniquitous Pharaoh in the Qur'an (12:30, 51), a title adopted (ironically) by some later Muslim rulers of Egypt. Despite Hitti's claim (*Memoirs*, p. 57, n. 91), it was not 'a title borne by the Fatimite caliphs', though there was one caliph called 'Aziz.

95. *Amin al-Dawla*: Gumushtagin, Ridwan's host. Here, Ridwan enlists the aid of Gumushtagin in his attempt to return to Egypt and seize power there (contrary to what I stated in Cobb, p. 33).

96. *first arrived in Cairo*: Usama arrived in Cairo in November 1144. Ridwan had returned to Cairo as Zangi was besieging Baalbek in 1139. It is thus five years since Ridwan was captured and imprisoned.

97. *Wednesday night*: (Arabic *laylat al-khamis*) 'the night of Thursday', 13 April 1148, according to Derenbourg (*Vie*, p. 210, n. 2).

98. *crossed over into Giza*: That is, from the right bank, where Fatimid Cairo is located, to Giza (and the nearby Pyramids) on the left bank.

99. *Master of the Gate*: (Arabic *Sahib al-Bab*) traditionally the next-in-line to become vizier. This, in fact, was Ridwan's post before his rise to power.

100. *al-Aqmar Mosque*: The 'Moon-Lit' Mosque, whose elaborate white-grey decorations still dazzle. The mosque was built some decades earlier, in 1125, in the northern part of Fatimid Cairo.

101. *The Egyptians ... acquire his valour*: Cannibalism, though not

unknown in Usama's world, is of course strictly forbidden in Islam. The account is, in any case, almost certainly just a literary device by which Usama underlines the depth of the scheming Ridwan's fall from grace.

102. *even if the divine decree had not been executed*: That is, on 'Abbas, whose own story started this digression about Ridwan.

103. *On that day*: That is, the day the Franks attacked Usama and killed 'Abbas at al-Muwaylih en route to Syria: Usama has returned to the main thread after the digression about Ridwan.

104. *twenty ratls of blood*: A *ratl* is a unit of weight, though it was occasionally, as here, employed to measure volume. In this case, it is roughly equivalent to a pint or .568 litres, so twenty *ratls* is about eleven litres of lost blood. Since the human body only contains about five litres of blood, the man is clearly exaggerating for rhetorical effect.

105. *entered the service of Nur al-Din*: In June 1154. By this time, Damascus had finally submitted to Nur al-Din, who made it his capital, though he spent much of his time on campaign in the north.

106. *Aswan*: Then, as now, the southernmost city of Egypt and bridgehead into East Africa. Note that, for Usama in Syria, it is easier to cross to Aswan from Mecca in Arabia than to return to Cairo and proceed up the Nile.

107. *the king of the Franks*: Baldwin III of Jerusalem (r. 1143–63), the first Palestinian-born King of Jerusalem who, among other things, finally captured Ascalon from the Fatimids in 1153, just before Usama's arrival in Damascus. In contrast to his relations with Baldwin III, Usama had been on rather good terms with his father and predecessor as King of Jerusalem, King Fulk of Anjou, as he describes below.

108. *with his cross right on it*: Perhaps indicating the royal seal.

109. *in the region of Ra'ban and Kaysun*: Two cities located on the upper Euphrates in eastern Anatolia. Kaysun is also known as Kaysum. They belonged to Mas'ud, sultan of the Seljuks of Rum, and were the subject of some of Nur al-Din's military campaigns in 1155.

PART II

WONDERS OF WARFARE, AGAINST
INFIDELS AND MUSLIMS

1. *Mahmud ibn Qaraja*: Shihab al-Din Mahmud ibn Qaraja (d. 1123). His father, Qaraja, had been lord of Harran and then Homs. Upon Qaraja's death in 1113, Mahmud's brother Khir-Khan became lord of Homs and named him lord of Hama. He is not to be confused with Shihab al-Din Mahmud ibn Buri, Burid lord of Damascus (r. 1135–9). See *Kamil*, 10:373, 493.

2. *having no result*: (Arabic *ma taghabb*) the point is not that there was no respite (as in Hitti, *Memoirs*, p. 63), but that no one was gaining any ground.

3. *You do not even think ... extra measure*: Usama also cites this anonymous poem in his collection *Lubab* (p. 47).

4. *Malik ibn al-Harith al-Ashtar*: Malik al-Ashtar (d. 658) was a renowned warrior, partisan of the caliph 'Ali and general nuisance to all his rivals during Islam's early decades. On him, see *EI2*, s.v. 'al-Ashtar'. Malik's epithet *al-Ashtar* ('Droopy-Eyed') can, in fact, refer to two separate eye-conditions: entropion, the folding-in of the eyelid onto the surface of the eyeball, or ectropion, the folding-out of the eyelid so that it droops markedly down and away from the eye.

5. *in the days of Abu Bakr al-Siddiq*: That is, during the so-called Ridda Wars in Arabia shortly after the death of the Prophet Muhammad in 632. His successor, the caliph Abu Bakr (known also as al-Siddiq), led Muslim armies against those tribes that had renounced their allegiance to Islam.

6. *returned to Hama*: Much of the account that follows is not clear in the original and, thus, its reading is conjectural.

7. *quntariya-spear*: The *quntariya* is a spear of Byzantine origin (cf. Greek *kontarion*), probably with a wooden haft. Usama also uses the more generic term *rumh*, which is properly the classic Arab spear, slightly longer than the *quntariya*, and with a cane or reed haft.

8. *'Antara ibn Shaddad*: 'Antara ibn Shaddad al-'Absi was a famous poet of pre-Islamic Arabia (sixth century). As the verses cited indicate, his father was a proud 'Absi tribesman, but his mother a slave. On him, see *EI2*, s.v. ''Antara'.

9. *Apamea*: (Arabic Afamiya) an ancient city located a few kilometres northwest of Shayzar in the Orontes Valley. The southern-

most possession of the Crusader lords of Antioch, it was frequently used as a base for incursions further into Syria. Known also as Qal'at al-Mudiq, it is dominated today by an impressive medieval walled town and a vast field of Classical ruins.

10. *Il-Ghazi*: Najm al-Din Il-Ghazi ibn Artuq was a member of the Artuqid family and a prominent commander in the Seljuk army.

11. *the year 513*: The date Usama provides is incorrect. In fact, this is the date of another battle, not that of the Battle of al-Balat, better known in the West as the 'Field of Blood' or *ager sanguinis*, which took place on 28 June 1119.

12. *Roger*: Roger of Salerno was regent of the Principality of Antioch (r. 1112–19). Typically for the era, Roger had once been an ally of Il-Ghazi, when the two joined forces against the Seljuks at the Battle of Tall Danith in 1115. Roger's massacre of prisoners in the wake of that battle gained him widespread infamy.

13. *Wadi Abu al-Maymun . . . pillagers*: The precise location of Wadi Abu al-Maymun, 'The Valley of the Father of Bohemond', is not known, but it is clearly in the vicinity of Apamea. The 'pillagers' appear to be irregular troops whose job was to raid the hinterland of a city for animals, crops and other movable property.

14. *hauberk*: (Arabic *dir'*) a heavy shirt of armour made of mail.

15. *gambeson*: (Arabic *tijfaf*) a form of 'soft armour', a quilted felt garment worn, as in this example, beneath hard armour, the *dir'* or mail hauberk. Cf. Hitti (*Memoirs*, p. 68): 'wearing a coat of mail and the full armor of war'.

16. *bumped backwards from the seat of my saddle*: That is, he was jolted over and behind the low back support of his saddle-seat, not completely unhorsed as Derenbourg (*Vie*, p. 41) has it. Though taller than modern riding saddles, medieval Islamic saddles had a relatively low back and lacked the wrap-around support (the cantle) of medieval European saddles.

17. *saddle-blanket*: It is not clear what is meant exactly by the generic term *markub thaqil fidda*, as *markub* usually indicates a riding-animal itself, but here clearly indicates some part of its saddle-gear. That it is described as thick and of silver suggests a saddle-blanket akin to the gold-embroidered one described in an earlier account at the end of Part I.

18. *the dark mare*: Literally, 'the green mare' (Arabic *al-khadra'*) or perhaps as Gibb (p. 1007) ingeniously suggests, it is the horse's name: 'he was riding al-Khadra'.

19. *Thus I say . . . do no damage*: In fact, the technique that Usama is advocating is known from medieval Islamic manuals of war as

the 'Syrian thrust', though it is not entirely clear from his description if it is similar to the couched technique of medieval European cavalry of this time and later.

20. *that little bone that is in one's chest*: What Usama terms *al-'usfura*, which has perplexed most translators. As the term was used to designate the blaze on a horse's head or (colloquially) vertical pegs used on ploughs, it seems that Usama means the sternum here (as Miquel, p. 152, n. 29, suggests), and not a 'vein' as in Hitti (*Memoirs*, p. 70).

21. *With this hand . . . all things*: An allusion to Qur'an 3:26.

22. *man born to our household*: The kinship term Usama uses is *muwallad*, that is, a child of a slave or *mamluk*, and who is thus also a slave, born into the household of the owner.

23. *woman's get-up*: (Arabic *ma'raqat imra'a*) which kind of clothing is not stated. Usama's point (as is clarified below) is that he appeared not just comical, but unarmed.

24. *I am waiting . . . horses of those infidels*: A pious way of saying he's going to steal them.

25. *He wasn't wearing any trousers*: The absent article of clothing is specified as *sarawil*. That is, his legs were unprotected, a detail that becomes relevant below.

26. *Mu'in al-Din*: Atabeg of Burid Damascus and patron of Usama.

27. *at the time I was an enemy of Hama's lord*: This context allows us to fix the date of these events between 1136 and 1137, when Usama himself was working for the atabeg Zangi and his commander al-Yaghisiyani at Hama.

28. *for pity's sake*: The implication of the Arabic is that the gift would serve as alms.

29. *bodyguard*: The Arabic word is *al-jandariya*, from Persian *jan-dar*.

30. *Mudhkin*: Hitti reads this as 'Muthkir', and was unable to identify it. But as a village named Mudhkin in the vicinity of Kafartab is known from other sources, it would seem to be a variant spelling on Usama's part. Cf. Ibn al-'Adim, *Zubdat al-Halab min ta'rikh Halab*, ed. Sami Dahhan (Damascus: IFAO, 1968), 2:47. Usama's man is thus a local boy.

31. *Kafartab*: A small fortified town on the medieval road from Shayzar to Aleppo, once a possession of Usama's family.

32. *controlled by al-Yaghisiyani*: That is, Usama's commanding officer in Hama – this explains why one of Usama's men is involved.

33. *two farsakhs*: A *farsakh* was a measure of distance roughly equivalent to 6 km.

34. *one day ... Rafaniya*: The atabeg Zangi, Usama's lord at the time, was besieging a small fortified town, about 40 km north-west of Homs.

35. *brought from town*: The town where Usama's horses are stabled is Hama, where he was posted, just a few kilometres away. Oddly, Hitti (*Memoirs*, p. 74) leaves this phrase out altogether.

36. *at the end of this particular period*: That is, of this cluster of discrete battles and encounters, which punctuated Usama's early career, as he says explicitly in the introduction to this section, above. Thus, this was not 'the battle which was the last to take place in this war', as Hitti (*Memoirs*, p. 74) has it, since the battle described in this account, against the Muslim Banu Qaraja of Homs and Hama, was not part of Zangi's siege against Frankish Rafaniya, described in the preceding account.

37. *rolled out the red carpet for them*: (Arabic *wa-basatnahum*) an expression used to describe the cheery greeting of guests. Usama is being ironic here, a nuance lost in Hitti's 'we encountered them' (*Memoirs*, p. 74).

38. *kazaghand ... aventail*: A *kazaghand* (from Persian *kaz-agand*, 'stuffed silk') describes a multi-layered form of armour which included a layer of mail as well as internal padding and external (often decorative) fabric; an aventail (Arabic *litham*) is the leather or armoured piece that dangles from the back of a helmet, protecting the neck and throat, as should be clear from the rest of the account. It is thus not a 'visor' as Hitti (*Memoirs*, p. 74) has it.

39. *chisel-headed arrow*: The reading is uncertain. The root of the key term, *k-sh-m*, denotes anything 'cut off from its origin', especially a nose cut off from one's face. This would suggest that the arrow is of the blunted broad-headed type, normally associated with hunting rather than war. Such hunting arrows could be used in war against unarmoured foes, or against horses. This would coincide with Usama's intent here, as he says this wound was akin to the 'similar thing' that occurs in the next account, namely a trifling arrow wound that kills its victim against all expectation. His point is that, had the soldier been wearing an aventail, the arrow would have been harmless, but Fate had other plans.

40. *Kar'a*: I have been unable to identify this location (also read 'Lar'a'), but it is clearly a place between Apamea and Shayzar.

41. *out of fear of the Kurds*: The Arabic text reads *'ala khawf al-akrad*. Kurds were commonly recruited as soldiers in Islamic armies of this period in Syria, Iraq and elsewhere. But Samarrai (p. 70, n. 134) makes the interesting suggestion that this may be a misreading of a placename Harf al-Akrad or the like, i.e., the location to which Shihab al-Din has withdrawn.

42. *Jum'a*: The Numayri warrior of Shayzar whom Usama depicts above as a model of warrior's disdain.

43. *Burj al-Khurayba*: The reading of this toponym, *Burj al-Khurayba* or *al-Khariba*, 'the Tower of the Little Ruins' or 'Stoneheap Tower', is complicated here by the interposition of the name 'Musfan' in the manuscript, itself marked as if to suggest that the copyist saw it as an error of some kind. But this is probably the *Hisn al-Khurayba*, mentioned below.

44. *But I am in the home of my father*: Mahmud ibn Qaraja indicates here his loyalty to his hosts, Usama's family – he was not actually related to them. Usama's uncle plays along.

45. *and then through three on his right*: Hitti (*Memoirs*, p. 76) omits this last phrase.

46. *How close the funeral to the wedding*: Here Usama alludes to a line of early Islamic poetry, attributed to various authors, 'And so does Fate act: his funeral was the closest of things to his wedding.'

47. *Qays ibn al-Khatim*: An Arabian poet (d. 620).

48. *the Ansar*: Literally, 'Helpers'. These were those natives of Medina who supported the Prophet Muhammad and his cause when he emigrated to that city.

49. *Battle of al-Hadiqa*: Hadiqa was an area of orchards and gardens just outside Medina, where a pre-Islamic battle between the tribes of Aws and Khazraj was fought.

50. *court of the sultan Malikshah*: For 'court' Usama uses the Persian term *dar-gah*. Malikshah was sultan of the Seljuk dynasty from 1072 to 1092.

51. *the Cerdagnais*: Usama calls him *al-Sardani*, i.e., William Jourdain II (Guillem-Jorda II), count of Cerdagne and lord of Tripoli (1105–9). The attack would have taken place around 1108.

52. *al-Find al-Zimmani*: The sobriquet of the pre-Islamic poet Sahl ibn Shayban (seventh century).

53. *al-'Ala*: That is, the Jabal al-'Ala region of rocky uplands, not far

from Antioch, extending from the west bank of the Orontes River to the vicinity of the town of Idlib in northern Syria.

54. *Turcopoles*: (Arabic *turkubuli*) native mercenary troops employed by the armies of the Franks. Some were Muslim, others were converts from Islam or were native Christians. They are usually interpreted as light cavalry, but in fact served a variety of military functions.

55. *dagger in his boot*: Usama uses the Persian word *dashneh* to denote this dagger, which is a short, double-edged knife.

56. *Ibn Mula'ib*: Sayf al-Dawla Khalaf ibn Mula'ib al-Ashhabi was a notorious bandit and warlord in northern Syria, a constant thorn in the side of local rulers, including the Banu Munqidh of Shayzar. He was eventually murdered and the Franks captured Apamea not long after these events.

57. *javelin*: Usama uses the Persian word *khisht*, a light javelin used by footmen.

58. *In that chest . . . forty-three of them*: Copying the complete text of the Qur'an was considered an act of great piety. That said, it was not standard Muslim burial practice to include burial goods. By *masatir*, 'copy-books', Usama means the lightly ruled quires of paper that copyists practised in, not hefty bound tomes.

59. *The Great Commentary*: (Arabic *al-Tafsir al-Kabir*) a typical enough title for works of this kind. Such commentary and scholarly apparatus were commonly added in a small tight hand in different colours in the margins of a Qur'an copy.

60. *tenth and fifth parts*: The Qur'an consists of 114 chapters (or *suras*), which are divided into thirty sections (*ajza'*), which can be combined to form tenths (three sections) or fifths (six sections), both of which are standard units used in the recitation of the texts on ritual occasions.

61. *that same day*: 25 July 1104, the day of the battle with Ibn Mula'ib when Usama's father was wounded in his hand. To distinguish the two individuals involved, in what follows I have translated the Arabic term *mawla* as both 'lord' (for the king Ridwan) and as 'master' (for 'Izz al-Dawla Nasr).

62. *Ridwan*: Ridwan ibn Tutush was the Seljuk lord of Aleppo from 1095 to 1113. He is not to be confused with the adventurous Egyptian vizier al-Afdal Ridwan, whose tragic fate Usama relates in Part I.

63. *All servants and subjects*: The text reads *al-ghilman wa-awlad al-hilal*, that is, servants born of servile status as well as people born free.

64. *back in the days of my father*: That is, in the days of Tutush, Seljuk lord of Aleppo from 1078 to 1095.

65. *Instead, Sham'un told him*: Note that Sham'un does not tell him the story he wishes to hear (Usama tells it below), but instead the story of his saving his master just a few days prior.

66. *Sadid al-Mulk 'Ali*: Usama's grandfather, the conqueror and first lord of Shayzar.

67. *my uncle 'Izz al-Dawla*: Usama is mistaken here. 'Izz al-Dawla was the title of his uncle Nasr (d. 1098) and appears in the previous anecdote. He probably means his uncle Sultan, who bore the similar title, 'Izz al-Din.

68. *Tall Milh*: Tall Milh ('Salt Hill') is a small hill about 6 km to the west of Shayzar.

69. *I, just a youth*: This was perhaps an incursion by Count Bertrand of Tripoli in the summer of 1110, so Usama would have been about fifteen (see *Vie*, pp. 86–7).

70. *the dyke*: Usama calls it *al-sakr*, a low retaining wall presumably intended to hold back the waters of the Orontes during flooding. From the statement of his father, it seems it extended from the walls of the lower town, so Usama could use it to mount the walls safely.

71. *ones that rise and set*: Of course, all stars rise and set. He is perhaps referring to constellations, which rise and set as distinctive groupings, and provided at least a foundation for astrology and navigation. Note too that Usama expresses misgivings about astrology that were common (but certainly not universal) among the pious of his day.

72. *gate ... opened*: Medieval city gates were invariably closed at night.

73. *What's the name of this here town?*: The Arabic reads *Ayyu shay'in ismu hadha al-balad*. This is a good example of one of Usama's colloquialisms that has been 'Classicized'.

74. *And we turned ... choke-hold ... save him, though*: The original text indicates that 'one of them took the head of Jum'a under his armpit' – this is exactly how Usama describes a similar hold used in another context in Part I, during the massacres of the Fatimid royal family. Hitti and Samarrai (p. 80) both change the Arabic to make it 'the son of Jum'a' in the Frank's choke-hold, presumably because they assume Mahmud had been killed. But there is no evidence to prove such a conclusion.

75. *overlooks the plaza ... that road*: Usama's description still matches the topography of the town of Apamea today, which is

accessible only via a winding road overlooking a broad open area or plaza (Arabic *maydan*).

76. *cap on his head*: The cap was a *qalansuwa*, a thick quilted cap, almost a form of soft armour.

77. *Mayhap the body is cured by illness*: Here Usama quotes a verse of the poet al-Mutanabbi (d. 955).

78. *Dhakhirat al-Dawla Hittan*: Hitti reads this cousin's name as 'Khitam', but this is surely the Dhakhirat al-Dawla Hittan ibn Munqidh known from other sources as a prominent amir later in the days of Saladin. The two names look nearly identical in unpointed Arabic script.

79. *You may dislike something though it is good for you*: Qur'an 2:216.

80. *Upper Mesopotamia*: (Arabic al-Jazira) northern Iraq, where Mosul is, and which served as the primary base of operations for Zangi ('the atabeg').

81. *He had come with me into exile*: The text reads *wa-qad tagharrab ma'i*. That is, Ghunaym came with Usama from Shayzar. In the surviving text of the book, this is one of Usama's few references to his expulsion. Cf. Hitti (*Memoirs*, p. 88), 'kept me company on my sojourns in foreign lands'.

82. *Basahra' Castle*: Hitti (*Memoirs*, p. 89) reads 'Bashamra', a castle in northern Syria. But it seems a locality in Upper Mesopotamia is intended and so, following Gibb (p. 1007), I suggest Basahra', near Mosul.

83. *I saw the austringer ... French Moult*: The text reads *baziyar*, often translated 'falconer', but as the birds in questions are goshawks (Arabic *baz*), a hawk-handler or austringer is intended. In falconry, French Moult (Arabic *hass*) is a blanket term used to describe any ailment that would cause a bird to moult out of season or grow misshapen feathers.

84. *francolin*: (Arabic *durraj*) *Francolinus francolinus*, a tasty partridge-like bird that favours marshes.

85. *climbed up on the mill*: The Orontes River (which does indeed contain a few small islands along its course) fed a number of water-wheels on its banks, some used for milling grain, others for propelling water into irrigation-works. A few examples, primarily of Ottoman origin, can still be seen on the Orontes today (where children climb on them as a diving platform, not unlike the archers described here).

86. *man of courage*: Usama calls him *rajulan shuja'an*, a play on the man's title, Shuja' al-Dawla, 'Courage of the State'.

87. *Sarhank ... Khutlukh*: All prominent local amirs. Sarhank is the same champion that roused Jum'a's sense of honour in another encounter that Usama described above; Ghazi al-Talli's last name indicates his place of origin, but it is not specific: perhaps Syrian Tall Mannas or Mesopotamian Tall Bashir (Frankish Turbessel); Khutlukh bears a Seljuk title of Persian origin (*sipah-salar*), commander.

88. *leading down to al-Jalali*: Hitti (*Memoirs*, p. 92, n. 73) says that the Jalali is a tributary of the Orontes, but I have not been able to confirm this independently – there are certainly no major tributaries in the vicinity of Shayzar. Thus, one assumes that, to Hitti, the Jalali Mill mentioned above was named after the river. But the mill is far more likely to have been named after its builder, a local ruler with a title like Jalal al-Din or Jalal al-Dawla (a good candidate is an old ruler of Aleppo, Jalal al-Dawla Nasr, r. 1074–6). If that is the case, then the mill is once again meant here and not a tributary.

89. *went down*: Hitti (*Memoirs*, p. 92) has misunderstood the topography here: the horseman finds himself *'ala shafir al-wadi*, which is at the side of a canyon (i.e., the Orontes Valley), as with a bank of a river, not 'on the very edge of a precipice'. Usama's point is that the horseman falls, but finds himself on the side of the canyon convenient to his comrades' location at the Jalali Mill (with the cattle), and so goes down to them in safety.

90. *Bandar-Qanin*: Location unknown. The word *bandar*, however, is of Persian origin, meaning town, especially a market-town.

91. *projecting window*: The window is called a *rawshan*, a Persian term used to describe the projecting bay-windows that are often covered with intricately carved wooden screens or *mashrabiyat*.

92. *Bohemond's son*: Usama simply calls him *Ibn Maymun*, that is, Bohemond II, Frankish lord of Antioch (r. 1126–30), and son of Bohemond of Taranto.

93. *Rabiyat al-Qaramita*: 'Carmathian Height'. The Carmathians, or Qaramita, were an extremist Shi'ite sect prominent in the history of Syria during the tenth century.

94. *Banias ... Damascus*: The town of Banias, located at the head of the Jordan River, was captured by the Franks in 1140. It was well known for these surrounding woods, which Ibn al-Qalanisi (*Ta'rikh*, p. 520) mentions as the subject of Frankish raiding. Banias should not be confused with the Syrian coastal town of the same name, conventionally spelled Baniyas. The truce between Frankish Jerusalem and Burid Damascus, for which Usama was

to some degree responsible, was settled in 1139, while Usama
served the Burid atabeg Mu'in al-Din (1138–44).

95. *Fulk, son of Fulk*: Fulk V, count of Anjou, Touraine and Maine,
and King of Jerusalem (r. 1131–43) by virtue of his marriage to
Queen Melisende.

96. *Tancred*: Usama calls him *Dankari*. He was a nephew of
Bohemond of Taranto and served as his regent over Antioch
almost continuously from 1101 to 1112.

97. *noble horse of the Khafaja*: The Khafaja was a largely nomadic
Arab tribe of Syria whose horses were greatly prized.

98. *serjents*: Usama represents the French term in Arabic as *sarjand*.

99. *Badrahu*: Derenbourg transcribes this as 'Badrhawa', but the
long *alif* at the end of this name is not a letter, but an example
of *alif al-wiqaya*, a mark used to prevent a final letter *waw*
from being misread as the word for 'and'. I have transcribed the
name accordingly. Either way, it is difficult to interpret. On
the basis of his reading, Derenbourg (*Vie*, p. 57, n. 2) suggests
'Pedrovant', but my reading suggests a simple 'Pedro' will do.

100. *water*: The Orontes River.

101. *Yahya ibn Safi Left-Hand*: The man's epithet is *al-A'sar*, 'the
Left-Handed', or, possibly, 'the Unlucky'.

102. *al-Ruj*: This name, variously applied by different texts to a district, valley, castle or town, has caused no end of grief to medi-
evalists. Fortunately, Dussaud (pp. 165–70) seems to have sorted
it all out. In this instance, Usama means the vast and rugged
district south and west of Aleppo.

103. *Mawdud*: The isbasalar Sharaf al-Din Mawdud was the Seljuk
governor of Mosul and the commander of the sultan's armies
sent against the Franks.

104. *The right thing . . . our tents and baggage*: The point here is that
Mawdud's original camp on the river was exposed, so he is
enjoined to set up tents wherever he can behind the safety of
Shayzar's walls (and not 'on the roofs of the lower town', as
Hitti, *Memoirs*, p. 97, bizarrely puts it).

105. *Tall al-Turmusi . . . Tall al-Tulul*: Tall al-Turmusi ('Lupin
Mound') is to be identified with the 'Termeise' mentioned by
Dussaud (p. 208), about 6 km downstream from Shayzar. Tall
al-Tulul ('Hilly Mound') is located just north of Tall al-Turmusi.
Tall al-Milh, mentioned in a battle above, is also quite nearby,
suggesting that this area, a broad triangular plain on the north
bank of the Orontes, was a common battlefield for Shayzar's
armies. These mounds, it should be noted, are common features

of the Syrian landscape, often the ruin-mounds of ancient, now-deserted settlements.

106. *one of our Bedouin troops*: Hitti (*Memoirs*, p. 99), reading *min al-maghrib*, has 'one of our combatants from al-Maghrib [Mauretania]', and likewise Miquel (p. 191). But Samarrai's reading (p. 92) of *min al-'arab*, 'from among the Arab tribesmen', is surely correct, given that the man's father (as revealed below) was a camel-merchant living in Tadmur/Palmyra.

107. *Palmyra*: Known in Arabic as Tadmur, Palmyra is an ancient caravan city whose superb ruins still dominate their verdant oasis in the heart of the Syrian desert, about 240 km northeast of Damascus – a journey long enough to suggest the value of eight camels.

108. *saw something . . . described to him*: This is Usama's polite way of saying she was ugly.

109. *Another example . . . in the year 565*: This was during the period when Usama was serving under Qara Arslan, lord of Hisn Kayfa, in Diyar Bakr, in Upper Mesopotamia. The poet al-Mu'ayyad al-Baghdadi was a minor man of letters (d. 1202), and so probably a young man when he related this story to the old warrior-poet Usama.

110. *young toughs*: The narrator calls them *'ayyarun*. They are addressed below as *fityan* (literally, 'youths'), which I have rendered with the Turk's overly familiar 'boys' and *shabab* ('young men'). These terms suggest that these are the sort of young men often found in cities and towns of the medieval Near East, who formed semi-official gangs or militias. They frequently took upon themselves the defence of their cities and the 'protection' of their neighbourhoods.

111. *Turkish attendant . . . bag*: The term used to describe the Turk is *ghulam*, which probably indicates that we are dealing with a Turkish soldier of slave origin, a *mamluk*. His charge, the girl, is referred to as a *jariya*, a female domestic servant or slave, and evidently one in service to a wealthy household. The saddle-bag (*khurj*) must have been a large bundle, since the Turk later asks for help unloading it.

112. *al-Anbar*: A town in Iraq on the Euphrates, some 80 km to the west of Baghdad.

113. *Pfft*: By this explosive interjection, I attempt to convey the scatological onomatopoeia of the Arabic verb used here, *darata*, meaning both 'to scoff' and 'to fart'.

114. *Bursuq . . . by order of the sultan*: Bursuq was named commander

(*isbasalar*) by the Seljuk sultan Muhammad I, replacing Mawdud, whom Usama mentions earlier. This campaign took place
in September 1115.

115. *prominent amirs*: The names of some of these commanders
deserve some notice. The Commander of the Armies (*amir al-
juyush*) Uzbeh is also known in other sources by the roughly
equivalent appellation of Juyush-Bek. Usama is confused about
Sunqur Diraz ('Sunqur the Tall' in Persian): he is not lord of
al-Rahba, but the similarly named Aq-Sunqur (in Turkish 'White
Falcon') was. As Aq-Sunqur was a *mamluk* of Bursuq's, it is
probably this latter man that was present, and not Sunqur Diraz.
The Zangi mentioned here is not to be confused with Usama's
first patron, the mighty atabeg Zangi. This Zangi is a mere
commander, a brother of Bursuq. Finally, Isma'il al-Bakji (in
Persian 'Isma'il the Grand'), known from other sources, is a
correction on Hitti's part: Usama or the scribe had misread the
name as 'al-Balkhi'.

116. *Theophilos*: As a Theophilos (Arabic *Thiyufil*) is mentioned
below as the Frankish lord of Kafartab some nine years earlier,
Hitti reads his name here too, though it could also be *Manwil*,
Manuel. In either case, his name suggests that he is a Greek
rather than a Frank.

117. *entered the fosse and began digging a tunnel*: In preparation for
sapping the walls, discussed in detail below. Khurasan was a
region of the Seljuk sultanate, comprising northeastern Iran and
Afghanistan. The fosse (Arabic *khandaq*) was the defensive
trench dug outside the city walls.

118. *barbican ... tower*: Both 'barbican' and 'tower' refer to the same
structure in this account, though Usama seems to use the term
'barbican' (Arabic *bashura*) to refer specifically to the outer
entrance of this structure, a structure which in its entirety is a
'tower' (*burj*).

119. *inner wall remained as it was*: That is, they had hoped to damage
the inner curtain-wall of the citadel, but instead only collapsed
the outer walls of the barbican-tower that extended from the
curtain. The main defensive wall remained an obstacle.

120. *reached its highest point*: That is, by climbing the rubble of the
outer barbican-tower walls, the infantry are able to climb over
the inner curtain-wall and assault the citadel.

121. *on the parapet between the two tower walls*: This is a somewhat
vague phrase, *badan min haytan al-burj*. Other sources of the
era use *badan* to describe stretches of city wall. As the top of

a wall, connected somehow to the two walls of the damaged
barbican-tower, is describe here, and as *badan* means, literally,
a coat of armour, I assume some sort of defensive outcropping
on top of the barbican is intended, perhaps what is known as a
'hoarding' in the West or a machicolation of some kind.

122. *naphtha*: This highly flammable substance was used as a grenade-
like weapon in 'naphtha-pots' by ground troops, as well as in
naval combat as in the famous 'Greek fire'.

123. *doubled hauberk*: In fact, probably just two hauberks (Arabic
zardiyatayn) at once, a common practice in the West as well.

124. *But the Turk ... spear had been*: The Arabic is perplexingly
pronominal: *wa-masha ila al-ifranji wa-qad dakhala 'ala al-rumh
ilayhi*. Having knocked the spear aside with his shield, the Turk
steps into the Frank's zone of attack before he can recover.

125. *like a man at prayer*: The text reads *ka'l-raki'*, i.e., like a Muslim
at prayer, which would also suggest he had his hands held at his
head.

126. *al-Sayyid al-Sharif*: This amir, presumably one of Bursuq's men,
has not yet been identified.

127. *Danith*: A small town between Aleppo and Kafartab. The following reference is to the first Battle of Danith, a serious Muslim
defeat.

128. *Lu'lu' the Eunuch*: Lu'lu' al-Khadim, also known as al-Yaya
(Turkish *yaya*, infantryman), became effective lord of Aleppo
after the death of Ridwan ibn Tutush in 1113 until his own death
in 1118. Cf. Hitti (*Memoirs*, p. 105, n. 109), where his date of
accession is incorrectly given as 1117, and he is called 'Badr
al-Din'. This was in fact the title of another Lu'lu', the atabeg of
Mosul, in the thirteenth century, and last of the Zangids.

129. *lord of Antioch*: Roger (Arabic Rujar) of Salerno (r. 1112–19).

130. *Commander of the Armies*: That is, the amir al-Juyush Uzbeh,
whom Bursuq sent to Aleppo as a result of Lu'lu''s ruse.

131. *one of the three men ... mentioned earlier*: Evidently in the
opening portion of the text that is missing from the manuscript.
This is a reference to the assault on Shayzar by the Nizari
'Assassins' in the spring of 1114.

132. *Chief Sahri*: By 'Chief' I translate the title *ra'is*, which, despite
Hitti's claim (*Memoirs*, p. 107, n. 112), is not a menial title as it
was in Hitti's post-Ottoman context, but a title indicating a
ruler's local headman through whom he governed the local populace. In large cities like Damascus, the *ra'is* was often one of the
most powerful men in the city.

133. *Hisn al-Khurayba*: 'Fort Stoneheap'. This may well be the same place as the Burj al-Khurayba ('Stoneheap Tower') that Usama mentions elsewhere.

134. *Yunan*: This Yunan (or Jonas) is, like Chief Sahri above, called 'Chief' (Arabic *ra'is*, actually colloquial *rayyis*). As such, Yunan is not a 'muleteer', as Hitti (*Memoirs*, p. 108) calls him, but a neighbourhood headman in Frankish Tripoli, as his authority over the robber-gang, whom he calls 'boys' (Arabic *fityan*), may also indicate. He is described as a 'Nasrani', a term that is typically used to denote native Christians.

135. *Mount Sinai*: (Arabic al-Tur) the rustic province of Sinai was Fatimid Egypt's easternmost frontier. As Rotter (p. 100, n. 20) points out, the text should be corrected here, as the original Arabic reads *min Misr*, '*from* Egypt'. I have rearranged a few of Usama's sentences here for the sake of clarity.

136. *The son of the governor . . . story*: This anecdote, and the few that follow it, are classic examples of the genre of tales known as 'Relief after Misfortune' stories (*al-faraj ba'da al-shidda* – Usama uses these very words), a popular genre in medieval Arabic literature to which whole books were devoted.

137. *I used to travel . . . Fulk*: Jamal al-Din Muhammad was Burid lord of Damascus from 1139 to 1140, though real power was held by Usama's patron, the amir Mu'in al-Din. The truce with the Kingdom of Jerusalem under King Fulk V that Usama mentions was a product of Mu'in al-Din and Usama's efforts and began in early 1140. See Cobb, pp. 28–30. The Baldwin mentioned here is King Baldwin II, father of Fulk's wife, Queen Melisende. As Usama clarifies below, the favour Baldwin owed Usama's father was connected to his stay at Shayzar in 1123 as a hostage after being captured in battle.

138. *William Jiba*: Usama calls him *Kilyam Jiba*. The man is otherwise unknown and his surname is conjectural. As Usama clarifies below, the setting of all this is the city of Acre.

139. *Acre*: (Arabic 'Akka) chief port of the Latin Kingdom of Jerusalem. After its capture in 1104, it attracted the commercial interests of the major Western maritime powers. It was an ideal base for someone like William Jiba.

140. *The amir Qara Arslan . . . Amid*: Qara Arslan ('Black Lion') was lord of Hisn Kayfa in the province of Diyar Bakr, which straddled Upper Mesopotamia and eastern Anatolia. Amid, its historic capital city, is now known by the name of its former province: Diyarbakr, in eastern Turkey. Qara Arslan was a member of the

Artuqid (or Urtuqid) dynasty, a long-lived and far-flung family of Turkish warlords. Usama was in Artuqid service from 1164 to 1174, composed many of his works and may have started the present one there. See Cobb, pp. 49–56.

141. *Yaruq*: The servant is said to be *ifranji* (Frankish) but his name is Turkish.

142. *Kamal al-Din 'Ali ibn Nisan*: Ibn Nisan was technically the vizier of Amid, but he in fact held real power in the city. In cities of the era, *al-baladiya* indicates the locally raised militia of the town and not 'the inhabitants', as Hitti (*Memoirs*, p. 113) and Miquel (p. 213) have it.

143. *Bridge Fortress . . . tribe*: The Bridge Fortress (Arabic *Hisn al-Jisr*) is the Gistrum of Frankish sources. It was a small fort, built by the Banu Munqidh, housing a local garrison at the bridge across the Orontes, just below Shayzar. The Banu Kinana were an Arab tribe of ancient prominence. The Banu Munqidh were a clan of this same tribe. Ibn al-Ahmar (Red's Son) is otherwise unknown.

144. *Kafarnabudha*: This village (known now as Kafarnaboudi) lies between Shayzar and Kafartab.

145. *as mice seek out those wounded by leopards*: On the belief that mice had a peculiar attraction to leopard-wounds, see below.

146. *A digression*: Usama also tells this story in his collection *Lubab* (p. 101).

147. *Ibn al-Munira*: Born in Kafartab, Ibn al-Munira later settled in Shayzar, probably fleeing the Frankish capture of his town during the First Crusade. He was a respected grammarian and religious scholar (d. 1110). Thus, Usama would have been younger than fifteen years old at the time of this conversation.

148. *Judge's Mosque*: This reading is based upon the version of this story in Usama's collection *Lubab* (p. 199), which reads *Masjid al-Qadi*.

149. *The Franks . . . Banias . . . patriarch*: It is not clear exactly which siege of Banias is intended here, but by context the patriarch can be identified as William, patriarch of Jerusalem.

150. *contrasting example*: Usama relates this account in his collection *Lubab* (p. 199).

151. *Zahr al-Dawla . . . elegant frame*: The man's title means 'Flower of the State', hence Usama's reference to the man's 'elegant frame'.

152. *He then told him the purpose of his journey*: But he does not, to our frustration, tell Usama.

153. *Fadl ibn Abi al-Hayja'* ... *Abu al-Hayja'*: As Usama clarifies, his source Fadl is the son of the Kurdish lord of Irbil, Abu al-Hayja', who is the ultimate source of this account. Irbil is a town in Upper Mesopotamia, about 80 km east of Mosul.

154. *sultan Malikshah ... amir Ibn Marwan*: Malikshah was sultan of the Seljuk dynasty from 1072 to 1092. We are dealing here with a story from an older generation. The Kurdish Marwanid dynasty controlled much of Diyar Bakr in the tenth and eleventh centuries before losing their lands to the Seljuks. The reference here is probably to Malikshah's first visit to Syria in 1082, meaning the 'Ibn Marwan' in this account is the amir Mansur (d. 1096).

155. *Khilat*: Also known as Akhlat, this is a fortified town at the northwest corner of Lake Van in Armenia. During the twelfth century, the region was governed by the Turkoman Shah-i Arman ('King of Armenia') dynasty. The account here describes Zangi's betrothal to the daughter of the ruler Suqman al-Qutbi, whose widow, Inanj Khatun, seized power from Suqman's ineffectual son Ibrahim in 1128.

156. *Bitlis*: (Arabic Badlis) a town about 25 km southwest of Lake Van, not far from Khilat, in eastern Anatolia. With the Seljuk conquest of the region in 1084, the city was granted to a Turkish commander, Muhammad ibn Dilmaj, whose descendants ruled until 1192. It is not certain which Ibn Dilmaj is intended here. These events took place in 1131.

157. *training-grounds*: A *maydan* is an open plaza generally used for equestrian drills and training. They were a common feature of the horse-warrior cities of the medieval Near East, almost always extramural, as seems to be the case here.

158. *Malik ibn Salim*: One of the last of the 'Uqaylid dynasty, a clan of Bedouin origin that once controlled most of northern Syria and Mesopotamia. After the Seljuk conquests, their domains became ever more circumscribed in marginal areas of Mesopotamia, such as al-Raqqa and al-Qal'a (a short form of Qal'at Ja'bar, 'The Citadel of Ja'bar'). These nearby towns of the middle Euphrates are a little more than halfway between Aleppo and the modern city of Deir ez-Zor. The impressive ruins of the castle at al-Qal'a can still be seen, though where once they dominated the river plain, they now occupy an artificial peninsula in Lake Assad.

159. *Joscelin*: (Arabic Juslin) Joscelin of Courtenay, lord of Tall Bashir and soon to be named count of Edessa. The events described here took place in 1120 or 1121.

160. *The atabeg . . . had assembled in Apamea*: This was during the massive offensive of 1115 ordered by the Seljuk sultan. Tughdakin (or Tughtakin) was the atabeg of Damascus. His descendants ruled after him as the Burid dynasty. Fearing his autonomy in Syria would be lost in the process of a Seljuk campaign against the Franks, he, along with Il-Ghazi, the Artuqid lord of Mardin (in Upper Mesopotamia), made common cause with the Franks of Antioch (themselves assisted by Tripoli, Edessa and Jerusalem) and repulsed the Seljuk army at Danith.

161. *I myself have witnessed . . .*: Usama included another version of this anecdote in his *Kitab al-'Asa*, ed. Hasan 'Abbas (Alexandria: al-Hay'a al-Misriya al-'Amma li'l-Kitab, 1978), pp. 337–8.

162. *Mahmud ibn Salih*: Mirdasid ruler of Aleppo (1060–74). The ascetic Usama is describing in 1138 must therefore be a *descendant* of one of that ruler's *muwallads*, rather than one himself.

163. *Constantinople*: (Arabic al-Qunstantiniya) capital of the Byzantine empire.

164. *Franks attacked us on the road from Egypt*: A reference to the attack at al-Muwaylih, in Jordan, described in Part I. Usama survived the assault, but his patron, the disgraced vizier 'Abbas, was killed. His son Nasr (called here Nasr al-Kabir) was not killed during the battle but only after he had been ransomed back to the new ruler of Egypt.

165. *unable to walk*: One must recall here that Usama was gravely injured during his flight from Egypt. Usama refers to his poor horse here as *ikdish*, a colloquial term of Persian origin meaning 'mixed breed', but used (as *kadish*) to describe a nag or workhorse.

166. *Hayzan*: Also Layzan, a town in Sharwan province in the eastern Caucasus, near the Caspian Sea. The narrator seems to have been imprisoned during a conflict with the local Muslim lord of the place, perhaps during the Seljuk invasion of Sharwan beginning in 1118.

167. *Companions of the Prophet*: The generation of pious men who were contemporaries of the Prophet Muhammad. Their exemplary behaviour is as much a guide to proper Islamic conduct as is the Prophet's.

168. *Frankish king of the Germans . . . marched on Damascus*: Though it is hard to tell from this account, this is a reference to the Second Crusade and the ill-fated Frankish assault on Damascus in July 1148. The king of the Germans (*malik al-Alman*) was Conrad III (note that he is, like anyone hailing from Europe,

described as a 'Frank'), whom Usama makes the leader of the Crusade, ignoring Louis VII of France.

169. *most virtuous of all Muslims*: The story of these two men was a favourite of Muslim chroniclers of the era. Indeed, al-Findalawi, a jurist (*faqih*) of the Maliki school of Islamic law, became something of a local hero.

170. *cavalier*: The man's name, Faris, means, literally, 'horseman, cavalier, knight'.

171. *Asfuna*: A small fortress near Ma'arrat al-Nu'man that had once belonged to the Banu Munqidh.

172. *Fakhr al-Mulk ibn 'Ammar*: The independent ruler of Tripoli, who was ousted when the Franks captured the city in 1109. After passing through as an exile to Shayzar, Damascus and Baghdad, he took power near Tripoli in the town of Jabala as described here. See *Kamil*, 11:152–4.

173. *Shihab al-Din . . . Tall Mujahid*: Yaghisiyani and his son Ahmad, governor of Hama, are also mentioned in Usama's account of his return to Shayzar in 1138 during the joint Byzantine-Frankish siege in Part I. Shihab al-Din Mahmud reigned as lord of Damascus (1135–9). Tall Mujahid ('Holy-Warrior Mound') is unidentified, but it would appear to be in the vicinity of Hama.

174. *Ghazi al-Talli*: Described in another anecdote above as a prominent amir. My translation of what follows differs significantly from Hitti (*Memoirs*, p. 128) and is inspired largely by Gibb (pp. 1008–9).

175. *The battle was between them and . . . Malik ibn Salim*: The opponents of the Banu Numayr tribe here are minor princes of the 'Uqaylid dynasty. The events described here took place in 1107–8.

176. *Darayya*: One of the villages of the Ghuta, the oasis that surrounds Damascus.

177. *left Baalbek . . . service of the atabeg*: In effect, the lord of Baalbek, a member of the Burid dynasty, has joined forces with Zangi to make war on his own brother, the Burid lord of Damascus.

178. *Dumayr*: A little village with a fort, probably of Roman origin, just to the north of Damascus, clearly visible on the road to Palmyra today. Usama gives a valuable clue about the slowness of troop movements here: the army left Darayya in the Ghuta in 'the early part of the night' and was only a short distance north of Damascus at Dumayr when morning broke.

179. *Sharuf*: This would appear to be a tributary of the Orontes from this description, and is undoubtedly to be identified with the

River Sarut that debouches into the river between Hama and Shayzar.

180. *Mahmud ibn Qaraja ... Khir-Khan ibn Qaraja*: The brothers Mahmud and Khir-Khan ibn Qaraja were lords of Hama and Homs respectively, owing allegiance (technically) to the Seljuk sultan.

181. *compound spears*: Comprised of *rumh*-spears rather than the *quntariya*-style spear.

182. *Baldwin, king of the Franks ... Timurtash*: Baldwin II, count of Edessa (r. 1100–1118) and King of Jerusalem (r. 1118–31), was captured in battle in 1123 and was released, after passing through many hands, with the intercession of Usama's uncle Sultan (see Ibn al-'Adim, *Zubda*, 2:22, and Cobb, pp. 15–16). Timurtash (d. 1154) was the Artuqid ruler of the city of Mardin. In 1124, he took control of Aleppo, where Baldwin was being held prisoner.

183. *the Bridge*: That is, Hisn al-Jisr, the 'Bridge Fortress', the small fortress at the bridge that crossed the Orontes just below Shayzar.

184. *God ... made His creatures of various sorts*: An allusion to Qur'an 71:13.

185. *an omen may employ speech as its agent*: The text reads *wa'l-fa'l muwakkil bi'l-mantiq*, a phrase that perplexed Hitti (*Memoirs*, p. 135: 'a good omen is superior to logic') and Miquel (see his intricate note 18, p. 244); Rotter (p. 125) chose to drop it altogether. But the language is straight out of the lexicon of commerce: it refers to the anecdote preceding it, in which Muhasin *says* he will be stung, and so is stung, fulfilling the omen.

186. *Sabiq ibn Waththab*: Sabiq ibn Waththab ibn Mahmud ibn Salih, one of the surviving children of Waththab ibn Mahmud, a member of the Mirdasid dynasty of Aleppo and northern Syria, who played a prominent role in that dynasty's downfall on the eve of the First Crusade. Waththab survived the downfall of his family and he and his sons became minor lords in northern Syria.

187. *In those grasslands*: (Arabic *al-ghalfa'*) not a 'thicket of brambles' as Hitti (*Memoirs*, p. 135) has it (cf. Miquel, p. 245: *fourré*), but ungrazed lands abounding in various kinds of herbage. The man's fear of entering a wide open space hiding a lion is thus very understandable.

188. *horse-herdsman*: The text reads *juban al-khayl*, horse-herdsman, an adaptation of the Turkish *chuban*, herdsman.

189. *table-master*: The title is Persian *khawan-salar* – effectively the servant in charge of the kitchen.

190. *took to circling the pool*: This residence, like many traditional homes in the region today, is a building with rooms leading off an interior courtyard with a pool, fountain or cistern in the centre.

191. *it was granted a full pardon*: The text reads '*utiqa dhalika al-khuruf min al-dhabh*'. Usama uses the legalese of granting a slave freedom for humorous effect here.

192. *senile old fool*: Following Samarrai (p. 129), I read the word in question as *al-mufannid*, a weak-minded man or liar, someone whose word cannot be trusted. The reference (as Hitti, *Memoirs*, p. 137, n. 13, notes) might be to the leader of the Nizari 'Assassin' sect, the famous 'Old Man of the Mountain', whose headquarters was at Masyaf, in the mountains west of Shayzar, and for whom Usama had no great love. Hitti's reading, *al-mu'abbad*, 'the one worshipped', seems redundant given the rest of Usama's condemnation. Then again, it may be a reference to the leader (Arabic *muqaddam*) of the adherents of various sects in the Wadi al-Taym area around Baalbek, described by Ibn al-Qalanisi (*Ta'rikh*, pp. 351–2) and Ibn al-Athir (*Kamil*, 10:656).

193. *Latakia once belonged to my uncle*: As Usama's uncle Nasr became lord of Shayzar in 1082, and as Latakia was lost to the Banu Munqidh in 1086, these events must have taken place in that interval, some ten years before Usama's birth. The brothers in question then will have been old retainers of his household when they related the tale.

194. *Ma'arzaf*: A village with a small fort about 15 km southwest of Shayzar.

195. *Hunak*: A village about 35 km northeast of Shayzar, just off the modern road to Ma'arrat al-Nu'man.

196. *landlord*: The text uses the Arabic *muqta'*, i.e., in Western terms, he holds the village as fief.

197. *holy-warrior leopard*: The text reads *al-namir al-mujahid*, the leopard who goes on jihad.

198. *Qadmus ... Banu Muhriz*: Qadmus was a fortress in the Jabal Ansariye which later was captured by the Nizaris. The Banu Muhriz were one of the many local families that held small principalities in the region in the early twelfth century.

199. *variety of wild beast called a tiger ... ibn Zafar*: Usama uses the accepted term for tiger, *babr*. Though not unknown to medieval Muslim zoologists, the tiger was considered something of a natural wonder (and rightly so). There are, of course, no tigers in Africa, so it is not clear what his informant, Ibn Zafar, actually saw. Ibn Zafar was a well-travelled man-of-letters, born in Sicily,

raised in Mecca and settled and died in Hama in 1170 (see *Siyar*, 20:522–3).

200. *weighing twenty or twenty-five ratls*: As a unit of weight, the *ratl* varied slightly over time and space. In late medieval Egypt, the *ratl* was equivalent to about 434 grams or about a pound. In Syria, the *ratl* was slightly heavier. Even still, these are payloads that could inflict serious damage.

201. *The Franks March on Damascus*: This sub-heading, the only one of its kind, appears in the margin of the manuscript. It was probably added by the copyist.

202. *The Franks . . . march on Damascus and capture it*: This is the 'Damascus Crusade' of Baldwin II in 1129. Bohemond II of Antioch had captured Kafartab in 1127.

203. *lord of Edessa and Tall Bashir . . . Antioch*: Edessa (Arabic al-Ruha) was the centre of a short-lived Crusader principality on the Upper Euphrates, some 170 km northeast of Aleppo. Both Edessa and nearby Tall Bashir (Frankish Turbessel) were controlled by Joscelin I. Antioch was ruled at the time by Roger of Salerno.

204. *burgesses*: Usama uses the word *al-burjasiya*, a Frankish loan-word, literally, bourgeoisie.

205. *Mudhkin*: A town near Kafartab.

206. *public wailer at our funerals*: Ritual wailing was a commonly accepted public role for old women in many cultures of the ancient and medieval Mediterranean.

207. *blow of the mangonel-stone upon that old man's head*: Usama refers here to the anecdote above about the mangonels at the Byzantine siege of Shayzar; he is returning to this sub-section's main theme of wondrous blows.

208. *attempt on the citadel of Shayzar*: Usama refers here to the attack on Shayzar by the Nizari Isma'ili 'Assassins' in 1114.

209. *The Batini*: Usama uses this term as a synonym for the Nizari Isma'ilis, because of their belief that the Qur'an possesses an inner esoteric truth (*batin*) known only to an elect few.

210. *Abu Qubays Castle*: Located in the mountains west of Shayzar. As we shall see, this Iftikhar al-Dawla was an ally of Usama's uncle Sultan.

211. *brief exposition by way of introduction*: Usama seems to have got carried away with his long and detailed 'brief exposition' here, which is really just intended as background to explain the presence of Bohemond II and the Franks in his story about the witch Burayka, below.

212. *Roger*: Usama calls him *Rujar*, i.e., Roger of Salerno (r. 1112–19).

213. *Baldwin the Prince*: Usama calls him *Baghdawin al-Bruns*, i.e., Baldwin II, King of Jerusalem (r. 1118–31). The epithet might also be read *al-ru'ayyis*, 'the little chief'.

214. *Danith . . . 14 August 1119*: In fact, Usama has his chronology and geography confused. Roger met his death at the 'Field of Blood' or *ager sanguinis*, at al-Balat, not nearby Danith, and on 28 June 1119, not 14 August. In fact, there were two battles at Danith, the first being a less-renowned Muslim defeat that took place in 1115, as Usama relates above. The second, more famous 'Battle of Danith' of 14 August is the battle between Il-Ghazi and Baldwin II that Usama describes below. Moreover, it should be said, this second Battle of Danith was not 'a draw' as he later states, but a victory for Baldwin II.

215. *Robert, the lord of Sahyun, Balatunus*: This is Robert FitzFulk 'the Leper', an Antiochene nobleman and lord of Sardana. Sahyun (Frankish Saone) is an ancient and imposing castle high in the mountains east of Latakia, now known as Qal'at Salah al-Din ('Saladin's Castle'). The castle of Balatunus lies just to the south of Sahyun.

216. *when the army of the East arrived under Bursuq*: A reference to the great Seljuk campaign against a Frankish-Muslim coalition in 1115. After the initial furore of the First Crusade, such alliances between Muslim rulers and Frankish lords were quite common.

217. *After Balak was killed, Baldwin came into the possession of Timurtash*: Nur al-Dawla Balak was the nephew of the aforementioned Il-Ghazi. He had captured Baldwin II in battle in April 1123. Baldwin changed hands a few times before being ransomed, thanks to the intervention of the Banu Munqidh of Shayzar. Balak died in 1124. His cousin Timurtash had succeeded Il-Ghazi as lord of Aleppo in 1122.

218. *exempted us from paying it*: A reference to the annual tribute imposed by Tancred of Antioch upon Shayzar since 1110.

219. *al-Suwaydiya*: The port of Antioch.

220. *son of Bohemond*: Usama calls him *Ibn Maymun*. This is Bohemond II, son and heir of Bohemond of Taranto, founder of the Principality of Antioch. He arrived to take his throne in October 1126, when he was only seventeen or eighteen years old.

221. *illicit profit . . . stipend by which he was employed*: A hypersensitive concern over the licitness of one's livelihood was a distinctive mark of the pious in Usama's time, and money that came from

government sources, with its inevitable ties to oppression and moral compromises, was a prime target for such attitudes. Usama is lampooning the idea, noting that the man would rather take money from a witch than from his soldier's stipend.

222. *So I put down my sword*: The text reads *fa-wada'tu sayfi . . .*; Hitti (*Memoirs*, p. 152) oddly has 'Taking up my sword . . .'

223. *cotton-carders*: Al-Dhahabi, *Duwwal al-Islam*, ed. F. M. Shaltut (Cairo: al-Hay'a al-Misriya al-'Amma li'l-Kitab, 1974), 2:31, notes that the community of Isma'ilis that had settled at Shayzar used to card cotton there.

224. *may God do something with you, and do it again*: A polite way of saying she cursed him roundly.

225. *peregrines . . . zaghariya-hounds*: Peregrines (Arabic *shahin*), *Falco peregrinus*, and the lesser-known sakers (Arabic *saqr*), *Falco cherrug*, are varieties of falcons commonly used on the hunt. Cheetahs were quite frequently used as hunting allies on the ground. *Zaghariya*-hounds are hunting-dogs, possibly of European origin.

226. *night of Nisf Sha'ban*: Sha'ban, the eighth month of the Muslim calendar, could be marked by additional fasting, remembrance of the dead, and prayers, especially on the Nisf, or middle day, of the month (as described here).

227. *eyesight like that of Zarqa' al-Yamama*: Zarqa' al-Yamama was a figure of Arabian legend, whose eyesight, it is said, allowed her to see three days' distance away.

228. *after Ibn Mula'ib was killed*: In 1106, at the hands of Isma'ili assassins. See Usama's account in the Lost Fragments from *The Book of Contemplation* in Other Excerpts below.

229. *Nada al-Sulayhi*: Unidentified. His name may also be read 'Bada'.

230. *Rafaniya, which belonged to them at the time*: The Franks had taken Rafaniya in 1126 (see *Vie*, p. 481, n. 1).

231. *manager of his household*: The text reads *qahramanat darihi*, the highest-ranked female servant.

232. *Saruj*: In Upper Mesopotamia, southwest of Edessa, conquered by the Franks in 1101.

233. *The 'Wonders' of the Frankish Race*: Usama makes heavy use of the word *'ajiba* in his writings, a common term for any marvel or subject that generates wonder, both positively and negatively. I employ quotation marks in this section heading to convey this ambiguity.

234. *al-Munaytira*: A Frankish fortress and town high in the Lebanese mountains, near Afqa in the north of modern Lebanon.

235. *dryness of humours*: The text reads *nashaf*, 'dryness'. This makes complete sense given the generally Galenic framework in which physicians in the medieval Levant operated. Hitti, however, prefers to read this as Persian *nishaf*, 'imbecility'.

236. *Their king*: Fulk V of Anjou, King of Jerusalem.

237. *al-Aqsa Mosque*: The main mosque of Jerusalem, located on the Haram al-Sharif or Temple Mount platform. Under Frankish rule, the Christian military order of the Templars (Arabic *al-dawiya*) used the al-Aqsa Mosque as their headquarters.

238. *praying towards Mecca*: The text reads *ila al-qibla*, 'towards the [proper] direction of [Muslim] prayer'. In Jerusalem this is due south. In the Middle Ages, most Christians, following ancient practice, prayed towards the east.

239. *Dome of the Rock*: The magnificent domed structure near the centre of the Haram al-Sharif or Temple Mount platform in Jerusalem, not far from the al-Aqsa Mosque. The Franks converted it into a church during their occupation of the city.

240. *May God be exalted far beyond what the infidels say!*: The Frank offends both Usama's theology and Christology. For Muslims, God is transcendent: He would never take so base and material a form as a human being, nor is He ever afflicted with youth or age. Consequently, there can be no Son of God. Thus for Muslims, Jesus is the son of Mary and will return as the Messiah, but he is a strictly human prophet. On Muslim conceptions of Jesus, see Tarif Khalidi, *The Muslim Jesus: Sayings and Stories in Islamic Literature* (Cambridge, Mass.: Harvard University Press, 2001).

241. *regard for honour or propriety*: By 'regard for honour' here I translate *nakhwa*, translated above as 'courage for the sake of honour', i.e., this is a specific emotion, a sense that one's honour must be policed. With 'propriety' I translate the roughly synonymous *ghayra*, often translated 'jealousy' but connoting a sense of earnest concern for one's reputation.

242. *Whenever I went to Nablus . . . sense of propriety!*: As the reader may notice, this anecdote, a much-beloved one among Usamologists, is probably too good to be true, bearing all the structural and rhetorical hallmarks of a joke. So Usama's claim to have 'witnessed' this, as with modern urban legends, must be taken with a grain of salt. Nablus is Classical Neapolis, ancient Shechem, some 50 km north of Jerusalem. As Usama notes throughout the text, it was a town where Muslims and Franks mixed with some frequency.

243. *Ma'arra*: That is, the town of Ma'arrat al-Nu'man, about 40 km north of Shayzar, captured by the Franks in 1098, lost, and then recaptured in 1105.

244. *madame ... 'the lady'*: Usama uses the term *al-dama*, which he (or Salim – it is not clear) translates accurately into Arabic as *al-sitt*, 'the lady'.

245. *Tyre*: Port city in the far north of the Latin Kingdom of Jerusalem, captured in 1124.

246. *William de Bures*: Usama calls him *Kilyam dabur*, William (or Guillaume) de Bures. He was granted the lordship of Tiberias, one of the principal fiefdoms in the Kingdom of Jerusalem, in 1119, and served as constable and regent of the Kingdom when Baldwin II was held captive in Aleppo in 1123. As Usama explains, by 'us' Usama refers here to himself and his lord Mu'in al-Din of Damascus.

247. *Let this go and bring the conversation back to Harim*: A hemistich from the sixth-century pre-Islamic poet Zuhayr ibn Abi Sulama al-Muzani, by which Usama states his desire to change the subject.

248. *And let us stop discussing ... move on to something else*: A line that has perplexed Usama's editors and translators. My reading follows that of Miquel (p. 300, n. 16), which is largely the result of context. Cf. Gibb (p. 1006) and the oddly anatomical Hitti (*Memoirs*, p. 167).

249. *vicomte*: Usama renders the Frankish term as *al-biskund* and gives its Arabic synonym as *shihna*, governor.

250. *they did some work on his eyes*: Usama uses a euphemism *fakahalahu*, 'they applied kohl to him', a verb normally used to describe the application of dark make-up around the eyes, using small metal wands to apply it, as was the fashion. But despite Gibb's claim (p. 1009), the term was also used as a bit of gallows humour to describe the practice of sticking sharp, red-hot sticks into the eyes, blinding the victim but leaving their eyeballs whole: see E. W. Lane, *An Arabic-English Lexicon*, 8 vols. (London and Edinburgh: Williams and Norgate, 1863–93), s.v. *kahala*.

251. *Burhan al-Din ibn al-Balkhi*: Contrary to the opinion of Miquel (p. 302, n. 23), Ibn al-Balkhi (d. 1154) was not 'un personage inconnu', but one of the greatest religious scholars of his day. See *Siyar*, 20:276.

252. *Chief Tadrus ibn al-Saffi*: Despite Usama's name-dropping, this urban 'Chief' (*ra'is*) is quite unknown. Derenbourg (*Vie*, p. 474, n. 4) suggests his name might be a rendering of a Greek name

such as Theodoros Sophianos. Unfortunately, this creation has
been taken as a real person in subsequent scholarship.

253. *'Urs*: Derenbourg (*Vie*, p. 475, n. 3) suggests 'Hurso'.

254. *bourgeois*: Usama's narrator uses the term *burjasi*, which is
glossed here as *tajir*, 'merchant'.

255. *meaning his master*: Usama's uncle, Sultan. But the attendant
(*ghulam*) could hardly be so direct about Sultan and so named
Homs as his master's residence to deflect any rage. Sultan clearly
saw right through him.

256. *Lu'lu'*: Not to be confused with Lu'lu', ruler of Aleppo (1113–18).

257. *Sayf al-Din Sawar*: Governor of Hama for the Burid dynasty of
Damascus in 1128–9. He later sought service with the atabeg
Zangi. See *Ta'rikh*, pp. 374, 382, 450.

258. *saw our men crossing the ford*: That is, the men (presumably
civilians) from Shayzar were crossing through the water *away*
from the oncoming Franks towards the safety of Shayzar's walls.
To avoid drowning, some went on the shoulders of others.

259. *Commander*: I am translating the Persian title *salar*.

260. *Exalted is He who created His creatures in various sorts*: An
allusion to Qur'an 71:13.

261. *Khatun*: Turkish for 'Lady'; it may in fact be the woman's title,
her status as daughter of the powerful Seljuk amir Tutush providing sufficient identification for the men in her life.

262. *Masyaf Castle ... heat of Shayzar*: The castle (which Usama
calls Misyath), southwest of Shayzar in the salubrious climate
of the Nusayri mountains, was taken from the Banu Munqidh
by Nizaris in 1140 and became one of their most redoubtable
lairs.

263. *the Bridge*: That is, from the Bridge Fortress, where a garrison
of Kinani tribesmen kept watch, as we have seen.

264. *mail chausses*: (Arabic *kalsat al-zard*) pieces of armour designed
to protect the legs.

265. *horse armour*: The Arabic (*zardiyatihi*) implies *mail* horse
armour.

266. *In the year 539 ... Damascus*: This is the campaign of the
atabeg Zangi of Mosul and Aleppo against the Burid dynasty of
Damascus.

267. *al-Qutayyifa ... al-Fustuqa*: Al-Qutayyifa lies about 40 km
northeast of Damascus, on the road to Palmyra. Al-Fustuqa was
a khan (essentially a caravanserai) lying further down the road
towards Damascus (see *Vie*, p. 149, n. 4).

268. *'Adhra' ... al-Qusayr ... the khan itself*: 'Adhra' is a village in

the Ghuta, the oasis settlements ringing the city of Damascus. Al-Qusayr ('Fortlet') is here not the small town on the road to Homs – despite the statement of Samarrai (p. 169, n. 374) – but rather Khan al-Qusayr, located just outside the Ghuta on the Palmyra road. The 'khan itself' is al-Qusayr's khan.

269. *just to ruin my reputation*: Hitti has *la-tuksar, ya Musa*, 'in order to be destroyed, O Musa!' But al-Yaghisiyani's name is Muhammad, not Musa. I follow here the reading of Samarrai (p. 169): *li-tuksar namusi*.

270. *dirty little so-and-so*: Usama's demure *kadha wa-kadha* surely, and regrettably, hides al-Yaghisiyani's more pungent expletive.

271. *officers of the guard*: Usama uses the Persian term *shawish*, sergeant, guardsman.

272. *valley of Halbun*: The village of Halbun lies to the northwest of Damascus, in the rough highlands beyond Jabal Qasiyun, the wizened escarpment that overlooks the city.

273. *to enter the service of Nur al-Din*: Nur al-Din had captured Damascus from the Burids in April 1154 and made it his capital. Usama was by now already in his service, having entered immediately upon his eventful flight from Egypt (as detailed in Part I), but he is perhaps here assisting Khusraw ibn Talil to make the transition. Khusraw became a prominent amir under Nur al-Din and later under Saladin.

274. *Church of Baal*: The unpointed Arabic text has produced some contorted interpretations of this phrase (see Miquel, p. 330, n. 16, for a list); I follow Samarrai (p. 172). By 'church' here I am literally translating *kanisa*, though Usama clearly means the awe-inspiring ruins of the Hellenistic Temple of Baal in Baalbek, as famed in his day as in ours.

275. *I was present ... defeat at Amid*: These events took place in 1134. Al-Sawr was a small citadel on the banks of the Khabur River in the province of Diyar Bakr, about 50 km northeast of Mardin. By 'crossbowmen' I translate *jarkhiya*, the *jarkh* being a large and unwieldy, yet nevertheless portable, form of crossbow used in siege and naval warfare. Amid was the chief city of the region and an Artuqid capital.

276. *citadel of al-Bari'a*: Frankish Montferrand, also known as Barin; this fortress is located northwest of Homs, quite close to Rafaniya. This is a reference to Zangi's campaigns in the area in the summer of 1137, which probably included the battle that is described on the first remaining folio of the manuscript (see Part I).

277. *Abu Bakr al-Dubaysi*: This amir (d. 1157) was lord of Jazirat ibn 'Umar (modern Cizre in Turkey).

278. *I have three retainers*: Kujak is listed as a great Seljuk amir in an earlier anecdote; Sunqur is otherwise unknown, though Hitti (*Memoirs*, p. 186, n. 33) says he was 'one of Zanki's viziers'. Samarrai (p. 176) reads his name as 'Juqur' and identifies him with Zangi's deputy in Mosul, Abu Sa'id Juqur al-Hamadhani (d. 1144).

279. *battle at Baghdad*: This was a battle between the atabeg Zangi and the 'Abbasid caliph al-Mustarshid, in 1132.

280. *Qafjaq's location ... in the mountains of Kuhistan*: Qafjaq was a Turkoman amir. Kuhistan refers to the mountainous region straddling the borders of modern Iran and Afghanistan, bordered on the west by the Dasht-i Kavir and on the east by the Hari Rud.

281. *parcham-ornament*: Usama uses the term *barjam*, from the Persian *parcham*, the tail of a sea-cow, which was hung from the necks of horses as decoration.

282. *al-Karkhini*: In Upper Mesopotamia, between Daquqa and Irbil.

283. *as if he were plundering Romans*: Usama refers here to a point of Islamic law: Jews and Christians living under Islamic rule, as *dhimmis*, are supposed to be protected from being treated as prisoners of war.

284. *Only a few years had passed*: Actually, more than a 'few years', as Usama's account about the Batinis is situated in 1114, twenty-five years earlier.

285. *not like the generous host*: A play on the man's name, Jawad, which means 'the generous'.

286. *We mounted up ... It's a trick!*: Hitti (*Memoirs*, p. 193) leaves out this sentence.

287. *I used to take such relief ... dying of thirst*: This passage alludes to Usama's nearness to, yet exile from, his home at Shayzar (by now demolished).

288. *Called me to him*: The rest of this purple passage is given up to praise of Saladin, founder of the Ayyubid dynasty and Usama's last patron. He invited Usama to join him at his court in Damascus in 1174.

289. *I prayed ... I do answer*: Apparently a poem of Usama's own creation. The 'two angels' mentioned here are the two angels that record the deeds of men prior to Judgment.

290. *God is enough for us, He is the best protector*: Cf. Qur'an 3:173. These final lines may well be the work of the copyist, not of Usama himself.

PART III

CURIOUS TALES: HOLY MEN
AND HEALERS

1. *Section*: In the original manuscript, Usama inserts here the word *fasl*, 'new section', which is the only indication as to how the work was organized. This section and the one following it are best seen as appendices of anecdotes added to *The Book of Contemplation* after its completion.

2. *Whatever good things you possess come from God*: Qur'an 16:53.

3. *preacher of the city of Is'ird*: Siraj al-Din Abu Tahir Ibrahim ibn al-Husayn ibn Ibrahim is otherwise unknown. Is'ird (modern Siirt) lies today in eastern Turkey, about 100 km southwest of Bitlis. The ultimate source of the account, Abu al-Faraj al-Baghdadi, is better known as 'Abd al-Rahman ibn al-Jawzi, a celebrated jurisconsult and historian (d. 1201).

4. *Abu 'Abdallah Muhammad al-Basri*: Samarrai (p. 185) reads the man's name as 'al-Tabari'. In either case, he is unknown.

5. *lawful*: The text reads *halal*, lawful to consume according to Islamic law, evoking Qur'an 2:168.

6. *A man from al-Kufa . . . descendant of the Prophet*: Al-Kufa was one of the principal cities of Iraq, famed especially for its religious learning, located about 150 km south of Baghdad. Usama names the man as a descendant of the Prophet, in Arabic *sharif*.

7. *Chief Judge al-Shami al-Hamawi*: This is Qadi al-Qudat al-Shami, Abu Bakr Muhammad ibn al-Muzaffar ibn Bakr al-Hamawi al-Shafi'i (d. 1095), acclaimed ascetic and chief judge of the Shafi'ite school of law for Syria (see *Siyar*, 19:85–8).

8. *Hisn Kayfa . . . Muhammad al-Samma'*: Hisn Kayfa, situated on the right bank of the Tigris in Upper Mesopotamia, was Usama's place of residence from 1164 to 1174. Al-Khidr, after whom the mosque is named, is a greatly revered saint-like figure in Islam, often likened to Elijah. Muhammad al-Samma' is otherwise unknown.

9. *He had his own prayer-room . . . one of the saints*: Usama calls the prayer-room a *zawiya*, a term usually designating a complex devoted to a Sufi brotherhood, especially in North Africa, but in origin meaning simply a 'corner' or small cell. Usama calls the man *min al-awliya'*, 'a client/friend [of God]'; technically there are no saints in Islam, but such holy men approximate the mix-

ture of piety, closeness, mortality and the miraculous associated with the cult of saints in Christianity.

10. *Muhammad al-Busti*: Abu 'Abdallah Muhammad ibn Ibrahim al-Busti, a Sufi master (d. 1188). See *Siyar*, 20:283.

11. *practise daily fasting*: The daily fast (*sawm al-dahr*) was a non-canonical form of excessive fasting that was becoming increasingly popular among the pious in Usama's day.

12. *eating dead animals*: That is, animals not killed in the ritually prescribed manner. The point is not that he *actually* took dead animals as his food, but that he is doing it *as if* it were the case, to make his fasting even more difficult (*aj'alu ma akluhu ka'l-mayta*).

13. *Ma'arra*: That is, the Syrian town of Ma'arrat al-Nu'man.

14. *making the station*: The text reads *al-waqfa*, one of the rituals of the pilgrimage to Mecca, involving standing in prayer at nearby Mount Arafat. The point of the tale is to highlight the miraculous nature of the news of the man's death – a man who prayed over a dead man in Mecca could not possibly arrive in Syria the next day to tell the news, unless God was involved.

15. *Shihab al-Din ... ibn Sabuktakin*: The name of Usama's source deserves some comment. The man is, so far as I have been able to tell, unknown. But his ancestor, who bears the Turkish name Sabuktakin, was a freedman (*mawla*) of Mu'izz al-Dawla ibn Buwayh (d. 967), who was one of the princes of the Buwayhid (or Buyid) dynasty that controlled Iraq and parts of Iran. As his anecdote suggests, he is certainly a man of some station. Usama heard this story in the Upper Mesopotamian city of Mosul while he was based in Hisn Kayfa.

16. *Commander of the Faithful ... al-Anbar*: Al-Muqtafi reigned as 'Abbasid caliph in Baghdad from 1136 to 1160. Al-Anbar is more or less due west of Baghdad, on the east bank of the Euphrates; al-Sandudiya (or Sandawda') lies on the west.

17. *Commander of the Faithful 'Ali*: 'Ali ibn Abi Talib (d. 661), cousin and son-in-law of the Prophet, fourth Sunni caliph, first Shi'ite imam and a figure of tremendous religious authority.

18. *sword with an iron hilt*: This suggests a sword of some antiquity, perhaps a relic or bit of caliphal regalia, as this style of sword had long since given way to swords with leather-covered wooden hilts.

19. *our lord al-Mustazhir*: 'Abbasid caliph (r. 1094–1118).

20. *Ask him something useful ... into his mouth*: It is not entirely clear where al-Muqtafi's speech ends in the text, or if Usama is

interpolating. I have assumed that this is all intended to be part of the caliph's dialogue.

21. *one of those who desire only the fleeting life*: An allusion to Qur'an 17:18–19, which contrasts those who cling to this life with those who piously yearn for the afterlife.

22. *the caliph said to me*: That is, to the ultimate narrator of this complex tale, Shihab al-Din Abu al-Fath.

23. *Official procedure ... authorized for him*: The point of this last paragraph is that the amount of the award was never specified in the document, so the caretaker was in possession of, as it were, a blank cheque from the caliph himself, had he only known.

24. *Khawaja Buzurk*: A Persian title (*khwaja buzurg*) meaning 'Great Lord', and borne by several prominent viziers of the Seljuks, in this case the mighty vizier Nizam al-Mulk, who effectively ran the sultanate until his death in 1092.

25. *From a foreign land*: The text might also be read 'From Ghazna', a city in Afghanistan.

26. *Malikshah*: That is, Khawaja Buzurk's lord, the Seljuk sultan Malikshah (r. 1072–92).

27. *sura of tabaraka*: That is, the Qur'anic chapter (*sura*) that begins with the word *tabaraka* ('blessed be'). This could be either sura 25 or 67.

28. *Qur'an-master*: (Arabic *muqri'*) a man who instructs Muslims in the art of reciting the text of the Qur'an.

29. *Ibn Mujahid*: Ahmad ibn Musa ibn Mujahid al-Muqri' died in Baghdad in 935 (al-Jazari, *Ghayat al-Nihaya fi Tabaqat al-Qurra'* (Cairo: Maktabat al-Khanji, 1932), 1:139).

30. *My womenfolk asked me for a daniq ... to rub her palate*: A *daniq* is a trifling measure of weight also used to denote a fractional piece of currency, either a fraction in theory (e.g., one-sixth of a dinar, though this value varies), or in practice, i.e., a piece physically cut from a larger coin. The point is that the man didn't even have the minuscule amount he needed, not two pennies to rub together, but was rewarded with a fortune. The palate-rubbing ritual (*tahnik*) was frequently performed on newborns, sometimes using dates rather than honey, and symbolized the entrance of the child into the new community.

31. *'Ali ibn 'Isa*: 'Ali ibn 'Isa, the so-called 'Good Vizier', held office twice for the 'Abbasid caliph al-Muqtadir (913–17 and 927–8).

32. *fuqqa'-vendor*: Fuqqa' was a beer-like beverage made of barley, whose name derives from the head of suds, *faqaqi'*, that appears on its surface.

33. *As you can see*: Presumably one can tell the man's trade because
     he is carrying his wares with him.

34. *Zayn al-Din 'Ali Kujak*: One of the atabeg Zangi's commanders,
     named governor of Mosul upon the atabeg's death. He himself
     died in 1167.

35. *Abu al-Khattab al-'Ulaymi*: Abu al-Khattab 'Umar ibn Muham-
     mad ibn 'Abdallah ibn Ma'mar al-'Ulaymi, a merchant and well-
     travelled scholar of *hadith* (Prophetic Tradition), he died in 1178
     (see *Siyar*, 21:49–50). His title of 'hafiz' indicates that he had
     memorized the Qur'an by heart.

36. *al-Qadi Abu Bakr ... known as Qadi al-Maristan*: An accom-
     plished judge and student of *hadith* who, as a prisoner of the
     Byzantines, learned to read and write Greek. Among his many
     students was the scholar and historian Ibn al-Jawzi. He died in
     1140 (see *Siyar*, 20:23–8). A *maristan* or *bimaristan* was an
     institution set aside for the housing and care of the mentally and
     physically disabled, a regular feature of the larger cities of the
     Islamic world.

37. *During my pilgrimage ... pilgrim-garment*: By 'pilgrimage', the
     pilgrimage to Mecca is implied. This rite, incumbent upon all
     able Muslims, involved numerous rituals, most famously the
     circumambulation (*tawwaf*) of the Ka'ba, the large black cubical
     stone structure associated with Abraham (called here simply *al-
     bayt*, 'the House'). Pilgrims were also obliged to dress in special
     simple unstitched garments signifying their new state of ritual
     purity. And unstitched garments, as this pilgrim realized, have
     no pockets.

38. *in the Sacred Precinct*: (Arabic *haram*) here meaning the sancti-
     fied zone surrounding the Ka'ba and other pilgrimage stations in
     Mecca. Entrance is forbidden to anyone not in a state of tempor-
     ary consecration, established by a sequence of rituals including
     a statement of intention, ablution, ritual dress and abstaining
     from certain acts. Mecca, Medina and Jerusalem all possess such
     sacred precincts.

39. *the bride was exhibited before me*: This refers to a traditional
     wedding practice in which the bride, in all her finery, at the head
     of a procession is presented to her husband.

40. *Lawful enjoyment has bent the nose of jealousy*: Meaning, 'You
     don't have to be worried about my intentions when I ask you,
     since you are lawfully married to her.'

41. *Yuhanna ibn Butlan ... his clinic in Aleppo*: Ibn Butlan was one
     of the most celebrated physicians of his day (d. 1063; see *EI2*,

s.v. 'Ibn Butlan'). Though it literally means 'shop', I translate *dukkan* as 'clinic' here as Ibn Butlan appears to be using the space to treat patients and instruct his students.

42. *But doctor ... with all its coldness*: Usama addresses the physician as *hakim*. Oddly, he refers to the melon as a *rumman*, a pomegranate, for reasons which are unclear, perhaps as a way of depicting his dismissiveness at the time. When he says the melon is cold, he does not mean chilled, but rather that cold humours dominate in the fruit, and so will further imbalance his already imbalanced system. The miracle-melon described is apparently a variety of the luscious, thick-skinned musk melon or kharbuja, *Cucumis melo*.

43. *On Sleep and Dreams*: This book, unfortunately, no longer survives. See Cobb, pp. 51–6.

44. *If We extend anyone's life, We reverse his development*: Qur'an 36:68.

PART IV

EPISODES OF HUNTING

1. *I put my trust in God, may He be exalted!*: This section, commencing on a new folio with this invocation and the following introduction, is clearly another 'appendix' added to *The Book of Contemplation*, but separate from the appendix devoted to 'Curious Tales' of 'Holy Men and Healers' that precedes it.

2. *To God belongs ... idleness*: These lines are presumably Usama's own work but they do not appear in any of his other collected poems.

3. *cast off*: With the bird on the fist, pushing the bird in the direction of its quarry.

4. *making a 'desert run'*: Reading uncertain (*d-sh-t kh-y-z*), though Hitti (*Memoirs*, p. 222) intrepidly translates it (without explanation) as 'and had perched on an elevated place'. I agree with Miquel (p. 386, n. 5) that we are probably dealing with a Persian technical phrase here, and one certainly can see the Persian word *dasht*, 'desert'.

5. *I have observed ... swiftness of flight*: Hitti routinely mistranslates *baz* as 'falcon', when what is intended is any variety of hawk, in this case, the smaller, stubby-winged goshawk. As Smith (p. 241, n. 17) explains, the 'mountain' peregrines, *shawahin kuhiya/jabaliya*, are those nesting locally, as opposed to 'over-

seas' peregrines that have come from other regions. What is described here is the use of smaller goshawks in the more enclosed space of the river-banks, followed by a 'mopping up' by the swift, long-winged and swooping peregrine falcons in the open reaches of the adjacent desert.

6.   *sparrow-hawk*: (Arabic *bashiq*) *Accipiter nisus*.

7.   *Nisibis*: A town located in the upper basin of the Hirmas River, which is a tributary of the Khabur River in Upper Mesopotamia.

8.   *Sinjar*: A city at the foot of Jabal Sinjar, about 110 km west of Mosul.

9.   *caracal*: (Arabic *washaq*) *Felis caracal*; sometimes called a 'desert-lynx' or a 'Persian lynx', they are among the largest and fastest of the 'small cats' and, like cheetahs, were used as hunting-cats.

10. *'overseas' peregrines*: Peregrines not raised locally (see Smith, p. 241).

11. *intermewed goshawk with red irises*: A bird that has moulted in its cage, or mews, and has been kept on for the next season. As Smith (p. 243, n. 30) notes, hawks have yellow irises. But they turn red as they grow old. The implication, then, is that this is a bird that has seen many seasons.

12. *gorged*: The text reads *ashba'a*. Gorging is the practice of rewarding a bird by letting it eat its fill. Captured game must first be slaughtered according to the niceties of Islamic ritual law before it can be eaten.

13. *grey heron*: (Arabic *balshub* or *balshun*) *Ardea cinerea*.

14. *stoops*: The act of a bird flying high, then, with wings folded back, dropping quickly on its quarry.

15. *al-bujj ... flamingo*: The Arabic *nuham* is the generic term for the greater flamingo, *Phoenicopterus ruber roseus*, known throughout the Mediterranean.

16. *cow of the Children of Israel*: Cf. Qur'an 2:67–71.

17. *They also have an animal ... barley*: Behind the fanciful details, one can still recognize here the hippopotamus, whose Greek name does indeed mean 'river-horse' (Arabic *faras al-bahr*).

18. *tail-feathers*: In fact, all birds of prey have twelve tail-feathers. The Genoese may have simply meant that finding a sprinting bird that can hunt the high-flying crane is a rarity. This account is of some importance as it shows clearly that birds and hounds were occasionally imported from Europe. This would then make the bitch a *zaghari*, a foreign hound.

19. *see-sees*: (Arabic *zarkh*) the manuscript glosses this in the margin with the phrase *wa-huwwa al-tayhuj*. The *tayhuj* or see-see

partridge, *Ammoperdix griseogularis*, is a native of Syria and
Iraq, among other regions.

20. *Najm al-Din*: This is the amir Najm al-Din Abu Talib ibn 'Ali-
Kurd. He was the son of 'Alam al-Din 'Ali-Kurd, lord of Hama,
already mentioned in Part II.

21. *He imped the wings*: Imping is the grafting of feathers onto birds
to increase their flying capacity.

22. *Valley of Ibn al-Ahmar*: As Usama goes on to show by naming
its villages in the next sentence, the Valley of Ibn al-Ahmar was
located in the Nusayri mountains due west of Shayzar. It was
named after the Banu al-Ahmar, an Arab clan that dominated
that region in the early eleventh century.

23. *including passagers, haggards and tiercels*: Hitti (*Memoirs*,
p. 229) misses the nuances of the hawking terminology here:
passagers (Arabic *firakh*) are young birds of prey caught on their
first migration, the perfect age, while a haggard (*muqarnasa*) is
a hawk caught after moulting and growing its adult plumage; a
tiercel (*zurraq*) is simply a male goshawk, about a third smaller,
and so much less useful, than his female counterpart.

24. *seels its eyes*: Seeling is the practice of sewing the bird's eyelids
shut with a single thread, in lieu of hooding, temporarily blinding
it to make it more tractable.

25. *saluki-hounds ... zagharis*: The ancient, graceful, greyhound-
like saluki (Arabic *saluqi*) is a common enough breed and perhaps
needs no introduction; the *zaghari*, however, is more of a puzzle.
A plausible theory is that it is a breed of hound introduced by
the Franks or perhaps the Byzantines – the name may well be
German, cf. the modern German word *Zeiger*, 'pointer'. But
Smith (p. 251, n. 57) rightly cautions against too easy an identification. Gibb (p. 1011), a voice from another age, points out
that the houndsmen are technically 'whippers-in' as they are
unmounted.

26. *our joy ... other game*: Usama is alluding to religious scruples
here: the pig, wild or otherwise (Arabic *khanzir*), is religiously
unclean in Islam, not to mention just plain dangerous. They are
not to be hunted, but simply killed.

27. *sons of Rupen ... the Passes*: A reference to the Christian
Armenian Kingdom of Cilicia or 'Lesser Armenia', which was
ruled by the Rubenid (or Rupenid) dynasty in territories extending throughout the fertile coastal plain along the northeast
corner of the Mediterranean. The dynasty included the two
princes named here, Thoros I (Arabic *Tarus*, r. 1102–29) and

Leon I (r. 1129–40). The cities named by Usama were all historic-
ally part of the Cilician Kingdom, though I read Usama's
Antartus (Tartus, a city on the Syrian coast) as a copyist's error
for Cilician Tarsus. By 'the Passes' (*al-durub*), Usama means the
famous 'Cilician Gates' through the Taurus Mountains.

28. *white-birds*: This last bird species (Arabic *baydaniyyat*), despite
the description of its habitat, has not yet been identified.

29. *salamander goose*: (Arabic *al-wazz al-samand*) exact identity
unknown. No one seems to be able to identify this bird, though
Smith (p. 252) does note that the behaviour described is an
accurate depiction of general goose behaviour. A possible candidate might be the Eurasian coot, *Fulica atra*, known in Syria as
salanda.

30. *argala*: The text reads *harjal*, which is unidentified. Miquel
(p. 400, n. 35) discusses all the options. Sharing his despair,
I simply follow Hitti (*Memoirs*, p. 235).

31. *sword and mat*: The text reads *bi'l-sayf wa'l-nat'*, that is, the
customary symbols of the executioner – his sword and the leather
mat which collected blood. Usama is here alluding to the hawk's
relentless ferocity on the hunt.

32. *Tall Saqrun*: Apparently a hill outside the old city of Hama, but
its location is unknown.

33. *ride out*: Large animals with low stamina like cheetahs used in
hunting were usually transported riding in a cart or even 'riding
pillion' on horseback.

34. *idmi*: This refers to the gazelle's colouring, which Smith (p. 248,
n. 49) describes as 'brown with black lines on the flanks, with
black eyes'.

35. *al-'Ala ... white gazelles*: This is the Jabal al-'Ala region near
Idlib in northern Syria. As for the gazelles, Smith (p. 248, n. 50)
notes that these are probably the *rim* gazelles common to the
Syrian desert.

36. *Abu 'Abdallah al-Tulaytuli*: His name indicates he is from Toledo,
though, as Usama goes on to explain, he was a refugee from
Tripoli. It is possible he was also a refugee from Toledo, the city
having been conquered by Christians in 1085.

37. *the Sibawayh of his age*: Sibawayh was considered the greatest
Arab grammarian (d. 796).

38. *House of Learning in Tripoli*: A princely library founded by the
lord of Tripoli, Fakhr al-Mulk ibn 'Ammar. Tripoli was captured
by the Franks on 12 July 1109.

39. *Yanis, the copyist*: Yanis later moved to Cairo to work in the

Afdaliya library there, in 1112 (see al-Maqrizi, *Itti'az al-hunafa'
bi-akhbar al-a'imma*, ed. J. al-Shayyal (Cairo: Lajnat ihya' al-
turath al-islami, 1948), 3:51).

40. *Ibn al-Bawwab*: The sobriquet of Abu al-Hasan 'Ali ibn Hilal,
one of the most celebrated calligraphers of his day (d. 1022).

41. *many books of grammar . . . Sentences*: Sibawayh was the author
of a central Arabic grammatical text known simply as *al-Kitab*,
'The Book'; Abu al-Fath Ibn Jinni, author of *The Peculiarities
of Speech* (*al-Khasa'is*) (d. 1002); Abu 'Ali al-Hasan al-Fasawi
al-Farisi, author of *The Explanation* (*al-Idah*) (d. 987); the *Salient Features* (*al-Luma'*) is probably the text by that name written
by Ibn Jinni; and the *Sentences* (*al-Jumal*) is probably the work
by al-Zajjaji (d. 950).

42. *his feet covered in sores*: The crucial word is illegible – Hitti
(*Memoirs*, p. 238) assumes his feet are 'covered in rags'. Following Miquel (p. 405), I think 'sores' makes more sense.

43. *al-Amir*: The Fatimid caliph in Cairo (r. 1101–31).

44. *sharp-set*: (Arabic *afrah/farih*) a bird in top physical and mental
form.

45. *al-Afdal*: Fatimid vizier (d. 1121).

46. *wood-pigeons*: (Arabic *dalam*) *Columba palumbus*.

47. *jesses*: (Arabic *sibaq*) the straps attached to the legs of birds, by
which they are held (normally) upright on one's wrist.

48. *This falconer . . . peregrines*: This sentence clearly introduces
the discussion of well-trained birds that follows, though Hitti
(*Memoirs*, p. 240) attaches it to the previous paragraph. As such,
I interpret the subject of most of the action (indicated by a vague
pronoun in Arabic) as the falconer, not Usama's father, as Hitti
has it.

49. *wait on*: (Arabic *adara*) a technical term from falconry, translated
also less technically above as 'circle around'. On the significance
of this, see Smith (p. 250).

50. *Isfahan*: One of Iran's principal cities and erstwhile capital of the
Seljuk sultans. It is likely that Usama's father's visit concerned
the return of family lands in Syria that had been taken by the
Seljuks.

51. *weasel*: The text reads *ibn 'irs*, technically, a weasel (*Mustela
nivalis*). Hitti (*Memoirs*, p. 242) translates this as 'ferret', which
is indeed better attested as a hunting-animal.

52. *bustard*: (Arabic *hubara*) despite the Arabic name and the somewhat imprecise statement of Smith (pp. 252–3), this is not to be
confused with the North African Houbara Bustard (*Chlamydotis*

undulata), but rather to be identified with MacQueen's Bustard of the Near East (*Chlamydotis macqueenii*), now hunted almost to extinction.

53. *Tall Sikkin*: 'Knife Mound', located to the southwest of Shayzar (Dussaud, p. 209).

54. *Khurji's horse*: Khurji, it should be noted, means 'maker of saddle-bags'.

55. *he was his sheikh . . . studied Arabic*: The parenthetical statement is Usama's, i.e., the sheikh was the teacher of Usama's father. Hitti reads the man's name as 'ibn Qatrmatar'.

56. *Your eyes, your eyes*: The text reads *'aynak 'aynak*, translated by Hitti (*Memoirs*, p. 244) as 'Look out! Look out!' But the warning is more specifically to the threat that a hawk – trained to harry and blind its quarry – may present should it accidentally attack a human.

57. *pike*: The text reads *al-bala* – a long pointed blade, apparently from Turkish *bala*.

58. *in the bed of a wadi*: The reading is uncertain. Hitti (*Memoirs*, p. 245) and Miquel (p. 417) read it as a toponym *fi ard al-Hubayba*, 'in the land of al-Hubaybah'; Rotter (p. 242) reads it as a topographical feature, *fi ard al-junayna*, 'in the little garden'. I follow Samarrai (p. 223): *fi ard al-khabiba*, 'in the earth at the deepest part of the *wadi*'.

59. *footed*: (Arabic *asada*) footing is when a bird grabs its quarry with its talons to subdue or kill it.

60. *starling*: (Arabic *zarzur*) *Sturnus vulgaris*.

61. *mutes*: 'Muting' (Arabic *salaha*) is the practice of projectile excretion as a means of defence, something bustards were famous for, even among pre-Islamic Arab poets, as Smith (p. 253) notes.

62. *young hawk, still downy*: (Arabic *baz ghitraf farkh*) Hitti (*Memoirs*, p. 246) confuses *ghitraf* with *ghitrif*, and so translates it as 'excellent'. But in fact quite the opposite is meant: it is a technical term for a young bird just taken from its nest, still covered in down (and thus untried).

63. *'ayma*: This species remains unidentified, despite Usama's close description. Given its size, it would appear to be some variety of stork.

64. *Abu al-'Ala' ibn Sulayman*: The celebrated Syrian poet Abu al-'Ala' al-Ma'arri (d. 1057). The mythical bird he mentions in his verse is the *'anqa'*, closer to the phoenix than a griffin – despite Hitti's claim (*Memoirs*, p. 246) – and famous for being elusive (and taken by Sufis as a symbol of nothingness).

65. *bells*: (Arabic *ajras*) the little bells worn by birds of prey to make them easier to locate from afar.

66. *the Ghab*: The text reads *al-Ghab*: not simply 'the forest' as Hitti (*Memoirs*, p. 247) has it, but rather the marshy basin known by that name, stretching along the Orontes from Shayzar past Apamea.

67. *javelin*: The text reads *al-khushut*, from Persian *khisht*, 'javelin'. Usama here seems to be referring to a specific variety of this weapon – this one would seem to be a light weapon.

68. *luzzayq ... kestrel*: Smith (pp. 253–4) is probably right to avoid identifying the *luzzayq* (or *luzayq*, *laziq*) with any specific species of bird, given the sparse details. It does not appear to be the hobby (*Falco subbuteo*), one of Smith's possible candidates, as that is commonly called *kawanj*. Given Usama's description, another candidate, the red-footed falcon (*Falco vespertinus*), seems the best bet, but, as Smith notes, it would be remarkable indeed for such a small bird to down a crane. It appears to be unknown outside this text. But Smith is surely too cautious not to translate *'awsaq* as kestrel (*Falco tinnunculus*), as the name is clearly used in that sense in Syria today.

69. *Wadi al-Qanatir ... bandits*: Wadi al-Qanatir, 'Valley of the Bridges' or 'Arches', remains unidentified, but it seems to be within the lands controlled from Shayzar. The bandits are described as *'abid*, 'slaves', a term sometimes (but not always) indicating slaves of African origin.

70. *Fakhr al-Mulk ibn 'Ammar*: The independent ruler of Tripoli, on the Syrian coast, until it was captured by the Franks in 1109.

71. *slapping one hand against the other ... save in God*: This exclamation of wonder or disaster, drawn from Qur'an 18:39, is invariably accompanied by this gesture, even today.

72. *white hawk*: The text reads *zurraq*, exact identity unknown. The medieval lexicographers describe it as between a goshawk and a sparrow-hawk.

73. *first of Rajab, while we were fasting*: Fasting outside the required fast of Ramadan was considered an act of special devotion; the month of Rajab was a popular month to do this for a variety of reasons. See *EI2*, s.v. 'Radjab'.

74. *liquorice-bushes*: Liquorice (*Glycyrrhiza glabra*), known in Arabic as *sus*, grows in low, thick bushes in Lebanon and northern Syria.

75. *asphodel*: (Arabic *khinath*) *Asphodelus ramosus*, King's Spear,

which grows in tall spikes bearing large white flowers. Its fruit, by the way, are said to be a favourite of the wild boar. Samarrai (p. 230) reads *khabab*, 'plants, growth', which also fits.

76. *boar*: Hitti (*Memoirs*, pp. 251–2) unaccountably thinks Usama has started chasing the *bull* at this point, a change of quarry that would be neither honourable nor cost-effective.

77. *hunting with sakers has a system ... horses*: On the technique described here and this passage, see Smith (pp. 254–5). In his translation he renders *al-kalba* ('bitch') as 'saluki bitch'. But it seems clear that this anecdote is about the well-trained dog that was just previously mentioned, the one that Usama's father received as a gift. And, as this follows on the heels of an account about *zaghariya*-hounds and their tractability, I suspect the bitch in question is a *zaghariya*, not a saluki. This would be further evidence that *zaghariya*-hounds were not pointers.

78. *Injustice ... some defect*: Usama also cites this memorably cynical verse from the poet al-Mutanabbi in his *Kitab al-Badi'*, p. 381.

79. *Praise be to God ... in Him we trust*: These final lines may not have been penned by Usama, but added by a copyist. The passage that follows clearly indicates that this manuscript is a copy of an earlier manuscript. The scene that it depicts in the history of that earlier manuscript is touching: in 1213, Usama's (now elderly) son, 'Adud al-Din Murhaf, instructed his own grandson faithfully to transmit Usama's famous work.

OTHER EXCERPTS

1. *From the Introduction*: Samarrai (pp. 16–17), citing al-Dhahabi, *Ta'rikh al-Islam* (British Museum MS 739B, ff. 16a-19b). See also *Vie* (p. 619).

2. *in the same year*: Al-Dhahabi (*Ta'rikh al-Islam* MS, f. 16a) here goes on to describe the rest of the book as follows: 'Then he sets out in detail the amazing experiences he has had during these battles, describing in it his courage and audacity, may God have mercy upon him.'

3. *A Summary History of Shayzar*: Samarrai (p. 15), citing the historian Abu al-Fida' (d. 1331), *al-Mukhtasar fi akhbar al-bashar* (Cairo: al-Matba'a al-Husayniya, 1907), 3:33.

4. *Bridge Fortress*: Abu al-Fida' (*al-Mukhtasar*, 3:33) adds: 'The aforementioned bridge is known in our time as the Bridge of Ibn Munqidh, and the place where the fortress used to be is today a

    mound clear of any building. It is located to the west of Shayzar, just a short distance from it.'

5. *Demetrios*: The text reads *Dimitri*.

6. *quntariya*: Usama uses this term, the same name given for the spears favoured by certain warriors at Shayzar in Usama's day. The word and the weapon are of Greek origin (*kontarion*), and would seem to indicate that these troops were some kind of elite infantry associated with this weapon.

7. *So my grandfather handed over . . . earthquake*: Nasr and Sultan are Usama's paternal uncles, Muhammad his paternal cousin. Almost the entire family was destroyed in the earthquake that levelled Shayzar.

8. *The Bravery of the Caliph al-Mustarshid*: Samarrai (p. 19), citing Ibn Wasil, *Mufarrij al-Kurub*, ed. Jamal al-Din al-Shayyal (Cairo: Matba'at Jami'at Fu'ad al-Awwal, 1953–7), 1:50–51. This passage describes the disastrous battle between the atabeg Zangi and the 'Abbasid caliph al-Mustarshid (r. 1118–35) near Baghdad.

9. *'Aqarquf*: A village about 30 km west of Baghdad.

10. *Usama Gives Advice to a Friend in Peril*: Samarrai (pp. 21–22), citing Abu Shama, *Kitab al-Rawdatayn*, ed. M. H. Muhammad (Cairo: Lajnat al-Ta'lif wa-al-Tarjama wa-al-Nashr, 1956–62), 1:138.

11. *al-Mawsili*: The man, whom Usama warns is spending too much of his prince's money on charity, was vizier in Mosul.

12. *Nineveh . . . training-grounds*: Nineveh was a small medieval town that had developed in the ruins of the ancient Assyrian city, across the Tigris from Mosul. The training-grounds (Arabic *maydan*) lay outside Mosul, to the north of the city walls.

13. *al-Sharif al-Radi*: One of the greatest Shi'ite poets (d. 1016). See *EI*2, s.v.

14. *Barmakids*: The family of viziers and financial administrators that dominated the caliphate of the early 'Abbasids. Their violent fall from grace under the caliph Harun al-Rashid (786–809) became paradigmatic of the fickleness of political position and the inscrutability of Fate.

15. *the Hijaz*: This is the Arabic name for the mountainous area of northwestern Arabia, where the Muslim holy cities of Mecca and Medina are located.

16. *Isma'ilis Capture Apamea*: Samarrai (pp. 22–3), citing Ibn al-'Adim, *Bughyat al-talab min ta'rikh halab*, ed. Suhayl Zakkar (Damascus: 1991), 1:131. Apamea, located just north of Shayzar, was the base of Ibn Mula'ib, who features prominently in *The*

Book of Contemplation as a thorn in Shayzar's side in Usama's youth.

17.   *Malikshah*: Seljuk sultan (r. 1072–92).

18.   *Abu Yusuf al-Qazwini*: 'Abd al-Salam ibn Muhammad ibn Yusuf ibn Bundar, Abu Yusuf al-Qazwini, Mu'tazilite sheikh and noted scholar (d. 1090).

19.   *al-Hakim*: Fatimid caliph (r. 996–1021).

20.   *Latakia*: Syrian coastal city, conquered by the Byzantines (whom Abu Yusuf calls 'Romans', following common practice) in 968.

21.   *Ibn al-Buwayn*: Abu al-Hasan 'Ali ibn Ja'far ibn al-Hasan ibn al-Buwayn, poet and scribe from Ma'arrat al-Nu'man (d. 1111 in Egypt). He was a scribe for Usama's grandfather, Sadid al-Mulk 'Ali, as Usama adds here as an aside.

22.   *he had left ... grown man*: If Murshid, born in 1068, was a 'grown man' when he made this trip, it would be after *c.* 1082 but before Abu Yusuf's death in 1090. Probably, the journey was made after 1086 (and so a decade or more after Murshid and the old man had first met) when the Banu Munqidh were forced to cede some of their domains to the sultan in return for their continued possession of Shayzar. Significantly, these possessions were returned in 1091.

23.   *Khawaja Buzurk Nizam al-Din*: That is, the sultan's all-powerful vizier, Nizam al-Mulk (d. 1092).

24.   *They said ... a seller of milk*: A verse from a poem by a poet called al-'Usfuri, mocking the pretensions of a poetaster he met.

25.   *as when Jacob satisfied his soul's desire*: An allusion to Qur'an 12:68.

26.   *al-Bulayl*: Or, possibly, al-Balil, which Yaqut, *Mu'jam al-buldan*, 5 vols. (Beirut: Dar Sadir, 1955–7), s.v., describes as 'a quarter of Siffin', Siffin being situated across the river from Qal'at Ja'bar.

27.   *House of the Chain*: On the Dome of the Chain, and the traditions surrounding it, see (with references to the literature) Amikam Elad, *Medieval Jerusalem and Islamic Worship* (Leiden: E. J. Brill, 1999), pp. 47–8.

28.   *stand beneath the chain*: That is, the chain was suspended from the underside of the dome.

29.   *a visit to the sheikh Yasin*: The text reads *ziyarat al-shaykh yasin* which connotes a visit made for the purpose of religious merit (as also in Usama's 'visit' to Jerusalem, above).

30.   *Mambij*: A Syrian town located near the Euphrates, northeast of Aleppo, about four days' journey from Shayzar

31.   *Shihab al-Din Mahmud*: Burid amir of Damascus (r. 1135–9).

32. *supervisor*: (Arabic *na'ib*) the supervisor of the *waqf*, or charitable endowment, set aside for the blind men.

33. *Ibn al-Farrash*: As Derenbourg notes (*Vie*, p. 176, n. 6), this is possibly the judge Shams al-Din Abu 'Abdallah Muhammad ibn Muhammad ibn Musa, aka Ibn al-Farrash.

34. *On the Utility of Deception in Battle*: This passage was inspired by Usama's reflections on al-'Asa, the steadfast horse of Jadhima al-Abrash, an ill-fated pre-Islamic Arab king, who was seduced and then murdered by the queen Zenobia. His kinsmen had their revenge on Zenobia by killing her after sneaking into her city, using a Trojan-horse-like ruse in which, as Usama's exasperated comments indicate, the soldiers hid in sacks to appear like cargo.

35. *At the Tomb of St John the Baptist near Nablus*: This account has already appeared in an English translation in Francesco Gabrieli, *Arab Historians of the Crusades* (Berkeley: University of California Press, 1969). But, as that translation is itself a translation from Gabrieli's Italian, which is, in turn, based upon Derenbourg's defective edition of Usama's original, I have produced a new translation of it here, which, I think, also clears up some of the confusing parts of Derenbourg (*Vie*, pp. 189–90) and Gabrieli's (pp. 83–4) readings.

36. *Yahya ibn Zakariya ... Sebaste*: Yahya is the Arabic name for John the Baptist, known to Muslims as a prophet mentioned in the Qur'an. Sebaste was a city built by Herod on the site of biblical Samaria, and was associated with John the Baptist since pre-Islamic times.

37. *like carded cotton*: A favourite simile of Usama's. Gabrieli (*Arab Historians*, p. 84) glosses this as 'as white as combed cotton'. But it seems to be the unkempt state of their hair, and not its whiteness, that is being described.

38. *They propped themselves ... recited to them*: Gabrieli (*Arab Historians*, p. 84) renders this, following Derenbourg (*Vie*, p. 189, n. 4), as

> They were facing the east, and wore (embroidered?) on their breasts staves ending in crossbars turned up like the rear of a saddle. They took their oath on this sign, and gave hospitality to those who needed it.

In the footnote, Derenbourg suggests it indicates that these are monks of the Chapter of St John (thus his reference to oaths and hospitality). More likely, they are monks leaning upon some kind of crutch-like piece of gear. This interpretation would fit better with the theme of the anthology (staves) and the point of the passage (that Usama is impressed by the strenuous devotions he sees these old men performing, despite their frailty).

39. *al-Tawawis*: The Khanqah al-Tawusiya, Damascus's first Sufi meeting-space, located in the Suq Saruja neighbourhood, north-west of the city, but now no longer extant.

40. *Ibn al-Sallar*: The all-powerful vizier of the Fatimid caliphate (r. 1150–53), who features in many of Usama's Egyptian anecdotes in *The Book of Contemplation*.

41. *patriarch of Egypt . . . Ethiopia*: Yoannis V was Coptic patriarch of Egypt from 1146 to 1166. By the twelfth century, the Coptic patriarch of Egypt usually appointed the Ethiopian patriarch himself. The Ethiopian patriarch alluded to in this account is Mika'el I.

42. *The First Crusade and its Sequel in the North*: This account collapses events stretching from 1096 to 1108, and is really a mere digression started by a similar tale involving the haggling over terms of ransom between Alexander and the emperor of China. Nevertheless, it is one of the only Muslim accounts describing what at least one Muslim took to be the goal of the First Crusade: not merely Jerusalem, but Baghdad and the East.

43. *Jikirmish*: Shams al-Dawla Jikirmish (also Chökürmish), Seljuk governor of Mosul (d. 1106).

44. *in battle*: Near Harran in 1104, see Claude Cahen, *La Syrie du nord à l'époque des croisades et la principauté franque d'Antioche* (Paris: Paul Geuthner, 1940), pp. 236–8.

45. *King Baldwin the Prince and Joscelin*: Baldwin of Le Bourcq was count of Edessa (1100–1118) and later King of Jerusalem as Baldwin II (r. 1118–31). Joscelin of Courtenay was Baldwin's cousin and later count of Edessa after him (1119–31).

46. *Bohemond . . . Jikirmish*: Bohemond left for Europe in the autumn of 1104; after failing in a campaign against the Byzantines at Durazzo in 1107, he died in Apulia in 1111. Jikirmish died in 1106.

47. *Jawali Saqawa*: Also spelled 'Chavli Saqaveh' or 'Saqao', Seljuk governor of Mosul until 1108, appointed by the Seljuk sultan Muhammad ibn Malikshah.

48. *lord of Antioch . . . ibn Tutush*: Tancred was regent of Frankish-held Antioch while Bohemond was absent in Europe. Ridwan ibn Tutush was Seljuk lord of Aleppo (r. 1095–1113).

49. *The blows of the swords . . . prisoner*: A reference to the conflicts of 1108, involving tortuous alliances between Franks and Muslims, and ending in battle near Tall Bashir, about midway between Aleppo and Edessa. See Cahen, *Syrie du nord*, pp. 247–51.

50. *the year 507 (1114)*: The text gives a date of 527 (1133), but this is a misreading for 507 (1114). This is the same Isma'ili attack on Shayzar which features in a number of anecdotes in *The Book of Contemplation*.

51. *Ibn al-Munira*: Born in Kafartab, he later settled in Shayzar, probably fleeing the Frankish capture of his town during the First Crusade. He was a respected grammarian and religious scholar (d. 1110).

52. *spurs*: (Arabic *mahamiz*) a valuable piece of any horseman's gear, but never easy to steal.

53. *woman's get-up*: A woman's wrap is probably intended, a favourite disguise of bandits. Cf. the disguise of the bandit al-Zamarrakal in *The Book of Contemplation*, 'Thief Stories'.

54. *Ma'arrat*: That is, Ma'arrat al-Nu'man, a town just to the northeast of Kafartab.

55. *scarred*: Reading *'alabat* for the edition's *ghalabat*.

Index

(Note: The Arabic definite article 'al-' has been ignored for purposes of alphabetization.)

PENGUIN CLASSICS

THE EPIC OF GILGAMESH

> 'Surpassing all other kings, heroic in stature,
> brave scion of Uruk, wild bull on the rampage!
> Gilgamesh the tall, magnificent and terrible'

Miraculously preserved on clay tablets dating back as much as four thousand years, the poem of Gilgamesh, king of Uruk, is the world's oldest epic, predating Homer by many centuries. The story tells of Gilgamesh's adventures with the wild man Enkidu, and of his arduous journey to the ends of the earth in quest of the Babylonian Noah and the secret of immortality. Alongside its themes of family, friendship and the duties of kings, *The Epic of Gilgamesh* is, above all, about mankind's eternal struggle with the fear of death.

The Babylonian version has been known for over a century, but linguists are still deciphering new fragments in Akkadian and Sumerian. Andrew George's gripping translation brilliantly combines these into a fluent narrative and will long rank as the definitive English *Gilgamesh*.

'A masterly new verse translation' *The Times*

Translated with an introduction by Andrew George

PENGUIN CLASSICS

THE BHAGAVAD GITA

> 'In death thy glory in heaven, in victory thy glory on earth.
> Arise therefore, Arjuna, with thy soul ready to fight'

The Bhagavad Gita is an intensely spiritual work that forms the cornerstone of the Hindu faith, and is also one of the masterpieces of Sanskrit poetry. It describes how, at the beginning of a mighty battle between the Pandava and Kaurava armies, the god Krishna gives spiritual enlightenment to the warrior Arjuna, who realizes that the true battle is for his own soul.

Juan Mascaró's translation of *The Bhagavad Gita* captures the extraordinary aural qualities of the original Sanskrit. This edition features a new introduction by Simon Brodbeck, which discusses concepts such as dehin, prakriti and Karma.

'The task of truly translating such a work is indeed formidable. The translator must at least possess three qualities. He must be an artist in words as well as a Sanskrit scholar, and above all, perhaps, he must be deeply sympathetic with the spirit of the original. Mascaró has succeeded so well because he possesses all these'
The Times Literary Supplement

Translated by Juan Mascaró with an introduction by Simon Brodbeck

PENGUIN CLASSICS

THE RISE OF THE ROMAN EMPIRE
POLYBIUS

'If history is deprived of the truth,
we are left with nothing but an idle, unprofitable tale'

In writing his account of the relentless growth of the Roman Empire, the Greek statesman Polybius (*c.* 200–118 BC) set out to help his fellow-countrymen understand how their world came to be dominated by Rome. Opening with the Punic War in 264 BC, he vividly records the critical stages of Roman expansion: its campaigns throughout the Mediterranean, the temporary setbacks inflicted by Hannibal and the final destruction of Carthage in 146 BC. An active participant in contemporary politics, as well as a friend of many prominent Roman citizens, Polybius was able to draw on a range of eyewitness accounts and on his own experiences of many of the central events, giving his work immediacy and authority.

Ian Scott-Kilvert's translation fully preserves the clarity of Polybius' narrative. This substantial selection of the surviving volumes is accompanied by an introduction by F. W. Walbank, which examines Polybius' life and times, and the sources and technique he employed in writing his history.

Translated by Ian Scott-Kilvert
Selected with an introduction by F. W. Walbank

PENGUIN CLASSICS

THE POLITICS
ARISTOTLE

'Man is by nature a political animal'

In *The Politics* Aristotle addresses the questions that lie at the heart of political science. How should society be ordered to ensure the happiness of the individual? Which forms of government are best and how should they be maintained? By analysing a range of city constitutions – oligarchies, democracies and tyrannies – he seeks to establish the strengths and weaknesses of each system to decide which are the most effective, in theory and in practice. A hugely significant work, which has influenced thinkers as diverse as Aquinas and Machiavelli, *The Politics* remains an outstanding commentary on fundamental political issues and concerns, and provides fascinating insights into the workings and attitudes of the Greek city-state.

The introductions by T. A. Sinclair and Trevor J. Saunders discuss the influence of *The Politics* on philosophers, its modern relevance and Aristotle's political beliefs. This edition contains Greek and English glossaries, and a bibliography for further reading.

Translated by T. A. Sinclair
Revised and re-presented by Trevor J. Saunders

PENGUIN CLASSICS

THE PERSIAN EXPEDITION
XENOPHON

'The only things of value which we have at present are our arms and our courage'

In *The Persian Expedition*, Xenophon, a young Athenian noble who sought his destiny abroad, provides an enthralling eyewitness account of the attempt by a Greek mercenary army – the Ten Thousand – to help Prince Cyrus overthrow his brother and take the Persian throne. When the Greeks were then betrayed by their Persian employers, they were forced to march home through hundreds of miles of difficult terrain – adrift in a hostile country and under constant attack from the unforgiving Persians and warlike tribes. In this outstanding description of endurance and individual bravery, Xenophon, one of those chosen to lead the retreating army, provides a vivid narrative of the campaign and its aftermath, and his account remains one of the best pictures we have of Greeks confronting a 'barbarian' world.

Rex Warner's distinguished translation captures the epic quality of the Greek original and George Cawkwell's introduction sets the story of the expedition in the context of its author's life and tumultuous times.

Translated by Rex Warner with an introduction by George Cawkwell

PENGUIN CLASSICS

THE CONSOLATION OF PHILOSOPHY
BOETHIUS

> 'Why else does slippery Fortune change
> So much, and punishment more fit
> For crime oppress the innocent?'

Written in prison before his brutal execution in AD 524, Boethius's *The Consolation of Philosophy* is a conversation between the ailing prisoner and his 'nurse' Philosophy, whose instruction restores him to health and brings him to enlightenment. Boethius was an eminent public figure who had risen to great political heights in the court of King Theodoric when he was implicated in conspiracy and condemned to death. Although a Christian, it was to the pagan Greek philosophers that he turned for inspiration following his abrupt fall from grace. With great clarity of thought and philosophical brilliance, Boethius adopted the classical model of the dialogue to debate the vagaries of Fortune, and to explore the nature of happiness, good and evil, fate and free will.

Victor Watts's English translation makes *The Consolation of Philosophy* accessible to the modern reader while losing nothing of its poetic artistry and breadth of vision. This edition includes an introduction discussing Boethius's life and writings, a bibliography, glossary and notes.

Translated with an introduction by Victor Watts

PENGUIN CLASSICS

THE BOOK OF THE COURTIER
BALDESAR CASTIGLIONE

'The courtier has to imbue with grace his movements, his gestures, his way of doing things and in short, his every action'

In *The Book of the Courtier* (1528), Baldesar Castiglione, a diplomat and Papal Nuncio to Rome, sets out to define the essential virtues for those at Court. In a lively series of imaginary conversations between the real-life courtiers to the Duke of Urbino, his speakers discuss qualities of noble behaviour – chiefly discretion, decorum, nonchalance and gracefulness – as well as wider questions such as the duties of a good government and the true nature of love. Castiglione's narrative power and psychological perception make this guide both an entertaining comedy of manners and a revealing window onto the ideals and preoccupations of the Italian Renaissance at the moment of its greatest splendour.

George Bull's elegant translation captures the variety of tone in Castiglione's speakers, from comic interjections to elevated rhetoric. This edition includes an introduction examining Castiglione's career in the courts of Urbino and Mantua, a list of the historical characters he portrays and further reading.

Translated and with an introduction by George Bull

PENGUIN CLASSICS

ON LOVE AND BARLEY: HAIKU OF BASHO

'Orchid – breathing
incense into
butterfly's wings'

Basho, one of the greatest of Japanese poets and the master of haiku, was also a Buddhist monk and a lifelong traveller. His poems combine 'karumi', or lightness of touch, with the Zen ideal of oneness with creation. Each poem evokes the natural world – the cherry blossom, the leaping frog, the summer moon or the winter snow – suggesting the smallness of human life in comparison to the vastness and drama of nature. Basho himself enjoyed solitude and a life free from possessions, and his haiku are the work of an observant eye and a meditative mind, uncluttered by materialism and alive to the beauty of the world around him.

These meticulous translations by Lucien Stryk capture the refined artistry of the originals. This edition contains notes and an introduction that discusses how the life and beliefs of Basho influenced his work.

Translated by Lucien Stryk

PENGUIN CLASSICS

THE CAMPAIGNS OF ALEXANDER
ARRIAN

'His passion was for glory only, and in that he was insatiable'

Although written over four hundred years after Alexander's death, Arrian's
Campaigns of Alexander is the most reliable account of the man and his
achievements we have. Arrian's own experience as a military commander gave
him unique insights into the life of the world's greatest conqueror. He tells of
Alexander's violent suppression of the Theban rebellion, his total defeat of Persia,
and his campaigns through Egypt, India and Babylon – establishing new cities
and destroying others in his path. While Alexander emerges from this record as
an unparalleled and charismatic leader, Arrian succeeds brilliantly in creating an
objective and fully rounded portrait of a man of boundless ambition, who was
exposed to the temptations of power and worshipped as a god in his own lifetime.

Aubrey de Sélincourt's vivid translation is accompanied by J. R. Hamilton's
introduction, which discusses Arrian's life and times, his synthesis of other
classical sources and the composition of Alexander's army. This edition also
includes maps, a list for further reading and a detailed index.

Translated by Aubrey de Sélincourt
Revised, with a new introduction and notes by J. R. Hamilton

PENGUIN CLASSICS

THE CONQUEST OF GAUL
CAESAR

> 'The enemy were overpowered and took to flight.
> The Romans pursued as far as their strength enabled them to run'

Between 58 and 50 BC Julius Caesar conquered most of the area now covered by France, Belgium and Switzerland, and invaded Britain twice, and *The Conquest of Gaul* is his record of these campaigns. Caesar's narrative offers insights into his military strategy and paints a fascinating picture of his encounters with the inhabitants of Gaul and Britain, as well as lively portraits of the rebel leader Vercingetorix and other Gallic chieftains. *The Conquest of Gaul* can also be read as a piece of political propaganda, as Caesar sets down his version of events for the Roman public, knowing he faces civil war on his return to Rome.

Revised and updated by Jane Gardner, S. A. Handford's translation brings Caesar's lucid and exciting account to life for modern readers. This volume includes a glossary of persons and places, maps, appendices and suggestions for further reading.

Translated by S. A. Handford

Revised with a new introduction by Jane F. Gardner

PENGUIN CLASSICS

THE ANNALS OF IMPERIAL ROME
TACITUS

'Nero was already corrupted by every lust, natural and unnatural'

The Annals of Imperial Rome recount the major historical events from the years
shortly before the death of Augustus to the death of Nero in AD 68. With clarity
and vivid intensity Tacitus describes the reign of terror under the corrupt Tiberius,
the great fire of Rome during the time of Nero and the wars, poisonings, scandals,
conspiracies and murders that were part of imperial life. Despite his claim that
the *Annals* were written objectively, Tacitus' account is sharply critical of the
emperors' excesses and fearful for the future of imperial Rome, while also filled
with a longing for its past glories.

Michael Grant's fine translation captures the moral tone, astringent wit and stylish
vigour of the original. His introduction discusses the life and works of Tacitus and
the historical context of the *Annals*. This edition also contains a key to place names
and technical terms, maps, tables and suggestions for further reading.

Translated with an introduction by Michael Grant

PENGUIN CLASSICS

THE AGRICOLA *AND* THE GERMANIA
TACITUS

> 'Happy indeed were you, Agricola,
> not only in your glorious life but in your timely death'

The Agricola is both a portrait of Julius Agricola – the most famous governor
of Roman Britain and Tacitus' well-loved and respected father-in-law – and the
first detailed account of Britain that has come down to us. It offers fascinating
descriptions of the geography, climate and peoples of the country, and a succinct
account of the early stages of the Roman occupation, nearly fatally undermined by
Boudicca's revolt in AD 61 but consolidated by campaigns that took Agricola as
far as Anglesey and northern Scotland. The warlike German tribes are the focus of
Tacitus' attention in *The Germania*, which, like *The Agricola*, often compares the
behaviour of 'barbarian' peoples favourably with the decadence and corruption of
Imperial Rome.

Harold Mattingly's translation brings Tacitus' extravagant imagination and incisive
wit vividly to life. In his introduction, he examines Tacitus' life and literary career,
the governorship of Agricola, and the political background of Rome's rapidly
expanding Empire. This edition also includes a select bibliography, and maps of
Roman Britain and Germany.

Translated with an introduction by H. Mattingly
Translation revised by S. A. Handford

THE STORY OF PENGUIN CLASSICS

Before 1946 ... 'Classics' are mainly the domain of academics and students; readable editions for everyone else are almost unheard of. This all changes when a little-known classicist, E. V. Rieu, presents Penguin founder Allen Lane with the translation of Homer's *Odyssey* that he has been working on in his spare time.

1946 Penguin Classics debuts with *The Odyssey*, which promptly sells three million copies. Suddenly, classics are no longer for the privileged few.

1950s Rieu, now series editor, turns to professional writers for the best modern, readable translations, including Dorothy L. Sayers's *Inferno* and Robert Graves's unexpurgated *Twelve Caesars*.

1960s The Classics are given the distinctive black covers that have remained a constant throughout the life of the series. Rieu retires in 1964, hailing the Penguin Classics list as 'the greatest educative force of the twentieth century.'

1970s A new generation of translators swells the Penguin Classics ranks, introducing readers of English to classics of world literature from more than twenty languages. The list grows to encompass more history, philosophy, science, religion and politics.

1980s The Penguin American Library launches with titles such as *Uncle Tom's Cabin*, and joins forces with Penguin Classics to provide the most comprehensive library of world literature available from any paperback publisher.

1990s The launch of Penguin Audiobooks brings the classics to a listening audience for the first time, and in 1999 the worldwide launch of the Penguin Classics website extends their reach to the global online community.

The 21st Century Penguin Classics are completely redesigned for the first time in nearly twenty years. This world-famous series now consists of more than 1300 titles, making the widest range of the best books ever written available to millions – and constantly redefining what makes a 'classic'.

The Odyssey continues ...

The best books ever written

PENGUIN CLASSICS

SINCE 1946

Find out more at www.penguinclassics.com